More Than a Pastime

More Than a Pastime
An Oral History of Baseball Fans

WILLIAM FREEDMAN

McFarland & Company, Inc., Publishers
Jefferson, North Carolina

> *The present work is a reprint of the library bound edition of* More Than a Pastime: An Oral History of Baseball Fans, *first published in 1998 by McFarland.*

LIBRARY OF CONGRESS CATALOGUING-IN-PUBLICATION DATA

Freedman, William, 1938–
    More than a pastime : an oral history of baseball fans / by William Freedman.
      p.   cm.
    Includes bibliographical references and index.

    ISBN 978-0-7864-9381-4
    softcover : acid free paper ∞

    1. Baseball fans—United States—Interviews.
    2. Baseball—Social aspects—United States.
    3. Baseball—United States—History.   4. Oral history.
    I. Title
    GV865.A1F72   2014
    796.357'0973—dc21   98-10297

BRITISH LIBRARY CATALOGUING DATA ARE AVAILABLE

© 1998 William Freedman. All rights reserved

No part of this book may be reproduced or transmitted in any form or by any means, electronic or mechanical, including photocopying or recording, or by any information storage and retrieval system, without permission in writing from the publisher.

Cover image: *Cheering Baseball Fans*, Edward Laning, 1944 (© 2014 PicturesNow)

Manufactured in the United States of America

McFarland & Company, Inc., Publishers
  Box 611, Jefferson, North Carolina 28640
    www.mcfarlandpub.com

To my brother Jim, a courageous Tiger fan in Newark.

To my son Etai, who mistakenly believes in the NBA.

To the memory of Ed "Dutch" Doyle, Mel Prosen, and Jack Kitch, three wonderful fans and people, who have passed on since our conversations and who have gone, I hope, to watch a better game.

To baseball, the chess and symphony of sport.

Acknowledgments

I want to offer special thanks to Annette Guardabascio of the New York Yankees organization, to Lila Canuelle, then of the Detroit Tigers organization, and to Norman Macht of SABR for their generous help establishing contacts and arranging interviews; to Barbara Moser of the Senior Times of Montreal for that and patience and all the rest; to Lois Olena for her splendid typing, her encouragement, and for asking who that Bobby Thomson fellow was; to Carl Prince (maybe), who got me started on this project by suggesting I do something else; and to Selma Khalili for letting me disappear to finish this book without disappearing me altogether.

I also want to thank, genuinely and apologetically, all those fans who spoke to me so meaningfully and eloquently about what this glorious game meant to them and whose testimony not I, but that heartless bruiser named Limited Space left out of this collection. To paraphrase Dan J., a fan whose interview does appear here, "Go and talk to them; they'll tell you it had a lot of meaning." Here are their names, in no particular order: Chris Rosen, Greg Kalik, George Kochanowicz, Lou Greenberg, Jean Burke, Arnie Price, Paul Katz, Jack Kitch, Al Guttman, *Fred Holdsworth, Mike Chamberlain, John Buford, James Freedman, Lloyd Johnson, Howard Weisband, Achituv Gershinsky, Norman Macht, Malcolm Macht, Dennis Callahan, Jonathan Prosen, Joe McGillen, Dan Hennessy, Sal Napolitano, Jonathan Friedland, Michael Murphy, Fred Schuld, James Carone, Joe Conforti, Ron Johnson, Gary Emmett, James Gordon, Paul Silverman, Charles Zabransky, Jim Torczyner, Stan Markowitz, Larry Lasher, Harold Laxer, Allyson Felix, *Vern Holtgrave, Chris Witt, Jack Kavanagh, Mark Alvarez, Zvi Shilon, *Jerry Davie, *Bill Zepp, Darryl Brock, Thomas Zocco, Stan Shapiro, Ralph Cahn, *Reggie Sanders, Dan Isaac, Ron Waxberg, Gerard, Lorraine, and Gabriel Givnish, Mark Stangl, Sid Feltman, Andrew Boyle, George Boutor, Larry Yaffa, Marc Stengl, Sam "Leaden" Bernstein, Marvin Hyatt, Joe White, Ron and Toby Gish, Mack McCarey, Lou Gamba, Bob Davies, Jonathan Spector, all the members of "Dutch" Doyle's group, George Robinson, **Gene Benson, Andrew Boyle, William Guhl, Patrick McMorrow, Robert Canuelle, and Kevin Mattison. And there are others, though only a very few, whose tapes I've unfortunately misplaced and whose names I cannot remember. To them an additional apology and thanks. A final apology to those fans whose interviews are included in this history but whose birthdates I may have misconstrued, though by no more than a year, I trust. When doing these interviews I often asked the fan's age rather than his or her date of birth. Later, attempting to calculate but having forgotten the precise year of the interview and lost contact with the fan, I was forced to rely on an imperfect memory.

*Former Detroit Tigers
**Former outfielder for the Negro Leagues' Philadelphia Stars

Contents

PREFACE	1
INTRODUCTION: SAVING THE GAME THAT SAVED THEM	3

I. Moral Landscape, Mentor, Proof — 37

The Moral Force of Victory: The Yankees on the Side of the Gods / Gene W.	41
Society's Rudder and Keel / Reno B.	46
Affection, Loyalty, Sacrifice: "I Followed My Friends to the Giants" / Peter A.	52
Being Human in the Clutch: The Guys Who Came Through When You Needed Them / "Dutch" D.	55
Something I Cared About, Something to Defend / Erik B.	59
"Go and Talk to the Kids: It Had a Lot of Meaning" / Dan J.	63

II. Striving for Excellence and Perfection — 69

Greatness Up for Grabs / Paul K.	72
Tragedy and Triumph: Up from Depot Street / Walter S.	76
Baseball and Christianity: Going All Out for that Great Reward / Clive C.	82

III. Empowerment — 87

"Taking Risks and Chances—The Way the Dodgers Did" / Mel P.	90
"Part of this Masculine Thing" / Carol T.	94
Status in the Neighborhood / Michael K.	99
Showing Them You Have It in You / Brandon M.	102
Enfranchised in America: We Are Who We Are / Bernie O.	104

IV. The Contained Aesthetic Object, the Mirroring Work of Art — 110

Style, Flair, Transcendence: The Gods of Baseball / Andy C.	113
From Wonder to Completion / Sanford F.	117
Baseball as Poem: The Self-Sufficient Mirror / John S.	122

V. Not Just Fathers and Sons — 127

Learning What the World Was Supposed to be Like / Rebecca A. — 130
"An Intimacy Between Me and My Father ... A Secret Society" / Vivian L. — 135
"My Way of Remembering" / Tom Z. — 141

VI. A Sense of Belonging — 145

"A Social Activity, Something to Do with Other People" / Abby L. — 148
At Home in Yankee Stadium / Pat and Sue J. — 151
"The Tie That Binds" / Sanford S. — 158
Paradise, the Bronx / Bennett K. — 162
A Part of History / Joe N. — 168

VII. Identification — 172

A Member of the Team: The Warming Brotherhood of Baseball / Elliott S. — 178
Catcher in the Rye / Tim C. — 180
Even Mr. Replay Can't Go Home Again / John D. — 183
"I Talk to the Players, I Talk to the Television": A Kind of Obsession / Eric K. — 186
Dominance from Within / Charles S. — 189
Yankee Goyim, Dodger Jews: "You Need to Know Who You Belong With" / Herb P. — 194

VIII. Formation of Identity and Character — 198

Identity through Difference and Continuity / Chris H. — 200
"You Sit Down and Think What Its Lessons Are": Becoming a Better Person / Fred C. — 203
"Yeah, but It Was Not a Piece of Cake": A School for Stoics / George P. — 206
Quirkiness in Action: Playing Life the Way It Should Be Played / Carl T. — 211

IX. Rescue, Fun, and All the Rest: A Concluding Miscellany — 216

They Kept Me from Going Under / Carl P. — 218
"Something in This Life That's Just for Fun" / Kathy D., Cindy D., and Valerie A. — 222
One of Fate's Threads / Lila C. — 227

EPILOGUE — 233
BIBLIOGRAPHY — 243
INDEX — 249

Preface

The following interviews were conducted during the four-year period from 1992 to 1996 and in nine locations: New York, northern New Jersey, Philadelphia, Baltimore and its environs, St. Louis, Detroit, Montreal, Phoenix, and the Bay area of northern California. The ages of the interviewees range from 10 to 81, and while Yankee and Dodger fans are disproportionately represented, 17 teams find their advocates among these fans.

An apologetic word about all those Yankee and Dodger fans. There are, I think, three main reasons for their over-representation in these pages. One, I did much of my interviewing in the metropolitan New York area and along the eastern seaboard and spent two days combing the ranks at a New York Yankee fan festival in 1992. Second, many of the fans are in their fifties today, as am I, which means they were introduced to baseball in the late 1940s and 1950s, when these two teams were dominant. And third, there was something undeniably special about those glory-day Yankees and those Ebbets Field Dodgers. More than other teams, they had, it seems, an identity, a distinct and identifiable character that separated them from the rest of the league by margins larger than those they took quite regularly to their pennants. One might say, as fans did, of the San Diego Padres, the Philadelphia Phillies, the Baltimore Orioles, or the Montreal Expos—that they rooted for these teams simply and undeniably because they were the home team. But while Yankee and Dodger fans also acknowledged the powerful, even irresistible home-town influence, there was always a great deal more to their attachment. The Yankees and Dodgers came equipped not merely with histories, but with emblazoned identities, personalities, and traditions. They were uniformed symbols of victory and success, morality and social conscience, polished perfection and dogged struggle, American purity or accented ethnicity. Their fans, therefore—only those who clung to the perennially tragic Red Sox could rival them—had more to begin with, a richer inheritance to trade on; and their testimonies, typically resonant with that richness, were more resistant to the editorial scythe.

The subject of this book and the interviews that comprise it is the role and importance of professional baseball in the lives of American children and adolescents. The principal focus of the interviews, therefore, is on baseball as it is remembered, their principal effort to discover what baseball meant to the children who soared and suffered with their teams.

The responses suggest three major hypotheses: that how the youthful fan regards the game, his favorite team and players is a resonant expression of his personality, his family and social situation, and his needs; that baseball, far more than a pastime or idle entertainment, serves a number of extremely important emotional and developmental functions—moral, aesthetic, mythic, social, and psychological—in the lives of its fans; that one of baseball's less frequently heralded virtues is its extraordinary richness, its capacity to turn a different face to almost every child and to satisfy that remarkably wide range of personalities and requirements.

Partly an instrument for the expression of the young fan's forming personality, partly responsible for its shape and direction, baseball, these interviews suggest, has an importance we have hardly begun to understand. What they demonstrate at least as clearly is how wonderfully thoughtful, impassioned, and eloquent fans become when they speak about this quite amazing game.

It has become customary, perhaps even a bit fashionable, to respond to the growing number of enthusiastic tributes to baseball's special significance and power with a raised eyebrow above a jaundiced eye. Such paeans, of which Ken Burns's television documentary *Baseball* is only the best known, are skeptically described by cooler, ostensibly more realistic critics as "glutinized," "saccharine," or simply "overblown." One of the conclusions of this book, as I've indicated, is that baseball often is what we need and needed it to be. A prismatic mirror of the self, it reflects the viewer as it broadcasts itself. Cynical commentators, therefore, are of course entitled to their perceptions; their view is as sincere and legitimate as any. But what these interviews demonstrate quite conclusively is that the professional eulogies skeptics deride are not manufactured extravaganzas far removed from the experience of the ordinary fan. On the contrary, they reflect quite accurately the passion fans bring to the game, the importance they attribute to it, and the quite extraordinary claims they make on its behalf. If the fans I interviewed are at all representative—and I believe they are—it is the skeptics who are the aberrations, those unashamed enthusiasts the norm.

Introduction

Mantle's Body and the Game's

In one body—supple, powerful, and amazingly swift, yet covertly eating itself away with the poisoned substances of its own indulgence—Mickey Mantle anatomized the game of baseball in the last half of this century. Straw-haired and blue-eyed, a rural Oklahoman with the looks and innocence if none of the survivalist savvy of Huckleberry Finn, Mantle *was* baseball as the rural idyll it had always seemed. He was country simplicity and power come to the big city to surprise and win its as yet unjaded heart. Born to a mining family at the nadir of the Depression and raised in a small country home without indoor plumbing, Mantle—his name an emblem of his mission—would play out the American dream on a dozen playing fields before the millions of fans he made believers. Brought into the major leagues as an adolescent at the start of the '50s, he seemed to represent not only the game in its vaunted golden era but the candid innocence and simplicity, the still youthful assurance, and the all but limitless power and potential of postwar America. And like that fantasy of omnipotence—indeed like the Yankees and like baseball itself—he began to unravel in the latter part of the following decade. All the while, of course, like both baseball and the America it seemed synonymous with, Mantle was fooling us. His childlike purity and goodness was, in substantial measure, a myth created and sustained by a press both timid and worshipful. Like baseball and America, Mantle played on damaged knees. Like them both, he was a poor father to his children and his own encroaching future. Like them both, he was imbibing substances—alcohol in his case, expansion, free agency, artificial turf, and Vietnam in theirs—his body couldn't assimilate. "God gave me the ability to play baseball," Mantle lamented near the end. "God gave me everything, and I just wasted it." The words seem prophetic. They seem the words of the confessional oracle of the game itself, acknowledging what the last 30 years of its history make all but undeniable. "The next drink you take may be your last," Mantle's doctor reportedly warned him before he committed himself for treatment. And witnesses of the most recent and pernicious of baseball's damaging strikes and its aftermath are aware of the warning's applicability to the game.

Disenchantment

Mickey Mantle died of his self-destructive habits. His cancer, doctors said, was among the most aggressive they had ever seen. Once it had begun to spread there was no stopping it, no hope for the once magnificent body that crumblingly housed it.

Unlike Mantle, the game of baseball is still with us. It is World Series time as I write this, the stadiums in Atlanta and New York are packed; fans in both cities are poised to burst into the streets as loyal enthusiasts have always done once victory is secured. But these are the '90s, not the '50s. The signs of illness and decay are visible and stubborn. They are held before us by a press no longer dedicated to their concealment, exacerbated perhaps by an increasingly cynical populace given almost chronically to anger and more inclined to denigration than belief.

Baseball is alive, but especially after the devastating 232-day strike of '94 and '95, it is not well. During those two years, attendance at major league games declined, on an average, by 19 percent in comparison with 1994, and while there was a substantial recovery in 1996, the game's condition remains unstable, its prognosis less than fully promising. A 1996 Baseball Server poll showed fan alienation at alarming levels—55 percent among men, 31 percent among women, and rising from 30 percent among the lowest income group to 55 percent among those with the highest incomes. Although fan attendance was about 20 percent higher in 1996 than in the preceding two years, teams that can least afford the drop-off—Kansas City, Milwaukee and Minnesota in the American League, Cincinnati, Pittsburgh, and San Francisco in the National—seem to have leveled off at attendance rates 25–40 percent lower over the past three years than in the three preceding. Pittsburgh's decline is approximately 40 percent, San Francisco's almost one-third, Kansas City's about 35 percent, and so it goes. While some large-market teams rebounded in 1996, these did not.

National and local TV ratings for baseball were down by about 20 percent overall in 1994 and '95, and in July 1994 NBC and ABC announced their withdrawal from the baseball network. Advertising had taken a commensurate plunge. Licensed product sales fell 23 percent during the strike, and as one advertising and marketing consultant ominously warned, "Baseball will never get some of its advertisers back. They'll find other places to put their money."[1] So far, it seems, they have. Stuart Elliott, in a recent article in the *New York Times*, speculated that even the Yankees are unlikely to escape relegation to the minor leagues of advertising, since the game's recent setbacks have damaged its standing among marketers as well as consumers. "Attendance is 15 percent below pre-strike levels and ratings are way down," observed the president of a sports celebrity service in Chicago. "So we just don't get the calls for baseball players.... Baseball is down to hockey's level, [and] that's a long way down."[2]

The understandable inclination, of course, is to blame the strike and predict the inevitable diminution of its effects. In response to an August 1994 poll that showed a sharp decline in the number of people identifying themselves as baseball fans, Gene Orza, the associate general counsel to the Major League Baseball Players Association, blamed the strike. "A lot just threw up their hands," he surmised, "and said they weren't interested."[3] But Orza's seems like wishful thinking, for the decline in fan interest is not a poststrike seizure, but a steady cellular erosion afflicting the body of the game. A similar survey of fan interest conducted in 1991 found that the fan base had already dropped substantially from its 1989 figure, while a number of polls taken over the past decade show baseball losing its place as the national pastime, slipping behind both basketball and football in popularity. Similarly, as Andrew Zimbalist reports in *Baseball and Billions*, national TV ratings were low and dropping during each of the first two years of the contracts with CBS and ESPN. CBS, it is estimated, lost $100 million, ESPN some $40 million on their 1990 contracts. For quite some time now, Michael Jordan, not Tony Gwynn, has been selling Nikes, while Shaquille O'Neal, not Greg Maddux, guzzles orange juice.

The fan revolt of late 1994 and '95 was not a sudden uprising born of a single cause, but the triggered outburst of a seething discontent bred of a long and growing list of grievances. It is true that both fan attendance and TV ratings rose acutely during the prestrike segment of the 1994 season, baseball's year of early glory and protracted shame. But that, rather than the fan withdrawal that followed the strike, seems the aberration. Fans pounced on the strike with a readiness suggestive of an ambush. One heard in their reactions the sounds of a gradual softening of commitment and the snap of a final straw.

What one heard with greater and greater frequency during and after the strike was an emotional confusion that wavered between resentment and indifference. "Sure I'd like to see them play," remarked one previously unshakable Cubs fan, "but if they don't for another 10 years I won't care."[4] An Oriole fan, responding with more adrenaline than ennui, announced, "From now on, I won't even come to a game. I don't care anymore."[5] The same poststrike poll that showed a sharp decline in the number and percentage of fans discovered that only one-fourth of the fans polled admitted they missed the game a lot, while 31 percent said they missed it "some," and 43 percent said "not so much."[6] Since these presumably are the same fans who before the strike were filling the stadiums and lifting baseball's TV ratings to encouraging altitudes, one is led to the inference that the depletion of the game's fan base was preceded and anticipated by its softening. More fans were watching and attending games, but when the games were taken away, their world did not empty or collapse; the air was not drained from their lungs or purpose from their lives. "You were my whole world in 1952," wrote Marlene Starry to Mickey Mantle, urging his recovery.[7] "When nothing else was, baseball was happiness," remarked one of the fans I interviewed for this book. "Was it important to me?!" exclaimed another, astonished at the question. "Baseball was all there was!" This kind of fan, it seems, is disappearing. In his or her seat sits the fan for whom baseball is principally and merely entertainment. When pennant races are tight, when players are threatening and breaking records, and for as long as mascots are cavorting in the aisles while scoreboards generate electronic POWS and BOOMS, this fan will show up at the stadium or screen. When darkness falls he will turn, all limbs and organs intact, to other sources of entertainment, and he will miss baseball just this much, no more. Baseball, in other words, has fallen to the status currently occupied by virtually everything else in America, including news and weather, hurricanes and wars. It has become just another form of entertainment, and when it is removed from the horizon, the consumer of simple pleasures directs his dull gaze elsewhere. He does not really care.

This decline in caring is particularly sad and portentous in light of William Saroyan's poignant observation that "Baseball is caring," that "more Americans put their spare (and purest?) caring into baseball than into anything else I can think of," and, above all, that "It is good to care." For Saroyan, writing in 1956, the year of Mantle's Triple Crown, baseball was a game that was infinitely more than a game. "Well, is it a game?" he muses. "Is that all it is? So the Dodgers win it again in 1956. So the Yanks win. So what? What good does *that* do the nation? What good does that do the world? A little good. *Quite* a little. And there's always next year." Now we are not so certain. Perhaps, after all, there may not be a next year, not for baseball, not always. For Saroyan and many of the rest of us in 1956 such a prospect was unthinkable. The novelist and playwright seemed to be indulging only in the mildest hyperbole when he remarked, "If there's no game, there's no pennant race and no World Series. And for all any of us know there might soon be no nation at all." Caring is important, critical, essential. People who stop caring about one thing they once deeply loved and pledged devotion to may stop caring about another. They may stop caring about anything larger than their own living rooms and TV screens, anything that does not gratify their most immediate whims and needs. And if we look thoughtfully around and inside us we will recognize, perhaps, the pertinence of Saroyan's at-first-glance outrageous exaltation of the game's importance. Baseball was caring and the object of caring. Today, both are waning like a conquered demythicized moon.

One senses in the fervor of some of these declarations of indifference the pain of the jilted lover or the disillusioned child. Fans react differently to the abuses the game has subjected them to over the past three decades, some with hurt bitterness and anger, some with a calmer withdrawal and detachment. But what drives most of these responses, I believe, is condensed in the remark of a Hollywood screenwriter and producer. "Normally I would take the kids to games at Dodgers Stadium," offered Roy Friedland, "but I'm not doing it this year. I'm disenchanted, and that's the only way I know how to show it."[8] The key word here is "disenchanted." Pointing to the visceral power of the game that once charmed us so completely, it also helps explain the depth of fan anger and disappointment. The charm, the spell, has been broken. Innocence has been exposed as a sordid experience. Something magical has fallen to earth. Fans are wary. Owners seduce them back with bat days, ball days, hat days, and banner days, with enhanced accommodations and more accommodating stars. But the cancer of disenchantment is spreading—quickly and perhaps irreversibly. Once faith is broken, especially where innocence and purity were an essential part of the original contract or understanding, it is all but impossible to restore.

Some Causes of Decline

The causes of fan disenchantment proliferate like teams in an overexpanded league. One may begin with the predatory greed of team owners who, as one skeptic put it, talk like lovers of the game and behave like real estate tycoons blackmailing cities for tax breaks, new stadiums, and an assortment of other perks lest, like those we used to call sore losers, they take their bat and ball and go elsewhere. Television has a hand (or antenna) here, as in almost every other American pie. Television itself, as many have remarked, became in the 1960s the true national pastime, pushing baseball out of the ring with its sumo wrestler weight and favoring more completely visual and explosive sports like football and basketball. Bringing major league baseball to virtually every home in the nation, it has also participated in the slow murder of minor league ball. And pressing as it does for speed and the "big moment," television tempts us toward a fatal tampering with the regal pace of this wonderfully slow-moving game and toward the introduction of more and more playoff games and wild-card matchups. It is also perhaps the most powerful vehicle in the U-haul move of teams from market to market. As the principal source of baseball revenues, television contracts in large market areas can assure a financial windfall regardless of a team's performance. Hence the flight from less to more lucrative marketplaces, from smaller to more densely populated areas. Hence too the diluting expansion of both major leagues.

If owners are not skipping town because they have been refused a better yard to play in, they leave in search of richer markets. And on the road from one city to the next they are bumper to bumper with free agents for whom team loyalty has the antiquated ring of a duel to defend the honor of a slighted damsel and the power to resist anything but a larger offer. In the newly franchised cities there is no history or tradition. There are no stories of 41-year pennant droughts or 80 years without a Series victory, no feverish prayers for redemptive victory. With the frequent movements of franchises and free agents, fan loyalty weakens where it does not die. One cannot develop or risk vital attachment to a team or player who may be gone with the next year's snow. And where longevity permits the formation of such a bond, the geometrical leap of player salaries toward figures accessible to the average fan only in the lottery erodes it. Where players once lived in the neighborhoods, now they own them. According to a *USA Today* poll, 84 percent of fans thought ball players were overpaid—and that was in 1991! When a fan finally manages to set aside this disparity or injustice in order to get on with the business of worshipful love and idealization, he is shot to earth by news of bickering—for $15 million over a four-year period, rather than $10.5 over three.

And then of course there are the sleaze charges—seven drug suspensions for Steve Howe, three for Darryl Strawberry, who also beats his wife for variety and shortchanges the IRS. Wade Boggs is caught philandering, Vince Coleman throws a firecracker for amusement, injuring a little girl, Jack McDowell gives the finger to his disapproving fans, Albert Belle is a symphony of obscene gestures and complaints, Danny Tartabull is accused of faking injuries to avoid playing, and the rot seeps backwards. Former all-star and four-time batting champion Bill Madlock is arrested for passing bad checks, and the golden age itself proves a tarnished bronze. Duke Snider and Willie McCovey, superstars of the innocent '50s and ebullient '60s, are indicted for failing to report tens of thousands of dollars earned at autograph signings and sports memorabilia shows. "For the first time," as the *New York Times* article reported, "the stars from the game's gilded age were enveloped in a crime that up to now has only involved players from its more troubled present."[9] A Bay Ridge bartender undoubtedly spoke for many when he remarked that while what Snider did was wrong, "he's no different from anyone else in baseball these days. There's money out there to be had, and Duke just got on the bandwagon. He also just happened to get caught."[10] For Mr. Mullane, Snider's only real crime was stupidity. But for many others the *Times* reporter spoke to this was simply one more nail in the coffin of major league baseball, which they described as an institution racked and ruined by greed.

No longer the Field of Dreams, it has become for many, in the flourishing catch-phrase, the Field of Greed. Players, as Robert Lipsyte argued in a recent essay, no longer represent anything beyond or larger than themselves. Once we found inspiration in the dignity and integrity of figures like Joe DiMaggio and Jackie Robinson. And while we know now that many of our shiniest models were tarnished or stood on shaky pedestals, they were polished and held erect for our benefit, and we profited from what was, after all, only a partial illusion. Neither we nor they were as enviable as we once thought or now remember them. But neither were we as tawdry as we have become. As a mirror of our culture, writes Lipsyte, sports shows us spoiled fools as role models, cities and colleges held hostage to selfish financial interests, and games that exist for no higher purpose than to sell products. "The values of sport—honoring boundaries, playing by the rules, working together for a common goal, submitting to authority—were the same values that shaped the American character for the long, winning season.... And now it has ended."

Labor strife, which culminated in the strike that killed the World Series for the first time in 90 years, is one of the game's sorriest and most persistent problems. This last was the eighth in the past 23 years. In fact, since 1979, no contract expiration date has passed without a strike or lockout, and the one just "ended" has only been set aside, not settled. Burned too often, fans are frequently heard to say they will not return to the ballparks or to the conjugal commitment that once bonded them to the game until their "spouse" assures them (s)he will not walk out on them again.

In the wake of all this blight, some few remain sanguine or graspingly hopeful. Mark Harris effused as late as 1991 that he "can almost say with Pete Rose, 'I can't think of a single thing wrong with baseball,'"[11] but his is a lonely if not a desperate voice. Roger Angell believes that if fans will force themselves back to the ballparks—hold their noses while they eat hot dogs, so to speak— they'll be drawn back by the subtle beauty and hypnotic rhythms of the game he still, if ever so much more skeptically, adores. Tim McCarver points to baseball's remarkable resilience, its almost magical capacity to captivate people, and anticipates a return of the disaffected. As does Bobby Murcer who, pinch-aphorizing for Yogi Berra, observed: "Baseball fans are baseball fans. And good baseball can excite and thrill them again as it has in the past."[12]

If the playoff and World Series temperatures are any indication, the hopeful may be right. And yet there is no guarantee. Back in 1992, then baseball commissioner Faye Vincent predicted that "baseball was poised for a catastrophe," and he was painfully prophetic.[13] Others, fans and pundits alike, share Roger Angell's gloomy suspicion—he is clearly torn—that baseball "may well be on the point of altering itself if not out of existence then out of any special place in the American imagination." If he is right—and there are many reasons to believe he is—the principal losers will be neither the ball players nor the owners; nor will it be the drivers and concessionaires, who will find other venues for their wares. The greatest loss will be not financial, but personal, moral, and emotional, and it will be suffered by the fans of this still alluring, however pockmarked game. It will be paid for by those who will lose what the fans I interviewed acknowledge with boundless gratitude to have been given by the game; more expensively still by those who will never stand in its shower. For what virtually every one of these interviews (and many not included here) reveal is that for the devoted fan—particularly the fan as child or adolescent, but for the adult fan as well—baseball is rarely if ever merely entertainment. Rather, as Robert Frost said of the kind of work that unites vocation and avocation and is done for love, baseball "is play for mortal stakes." Touching the lover at every point that stirs and defines him, it is watched or played, as Frost writes, "For Heaven and the future's sakes," but more richly and palpably for one's own.[14]

If baseball continues to forfeit its special place in our lives and imaginations, the loss to its fans will be in both senses of the word "immeasurable"— financially incalculable, yet enormous. Those who will never develop the special intimacy with baseball that drives the avid fan from inexplicable ecstasy to unaccountable depression will of course never feel the deprivation because nothing will have been taken away, only tacitly withheld. Even those who experience the loss will not accurately measure or define it, for the effects of baseball on the lives of fans remain for the most part and to most of us a mystery. What baseball does to us, how it forms, alters, and affects us, eludes our understanding—or does until we are questioned, probed, and prodded, as I like to think fans were in these interviews. We will not know what we have lost, what we have perhaps already begun to lose, because we have not yet fully comprehended what we had. Baseball plays a hundred unidentified, unrecognized, and often inarticulable roles in the lives of its fans. Its influences and ramifications, as these interviews testify, are subtle, powerful, and far-reaching.

The Grip of the Game

That baseball has always had a strangely powerful grip on the American psyche, heart, or spirit is an old acknowledgment for which no explanations have proven adequate. All sports mystify us with the force and endurance of their grasp, though only a few writers have put the question directly or gambled on an answer. For Howard Nixon the capacity of sport to inspire commitment or devotion among its fans and participants depends "on its capacity to function as an escape or fantasyland in which idealized values, aspirations, and imagery predominate." For A. A. Brill the explanation lies, rather, in the aggressive component of sport, an active expression of the "mastery impulse" to which we're all, particularly as children and developing youngsters, inclined. For others, it is a matter, in one form or another, of excellence and perfection. "Why are so many so deeply involved, so caught up emotionally in athletic events?" asks the philosopher Paul Weiss. His answer, offered, as all are, with more confidence than is justified, is that sport attracts and fascinates us because "it offers a superb occasion for enabling young men to be perfected." "What accounts for the passions so many people feel about professional sports?" asks Norman Podhoretz. "What you've got here," he suggests, "is a kind of passion for a world in which the standards are clear [and] excellence is relatively uncontroversial as a judgment of performance…. We want that kind of world." "What 'grabs' so many millions?" Michael Novak asks in awe. "What is the secret power of attraction? How can we care so much?" Because sport is, somehow, a religion, a form of godliness, he adds, elaborating Weiss, the attainment of form and perfection, a form eternal in its beauty.

All sports, it seems, surprise us with their capacity to fascinate and addict us, to win our allegiance and engage our passions. But in this, as in all things, there is something special about baseball. We feel somehow that baseball's hold is superior and different, that its hand reaches deeper inside us, takes hold of a body part or psychic organ which others cannot reach, that it touches us more resonantly along a wider range of need and feeling.

Between its periodic explosions of speed and power, baseball moves slowly. It is a long time, as sport moves, between pitches, a longer time between batters, a still longer time between innings. The slow deliberateness of the game's progression distinguishes baseball from other ball sports, in much the same way that bridge distinguishes itself from blackjack. It is the difference between strolling through a museum, stopping first before one great painting, then another, and absorbing them slowly, one by one, and watching a film, whose images pass before our eyes at the rate of 24 frames per second. Even if each frame were a Rembrandt—and watching Michael Jordan leave the hardwood, hang and pivot in midair, and sink an underhand lay-up from the opposite side of the basket is a kind of Rembrandt—it is not the same. The thrill is exalting but ephemeral. Eye and mind are immediately drawn back into the rapid-fire stutter of the game which, like virtually every other ball sport except baseball, is a series of quickly bursting separate thrills and letdowns (oohs and ahs) whose dramatic accumulation is the almost exclusive product of the changing score.

A duel between a pitcher and batter, where the batter, with two strikes on him, protectively fouls off studied pitch after pitch, can take several minutes, all to no more apparent purpose than to keep one batter alive. If there is a speedy runner on first, a threat to steal, a second duel opens between the pitcher and the runner, doubling or tripling the time of this single at-bat. If the pitcher throws repeatedly to first to hold the dancing runner near the bag, fans often grow impatient, though the more patient among them know they are watching baseball if not at its most dynamic, at its most distinctive. There is time between pitches, time between tosses to first, time between batters, time between innings, time for everything to register and sink in. Images record themselves—the runner edging nervously off first, looking forth and back, unnerving the pitcher who, in his symmetrical turn, looks back and forth, bird-like, between the batter and the runner, the catcher and the ball, before making his selection and at last turning the ball loose. One can almost imagine him punching his chess player's time clock after each pitch and awaiting the opposition's next move as he settles into a defensive mode.

This is but one of a thousand images every game projects, and each is framed for our consideration, frozen in physical and mental space. If a runner we think safe is called out, we have time to consider the consequences before the next significant action takes place. Our mind and attention are not drawn, as in football or soccer, basketball or hockey, into the uninterrupted or briefly broken rush of the game. We have time for our anger or delight, our sense of injustice or relief. We have time to consider the implications of the call, the short- and, with time, the long-term implications. We know how it affects the inning and perhaps the game, know how it lightens or adds to the pitcher's burden, and can trace its ramifications—a weaker hitter will open the next inning as a result, a pitcher or extraordinary fielder will be hit for—across the entire span of the game. And everything is cumulative. What happens at any given moment influences irreparably and substantially what happens at every subsequent moment. No pitch or play, however seemingly inconsequential, is without its radiant effect. As in chaos theory, every flutter of a butterfly's wing (or pitcher's or umpire's arm) alters irreparably the arrangement of the universe and its future, in this case the mutable world and future of the game.

More privileged than others, the baseball fan has time for all this, time too to adjust even to expectation and personality, to fit what he has seen into his habitual patterns of judgment and response: This confirms what I have long suspected about the superiority of shrewdness to power; this unsettles my notions about the ultimate triviality of luck; out there the city and its traffic, in here the serene and peaceful green; I am among good friends. Whatever effect the play has on us is magnified, extended, and multiplied in duration and force. Whatever this game means to us—as partisans, esthetes, idol worshippers, or probability theorists, as fantasizers, power-seekers, or as witnesses of cosmic or psychological forces at their just or unsavory work—there will be time for that meaning to ease its way inside us, take its place, and begin its slow stalactitic drip. In baseball, every situation—part painting, part drama—hangs before us, moving yet framed for our absorption and contemplation. There is time, in these nearly frozen moments, for subject and object to meet, look one another over, and make acquaintance. In games of breakneck speed and continuous motion, the viewer is overwhelmed, sucked into an experience that, by demanding his constant attention to unbroken action, sweeps him up and, in large measure, cancels him. The fan is absorbed, taken in, swept along, charged—call it what you will, but all tip the balance of participation away from the spectator toward the game. In place of that measured balance of contemplation and identification, absorption and distance, that characterizes the response to fine art, the fan "loses himself" in the rush of sensory pleasure and excitement. The spectator of these sports is, relatively speaking, more a mechanism of response, less a creative contributor to the experience and the game. In baseball, owing to its slower pace, dramatic development, and greater complexity, the observer's personal history, character, and inclination are tapped and let run, if never drained. We meet the game on even terms and create an experience out of that meld and meeting. Who we are has time and provocation to become part of what we see.

Baseball, then, plays more instruments in the orchestra of human response, plays them more sonorously, and sustains its tones with a more lyrical and full-throated ease. Those of us who share this treasured affliction understand very well what novelist Wilfred Sheed means when, in *My Life as a Fan*, he reports that he was "insane with grief" and "sick with sorrow" when the Cardinals beat the Dodgers for the 1942 National League pennant. We nod when he finds it "strange [that] he could hurt so much," but though he may be, we are not surprised. Like Sheed, we have been intoxicated by this game, enslaved to it. And while other sports have their adherents, their champions of suffering and addiction, we take as incontrovertible truth sportswriter Jim Murray's observation that "No one bleeds like a baseball fan whose team is in a long slump."[15] Nor, we want to add, do others experience to a comparable degree the bliss or ecstasy that comes with a ninth inning victory, the feeling of awe that overtakes us when we enter the ballpark and are flooded with green, the beauty inherent in a smoothly executed double play, the rising tension of a slowly building rally or a foul-off duel between a canny pitcher and dogged hitter locked at three-and-two. Other sports, we are convinced, have no equivalent for the fierceness of that head-to-head competition, the elegant cooperation of the squeeze, the hit-and-run or pickoff. They have no substitute for the rich embeddedness of everything that happens in the thickening strata of the season, the geological history of the game, the meticulously cherished tales and records of every past and passing citizen of the ancient nation of baseball.

Red Smith reports the following:

> I had a bartender friend in Philadelphia years ago, a devoted baseball fan, who told me, and he said this with tears in his eyes, that the most beautiful thing in the world, more beautiful than any blond, more beautiful than a mountain lake at sunset, was bases filled, two out, three and two on the batter, and everybody moving with the pitch.[16]

If you are a baseball fan, you will know at once that (a) this man is in dire need of therapy, (b) this man is at the same time very nearly right, and (c) that whatever he or she may claim, no fan of any other sport is likely to have felt or spoken quite this way. And as these several truths wash over you, you will feel a goose-bumping thrill of appreciation dance across your skin, a smile spread irresistibly across your face. Like Thomas Boswell, one of baseball's clearest and wisest voices, "we can't quite say why baseball seems so valuable, almost indispensable to us."[17] But we know with unshakable conviction that the game has earned its special place and value. Checkers is an enjoyable game, and when it is played by two masters we can recognize its richness and possibilities. Backgammon and bowling no less. But they are not chess. And baseball, as someone has said, is quite simply the world's most interesting game, a game of chess for sprinters and gymnasts, individual and cooperative, deliberate and eruptive all at once.

That we cannot quite say why baseball means and matters as it does has not prevented at least a few from seeking the measure of its depths. Here is one list of hypotheses:

(1) It is sufficiently complex to fascinate the poet, sufficiently obvious to please the peasant.

(2) It offers a sensitive balance of physical skills, problem solving, and chance.

(3) It is hard to play well, yet easy to learn.

(4) It is fun to watch, yet challenging to study.

(5) It is a game steeped, more than any other, in rich mythological currents and metaphorical contexts.[18]

Here is another:

(1) The relationship between baseball and its fans is usually longer than that for other sports, extending over years or even decades.

(2) The fan's relationship to the game often resonates with the fact that

he first played it with his father and that that act is memorialized among the most noteworthy and celebrated rituals of father-son relations.

(3) It is a year-round sport, played for eight consecutive months and then discussed, debated and dissected the remainder of the year.

(4) To be a baseball fan is to be a perpetual cheerleader, judge, critic, and sage all in one. Everybody talks about baseball.

(5) The fan's attachment to the game is enhanced by his attachment to the parks that house them. No other sport lavishes so much attention and love on the fields and structures where the game is played.

(6) Although prices have risen, tickets remain, compared to other sports, a bargain. Families, including those of modest means, can attend.

(7) The ballpark experience is cathartic: fans enjoy unusual latitude and are accorded a larger role than elsewhere.[19]

The lists are extensive, complementary, persuasive, highly suggestive, and finally—like any two hundred lists that might be added to them—inadequate. A common attempt to fill some of the more conspicuous voids explains baseball's popularity by its compatibility with the American character. Despite its probable origin in the British game of rounders—no, Abner Doubleday did not invent it one day in Cooperstown in 1839—baseball has become the preeminently American game, the national pastime as it has long been called, though it begins, sadly, to cede that place to others. "Next to religion," declared Herbert Hoover, "baseball has furnished a greater impact on American life than any other institution." "Whoever wants to know the heart and mind of America," remarked Jacques Barzun portentously, "had better learn baseball."[20] Far more numerous than those who have tried to explain baseball's popularity and power in broadly human terms are those who have sought to explain it as a reflection or metaphor of the American character. The belief is, if we can somehow identify what it is that makes baseball so distinctly and comprehensively American, we will have gone a long way toward understanding the game's almost emblematic connection to the country and its uncanny hold on its population. If the stars and stripes had not beaten them to it, the bat and ball might have graced our nation's flag, though come to think of it, 50 baseballs in the upper left hand corner, bordered below and to the side by a field of bats laid out in rows is a near enough cousin to the one we have.

The attempt to identify the American characteristics of baseball, like the effort to isolate the distinctively American character itself, has become a kind of miniature national pastime. And both have been too glibly successful to be informative. A 1942 study of the myriad efforts to define the American character concluded, as we might have guessed, that "almost every conceivable value or trait has at one time or another been imputed to American culture by authoritative observers."[21] And so it is with the alleged Americanness of baseball. For some it is a prime expression of the pastoral idyll. An implantation of Edenic green in the heart of urban turbulence, it signals a return to the purity, innocence, and simplicity of an earlier rural America. It offers, in this view, a pastoral vision of peace and harmony. Or, if not quite pastoral, then an Enlightenment expression of order, reason, and balance, a kind of playing-field version of John Locke or the Federalist Papers.[22] Others see it differently, though they plant their claims in soil no less American. For Mark Twain, baseball was, unpastorally, "the symbol and expression of the drive and push and rush of the booming nineteenth century."[23] Or, as another put it, mingling Enlightenment orderliness with robber-baron drive, the game was an embodiment of American life in its exalting energy, opportunism, and execution, while paying lip service to management, strategy, and planning. While for some baseball is a symbol of the American deference to rules, boundaries, and the governance of law, to others it represents the fulfillment of the American promise to reward virtuous striving or the American inclination to pay lip service to the law while rewarding theft.

Robert Frost claimed he never felt more at home in America than at a ball game because the game, like America, was a full-bodied exhibition of prowess, justice, and courage.[24] Others, in a similar vein, have found in the national pastime the nation's own exaltation of freedom and liberty, fortitude, bravery, and patience. One writer reads baseball as prototypically white and Protestant, a representation of the mythic world of the solitary, lone individual and his need for physical space; another emphasizes its alleged democracy of spirit, its submergence of the individual in the union, and subordination of solo effort to team play. For baseball's late commissioner Bartlett Giamatti and the documentary producer Ken Burns, baseball, like America, is about coming home. It is, in Giamatti's fine phrase, "the romance epic of homecoming America sings to itself." In his *Baseball and the American Dream*, however, George Grella finds in the open-endedness of this timeless game echoes of the old American yearning not for home, but for infinity and eternity.

Perhaps Giamatti is nearest the mark when he describes baseball as a compound whose mix encompasses the contrarieties and contradictions of the American character—a mix of moral energy and pragmatic efficiency, optimism and guile, respect for law and admiration for the maverick. To which one might add, as some do, a respect for both the individual and the group, for cooperation and competition, for equal opportunity and unequal dispensation, and on and on and on.

Baseball Wears the Colors of the Spirit

To say that such a reading is nearest the mark is to suggest ultimately that there is no mark, only a near infinity of marks, many of them in targets fixed at opposite ends of an all but unbounded range. These efforts to explain the appeal of baseball to its fans are typically sociological in their orientation. They treat the game, not without some justification, as a reflection of the character, history, and values of the nation or of one or more of its many subgroups and populations. What has been slighted, I believe, is the critical personal and psychological component of that appeal. Baseball reflects our character and culture as a nation. But it also and more fundamentally addresses our personal cultures: our individual desires and needs, our proclivities and obsessions, even our pathologies. If baseball is a distinctively American game, it is so only in the sense that the nation is the sum of its individual citizens and that "American," therefore, is a shorthand term for virtually every conceivable attribute or value. Baseball has become so intricately entangled with our nerves and sinews because it appeals to almost everything that is in us. As the interviews that follow collectively reveal, it offers itself, in the jargon of contemporary literary theory, as an "open text," one that can be read in as many ways as there are readers, one that will be read, to psychologize the theory, largely as a reflection and projection of the personal inclinations, needs, and passions of its fans. What differentiates baseball from other such reflectors is that the richness and complexity of the game enable it to answer almost every signal as its archetypal picks strum our most deeply resonating nerves. Baseball, writes Roger Angell in *The Summer Game*, "is so rich and various in structure and aesthetics and emotion that I have not yet come close to its heart." It is a telling confession, coming as it does from the archer with the fullest quiver and the keenest aim. But it is an enduring virtue of the game that while none of us has approached its heart, the game has a sufficient array of other vital organs to occupy us for a lifetime. Also, that every attempt to find its heart brings us closer to our own.

For this reason it is dangerous to generalize about fans, even about those routinely stereotyped Yankee and Dodger fans of the 1950s. Even the usually unimpeachable Mr. Angell runs into trouble when, in the same collection, he yields to the temptation to draw dark circles around crowds of fans. Listening to Yankee fans speaking contemptuously about the Mets, Angell claims to recognize the tone.

> It was knowing, cold, full of the contempt that the calculator feels for those who don't play the odds. It was the voice of the Yankee fan. The Yankees have won the American League pennant 20 times in the past 30 years; they have been the world's champions 16 times in that period. Over the years, many of their followers have come to watch them with the stolidity, the smugness, and the arrogance of holders of large blocks of blue-chip stocks. These fans expect no less than perfection. They coolly accept the late-inning rally, the winning homer, as only their due. They are apt to take defeat with ill grace, and they treat their stars as though they were executives hired to protect their interest. During a slump or a losing streak, these capitalists are quick and shrill with their complaints: "They ought to damn well do better than this, considering what they're being paid!"

As a Yankee fan who lived and, yes, occasionally died with that team, I can attest that Angell is wrong. No less typically than the fans whose waters he believes he has fathomed, I never expected perfection, only ultimate, if often hard-won and near-missed, victory. Angell knows there is no perfection in baseball. He has just spoken of the ability of any cellar dwelling club to beat a Series winner on any given day, and he knows well that a 3-for-10 hitter is Hall of Fame material. There was, moreover, nothing cool or smug about my expectations or my rooting, and nothing at all was experienced or accepted coolly.[25] To universalize such a response is to suggest that Americans approached World War II or Korea with a cool smugness, expecting no casualties, fearing no losses.

As a fan I differed from those who pledged their hearts to other teams, mainly because I had a tradition of dominance and nobility to protect. As Yankee fans we were keepers of the flame, guardians of an historic and elegant tradition. We had not only something to care and hope for, but something to protect and preserve: an unparalleled record of achievement. For such a fan the pain of loss is, if anything, intensified, though it may be felt less often. To other fans the absence of a pennant is just another season, just another loss. To a Yankee fan in the 1950s it was a blemish, a blot, a rust-spot on the splendid chassis polished with such meticulous dedication over the previous three decades. Burdened with the weightiest sense of continuity and tradition, the Yankee fan—this one at least—felt most vulnerable to the merest sign of weakness. And he knew how many others were out there, waiting eagerly to saw and hammer at the crack. Angell is undeniably one the most astute of baseball fans, observers, and writers. That he draws such an uncharacteristically pinched circle around the fans of a team he felt no love for, shows how risky generalizations about fandom are, how unlikely we are to be right when we sweep into any one container the emotions and motives of fans.

One of the defining characteristics of contemporary thought is that it has abandoned the notion of clear and objective meaning. Historical events, works of art, human events and activities of every kind are no longer thought to contain fixed meanings it is our task to tease out. In this post-modernist view, as it is called, there is no single correct interpretation of texts, incidents or events, but almost as many interpretations as interpreters. In this newly open world, while no object contains its own point or dictates its proper effect, there are degrees of openness. The richer, more multifaceted, and more ambiguous the object, the wider the range of potential interpretations. Different readers, as Mary Rosenau points out, are expected to offer different interpretations of whatever it is they fix their gaze on because the world, as we have come to perceive and not quite understand, has traded its virginal simplicity for a spiraling multiplicity. And in this expanding world, some animals are more multiple than others. Baseball, in these terms, is a radically open text, a game as broad and varied as its audience, as rich as the imaginations we bring to it.

This is not to say there is no game out there, nothing to stimulate, direct, or limit our responses. Baseball is not a blank slate on which we may write ourselves however we please. Rather, as these interviews make clear, it is a prism so multifaceted in its composition as to seem almost unlimited in the number of angles it can produce, the number of images it can capture and reflect. For

Shakespeare, art was a mirror held up to Nature. But our futile attempts to hold that mirror steady, to read that colossal poet (among others) in any one way, however comprehensive or complex, has helped us see that the greatest art is less a mirror held up to Nature than a prism held up to natures, the infinitely varied natures of those who gaze into it. And in this sense, if I may be presumptuous on behalf of this amazing game, baseball resembles great art. It is unique among sports—indeed, I would argue, among all the institutions of popular culture—in its cornucopic nourishment of almost every requirement and taste.

Sport in general, baseball in particular, has been frequently compared to art. Like a work of art, baseball is separate from the real world yet resonant of it. Attending to itself, to its own craft and indigenous beauty, it generates meanings reminiscent of our world and pertinent to our lives. Like a kind of poem, baseball has a beauty and rhythm appropriate to it; like drama it unfolds slowly and with mounting tension in search of resolution; like a complex narrative, every game and season tells a different story. Like works of classical art, baseball is highly structured, orderly, even symmetrical. Like pastoral, it is small, pleasing, whole, and separate, the image and music of another world. But without attempting to set this sport on a higher plane than the greatest art—there are limits, after all, even to my own admiration—one may argue for the greater immediacy and power of its appeal.

Baseball, like all sports, though in richer and more substantial ways, is an art that partakes of reality, acting as a transitional object and space between the imaginary and the real, as it does between childhood and maturity. Unlike the work of fiction, professional sport is at the same time real. The game is an artificial yet genuine struggle, a drama whose outcome is at once inconsequential and fateful, trivial and crucial. In baseball we see the beautiful in the service of the purposeful. Since it is a "game," an invention, construct or artifice, the importance of each reenactment fades with time and, at least apparently, does not exceed its own boundaries. But it is also real, as are the stakes. For it pits one individual against another, one group against another, one city against another, us against them, those we identify with and suckle power from against those we suspect, disdain, or care nothing for. Like art, baseball is an object of disinterested concern. But unlike art ideally construed, the disinterestedness is not distanced, not fully aesthetic, less than perfectly detached. It engages us contemplatively, yes, but finally more fully: morally, attitudinally, and emotionally, on every level and in ways not easily isolated from our daily lives and concerns. Baseball has art's otherness and nonreality, its insulated separation from the real world. Like poetry as Auden described it, baseball makes nothing happen. But sport involves real people playing this demanding game for mortal stakes, wearing the "skins" of rival animals and competing in ways that measure and determine their worth, to themselves and others. To identify with them in their striving, their enterprise, their plying of skill, their ecstasy in triumph and anguish in defeat, is to be more fully and humanly engaged than perhaps readers of fiction are when identified with literary heroines and heroes. It is to care, in this enclosed protected world, about real people, performing real activities for real stakes, however far removed their activity from ordinary life and its extraordinary consequences. And since our pride as individuals, as members of small groups or entire communities is at risk, the outcome is of more than surrogate significance.

The team's success or failure is, for the young fan, no small determinant of his well-being. To contemplate the sport, to witness it with the fan's devotion and involvement, is to partake of an activity that while it may lack the grandeur of the finest art, involves real human beings in genuine as well as representative and metaphoric action. Watching a game is not, as Roger Angell claims in *Five Seasons*, akin to the appreciative observation of very young children at play. It is the activity, rather, of rival parents watching their own children at embattled play in the same playground, free to expose their secret glee at their child's demonstrated superiority, or their otherwise hidden rage, pain, or disappointment at his or her incompetence or failure.

Baseball speaks meaningfully to us, then. It reaches our hearts and plays, along the way, across the entire network of our needs, emotions, and beliefs. Baseball speaks systematically to those who crave order, stability, tradition and predictability—no sport is so rule-governed or tradition-bound—more freely to those who crave the openness of its liberation from time and the infinite variety of its possibilities. It has a language for those who relish individual competition and challenge—a man with a rock facing a man with a club—another for those who love cooperation, teamwork, and self-subordination: no other game contains a play called "the sacrifice." Baseball is generous to those who wish or need to see their own ordinariness mirrored, ratified and enhanced. Baseball players are not giants; neither seven feet tall nor three feet wide, they look more like ourselves than participants in other major team sports. Yet the sport is, if anything, still more responsive to those drawn to the loftiness of myth, heroism, and legendary accomplishment. The Hall of Fame, the original which other sports have more feebly followed, speaks for itself. Its halls reverberate with history and heroism, and no other sport is so rich in legendary figures and moments. Mention the names Babe Ruth, Walter Johnson, and Joe DiMaggio, and try them against Bob Cousy, Wilt Chamberlain, even Michael Jordan, and listen for the difference. Or rub Ty Cobb, Honus Wagner, and Ted Williams against Jim Brown, Johnny Unitas, or Joe Montana and listen again. It is like playing a Stradivarius alongside a great but unanointed modern instrument. The difference is in the history, the resonance, the fullness of sound, and like the Strad, its splendor defies satisfactory explanation and is enhanced by that mystery.

Baseball has much to satisfy those who require or thrive on controlled planning, strategy, and cerebration—only chess can match it—almost as much for those who relish down in the dirt physical grubbiness, contact, and the threat of violence: manager and umpire nose to nose and raging, the high slide, the crash of runner and catcher at the plate, the knockdown pitch that starts a riot, the bench-clearing brawl. There is something too for those, microcosmically oriented, who find solace in its optimistic life-lessons, who view the game as a framed and brightened mirror of social, psychological, or political reality—the return home, the open-ended possibility of last-minute (or ninth-inning) triumph and redemption, the perpetual promise of a better next year.

No other game offers so many transportable metaphors, so many parallels to our own condition: "Out of left field," "Can't get to first base," "Off base," "Take a raincheck," "Play hardball," "Touch all the bases," "Bush league," "Bat this around," "Keep your eye on the ball," "Right off the bat," "Go to bat for," and so on. And the game, as we know, is for better and for worse a microcosm of the culture that surrounds and feeds it. In 1947 it became a spur and harbinger of racial integration. As a mirror of today's culture it reflects our corporate and personal greed and exposes us, as Robert Lipsyte claims, as spoiled, destructive children. Yet no other game offers such totalizing absorption and escape: the tailored park in the city's teeming heart, fantasy camps, the madly insulated and embroiling world of rotisserie baseball, the rural idyll of an earlier simpler America. Responding largely to the length of baseball's season and the daily reliability of the game, more than one fan I spoke to referred to baseball as a separate and insulated world (like a work of art), a world parallel to the one we live in, yet superior to and protectively separated from it. In fact, it is arguably the shattering of that wall, the erosion of baseball's special status as an idyllic refuge where order is maintained and continuity assured that threatens the game and the special place it occupies in our imaginations.

Nor need all of baseball's accommodations be expressed in balanced antitheses. It also has something of real depth, responsiveness, and value for those who seek a rich source of conversation, reminiscence, or family bonding, or for fans who find in its cooperative harmonies images of a family they do not have but dream of. It is also a persuasive reality instructor or socializing agent, teaching all the hard-won lessons of maturity: the value of patience ("wait till next year"), the capacity to deal with frustration and defeat, the value of loyalty to the consistently defeated sources of their frustration, appreciation for a success measured in modest terms (3 out of 10 is a distinguished average), and one could go on.

A Fan for All Reasons

Since I am stressing the multiplicity of nerves the game harshly or delicately touches, a question arises: Are there limits to what we might call "relevant" appreciation or response? Who qualifies as a bonafide baseball fan? What sorts of responses to the game are "legitimate" marks of fandom, which so extraneous to the game or irrelevant to its nature that they are simply "not in the ballpark?"

Virginia Gale, a local Chicago television personality in the 1950s, urged her female listeners to visit Wrigley Field with this message:

> It's like an afternoon vacation in the country and there's nothing more relaxing. Gee, you can sit in the sun if you want—or relax in the shade. There are plenty of seats for you and your friends. And comfortable, too. And lots of good food and refreshing drinks. And what a wonderful way to forget about washing, ironing, cooking. It's a fun place made for comfortable clothes and just relaxing. Get away from it all and have fun at Cubs Park—beautiful Wrigley Field.[26]

Is a woman who answers Ms. Gale's call a baseball fan? Is she enjoying or appreciating the game or something so peripheral to it as to make of her more a sunbather than a fan? At first glance the answer seems obvious. If this is fandom, everything is fandom; it doesn't wash. And yet it may, or very nearly. That everything or nearly everything even remotely connected or connectable to the game constitutes a potential aspect of fandom and a pertinent source of appreciation is precisely the point. But while Ms. Gale may be stretching things— even the elastic bodysuit we call baseball has its limits—much of what she recommends is quite remarkably reminiscent of the language of several unmistakably perfervid fans I spoke to. Their love for the game is quite inseparable from their enthusiasm about the beauty of the ballpark, the sounds of the crowd, the hawking vendors and the pouring of beer, the sense, perhaps above all, of unity and camaraderie they experience with those around them: an extended family, as one put it, a sea of friends. They too are getting away from it all and having fun at the park, and their fan credentials seem perfectly in order. As of course is Thomas Boswell's. Boswell's is inarguably one of the most lucid and knowing voices in the baseball archives, and yet he has this to say:

> Baseball was meant, and still is meant to be irresponsible, anti-adult, silly, lyric, inexplicable, slightly rebellious and generally disreputable. The ballpark is the place you go to play hooky.... That's baseball. Peanut shells on the floor, as much noise as you can make.... They call baseball the summer game, which, to a child, means vacation and laziness and multifarious mischief.

If that is baseball—and who among us can say with authority it is not?—Ms. Gale's women are in for a splendid afternoon of nothing else, and we are urged if not compelled to admit that this ballpark is larger than we had imagined.

We are perhaps a little closer to a seat we feel comfortable in when Roger Angell, letting us know in *Season Ticket* what, among a thousand other things, he finds precious and irreplaceable about this game, reminds a friend of an experience they shared at a game they attended together several years before: a spider working on a web, inning by inning at a Tigers-Jays game in 1984, the floodlights illuminating the tiny construction "as it grew in size and beautiful design ... and was stretched to its planned and perfect mooring." Although he never says so, Angell is probably weaving his own small construction here, an analogy between the beautifully designed web, growing in size inning by inning until it finds it destined shape, and the game itself. But that is resonant background to the more evident and explicit point: that baseball is a meeting of friends around often trivial but memorable images the game or its surroundings generate. Baseball for Angell is a piece of sculpture, as he puts it, that changes as you walk around it. And along its surfaces, some of them small as a fingernail but no more forgettable for that, are the moments of frozen beauty the game or attending it provides. Baseball, for this and other fans, is a place of purity, a golden vacuum to which beauty attaches itself as though it recognizes its long-sought mate. It is a park or paradise in which wonderful things can happen—anything from an unassisted double play to a spider's spinning—pristine images, waiting, poised for the magic moment that will memorialize them.

Because baseball is a relatively slow and deliberate game, because its players are stationed at relatively fixed and widely spaced positions, because almost everything that happens on the playing field is a vivid snapshot, baseball for Angell and many of the rest of us is a game of frozen moments: the close play at third base that shuts down a last-ditch rally; the pitch high and away hinting the pitcher has lost it, though the manager, to his and our chagrin, does not notice and stays with him a single pitch too long; Billy Martin racing from second almost to home plate to catch that pop-up, Sandy Amoros taking Berra's liner off his shoetops. These are the moments we cherish, ponder, and on a hundred occasions revive for reconsideration or a wordless awe. One remembers where he was and precisely how the scene was set, and he knows in his mind and nervous system what it meant. These are the peak moments the existentialist takes as his raison d'être and which a certain kind of baseball fan takes as his due. This is baseball as sculpture, photography, aesthetics—one of the 691 dozen ways the game can capture and reward us. The stadium and the game are intrinsically good, a kind of early evening summer background against which brilliant, subtle, and dramatic strokes are brushed. Nothing ill can happen here, or if it does it will be reframed, like a plain-looking girl in a chorus line of beauties or a slightly straying stroke in a Vermeer. Usually it is a critical play that decides the game or bespeaks a grace or promise worth remembering. But it may also be a spider. Is the web an appropriate object of fan appreciation? It is what it is, we know, because it found its illumination and design at a game between the Tigers and the Jays in 1984. Who among us will rule it out?

I am at the outer edges here, playing riskily at the margins of fan experience in order to show how uncertain and flexible they are, how far removed from the familiar center. We are on much safer ground, of course, with George Will's almost as lyrical appreciation of the remarkably complex strategies and thought processes that preoccupy the game's most meticulously mental players and managers and that make baseball, in Will's cerebral eye, the preeminent thinking man's game. In the reports of the fans you will read in the following pages you will find more near the center than at the margins, but much that hovers between them. All of these people are card-carrying fans, many come upon at ball games, conferences, and memorabilia shows. Everything they report is the testimony of devoted, lifelong fanatics about what the game meant to them when they were young or means to them now. Their testimony speaks, in its extension, to the range of that experience, the number of points at which baseball touched and touches them. It speaks, in its intensity, of the radiant power of its touch.

Early introduction to baseball is the gift of a personal garden, a field large as any major league diamond to roam and choose a position in, a stadium crowded with other fans yet with every seat still available. A mask on the back of the Wheaties box to fit every face (to change my metaphor), it comes, as few other "free offers" or impositions come, without instructions. You assemble it largely unaided and wear it in ways that suit you. A father may tell you how to watch a game. His own personal preferences for teams and players may influence yours, as will those of others: your peers or those older and wiser than you who have lived with the game a good deal longer, grown familiar with its personality and habits. One will remind you that a game, like the season it inhabits, is an unfolding story, another that the special beauty of the game is in its timelessness or that it is, alternatively or at once, the most aesthetic, casual, or cerebral of pastimes. Some will advise you to keep your eye on the way the third baseman moves to his left, on the grace of the catcher rising and throwing in one motion to nail the runner trying to steal. Some will bid you to attend to the meditative slowness of the game and to fill its spaces with calculations and probabilities. Others will urge you to consider its history and tradition, the glorious names that still echo in the rafters, the ghosts that haunt the field. They will remark on the wonderful continuity of the game, the all but unaltered and unalterable sameness that allows for sensible comparisons between Ruth and Aaron at the plate, Cobb and Henderson on the basepaths, Johnson and Ryan on the mound. But in the end, though perhaps you do not know it yourself, you will choose your own game, watch with more than your eye the game that answers to your needs, that resonates to an internal music you have perhaps never identified, listened to, or recorded.

Perhaps we approach almost everything this way: our first reading, our early encounters with popular, rock, or classical music. But the world being too much with us, too pedantic an instructor, we will learn how to narrow our sights. Teachers will teach us how to understand a story, what to look for in a plot or character or scene. Others will tell us what to listen for in music, how to distinguish a canon from a fugue. And since their authority is formalized, institutionalized, we will begin to adapt. We will watch through their lenses, listen with their ears. We will distinguish literature from mere fiction in all the proper ways, poetry from verse, "great music" from rock 'n' roll. And if we are among those who attend universities, we will make finer distinctions still. We will learn the latest ways of reading and listening and looking at art, and they will become our own. We will become neo–Aristotelians or New Critics, Deconstructionists or New Historicists, and though somewhere underground the old fresh currents may still be running, they will run more quietly and thinly as topsoil sifting down from the surface relentlessly dries the streams.

The great news is, there is no academy of baseball, no received view, no current or outdated fashion. One who still concerns himself deeply and significantly with the aesthetics of the game is not an anachronism; one who abandons a previously favored player because he seems unconscionably greedy, indifferent to fans, or cruel to his wife or girlfriend will not be dabbling in irrelevancies. Few will tell him that baseball properly appreciated leaves no room for such considerations, that they should not affect the fans' rooting or esteem. Or if they tell him so, they will not be listened to. The heart will follow what it needs and recoil from what repels it, and it will do so argumentatively, insistently, and without embarrassment. The baseball fan, unlike the academic reader, looker, or listener, will not respond impressionistically one year, formalistically the next, and post-modernistically a third. Or if he does, it will not be because fashions of baseball appreciation and analysis have changed, but because he or she is changing, and because what one sees and cares about and loves is a reflection of who one is. If he responds atonally to the music of baseball, it will not be because he has been exposed to (Moe) Berg or Bergians, Webern or Webernians, but because something is dissonant or askew in his personal or social life; or, conversely, because too little is and because he requires some surprising disharmonies to liven things up.

There are plenty of baseball writers out there—some of them splendid masters of prose, grand dramatists, subtle masters of the art of narrative, even lyrical poets of a more than respectable order—but they do not tell us what to see. Many will tell us what they watch for and perceive, and they will do so, as for example Roger Angell does, with a prose that makes one ache for his gift. But the wise reader knows when he hears another tell him what baseball is or how it should be loved that the pundit is speaking for himself, passing off the beating of his own heart as the pulse of a nation. Here is Daniel Guterson in a recent essay on the damaging commodification of sport: "The fan's fiercely felt allegiance to sport—I recognize this as occurring in my own heart—is a fiercely felt allegiance to life itself, a panicked hold he keeps on youth as with time his intimations of mortality resonate with ever-deepening seriousness." The comment is revealing in its subtle slide from personal awareness to projective generalization. What Guterson recognizes as occurring in himself he confidently attributes to "the fan" and offers as an explanation for all our fierce allegiances. It is always so. Explanations of baseball's or sport's attractions are occurrences of the private heart, read by the excited owner as the pulse of a nation, a generation, or an age. When the drummer is not ours, we wonder if we are speaking of the same game. Where there is harmony, there is wide illumination, the quaint and heartening conviction that we are all, in some warmingly binding sense, scarcely distinguishable mirrors of a single soul.

For Ken Burns, baseball is "a mirror or a prism in which we can see refracted all of our tendencies as a people." But it comes as no surprise that the most vividly refracted images in his nine-part television documentary are unity and perseverance and home. "If you wanted to describe my work in a nutshell," he admits, "it's about *unum*. What is it that makes us cohere? The last 30 years have seen the disintegration of that which brings us together. Every film I've made reminds us of why we should be together.... And baseball, like the Civil War, is one of these really clean shots right to the heart of who we are." Like his earlier documentary on the Civil War, the newer film is ultimately about "the intersection of love and family and what it is to be an American." When baseball and the Civil War wear the same uniforms we can be quite confident it is not because they have fortuitously selected them, but because they have the same insistent tailor. As Burns's brother Ric explained, their mother died when Ken was 11, and the pain of her early passing still haunts his work. All the films he has done, Ric suggests, are attempts to revisit this early trauma in order to deny or overcome it by celebrating the triumph of human community and will. It is no accident, therefore, that both histories are obsessed with the themes of unity, family, and home. Burns claims to have discovered something he was completely unprepared to find in baseball: "these feelings about family and memory and time in America, and this notion of home." But if he is surprised, we need not be, for we know that, as it always does, baseball returns the image of the self that inquires into it. What the literary theorist Wolfgang Iser says of works of literature is no less true of the hardly less rewarding experience of baseball. Formulating its meaning "enables us to formulate ourselves and thus discover an inner world of which we had hitherto not been conscious." Like Emerson's Nature, in other words, baseball wears the colors of the spirit.

It is rare that we are privy to such corroborative testimony as Ric Burns offers, but we rarely require it to recognize the personal component of ostensibly disinterested assessments of the game. Baseball, the bellicose Ty Cobb often said, "is something like a war." It's "a red-blooded sport for red-blooded men ... a struggle for supremacy, a survival of the fittest."[27] While the warrior Cobb perceived the game as a kind of battle, the Calvinist first commissioner of baseball, Kenesaw Mountain Landis, read it like a McGuffey reader. "Baseball is something more than a game to an American boy," he proclaimed, revealing more of his own Puritan moralism than of American boyhood. "It is his training field for life work. Destroy his faith in its squareness and honesty and you have destroyed something more: you have planted suspicion of all things in his heart."[28] No one who has read George Will's architectonic columns or watched him walk his voluminous political knowledge through the elegant labyrinth of his sentences should be surprised to learn that what he most appreciates about the game he loves is that it "rewards, and thus elicits, a remarkable level of intelligence from those who compete." For Will, being a serious baseball fan, like being a connoisseur of fine wines or a knowing political commentator, means to be "informed and attentive and observant," and accepting the responsibilities of such a student "makes demands on the mind of the doer." Roger Angell, on the other hand, speaks of baseball as a "comely" sport in *The Summer Game* and praises its "clean lines" and "perfectly observed balance," its "orderliness and constraint," its intriguing "convergence toward fixed points." And one knows, as one reads and savors these finely turned phrases and the elegantly crafted sentences that house them, that one is reading as much about the clean lines of Angell's comely temperament and prose as about the game they illuminate.

Baseball is moral and warlike, communal and comely, immortalizing and cerebral, and what shakes our head with wonder at the game is that neither these nor any of the innumerable other attributes or virtues ascribed to it seem inappropriate or unpersuasive. They are not arbitrary superimpositions of personality on an empty slate, but rich correspondences between the game and those who love it. In its alarming breadth and complexity, baseball answers what we ask of it and mirrors who we are. As the interviews in this collection bear witness, one's view of baseball is an expression, finally, of his or her view of life. Like a dramatic monologue by Browning it reveals a *weltanschauung*. Speaking about baseball, the fan speaks about himself, exposes himself, his personal history, his desires and values, his needs and urges. He tells us what he looks for in this world and what he shuns, what attracts him and what repels him, what matters to him and what seems trivial. He expresses, in short, his moral, intellectual, and emotional life. It may be that one's view of virtually anything—movies, shopping, vacations, letter writing, pets, anything at all—is inevitably self-reflective in this way, broadening as it describes itself into a description of self. Anything at all, in other words, may be an instrument of self-probing, a glass of self-examination, a mirror of self-exposure. But the special richness and complexity of baseball—its "ancient" history and mythic ambiance, its rule-governed order and reliable continuity, its pastoral urbanity, its special relation to time and space, its frozen and kinetic beauty, its mathematical measurability and virtual sameness through expanding time—all this and a great deal more broaden its inclusiveness and range. They seem to make of baseball a wider mirror, a scalpel that cuts deeper and more cleanly, an echo chamber with a rounder, fuller sound.

Some of us may write better than others, some may know a great deal more about the history and subtleties of the game. But what each of us sees is both there and here, in the game and in ourselves, principally and unalterably in the ever shifting relationship between them. The fan who cherishes the game as a pleasing escape or source of heroizing identification occupies precisely the same rung on the ladder of legitimacy and status with the fan preoccupied with the display of athletic near-perfection, with baseball's moral or mythic implications, or with the chess-like intricacy of its strategies. If he loves the game and can regale you with a thousand memories and tales, he has bought his ticket to the game and takes his seat.

Even among the manifestations of popular culture, sport is distinct in this way. The movie fan, too, is a creator and a fantasizer. In the dark he weaves the web he requires, receives the light from the screen that answers to the light and darker spots of his nature and need. He is free, for the duration of the film and in its wake to indulge what reveries he will and will perceive them in the production. He may witness, as some psychoanalysts suggest, a perpetual reenactment of the primal scene, where the child, concealed in darkness, watches the romantic machinations of undressing giants. She may identify with Sharon Stone, he with Sly Stallone, as richly and indulgently as the baseball fan identifies with Frank Thomas meeting the ball squarely with the fat of his bat or Greg Maddux permitting no batter to attend that meeting from the first inning to the last. She may attend to the intricacies of the plot, he to the brilliance of the performances, a third to the cinematographic shadings. But if they are "serious" fans, they will be reminded, in the morning when they read the reviews, in the afternoons and evenings when they pore through the literature, that their gaze was misdirected or misinformed. Even art forms as popular, some would say lowly, as cinema, fashion, and acid rock have arbiters and changing fashions, sanctified and deauthenticated voices. Its criticism is not educated personal response but (or passes itself off as) adjudication and assessment, canonization and disqualification. One learns what to look for and what not to be distracted or fooled by, what matters more and less, what counts for a sophisticated and a naive response. Baseball writers occasionally veer in that direction. George Will, for instance, in *Men at Work*, argues that "baseball more than any other sport is enjoyed by the knowledgeable" and that "its beauties are visible to the trained eye, which is the result of a long apprenticeship of appreciation." But even this elitist form of elevating qualification never disqualifies, for there are more beauties to this game than Will allows, perhaps more than he appreciates or perceives. Whether one looks down from or upon Will's position, there is always more to be seen—and that is one of the great glories and complexities of the game. Less, however, is not worse, only different. Different is not improper or irrelevant, only another aspect of that generous complexity.

Knowing Everything but Why It Matters

Baseball, as Thomas Boswell has remarked, has been studied in more subtlety, depth, and detail than any other sport. Each game is subjected to an intense and meticulous postmortem in the clubhouse. Athletic detectives, players ask, Who is at fault? Who deserves credit for victory and to what degree? Who blundered? What threads of the game's plot remain hidden? At what precise point was the game won or lost and for what discernible reasons?[29] Before and during the game, as George Will has shown us, players and managers plunge themselves into still more elaborate inquiries and analyses. As Mike Schmidt, speaking for many, admitted, "I don't know how many pitchers know that I'm sitting here in the dugout all through the game, thinking about what they're doing. But I am. I don't mind if they know it. I'm watching."[30] Pitchers, of course, are studying hitters with comparable interest, and fans—at least certain kinds of fans—are studying all we ever wanted to know about the game and much we didn't.

A glance at any issue of the SABR (Society for American Baseball Research)

Journal shows us just how microscopically the game is examined. The lead article in the 1994 issue details the historical evolution of the infield diamond. Another studies the combined hit totals of teammates over a number of seasons. Yet another essay offers yet another way to calculate the statistical probability of DiMaggio's 56-game hitting streak. A fourth writer correlates a player's fielding position with his place in the batting lineup, asking both where given fielders tend to bat and where given lineup positions field. Another exhumes a pitcher who, in 1933, his only year in the majors, compiled a 2-0 record with a whopping 9.53 earned run average. Still another, testing a sample of 201 pitchers, finds no support for the prevalent belief that southpaws mature later than right-handers (the "Koufax phenomenon"), and on it goes into the shimmering twilight of factual and statistical investigation.

Players, managers, fans, and experts have subjected every imaginable and some quite unimaginable aspects of the game to exhaustive examination. Everything, that is, except its fans, though they are, after all, the principal source and determinants of its worth. The subject we persistently neglect is the one that justifies all this attention and scrutiny: the effect and influence of the game on those who watch and love and pay to see it. We know, in short, everything there is to know about baseball except why it is worthy of our attention, what it does to and for those who keep it running while devouring these Holmesian analyses. We see this in Will's *Men at Work*. The book shows us men at work, studying their crafts, striving for excellence through the knowledge they are convinced is power, analyzing in scrupulous detail every pitch and angle of the game. The one unasked question is whether it is worth doing, except as a livelihood for its players, or merely because it is "fun," whatever that may mean. One can, after all, study a frigate composed of mutton bones to learn how it is constructed and why, according to the laws of physics, it floats. But this will not justify either its construction or the ensuing analysis. What we want to know in both instances— or should want to know—is in what ways, beyond time-passing pleasure, this obsession justifies the hours and years of our lives we devote to it.

Lip service, of course, is paid to the importance of fans, particularly when they threaten to turn away. In 1951, then baseball commissioner Happy Chandler said, "I have always regarded baseball as our National Game that belongs to 150 million men, women, and children, not to sixteen special people who happen to own big league teams."[31] The recent history of the game has of course emptied Chandler's perhaps sincere affirmation of all relevance. Fans, as Roger Angell sadly observes in *Late Innings*, are ignored by the media and simply counted by the front office, though the surprising fan rebellion of 1994–95 rekindled at least nominal concern. "I take my hat off to the fans," remarked Mets outfielder Brett Butler, "because it [fan apathy] should make everybody realize how important they are to us."[32] But the concern and respect for fans, real or feigned, has never translated into serious inquiry into their mysterious and variegated relation to the game.

Fans, whether of sport, film, or popular music, have never been taken very seriously. "The literature of fandom as a social and cultural phenomenon," writes Joli Jenson, "is relatively sparse." Film and rock-star fans, when they are shown the respect of professional attention, are deprived of that respect by the findings. They are presented, typically—in both essays and films about fans—as lone, obsessed lovers or as the flailing limbs of a millipedal crowd. Fandom, as Jensen argues, is defined as a form of psychological compensation, fans as alienated sufferers whose star or hero worship fills huge voids in an otherwise empty or painful existence.

With as few exceptions, sport in general has been thinly studied as a social and cultural phenomenon, its fans all but totally ignored. When sports fans are noticed at all, more often than not it is for their hooliganism at soccer matches. Baseball fans, voluble at the ballpark and sporadically quoted in the press and a few serious essays on the sport, are for the most part mute. In his essay "Causes and Effects of Spectator Sports," Michael Schwartz lists nine possible sources of fan appeal, nine tentative answers to the question "What draws people to watch sporting events?" Pleasure in observing excellence, the need for excitement, release of tensions and socially based frustrations, the affirmation of values, the desire for sociability, the establishment of sexual identity, group conformity, the need for continuity, and goal-direct consumption. As the interviews in this book plainly demonstrate, the list is at least several dozen shy. But the importance of the effort is overshadowed by the writer's acknowledgment that since very little worthwhile research has been reported, his and other theories of fan attraction remain conjecture.

To find out what baseball means and has meant to its fans, one of course must speak to them. Their reports and recollections may be partial and imperfect, but they are all we can hope for, unless we are prepared to test their galvanic skin response during a late-inning rally or apply electrodes to their brains while flashing images of crucial plays and favored players before their eyes. We have, then, only personal testimony to rely on, and one looks, for such testimony, to the many oral histories of baseball that grace the sports shelves in libraries and book shops. One looks largely in vain. For what one discovers very quickly about these oral histories, these interviews collected and compiled by Lawrence Ritter, Donald Honig, Eugene Murdock, and others, is that almost all of them restrict their platform exclusively to ball players. The choice is natural. We are inherently more interested in what Dizzy Dean or Ralph Kiner, Roger Peckinpaugh or Robin Roberts might wish to tell us about the game than what a lathe operator or teacher in Cleveland or a bartender or engineer in Baltimore might have to say. But if we are, we pay a price for our preference.

Baseball players, as virtually every fan knows or has been reminded, are irrepressible storytellers. They are, in Thomas Boswell's felicitous description, "tale tellers who have polished their malarkey and winnowed their wisdom for years."[33] Since stories are what ball players love to tell and what, apparently, their interviewers want to hear, oral histories of baseball are, almost without exception, anecdotal warehouses, each one a new and, in its own restricted terms, quite fascinating Arabian Nights of reminiscence. In the most famous and highly praised of these histories, Ritter's *The Glory of Their Times*, players reminisce, often interestingly and poignantly, about their teammates and managers, most often, since these are turn-of-the-century players, about John McGraw and Fred Merkle. Four different explayers give their version of the notorious "Merkle boner" of 1908, Snodgrass tells us about ... Joe Wood has a tale about ... Rube Marquand remembers when ... and everyone will tell you who was the toughest pitcher he ever faced or the hardest hitter to retire.

Ritter's and the oral histories that followed his lead are, as critics have warmly noted, "charming and delightful" (Red Smith), "vivid, gentle, and humorous" (Roger Angell), "immediate, vibrant, and authentic" (Mike Shannon). But these are surface virtues, the glancing beauties of spume and of sunlight's glitter on the crests of waves. There is nothing of the depths in these collections—no introspection offered or probed for, no analysis or insight, no attempt to move beyond the charming anecdote to the speaker's feelings about what he recollects, his thoughtful understanding of what he so vividly recounts. Players, after all, are also fans. They are lovers of the game whose love we can learn from. But only if we are prepared to press them beyond descriptions of the sequined gowns their lovers wore, the jeweled necklaces that sparkled at their throats. These books tell us "what it was like," as the catchphrase has it, only if by "what it was like" we mean who did what on that historic day, who was the zaniest guy on the team and what earned him that reputation, who was the toughest hitter to get out in the clutch, or whether that pitcher really threw a spitter? All the rain is on the roof and at the windows. The interviews tell us little about what it was like inside: how the sounds warm and cradle us, or how, above all, the rain outside beat in time or syncopation to the sounds within.

Eugene Murdock expresses disappointment in certain interviews and responses in his collection and warns us to be prepared for such letdowns. For example,

> In answer to my "hot" question to Elmer Smith, "How did it feel to see that ball you hit with the bases loaded in the 5th game of the 1920 World Series sail over the right-field fence, the first grand slam homer in Series history?", Mr. Smith smiled and softly said, "It was a nice feeling." End of subject. Interviewing Larry Kopf, who got the only base hit and scored the only run in the 10th inning of the Fred Toney-Jim "Hippo" Vaughn double no-hitter in 1917, I was similarly curious to know his reaction to the hit and run which won the game. He looked at me rather blankly and observed, "Sure, I felt pretty good about it, but it was nothing special." And taciturn "Lefty" Grove: "Weren't you upset at having to spend so many years with the Baltimore Orioles when you could have been in the majors?" "Hell, no. I was making more money."

Murdock singles these out as disappointments, but in fact few of the answers he elicits and seems content with are more personally revealing, more emotionally or analytically trenchant than these. Few interviewees in this or other ballplayer interview books do much thinking or are asked to.

These books charm and delight us. They are appealing additions to the lore, and no one who loves baseball would wish to be without them. But in a way they trivialize baseball even as they remind us how much we love it. By bathing the game in a radiance of nostalgic reminiscence to the exclusion of all else, they project the sport as little more than that radiance, more nimbus than substance, more glow than intense light or heat. Baseball has more to offer its players and fans than delightful tales, anecdotes and yarns, but its subtler gifts are often concealed under that brightly illumined surface. Too taken by the shape and color of the petals, we overlook the stems, the roots, the earth beneath them, where the life and energy lie hidden. Fascinated by the stories these inveterate storytellers tell, love to tell, and tell so well, we are invited to ignore their richer implications, their personal power, resonance and meaning. After hitting a couple of hard line-drives in a softball game against Canton when he was 20 and a semi-pro, Tommy Henrich felt

> somebody tapping me on the shoulder. I turn around. It's Billy Doyle (the Cleveland scout there to watch a fellow on the Canton club). "How would you like to play pro ball?" he asked. I think my eyes must have popped. "Are you kidding? I asked. "You're doggone right I would."[34]

That's it. This from a man who insisted a few minutes earlier in the interview that "You couldn't have kept me away from baseball. It was all there, right from the beginning," and who, though he admits he never dreamed he could be good enough to play professional baseball, wanted nothing more. "You're doggone right I would" has to stand as the reductive shorthand expression of the rush of thought and feeling that must have accompanied that moment. Disappointment receives the same short shrift. Hitting .346 in AA ball and hoping to be called up, Henrich is bypassed by the Cleveland organization in favor of Jeff Heath, a slugger playing only Class C ball at the time. "Jeff Heath sure turned out to be a fine slugger," Henrich acknowledges generously, "but at that time I felt a little put out, feeling that I'd earned the shot." "You're doggone right I would." "A little put out." These are the verbal wherewithal we are asked to be content with in these books of charming but finally unprobing recollection, even the best of them.

There are almost no exceptions to this rule of thumbing through.

What follows is all Kirby Higbe has to say—all, at least, Honig sees fit to reproduce (perhaps richer material has been omitted in deference to the primacy of anecdote)—about the cruel curtailment of Dizzy Dean's career.

> I knew that feeling [of power over hitters], and Dean knew it, too, until he hurt his arm. Then he pitched on heart alone, and he had plenty of that, buddy. You know what happened: Earl Averill hit a line shot off of Diz's toe in the 1937 All-Star game. When Diz went back to St. Louis he told Branch Rickey he wouldn't pitch for a while, until that toe healed up. But Rickey told him they'd been advertising Dizzy was going to pitch, that there was going to be a full house, and that Dizzy was going to pitch, bad toe or not. So he went

out and worked six or seven innings, favoring his toe, throwing off stride, and his arm just snapped on him. Right then and there he lost it all.[35]

How does Higbe feel about this wretched abuse of power that cost a great athlete his career? It is a presage of much to come, much we have grown too familiar with in this increasingly greed-ridden game, but we are not told or invited to inquire. Higbe's next sentence changes the subject, retells an anecdote that reminds us of Dean's earlier confidence and dominance. The order is significant. The chronologically earlier tale of Dean's supremacy falls like an embroidered curtain across the story of his career's callous ruination. The implicit attempt, it seems, is to inhibit all probing questioning of the game's demonic side by swaddling it in the youthful potency of the hero.

None of this is intended as criticism of Higbe, Henrich, or any of the literally hundreds of other ball players interviewed in these oral histories. The players give what they are asked for and are urged no farther. If they gave more, what they offered has been edited out, leaving us with what the readers who gravitate to these books in large numbers and the critics who unstintingly praise them seem to want: the systematic externalization of baseball as unexplored anecdote and reminiscence, the distillation of the game to a precious collection of gemlike moments. Baseball, associated in a hundred essays with the innocence of childhood and early America, is to remain innocent of analysis, introspection, and complexity. It is to be protected from psychology and insight like the object of adolescent romance, more beautiful and more perfectly adored for its lack of personality and depth.

Without slighting the importance of adolescence or the charm and delight of its fascinations, there is a maturer way to love this game, as there is a maturer way to love a man or woman we at first uncomplicatedly adore. Writing of W.P. Kinsella's *The Thrill of the Grass*, sportswriter Mike Shannon praises Kinsella in these terms: "Writers of typical play-by-play baseball stories get so caught up in the action that they forget that the ultimate subject of fiction must always be the human spirit. Kinsella doesn't forget." The human spirit, I would suggest, should be an important subject of oral history as well, but oral histories of baseball have a way of forgetting. Caught up in the action, the anecdotes, and the historic play-by-play, they forget the echoing relation of the game to the human spirit, how the game and its execution, the players and their performance, work their way inside us and take up residence in rooms as dark or bright, as starkly or richly furnished as those occupied by childhood friendships, adolescent romance, or the adult fear of aging. As the preoccupying object of the love and fascination of millions of children, baseball is a mirror, extension, and crafter of personality in its formative stages. And in its own astonishing subtlety and complexity, its openness to endless "reading," interpretation, and use, its generous responsiveness to every moral, emotional, social, and psychological task assigned it, baseball answers not only the call of youth, but the gruffer, raspier voices older fans shout down its labyrinthine halls.

None of my criticism of other oral histories of the game is meant to imply that these books do not have their value or do not please. Like virtually everyone, I assume, reading this introduction now, I have read these books myself and read them with considerable delight and pleasure. I too love to hear about the tyrannical John McGraw, the monomaniacal Leo Durocher, the ferocious Ty Cobb, the creaseless Lou Gehrig, love to read how this one said that to the other, how this one planted a mouse in the other's laundry or poured beer down his open mouth while he slept and snored. I too settle comfortably into history when I read that Johnson or Grove was the fastest pitcher X or Y ever faced, that Williams or DiMaggio or Kenny Keltner, for that matter, was the hardest for Z to get out in the clutch. I too want to hear who was carousing with whom and who was the most prolific of all carousers, who the most reliable of all friends, the most helpful of all teammates, and the meanest of all umpires. When you love something as fans love baseball, you love almost everything about it. As with the man or woman you love, every trivial tale or detail about him or her seems a treasurable gem. When you're starry-eyed with love and admiration, every twinkle seems a blazing comet. But to be in love is also to risk a protracted ride along the surface; it is to settle for too little and to be content with no more. The dazzled lover may overlook the character of the beloved in his obsession with appearance and detail. And, worst of all, perhaps, he may be himself ignored, relegated, as fans are, to the background, to the stands, to their sofas, to the role of silent listeners, consulted only at All-Star selection time or when their opinions about this or that increasingly common crisis can serve the composer of an article or fill a poignant moment on the air.

Fans, it is said, are the game's most important asset. But for all our homage to their value, we have listened to little they have to tell us that is more articulate or resonant than their acutest cheers or complaints. We know that baseball was, at least, the national pastime because it did something special to its fans, something no other sport has done or, it seems, can do. But we cannot name that "something," nor do we inquire. The game belongs to the fans, but the shelves belong to the players. And by focusing, as these oral histories do, almost exclusively on entertaining anecdote and reminiscence, they obscure the salient fact that baseball, while surely entertainment, is at least to its fans also a great deal more. We love and devour these stories because we love and devour the game that generates them so prolifically. What we have not asked ourselves seriously is where that love comes from or what it feels like. We have not searched, to alter Yeats, where all the ladders start: in the crowded, clattering bone-shop of the heart.

On the rare occasions when they are approached, fans typically acquit themselves quite brilliantly, only to be consigned to silence for another year or decade. Speaking to three Tiger fans in *Five Seasons*, Roger Angell learns what baseball means and has meant to them. "At the very least," he writes, "these prodigals have used their sport to connect themselves to their fathers and to their boyhood and to their city, the inner city that they long since lost and left—and also to connect themselves to friends with whom they could share a passion, a special language, and an immense private history. Baseball has been a family to them."

Peter Golenbock's *Bums: An Oral History of the Brooklyn Dodgers* is one of the few books that at least intermittently listens to fans. Joe Flaherty is only a shade more eloquent and astute than many when he explains what he believes the Dodgers meant to Brooklyn and what their departure left behind. Flaherty observes wisely:

> When the Dodgers left, it was not only the loss of a team, it was the disruption of a social pattern. The life went out of the street corners. What were you going to stand there and talk about? Conversations in bars stopped. Maybe Brooklyn was a minor borough compared to Manhattan, but Brooklyn had the Dodgers. With the Dodgers you could swagger. It was like being part of the Lafayette Escadrille, and when the Dodgers left, the feeling died. It wasn't just a franchise shift. It was the total destruction of a culture.

Players regale us with anecdotes. Fans, if they are listened to, may tell us what the game and its teams and players mean to us and why they mean so much: why we worship or despise them, live and die with victory and loss, as though they were our own and of mortal import. They can offer us the interior lining (often the eroding lining of our stomachs) that backs the visible patchwork of narratives most oral histories thrive on. Why do fans tell us so much more? Not, it need hardly be said, because they are inherently more sensitive, or insightful. Players, when called upon for more than mere storytelling, produce it. I interviewed, among more than one hundred fans, a half dozen or so ex players. Not superstars, but the kind who filled the ranks or had promising careers curtailed by injury—vaguely or perhaps unremembered names like Reno Bertoia, Bill Zepp, and Fred Holdsworth. When they are asked to think they do so very nicely, thank you. When they are asked for attitude and feeling, they respond with a sensitive awareness. Baseball, it turns out—should we be surprised?—means at least as much to players as to fans. But since most of the players called upon for testimony are celebrities whose every word is cash, interviewers are content with any word, usually with merely engaging anecdote and reminiscence. Since fans are of interest not for who they are or for the mere fact of speech, they are pressed to say more, press themselves to say more, and they deliver. A fan knows few will rush to the bookshop to read of how he once drank a beer with his friend Bob and fell over the pretzel bowl on his left shoulder when Mantle caught the line drive that saved Larsen's perfect game. But if the speaker's name is Whitey, and Bob is a man named Turley, the story will probably suffice.

The interviews that fill the remainder of this book are distinctly not anecdotal, though fans, like players, are inveterate storytellers and I often had to stop them from indulging their passion for unfiltered memories and tales. Stories are told here, but only for the purpose of going beyond them—to their personal resonance and meaning, their social, emotional, and psychological import.

It's the difference, I think, between literature and "a good yarn." I say this without fear of sounding arrogant because the praise, if it is due, belongs not to me, who merely poked and prodded, but to the fans who responded so richly. What I wanted and asked for was a sense of what baseball meant to these fans, ranging in age from 10 to 75, as children growing up with the game. For all but the youngest of them, this was an invitation to the past, a demand to recall, if they could, not glittering moments, but who they were and what mattered most to them as children. Roger Angell remarked in *Late Innings* that whenever a fan writes him he feels he is being offered not just a view of the game but a view of life, and so it was with us. Baseball is so vital a part of a fan's history and so thickly entangled with other critical aspects of his personality and past, that to hand a fan that string is to urge him or her to wind himself back to who he was and how, in large measure, he became who and what he is. An invitation to talk about baseball, it turns out, is an invitation to the rediscovery of self.

No one, of course, can reproduce the past, or himself as its inhabitant, "as it really was." Adult fans asked to recall their experience and sense of baseball as children, to consider what baseball meant to them back then, are summoned—as the game is said to summon us—to a simpler past, the timeless, frozen era of their own youth and at least a relative if by no means painless innocence. The recollection one receives is not pure. Reports of earlier experience are invariably colored, cleansed, or discolored by the adult lens through which they are perceived. What one receives, inevitably, is not childhood resurrected, but childhood recreated through the eyes of the adult. And yet, it does not lose value for that reconstruction or alteration; indeed it may gain value as it gains another dimension. What one learns from these fans is perhaps not precisely what baseball meant to them as children, but some composite picture of what it meant to them then, what it currently means to them as adults, and how the adult, partly formed by the experience he gropes imperfectly to remember, perceives that forming and formative child. Baseball is therapeutic, not only because, as Thomas Boswell observed, the sport cultivates a balanced temperament and generates a sense of elemental sanity and order, but because the adult, on the couch, as it were, not only when he is interviewed but whenever he thoughtfully remembers, struggles to make sense of the child he was and of the adult he has therefore become. Baseball, these fans often discover as they speak, meant far more to them as children than they had thought. It also played, they learn with us, a far larger role in the determination of who they currently are than they'd ever considered or imagined. A game indeed. But one watched, as it is played, for mortal stakes.

Notes

1. Quoted in "A Cash Cow Transforms Itself into a Dead Horse," Richard Sandomir, *New York Times*, Sept. 15, 1994.

2. Quoted in "The Yankees Conquered the World, Only to Find That Baseball Doesn't Sell the Way It Used To," Stuart Elliott, *New York Times*, Oct. 29, 1996.

3. Quoted in "Fans' Interest in Baseball Declining, Poll Says," Robert McG. Thomas, Jr., *New York Times*, August 20, 1994. According to a CBS News Poll interest in the game declined by one third in the five year period between 1991–94.

4. Quoted in "A sad end to an amazing season," Paul Glastris and Greg Ferguson, *US News & World Report*, Aug. 22, 1994.

5. *Ibid.*

6. Cited by Robert McG. Thomas, *New York Times*, Aug. 20, 1994.

7. Quoted in "Dear Mickey: Messages and Prayers for an American Hero," Ira Berkow, *New York Times*, June 25, 1995.

8. Quoted in "One year ago, baseball fell apart at seams," *USA Today*, Hal Bodley, Aug. 11, 1995.

9. "Tax Fraud: Two Baseball Legends Say It's So," Joe Sexton, *New York Times*, July 21, 1995.

10. Quoted in "In Brooklyn, Sympathy and Dismay," Randy Kennedy, *New York Times*, July 21, 1995.

11. Mark Harris, Introduction to *The Baseball Chronicles*, ed. David Gillen, p. xx.

12. Quoted in "Play Ball! Hello-ooo! Anybody Watching?", Ira Berkow, *New York Times*, April 23, 1995.

13. Quoted in Andrew Zimbalist, *Baseball and Billions*, p. xiii.

14. Robert Frost, "Two Tramps in Mud Time."

15. Quoted in Richard Skolnik, *Baseball and the Pursuit of Innocence*, p. 171.

16. Quoted in Michael Novak, *The Joy of Sports*, p. 176.

17. Thomas Boswell, *Why Time Begins on Opening Day*, p. 298.

18. Tristram Coffin, cited by Paul Zingg, in *The Sporting Image*, ed. Paul Zingg, p. 354.

19. Richard Skolnik, *Baseball and the Pursuit of Innocence*, pp. 167–71.

20. Hoover and Barzun are both quoted by Michael Novak, in his introduction to *The Joy of Sports*, p. xv.

21. Lee Coleman, "What is American: A Study of Alleged American Traits," *Social Forces*, XIX (1941).

22. Michael Novak, *The Joy of Sports*, p. 58.

23. Quoted in Paul Zingg, "Baseball in the History and Literature of American Sport," in *The Sporting Image*, p. 355.

24. Robert Frost, "'Perfect Day—Day of Prowess,'" in *Sports Illustrated Baseball*, p. 260.

25. See the interview with George P., p. 207, for a similarly nervous view of Yankee "invincibility."

26. Quoted in Robert H. Boyle, *Sport—Mirror of American Life*, p. 99.

27. Quoted in Geoffrey C. Ward and Ken Burns, "Game-Time," *US News & World Report*, Aug. 29–Sept. 5, 1994, p. 64.

28. *Ibid.*, p. 75.

29. Thomas Boswell, *How Life Imitates the World Series*, p. 9.

30. Quoted in Richard Skolnik, *Baseball and the Pursuit of Innocence*, p. 95.

31. Quoted in Andrew Zimbalist, *Baseball and Billions*, p. 1.

32. Quoted in "One year ago, baseball fell apart at the seams," *USA Today*, Aug. 11, 1995.

33. Thomas Boswell, *How Life Imitates the World Series*, p. 3.

34. Donald Honig, *Baseball Between the Lines*, p. 25.

35. *Ibid.*, p. 90.

I: Moral Landscape, Mentor, Proof

"Sport," claims existentialist writer Albert Camus, "is where I had my only lessons in ethics."[1] We are surprised by the "only" but recognize and nod at the asssertion. The connection between sport and morality or ethics goes back at least as far as Periclean Athens and the Greek belief that the space between the healthy body and the healthy moral spirit is, as Neil Armstrong would put it in a rather different context, both a small step for man and a giant step for mankind. Sport, we are accustomed to hearing, forges character, particularly male or masculine character. It teaches cooperation and generosity, discipline, toughness, and sacrifice, though the usual claim is that it teaches these virtues to the participant rather than the witness. Judge Landis brought the lesson home to baseball and its fans when he called baseball a training field for life work, a model of squareness and honesty for American boys to emulate and feed on. The jury foreman at the same Black Sox trial that elicited Landis's pious pronouncement echoed his judgment. The national game, he declared, "promotes respect for proper authority, self-confidence, fair-mindedness, quick judgment and self-control."[2] And while again the emphasis is on the participant rather than the fan, the assumption, as among the Greeks, was that continuous observation of moral phenomena has a salutary rub-off effect on the perceiver. To witness the good repeatedly is to wish and strive to emulate it and to absorb, deeper than wishing, its influence.

The contemporary philosopher Michael Novak is wise to warn against the "mushy thought" that we can transfer morality learned in sport to other areas of life. The rules in the real world, as he advises, are not so clear, nor so closely refereed, and there is far more room for slippage on the steeper slopes of the vastly more complicated world beyond the stadium, where no playing field is ever quite level. And yet, fans do make that transfer, though almost never in gruff or puffy Vince Lombardic ways. Baseball, to many of its fans, particularly its younger fans, is indeed a moral phenomenon, influence, or force, though in ways that vary widely with the character, needs, and background of the fan and in ways that define the game as subtle, rich, and fertile ground for moral expression, development and response.

The role of baseball in the moral life of the fan, particularly the young fan, is many-sided and complex. Much has been written about baseball, or sport in general, as a source of moral inspiration or instruction, a kind of hyperactive manual for personal betterment. But that is only one of its possible uses, one of several ways in which fans for whom the game is principally a moral event regard and exploit it. Surprisingly perhaps, it is not the road most often taken. To most of these fans, baseball is a moral playing field, a vividly bordered landscape on which moral action takes place and offers itself for judgment. For such fans—and there are six in this section—baseball is less a source of instruction than a kind of moral workbench at which he tests, hones, and exercises his moral sensibilities and standards.

As Peter A. makes clear, his orientation to baseball was always personal, a matter largely of personal affection and sympathetic feeling that attached him, like a loving brother or nurturing parent, to certain players. At the end of the interview Peter speaks of having been influenced by baseball, of having learned from it the supreme worth of loyalty, affection and sacrifice he describes so caringly as his recollections warm. But one feels, through most of the conversation, that these are virtues and values he had already internalized and that while it may have sharpened his sense of their importance, baseball was of value to him principally as an ever-present canvas on which he carefully and tenderly applied them.

"Dutch" D., who has passed on since we spoke, was a 71-year-old legend among fellow fans when we met. Whenever I asked a fan in Philadelphia who else I might speak to about the game, the unhesitant answer was "Dutch." When I spoke to Dutch, however, what I heard, along with a dozen splendid anecdotes, was talk of baseball not as a sport or game, but as a moral proving ground. Surely one of the most generous and caring family men who ever rode this planet, Dutch's baseball conversation was essentially a prayerful insistence on our mutual responsibility toward one another, on and off the playing field. He spoke repeatedly of the team as a family, of his fondness for players who came through for these "relatives" when it counted most or who took responsibility for the game. Revealingly, his attention alternated as he spoke between the ball field and his own quite superhuman sense of family responsibility and obligation, indicating that for him, as for Peter A., the playing field and its environs are a kind of home where one either meets his moral obligations or fails to. It was a source of palpable sorrow to this man that "a ball team used to be a family, but isn't any more." Still more, pressing the parallel, that the old feeling that we are all one family, here to care for one another, has been cruelly lost.

Dan J., who pronounces himself, past and present, an incurably "judgmental fan," acknowledges that what he "learned to look for in baseball, in a team, in the players, is their values." Although his life on the judicial bench of baseball undoubtedly strengthened and refined his developing moral sense, for the most part what he looked for and discovered as a fan was the enactment of values he had been raised, as a Catholic altar boy from an immigrant working-class family, to appreciate. As Dan realizes, the values he prized in Hank Aaron and other Milwaukee Braves—hard work and sacrifice, humility and understatement, and the delicate, often perplexed balance between sacrificial collaboration and the perhaps prideful desire for personal achievement—were forceful articulations of his origins. As the interview progressed, Dan's focus rose and expanded: from baseball as earthly moral landscape to the game as a cosmic demonstration of "natural justice" and, more potently still, as an alternative religion, one that lifted him when the other let him down.

For some fans, baseball is—or should be—morally instructive. In a rich and wide-ranging interview, Reno B., a former major league infielder and an unretired thinking man, speaks eloquently of baseball as a source of moral guidance. An Italian Catholic immigrant, Reno, like Dan, harvested his values from that rich but difficult ground. He seeks in baseball and elsewhere the virtues of a simple honesty and decency. And he speaks feelingly of the price he paid as a perhaps too sensitive young ball player in the hands of coarsely insensitive coaches and managers. His emphasis throughout is on what baseball can and should, but does not always provide us with: From player to fan, a graceful, almost poetic beauty and simplicity on the field and a role-modeling decency and sensitivity beyond it. From the professional organization to the player, a sensitive understanding of the cruel pressures of the game, particularly on young, less than tough-nosed athletes, and a willingness to guide and prepare them. From the game to society in general, an alternative in its beauty, peacefulness, and simplicity, to the violent harshness of our society. In this last and most critical function, baseball is, or at least may once again be, "a rudder for a ship that is losing its way."

Both of these categories—baseball as an expression of morality and the sport as a real or potential source of moral improvement—speak mainly of morality in the game of baseball. Values perceived in the game's form or structure or in the behavior of players or management are taken to heart, appreciated, and perhaps incorporated. But the relationship between the morally inclined fan and the game has other dimensions as well. One may also develop a moral attitude *toward* baseball, as Erik B. does; or one may speak, with Dan J. and Gene W., in unabashedly mythic terms, of the cosmic moral significance of the game itself or of the performance of a very special team.

For Erik B., contact with baseball was his "first encounter with something outside my family or school," and the way he related to it, he believes, "is what distinguished me as a person." Not so much for what he gleaned from baseball, for what lessons it taught him, but for what it seemed to demand of him and for how he answered the summons he thought he heard. For this very different, but equally moral and moralistic fan, his team, the Philadelphia Phillies, was the earliest object of extra-familial responsibility, the first object beyond his immediate environment that required his loyalty, service, and defense. Erik was their defender. When players were attacked for their inadequacies, Erik leaped to their defense. When others deserted the team for its own prolonged failures, Erik demonstratively stayed with them. Baseball played, in Erik's life, a transitional role. A way-station between narrowly personal and broadly social loyalties and commitments, it cut his path from smaller to larger worlds of moral action.

Baseball, for this fan, elicits and exercises moral virtue rather than displaying or teaching it, though in minor ways it performs these latter functions as well. For Gene W., the persistent and predictable triumph of the Yankees in their golden era is less instruction or elicitation than symbolic demonstration. So connected are the Yankees with the gods, their destiny with the moral fiber of the universe, that their victory is proof of the moral rightness of things. Their triumph, day after day, season after season, is a vibrant manifestation of a world functioning as it should, obeying laws of cosmic right and justice, and providing a reliable framework in which an otherwise uncertain child might find his way.

That as a child this fan regarded Yankee supremacy as a kind of "portent or omen," a sign that God was in his heaven and that all was right with the world, defines its almost astonishing importance. Baseball, of all things, is the mediator between heaven and earth, between the gods and the merely human. Like Mercury or classical tragedy, it bears messages about the moral state of the creation. It is hard to imagine that the game had many rivals at this height and perhaps initially difficult to give credence to what seems a quite outrageous claim. But while there is something quite distinctive about the idea of baseball as omen or portent, the magical cast and critical importance are repeated by fans throughout these interviews. Dan J. also read baseball as one of the few enduring demonstrations of God's justice in gratifying action and speaks of the game as a religion that may save us when the others fail. Erik B., like a number of other fans I spoke with, believed, quite magically, that his cheering and steadfast dedication were having a positive influence on the fortunes of his team and admits that "baseball was the world to me at the time." That is who he above all else was: a boy who played baseball and who cared about the Phillies.

Baseball, then, is a source of moral instruction, a worthy object and conduit for virtues already developing or formed, and a demonstration of the moral nature and reliability of the world. No mushy ideas about easy transfer here, but much that is central to the moral understanding, growth, and character of the child. And much, surely, of lasting value to us all.

Notes

1. Quoted in Michael Novak, *The Joy of Sports*, p. 172.
2. Quoted in G. Taylor Spink, *Judge Landis and Twenty-Five Years of Baseball*, p. 63.

The Moral Force of Victory
The Yankees on the Side of the Gods

Gene W. Born 1934. Sociologist. Raised in the Washington Heights section of Manhattan. New York Yankees.

My first memories of baseball go back to when I was about 5 or 6 years old, when my father took me to my first ball game. It was the New York Yankees against the Philadelphia Athletics. I remember my father apologizing for the fact that he was an Athletics fan. He was absolutely sure that the Yankees were going to win, but he felt a tremendous sense of loyalty toward the Athletics because he grew up in Philadelphia, and I sort of felt sorry for him. It seemed he was locked into a group of losers, and I didn't have any desire to repeat that experience. The idea of losing didn't appeal to me at all, and sure enough, when we went to the game the Athletics were kicking the ball all over the field. Every time there was a ground ball they would boot it around, and my father was holding his head, holding his head and laughing at the same time. He found it amusing, and it seemed he liked it. I asked him why he wasn't a Yankee fan, and he said he couldn't be because he had grown up in Philadelphia and felt loyal to their team. I felt sorry for him, sorry he'd grown up there and glad I was growing up in New York.

I liked the Yankees, and I thought of it as a kind of secret triumph for me over my father—you know, the fact that I could identify with a team that was really creaming his team. I sort of liked that. He never took my fanhood seriously. He was the fan in the family, and in his own mind he preempted the fanhood field. But while I don't think I was aware of it at the time, baseball as a way of triumphing over my father was an issue for me. Thinking about it now, it seems very much to have been there.

I don't think I chose the Yankees for that reason, though, not mainly for that reason. I remember asking the kids in school what baseball team they were for, and when the said they were for the Dodgers or the Giants I couldn't understand it. We had a lot of Giants fans because we lived right near the Polo Grounds. In fact you could walk to the Polo Grounds from where I lived. But somehow the Giants weren't me, and the Dodgers weren't me. It was the Yankees I felt a real sense of identification with.

Everybody was talking about the achievements of the Yankees. It was *the* subject, the achievements of all those great players, like DiMaggio, and there was something about Rizzuto that appealed to me very much. He was a little guy, a little guy who always came through, who always came up with the big play, the double play that got the side out. Stuff like that I really liked. I don't remember the pitchers of that period. They're not clear in my mind. I had a

Red Ruffing mitt, I remember, but they never really concretized for me as personalities. The personality that was really dominant was DiMaggio. He had a kind of aristocratic bearing about him: up from an ethnic group and into a kind of aristocracy. Like Rizzuto he was triumphing over some sort of disadvantage.

There was a little bit of scorn attached to being a Yankee fan when I was a kid because it was considered more adventuresome to be a Dodger fan, and there was something more solid about being a Giant fan. But for me, being a fan during the Second World War meant identifying with winners, and the Yankees were a kind of hopefulness about victory.

Victory became a central theme in my growing up. We had a Victory Garden in school. We didn't just plant seeds; there was a Victory Garden in the neighborhood. We dug up this old concrete that was lying around, and underneath we found real soil, so we planted a Victory Garden. There was also a Victory Scrap–heap of tinfoil and metal from the neighborhood, so it was all fused into one thing. And the people who identified with the Dodgers, well, they seemed a little unkempt and sort of scruffy and not well put together somehow. It was clear to me that whenever the Dodgers and Yankees would meet in a World Series the Yankees would win. The Dodgers would win a couple of games, but the Yankees would eventually come through.

There was another reason for choosing the Yankees, but they're all connected to winning and being a winner. In my childhood it seemed somehow significant that I was born near Columbia University, and in the earliest picture I have of myself I'm an infant lying on the grass in front of Lowe Memorial Library. I couldn't have been more than a couple of weeks old, but it was very important to my mother to take a picture of me lying in the grass with Lowe Memorial Library in the background. The place was suffused with the imagery of Lou Gehrig as the Columbia athlete who broke the window in Hamilton Hall, playing on South Field where he made his debut as a ballplayer. It became clear to me very early that Lou Gehrig was Columbia, that Columbia was the Yankees, and that the Yankees were me.

Gehrig's consecutive game string and the entire Yankee mythology animated my inner life. And then, when I was about 7 or 8 years old I started to read baseball books. You know, those quickie books that you read as a kid. There were never any particular or identifiable teams in there. The names were somehow amorphous, neutral, but they made the whole business of being a baseball player very real all the same; they gave it a moral dimension. The moral of these stories always was that you could be a good hitter, but if you had a moral flaw in you, somehow that affected your hitting or your pitching and baseball assumed a moral cast. Then when my father took me out for the kind of ritualistic things fathers do with kids around baseball it was quite clear to me that I was going through an important rite of passage with a distinctly moral dimension.

It was terribly important that I succeed in that. I remember spending hours throwing a ball against the wall in the hall of my house and practicing pick-ups. That was the ultimate challenge: whether you could pick up a ball on the short hop, whether you had the coordination to do that. I remember that was extremely important to me as a test, and there were others. The ultimate test of my ability to deal with my father was to stand against a wall and try to catch a hardball my father threw with all his might. That was the ultimate test, and I passed. So the moral dimension, the sense of worth and capability and courage, was very much a part of my identification with baseball and with the Yankees.

Since I thought of winning not only as a function of ability but as an expression of moral superiority, it was only right and proper that the Yankees win. There was something wrong with the world if they didn't. If they didn't win it wasn't only their being outplayed that had to be explained. It was almost a theodicy where you have to explain how God can be evil, and there had to be an explanation for it. I didn't really feel in my gut what that explanation might be because I never really had to face it. By the time the Yankees began to lose I was beyond the age of deeply caring. But at the time their winning seemed to make the world right and proper. It placed things in a kind of moral framework that seemed right. The fact that they won was proof of their moral worthiness, and it made the forces out there that were making this happen explainable. Something would have been wrong with the world if the moral superiority of the Yankees didn't get translated into victory. Just as there would have been something wrong, obviously far more terribly wrong, if the moral superiority of the Allies hadn't been translated into victory.

There's another aspect of the Yankees that I liked very much: their imperturbability. Their superiority was so obvious and taken for granted that they didn't have to prove it all the time. There's something about that I liked very much. It was a form of confidence and self-possession. The Yankees seemed more dignified than other teams. The others had to sort of hustle around more and get the breaks in order to win. The Yankees just did what was natural and they won. The other teams had to resort to a kind of subterfuge in order to win, but the Yankees just had to be themselves.

This is how I felt, but I never really talked to my friends about being a Yankee fan because it wasn't all that interesting. Somehow being a Dodger fan seemed more interesting, and it involved more risk, more danger, adventure, naughtiness. It involved being naughty in a certain sense, and talking about the Yankees was not naughty, so it was less interesting. That was the disadvantage of being a Yankee fan: there wasn't as much to talk about. When you said to another person, "So you're also a Yankee fan," that was the end of it. It was the end of the discovery, and there wasn't much beyond that. When a Dodger fan found another Dodger fan, on the other hand, it was the beginning of a relationship, the beginning of a conversation, the beginning of shared glories and anguish, whereas with the Yankees you had simply found another person like yourself. It was the discovery of personhood rather than the opening of a conversation.

What you assumed somehow was that the person you'd found was insulated in the way you were. If he was a Yankee fan he was probably a kind of loner. In a way I feel I missed something by not being a Dodger fan, but I couldn't change. When Martin Luther nailed his proclamation to the door of the church he said, "Here I stand. I can do no other." That was as true about me and being a Yankee fan as it was about Martin Luther and the Reformation. Yeah, it had its disadvantages, and I kind of regretted not being part of that sweaty enthusiastic naughtiness of being a Dodger fan. But being a Dodger fan was also associated with antiauthoritarianism, and I didn't regard myself in that way. It wasn't my self-image. The thing was to discover "the right" and to participate in it as passionately as you could, to connect up with it in a way that was beneficial to yourself and the people around you. There was a heavy component of moral quest, but there was also a very substantial component of self-interest, and the thing was to find the pattern that enabled you to serve both.

The Yankees fit right into that. They had the most august tradition, and they seemed to be the embodiment of rightness, somehow. It's difficult to be analytical about it because it was so patently and obviously true and plausible, and it's hard to get under the surface and ask why. It was just there.

As other people would open the newspapers and read their horoscope and feel good or bad the rest of the day, depending on the forecast, I'd search the morning papers to find out if the Yankees won in order to find out if the world was going to be supportive and sympathetic to my plans and activities that day or whether I was going to have to slug it out and deal with a reality that didn't quite go the way it should have gone. So the Yankees turned into a kind of portent, a kind of omen. The fortunes of the Yankees became a sign of the well-being and the rightness of the world, an index as to whether the world was going to support my projects and my being; their winning was a kind of psychological support.

When they lost I explained it away: everybody has a right to an off day. It was an aberration, and the question was always how many games in a row would they win before they lost. So the losing was just incidental to the winning. I explained away the losing the same way you would explain a circus perfomer's trying to jump on a horse. He misses a couple of times just to show how good he is when he does it, because if he did it all the time it would be a ho-hum kind of thing. Losing was a kind of necessary bone the Yankees were throwing to reality to demonstrate that winning was really their way.

For the Yankees, losing was almost an act of generosity. It was as if they could have won them all if they really wanted to. I felt deeply a sense of noblesse oblige. Losing, for the Yankees, was noblesse oblige, and I sort of liked that. It showed their humanness and their humility and their generosity. They were bestowing defeat on themselves because no one really could have beaten them unless the Yankees allowed them to.

Being a Yankee fan may not have been as exciting or as naughty as being a Dodger fan, but it was comfortable, and it was right. I was born to be a Yankee fan, and my younger son, who had a tremendous desire to internalize parts of me, also took to it naturally. We never had a discussion about whether it was right or wrong to be a Yankee fan. He just was a Yankee fan. It was passed down, like a family inheritance.

It was a possession, almost a sacred possession that bestowed good things, and I'm very grateful that I was able to be a Yankee fan. I can't imagine growing up in a moral universe of tremendous ambiguity and uncertainty. It must be terrible for people. Had I been born into a different moral baseball universe or into some analog of such a universe, I think my life would have been less charted, less certain, less directed. Being a Yankee fan gave a kind of direction to everything: to the belief that things would work out, that the universe is orderly and right, that good will triumph, and that things will be OK.

I was aware in the '50s of the association in the public mind between the Yankees and a kind of corporate selfishness, an association not with morality but with self-seeking, triumphant capitalism, and privilege. But that was merely an inconvenient fact I preferred not to think about. Or if I did think about it, I wrote it off as part of America and something I could forgive. There was also a kind of jarring note in their having guys like Stengel and Berra, people who didn't fit into the world I was describing. They were not aristocracy. They were the kitchen help who were let in through the back door and who managed to do great things. They were crypto–Dodgers in Yankee uniforms, but if the Yankees had to get characters like them in order to win, well, all right. The necessity was its own justification. But they weren't the real Yankees. They were like a joke, a comic relief. It was as though the king had allowed a court jester into his retinue to do naughty things to deflect anger that might have been aimed at him. It was a kind of sop.

But even when it came to sops the Yankees did it in style. Berra and Stengel were pure assets. They were winners, preeminent winners. There never was a winning manager like Stengel, and Berra played with winners and was a winner himself. You didn't feel they had been transformed magically into Yankees, that the Yankees had taken this raw material and alchemically transformed it into gold. They remained base material, but in the same way that the fool in the Roman Saturnalia remained a fool even as he was turned into a king for the day. The fact that these characters enabled the Yankees to gain more victories justified the whole thing.

Mickey Mantle, on the other hand, was a continuation of the traditional Yankee image. He was the embodiment of it. And Roger Maris was the ultimate expression of that corporate image, the faceless being who was also a home-run machine. You didn't really want him to break Ruth's record. It was an offense that he did, but the fact that he did it in more games than Ruth played partially enabled you to save the image of Babe Ruth. So you had the juxtaposition of characters like Mantle and Maris on one hand, Stengel and Berra on the other. There was enough left of the traditional Yankees to maintain that continuity with the earlier Yankees and the tradition of aristocracy.

Still, things were getting confusing, and when they got so confusing that there was no way to maintain yourself, to navigate yourself according to the old principles that defined the Yankees, then the game lost interest for me. I didn't feel betrayed, and I didn't make a sharp break. I just slid away. It was a process of physical change and aging. It was the way of the world. It was accepting the fact that the Yankees weren't the Yankees, and it was a kind of rite of passage into adulthood for me. It accompanied an inner process that declared: well, all of those fantasies were functional up to a certain age, but the world has to go on, and the world has changed. And this is what being an adult is all about. It's about the lack of absolute certainty about moral issues. It's where you can't really tell the good guys from the bad guys.

In a way, perhaps I didn't accept this fully, because I began to seek other arenas where moral issues were as clearly defined. The search for other arenas in which to impose that sort of childlike paradigm goes on. But on a parallel path is the realization that the world is more complex and that certainty is not to be gained. In a way I'm still walking both these paths, and the Yankees were important for both. They were the embodiment of that moral rightness I spoke of. But their slide away from that path and my gradual disassociation from them was also a mark, another rite of passage to another realm where the world doesn't lend itself to easy categorization. Still, the sense of enthusiasm and elation that comes with a world in which the Yankees are always victorious and on the side of the gods is very seductive, and I've been looking for it ever since. Basically, I've been trying to justify my Yankee fandom in different realms. From time to time I find those realms, while at other times I have to deal with the disappointment that comes with the realization that this realm is part of fantasy and not reality. But the beacon remains. The Yankee teams of my early childhood, they're that beacon, and they're always there. Shining.

Society's Rudder and Keel

Reno B. Born 1935. Former Major League infielder,* later a schoolteacher, now retired. Raised in Windsor, Ontario, Canada. Detroit Tigers.

My first recollections of baseball take me to a neighborhood in my hometown of Windsor, Ontario, and specifically to a street called Hickory Road. I was 4 or 5 years old and had recently arrived with my family from Italy, where I was born. My next-door neighbor, coincidentally, was Hank Biasetti, who

---

*Reno Bertoia played for the Detroit Tigers from 1953 to 1958. In 1959 he was traded to the old Washington Senators, which became the Minnesota Twins in 1961. During the 1962 season he was traded to Kansas City, then back to Detroit. 1962 was his last year in the big leagues. He spent a year in the minor leagues at Syracuse and finished his baseball career in Japan, "of all places," in 1964.

would soon become a big league ball player with the old Philadelphia A's, and this gentleman—and he was a gentleman—was the role model for every kid in the neighborhood. All the youngsters in the neighborhood followed his career, his rise to the big leagues, and he became my role model, more accurately my idol. I seemed destined to follow him everywhere. I went to the grade school he went to, the high school he went to, and the college he went to. And a few years after he'd made it to the big leagues and been sent down I followed him into the Majors. So that's how I got into baseball—by idolizing a young man in my neighborhood.

I was also fortunate to go to two very sports-oriented schools: Gordon MacGregor grade school and Assumption High School, and to live in a very ethnic but very decent neighborhood where everyone seemed to love sports and where we weren't sidetracked by the distractions that plague young kids today. I'm thinking of rock 'n' roll music, discotheques, all that. Hey, they're OK. That's their thing, and that's fine, but we didn't have them. Sports was our fun, and it organized our lives. It was the center, the focus; it was what we did, day after day, and I can't say I was ever bored as a kid. We were always playing some game or other, which we organized ourselves. We didn't have adults organizing to the nth degree. On weekends or during summer break we'd go to the park at about ten in the morning, stay there till noon, go home for lunch, come back till dinner, go home to eat, and come back again till we couldn't see the ball anymore. Our parents knew where we were, knew we weren't in trouble, and it was a healthy environment to grow up in. They talk about the '40s and '50s as being dull, but hey, I'll take them back anytime. And I'm not an old conservative either; we had some pretty good times.

What I really loved about baseball was the physical grace and beauty of it. The game is very graceful. I once heard someone compare it to poetry; whereas other games might be prose, he said, baseball is poetry; and you know, it is. They say simplicity is beauty, and that's what makes baseball special: the beauty of its simplicity. I hate the distractions: the obsession with ridiculous statistics, the exploding scoreboards, the frenetic music, you name it. And worst of all the obsession with money, paying a million bucks to a guy who's hitting .210. I made $15,500, so I guess I'm supposed to say that I can't compare myself to this guy. But what they're doing, if you ask me, though I don't like to say it, is polishing shit. All this garbage that's burying the game—it's a reflection of our society. It's all noise, static, tinsel, a distraction from the basic clarity and simplicity of the game.

It really is a basically pure and simple game. There are nine men on the field. There's one batter up, and there's the elementary battle between the pitcher and the batter. The ball's hit, and you can appreciate the gracefulness of the outfielders moving with it. When I was in the Tiger infield I'd watch the ball going to right center field, and I'd see Kaline go after it, catch up with it, and bring it in with such remarkable grace. Or I'd see an infielder make a diving backhand stop and come up throwing. That's the beauty of the game, and you don't need explosions to appreciate it.

To make the big leagues you were supposed to be an athlete, an all-around ball player who could run, field, hit, and throw. But you don't see much of that kind of versatility today. There are some great athletic bodies out there today, but the marketeers have turned the game into something it never was or was meant to be. It was a beautiful sport. The green grass, the levelness of the infield, the pool table look of it, and the naturalness of it all, which of course you lose with artificial turf. And on that beautiful setting, set into that landscape, those athletes in graceful motion. Watching an infielder dive for the ball, or an outfielder make a leaping catch at the wall—that's athletic ability in its most beautiful form. It's not the crunch of a football tackle or the crash of massive bodies on the line. I deplore football. I love to watch it but I deplore it, and I certainly don't want to hear it. I hate this new gimmick of putting a mike in some guy's helmet, so you can hear all the thuds and slaps and grunts. That's not sport to me. It's too violent, and sure, that's another reflection of the world around the stadium. We're a violent society in love with violent sports and games. The simplicity of baseball was a reflection of an earlier, simpler and less violent society, and it's a sport that might keep a society on an even keel, a last defense against chaos. That's probably too much to ask, it may be fighting windmills, but at least baseball brings some sense, some beauty, and a little sanity to our society. I know it did that for me when I was a kid. In a way, baseball organized my life, and though I came from a good family and lived in a pretty decent neighborhood, I think it kept me out of trouble. It did that for a lot of us, and I think it can do that for society in general if we learn how to appreciate it again, if we can get back to its beauty and simplicity.

I'm not an ostentatious person. I like simplicity, and it's what I look for—in choosing a mate, in friendships, everywhere. I don't like boorish people, and I don't like loudmouths, and what I like about baseball is what I like about people. When it's played right, there's no phoniness in it, no harshness, no brutality, no cruelty. If you ask me why I find these things so appealing I'm not sure. You know, this is the first time I've ever had this deep a discussion about baseball. It's very interesting. I think it was the way I was brought up. My parents were very down-to-earth people, immigrants who came over here and worked hard. My mother was a very, very good person, always wanting to help somebody, and she and my father taught me these values and passed them on to me. They taught me the value of simplicity and straightforwardness, of being honest, being who you are. The players I liked most were those sorts of people, or seemed to be. Guys like Johnny Pesky, Earl Torgeson, and Pat Mullen.

We're getting pretty deep into this and pretty deep into who I am. What I looked for in a ball player says a lot about who I am, but who I am wasn't always good for me as a ball player. If I had been a little bit more of an asshole, a little bit more of a dog-eat-dog type of guy, I might have been a more successful ball player. I was an average ball player. I played eight years in the big leagues, and I was happy to be there, but I could have been better had I had another attitude. If I'd have been a little bit more hard-edged, more aggressive, it might have made me a better competitor. My personality held me back; it even shortened my career.

I worried a lot, and if you were to ask me why I didn't have a longer career I'd say I worried myself out of the big leagues. If I had three hits in one day and made one error, the only thing I'd think about was that one error. That's my upbringing, too. That's my mother, and that's the Italian and the Catholic wanting to be perfect. I don't want to get too psychological here, but as youngsters in those days, we were raised on fear and guilt, and that stuff gets into your psyche. I was preoccupied with the fear of making a mistake. And when I did make a mistake I'd worry about it so much that it took me away from what I could do instinctively. I'd think only about the mistake, I'd try harder to avoid the next one, and boom, that would bring it on. You do that a few times and before you know it you're not playing, you're sitting on the bench. Next thing you know you're in the minor leagues and your career's over.

Baseball is a tough game mentally. And emotionally. You've got to have the physical ability, but a player's also got to have the right mental attitude and the emotional tools to cope with pressure. You've got to be able to keep your emotions in check. You've got to learn to focus on what's good and not be consumed by what goes wrong. I remember hearing Ted Williams talk about how bad he felt when he didn't get a hit in a critical situation. But you know, the best players in baseball fail seven out of ten times, and you've got to learn to deal with that.

I think ball players would be a lot better than they are if they were schooled not only in the physical aspects of the game, but in the mental and emotional aspects as well. The game is a roller coaster. You've got to learn how to stay in the car, how to ride with it, how to contain your feelings. I don't know about other sports, but I think baseball teams should have counselors in spring training to help those young kids prepare for what's coming. A lot of guys who fall by the wayside might have had better careers if some of their weaknesses had been addressed.

I knew nothing about the emotional stress of playing big league ball before I played it. When I watched a game I'd see these guys out there playing, things would happen, and there would be no changes on their faces. They're much more exuberant today, more expressive. In those days they showed almost nothing on their faces; they seemed to have everything under perfect control, and I thought "Gee, when I get to the big leagues I'll be just like them." But I wasn't. I was worrying all the time, and I couldn't figure it out. Why am I worrying? Why? It's not supposed to be this way. You're supposed to be a big league ball player and everything's supposed to be like it is on the television screen, where dramatic things happen, but where everyone does his job smoothly and automatically and doesn't feel a thing.

You need somebody to help you through this, to prepare you. When I signed with the Tigers, Muddy Ruel, the general manager, called me in for a talk. He's sucking on his pipe and he's saying, "Now, Reno," he says, "when you play in the big leagues there are lots of fans out there, screaming and going wild and maybe trying to get on you. But you pay no attention. Just make believe they aren't there. Pretend they're behind a wall." It's a nice idea, but it's unrealistic. I tried to do what Ruel said, but you know, they're there, the fans *are* there, and a guy who knows some psychology would have told the truth. He'd have said, "They're there and you have to cope with them." And maybe he'd have given us a few hints as to how to go about it, how an 18-year-old kid deals with the fact that 30,000 fans are watching everything he does and reacting in pretty uninhibited ways. No one told us that. We were raised in this horseshit way back then, told to simply ignore what you can't possibly ignore, and it's a wonder any of us made it through.

When I see a young kid, like this center fielder Milt Cuyler, I know how he feels. They're rushing him into playing only so they can showcase and trade him, and I know how that kid feels. They're ruining him, and as a former ball player I can empathize with what he's going through. I can empathize with the guy who falls into a slump; I can empathize with him when he's up there in a clutch situation, and when I hear people criticize a ball player for one thing or another I think—and sometimes I say it—you don't know what it's like till you're there yourself.

The game looks easy, but it's tough, and the closer you get to the batter's box the tougher it gets. If you're able to cope with failure emotionally you can deflect it and come back another day. But if you don't deflect it properly, it can eat you up. You know, it's very surprising. I'm talking along these lines of emotions and psychology, and while I don't want to make things bigger than they are, it's a wonder there's only been one suicide in baseball. He was a catcher for the Cincinnati Reds, I believe, a Jewish kid.* It's a wonder there haven't been more, with the tensions of the game, and I think one of the reasons might be the safety valves of drink, promiscuity, and today probably drugs. I can see why ball players are on drugs today. The drug of my day was alcohol, and a lot of guys were drinking. I remember a manager once telling me after a tough ball game, "Ah, go out and get laid, loosen up." That was his advice? To a 20-year-old kid, a good Catholic boy from Assumption High? That's his solution to the problem?

My personality got me in trouble in baseball. Maybe I'm a little too sensitive, but I believe the game should be a little bit more sensitive to the ball players. When I hear the owners talk with contempt about the players I don't like that. And I don't like it when I hear ball players say, "We don't care about the players of the past." Which at one time, for a long time, they didn't. They did nothing for us. They raised the pension a couple of years ago, and they're thinking about doing it again now, but there's got to be a little bit more sensitivity, not only in baseball but in our society. Look at the way our society is going. I mean, what the hell is happening with kids on the street in Detroit and in other big cities? Sports, if nothing else, should show some sensitivity towards

---

Willard Hershberger, who hit .316 in three years with the Reds and committed suicide on August 3, 1940.

us as human beings. There's got to be some place to escape to from all this cruelty, this harshness, something that can show us a better way. If anything in our society can do that it's sports. And if they're cruel to their own athletes, well, what kind of hope does that leave us?

As I said before, when I played I thought of baseball as something special. I admired the simplicity, the beauty, the ballet movements and gracefulness, and I believed it was somehow affecting the world around it in a positive way. But now it's turned around and society is ruining baseball. A lot of the new owners who have come into the game aren't really sports people. They're egotists, and a lot of them are greedy.

Society's changing. It's going where the money is. Baseball used to be a kind of rudder for society. It gave direction, showed it where it ought to go and helped it get there. Even with all that's happened to it, I'd still much rather take my grandchild to a baseball game than to a football game as an introduction to sports. It's a better model for them. Hey, you play it nicely, it's beautiful. Look at that shortstop moving to his right. In football it's "Look how the linebacker hit that guy there. The harder you hit him the slower he gets up." You know, I'm not so certain that's what I want to teach my grandchildren.

Baseball isn't a contact sport. Not that you didn't take the guy out at second base when you had to, but it's a secondary aspect of the game. Basically, baseball shows you how to live; there's something graceful and peaceful about it. It's a peaceful game. That's why I call it a rudder for a ship that's losing its way. What counts in baseball is that team spirit, that cooperation, the idea of crediting a good play whether it's your play or their play. One of the greatest compliments I ever got was from a guy on the other team, Pete Runnels. When we were crossing the field after I made a play at third base, "Reno," he said, "that's the best play I've ever seen." Runnels was a pretty good ballplayer, and it made me feel good to hear him say that. I'd do the same. We'd all do that. We saw guys on the other side make good plays, great plays, and we'd let them know it. "That was a hell of a play," we'd say, "a hell of a play."

Athletes are role models. Like it or not it's inherent in their position. And what are they doing with that influence? What kinds of role models are they? They're beating up women, they're selling drugs, they're spitting at people or throwing fire crackers at the fans. That's just wrong. I don't give a damn who you are, that's just wrong, and if you're in full view of society, a celebrity, interviewed on television or in the press every day, it's unconscionable to say, "I never asked to be a role model, and I'm under no obligation to be one." You're making millions of dollars from this sport, and all these kids are looking up to you with adulation. You have an obligation. You have to reflect the good values in sport, the good values period ... period. You don't have to be perfect. You don't have to be a choir boy. But you have to be sensitive, you have to be decent. There's a difference between an athlete and a jock. A jock is an insensitive, aggressive, macho, phallic asshole. An athlete is somebody who is educated, sensitive, and decent. I want to be thought of as an athlete.

Affection, Loyalty, Sacrifice
"I Followed My Friends to the Giants"

Peter A. Born 1926. Editor and Diplomat. Raised in Brooklyn, New York. Brooklyn Dodgers and New York Giants.

Perhaps the first thing I remember as a baseball fan is the voice of Red Barber doing the radio play-by-play of the Dodger games. For me, Barber was the world of baseball. His voice was the game's voice, and there was something very special about Red Barber. There was a certain warmth to him, a certain friendliness, a casual, inviting quality to his voice and manner. It was impossible to imagine a Dodger game, or even baseball in general, without Red Barber. My brother and I would listen to the games together and soak up that voice. We did everything together, and baseball was one of our favorite and most precious shared pleasures. My brother is now a mathematical economist and more statistically oriented than I am. His approach to baseball reflected that orientation. My own was always more personal, very much in terms of a personal affection I felt toward certain players.

Needless to say, growing up in Brooklyn I was a Dodger fan. There was really no other choice. Everyone I knew was a Dodger fan. My two favorite players were Dolph Camilli, the Dodger first baseman, and little Pete Cascorart. They were both real gentlemen, kind of soft-spoken. I can't tell you why I was so fond of Cascorart. He was a fine fielder, but far from an outstanding hitter. On the contrary, he was a rather weak hitter, and I think that's what drew me to him. I always felt drawn to the underdog. I always rooted for the underdog to do better, to win, to come out on top in spite of the odds, in spite of what everyone was saying about him. Also, of course, because Cascorart was a gentleman, or seemed to be. He was a very smooth fielder, and there seemed a kind of grace, a dignity, a gentlemanly quality to him. I don't know whether Cascorart and Camilli were really gentlemen, but that's how they impressed me at the time, and I guess that's what counts.

Towards the Dodgers as a team I felt loyalty, above all loyalty, which means I was always with them. Win or lose, they were my team. I would never abandon them. But in a way that's not entirely true because my loyalty was not so much to the institution as it was to individual players. I was very attached to these individual players. I had affection for them, and in addition to loyalty the other key term is affection. I had a very, very strong affection for certain players. It was as though they were my friends, as though I knew them personally and could somehow understand them and relate to them as human beings. I felt for them as I would feel for friends or relatives. My primary loyalty was to them rather than to the organization, so when the Dodgers traded a number of their players to the Giants, like Durocher and Stanky and Camilli and Dixie Walker, I felt betrayed. I felt that somehow my friends had been taken away from me and that whoever was responsible—it was Branch Rickey of course—had no right to do this. I understood that baseball was a business, and I knew that Rickey had a right to do whatever he wanted. It's part of the game, but a part of the game that I never liked, because there's a contradiction between this commercial aspect of the game and the human aspect that develops emotions like loyalty and affection. When these two things clash, you're bound to have a problem, and I had a problem. I recognized that formally Rickey had the right to sell these players, but felt that in the personal sense he didn't. In a personal sense these players belonged to me. They belonged to Brooklyn. They belonged to my neighborhood, and Rickey had no right to take them away from us. I was furious and frustrated, and in a kind of spiteful way, I think, I followed my friends to the Giants. It was as if I were saying, "I'll show you." By 1951 I was a Giant fan, and when Bobby Thomson hit that home run I was happy about it. There was an element of "I told you so" or "You had that coming to you" in my feelings. But I must admit that I never really became a Giant fan to the extent I had been a Dodger fan. The identification with the Dodgers, the loyalty to the Dodgers, the affection for the Dodgers was stronger than it ever became for the Giants. I was never quite able to get back to that level of intensity, that passionate involvement I felt with the Dodgers. Perhaps it was close, but it was never quite the same thing.

One of the things I loved most about baseball was the bunt. I loved Durocher for his bunting, and as a player I loved to bunt. I loved it, I think, because I loved the idea of sacrifice, the idea of moving somebody else along, of laying yourself down, giving yourself up, sacrificing yourself for the benefit of the team. That's why, to me, there was no more beautiful play than the bunt. The person who bunted knew that the chances were that he'd be thrown out. But he moved somebody up, he put someone into scoring position or brought someone home. That's a real sacrifice, and you know, there's a whole philosophy in that. If you ask whether sports or baseball can teach us anything, well, sacrifice is a value that played a role in baseball and that can be applied and is applied to other aspects of our lives. Now, at some point—I don't remember when this happened, but I think it was sometime in the '50s—they changed the rules. Since then a fly ball, on which somebody would tag up after the catch and score, would be counted as a sacrifice. I could never see that. It goes against the grain of the idea of sacrifice. The person who hits that fly ball doesn't mean to sacrifice himself. He's trying for a home run or an extra base hit, so why should it be scored a sacrifice? Sacrifice is a significant concept. It's a human attribute of great rarity and worth, and it shouldn't be cheapened. It can be Abraham offering up Isaac on the altar on Mount Moriah, or at least being prepared to do that. That is sacrifice. Or it can be a soldier going out to war and being prepared to lay down his life if necessary. That is sacrifice. Or it can be somebody giving a sum of money to charity that he might have spent on himself. That is sacrifice. It can also be somebody laying down a bunt in order to let a teammate score. That, too, is sacrifice, and it shouldn't be confused with trying to hit the ball out of the park and not quite making it.

I said earlier that what I felt toward the Dodgers until they sold my friends was loyalty, and I think the two ideas are linked. The loyalty you feel toward your team is like the loyalty you feel toward anything. It's like the loyalty you feel to a family member or to your country. The object of this loyalty is close enough to you for you to want to support it in every way, maybe to sacrifice something for it. You're involved with it, you follow its fortunes, you're happy when it's doing well and sad when something happens to it or when it's not doing well. And the same goes for affection. If something happened to an individual player, if he was injured or something like that, you knew that he could have been one of your own children, and his misfortune could even evoke tears sometimes. That's how I felt about Pete Rieser, for instance, a great ball player who never reached his full potential because he knocked himself silly banging into the wall to make great catches. And I remember Freddy Fitzsimmons, the pitcher who opened a bowling alley near Ebbets Field. If I were a bowling person, which I'm not, I would have wanted to patronize his bowling alley just because he was Freddy Fitzsimmons. There's a place in my heart for all these people, a little place for Freddy Fitzsimmons, a bigger place for Pete Cascorart, Dolph Camilli, and Leo Durocher. I'd do something for them if I could. I'd help them out if they needed me.

The press contributed to the affection we felt for the Dodgers. They would refer to them as "the Brooklyn Dodgers, affectionately known as 'the bums,'" and they kept referring to this affection, while the cartoonists would often use the image of the bum, the lovable hobo, to represent the team. So in a way they molded this image, which had a considerable influence on their readers, especially young readers who were impressionable. What the press manufactured became true for us. It became part of our feelings.

But there's another side to that "bum" image I didn't take to. When something went wrong on the field the lovable bum became the miserable bum, the object of ridicule. When they'd mess up, blow a big game, or go into a tailspin, the fans would give them what for. "Yeah, you bums," they'd shout, and they didn't mean it affectionately. I never did that, and I wouldn't do it. I might feel sorry or sad, but I would want to encourage them. I wouldn't hiss and boo them or call them bums. To me that's a form of disloyalty, and I want no part of it. When things go wrong it's not because somebody wants them to go wrong or because this or that player didn't try hard enough, though I guess on occasion that happens. I don't think a player should be booed because he fumbles a ball or because he lets it go between his legs. Maybe he was tired that day. Maybe he had an upset stomach and things are just not going for him that day. It's not that he wasn't trying. It's just that something went wrong, for whatever reason. Things sometimes go wrong, and if you really love somebody, if you love your wife, you don't upbraid her every time she takes a misstep or does something you might think is foolish or wrong. You want to encourage people that you love. You don't want to discourage them.

I guess you can see that my relationship with baseball was very personal.

Actually, it was a combination of the personal and the collective, though the personal element was stronger than the collective element. The people involved, the players, were more important to me than the team. I mean, if I had to make the choice, which I did at one point, I'd go with the players. Put simply, they were people for whom I had affection, and I related to them accordingly.

I'm not sure how rational that attitude was. I don't know if they deserved the affection I bestowed on them. In my more rational moments I'd ask myself, "What do I know about this guy, anyway? What kind of a guy is he?" And every once in a while—as when Dixie Walker made a fuss over Jackie Robinson's joining the team—something would happen that would make you think a little bit about it, whether it really made sense to attach yourself emotionally to this or that player or even to a group of players you knew so very little about. But in the final analysis I would set aside that kind of reasoning. It was something I thought about from time to time, but I didn't let it spoil my fandom and my emotional attachment. I said, "OK, so that's the way these guys are." I'd put it in a separate category, and I'd say, "I'm not all that concerned with what they do off the field." If I found out, as I did with Walker, I'd have to adjust my affections to a degree. But since I preferred not to know, preferred to live with my lovable images, I made no effort to disturb them. I wasn't inclined to enter into an investigation about what Dolph Camilli was doing when he was off the field or how well he behaved. I was a lover who wanted to stay in love and who knew deep down, unconsciously perhaps, that it's not always a good thing to know too much about those you love.

I hadn't realized this, just as I hadn't realized how much baseball influenced me as a child, instilling certain values in me. This has been a very far-ranging conversation. Some of the things I've spoken about here are things I'd forgotten long ago. You stirred up some memories. Thank you for that.

Being Human in the Clutch
The Guys Who Came Through When You Needed Them

"Dutch" D. Born 1921. Retired. Raised in Philadelphia, Pennsylvania. Philadelphia Athletics.

I was the baby of nine children. In 1928, when I was 7, my family moved from the neighborhood around 15th and Girard Avenue to an apartment one block from Baker Bowl, the Phillies' baseball field. On October 1st of that year, two weeks after we moved into the neighborhood, there was an outstanding fight, a heavyweight fight at Baker Bowl between Tommy Loughran, from South Philadelphia, and Jack Gross, an undefeated Jewish heavyweight from Jersey. The entire neighborhood was electrified. This was my first experience with the ball park: as a kid on the outside running around, so excited about the fight I just couldn't stand still. So I got started as a baseball fan because the stadium where that fight was held was also the home of the Phillies. One kind of excitement connected to another, so I guess you could say that boxing brought me to baseball.

The following year, 1929, my brother Jim, my oldest brother, took me one Saturday afternoon to see the A's play Detroit. Al Simmons hit two home runs off Earl Whitehill that day. George Earnshaw pitched and won the game for the A's and hit a home run, so those two immediately became my favorites: Earnshaw as a pitcher and Simmons as a hitter. There isn't much about Al Simmons' baseball career that I don't know. I feel that Simmons is as good a ball player as anyone who's ever lived—as a hitter and as a fielder. He did astonishing things.

As a person he was something else. You didn't go near him if he had a bad day. He'd be very unhappy, and he wouldn't sign autographs. But on a good day he would sign autographs just like anybody else, and he was nice to us kids. In all my years around the ball park—and I was around there an awful lot from 1936 to '54—there were only three ball players who I disliked, and they were Bill Terry, Joe DiMaggio, and Lefty Grove. They were genuinely mean people. I know about Terry. Our neighborhood tailor was a fine Jewish man named Mr. Tweer. Mr. Tweer used to press the suits of the visiting ball players, that is their dress suits, because everybody came to the ball park in a dress suit in the '30s. We got out of school at 3:15—I'm talking about grammar school—which is exactly when the ball games started. Mr. Tweer would wait for me at the ball park entrance with the pressed suits, and he would let me carry one back to the club house, which was in center field. All the other players were happy with the way Mr. Tweer pressed their suits, but not Bill Terry. He was never satisfied that his suit was pressed correctly, and he'd complain and complain. If Mr. Tweer pressed it on the first day of a three- or four-game stand against the Giants, he'd press that suit the next couple of days for nothing. Terry was mean. He didn't bother with kids, the opposite of Mel Ott, who was terrific to us.

I saw Joe DiMaggio come into the league, and I *know* Joe DiMaggio was mean. I always say that DiMaggio had the best manager—and I'm not talking about a baseball manager—of anyone in public life. Whoever took care of his publicity kept him in the limelight his entire life and kept his image clean and neat. I remember a young kid from Allentown who had this tremendous scrapbook on DiMaggio, one of the greatest scrapbooks I had ever seen. The kid was all excited, wanting to catch DiMaggio when he came to the park and ask him for his autograph, and I said to him, trying to calm him down, "Don't worry, he'll sign it, he'll sign it." So when DiMaggio came in the kid ran up to him and DiMaggio pushed him, knocked him away, and went into the clubhouse. Once, when the Yankees were playing cards in the clubhouse and the batboy came in to get their autographs for a player on the other team, all the other players stopped and signed willingly, but not DiMaggio. After making him wait a pretty long time, he looked up and said, "If you're gonna pester me about signing that lousy ball, give it to me and get outa here!"

Lefty Grove was another mean ball player. He was just mean. He mellowed later on, but through most of his career he'd never sign a baseball for us kids. I was talking to a bunch of friends of mine about this last night, and we were saying, we grew up in Baker Bowl, and we never remember a Phillies player that was mean to us. Not one. Nobody could come up with a single name. On the A's there was Simmons. He could be mean to people when he had a bad day, but he was my boy, and I would argue with anybody about Al Simmons.

Baseball, to me, was everything. I mean, that was my whole life. I went to the ball games every chance I got. I loved the A's. I just loved them. The guys I loved best were the guys who would deliver when the game was on the line, the guys who came through for you when you needed them. When the A's scored ten runs in that fourth game against the Cubs in the '29 Series and went ahead, Connie Mack brought in Grove, and he struck out four of six guys. In Yankee Stadium one time, they had the bases loaded in the ninth inning and the A's had a one-run lead. Mack brought Grove in from the *dugout!* No warmups. He just went out on the mound and struck out the side in ten pitches. There you've got it, see, and that's why I say Grove was the best pitcher I ever saw. Because Grove wasn't a strikeout pitcher unless he had to strike you out—after he learned to pitch. When he first came up he was wild and threw hard all the time. But when he learned to pitch he didn't strike you out unless he had to. A lot different.

I like the guy who does what he has to do to help the team. In 1930 Al Simmons had 14 home runs in the eighth or ninth inning to either tie or win the game. So he's my number one clutch hitter. To the gamblers the only player that was even money to get a hit with the game on the line in the last inning—it wasn't Ruth, Gehrig, Foxx, or Cobb—was Al Simmons.

I didn't like DiMaggio as a person but I liked him as a player. He could run the bases. On the record he was never caught going from first to third on a single. He knew how to run the bases, and he never looked for anybody else to win the game if it was there for him. That's what I didn't like about Ted Williams. Williams was one of the six best hitters I ever saw, but you could walk him in a tough spot with a hittable pitch, with the game on the line. He'd let you walk him and let someone else try to win it.

A guy has to take responsibility. He's gotta be there when it counts. That's the kind of player I was when I played baseball. If we were playing a tough team I was gonna be in the forefront. I didn't expect some other kid to win the game. I took that on myself; I took responsibility.

Even when I was a kid I took responsibility. I managed a baseball team from the time I was 12 years old. I stopped playing at 32, and I managed all those years. When I was a senior in high school I managed a team that had five guys over 25 years old. I've always been the kind of guy who takes responsibility and takes care of people if they need it. And I guess I like certain ball players because they take responsibility for the team. In a way they're taking care of other people too. It's a baseball thing, of course. But it's also a personal thing, and it's something that should go on outside the ball park.

It's no good saying, "Go away, kid, I have no time." There's always time if it's important enough to you. When I went back to college I got a night job on the Reading Railroad, midnight to eight, six nights a week, and sometimes I'd work the ball park selling programs to make extra money. I had two small children. I decided I would never sleep or do anything that would interfere with our meals together. So I would come home from school, have lunch with my wife and children, and then go back. In the evening I'd come home from school, sometimes study, eat dinner with the family, and then go to bed for my four hours of sleep. At the same time I never failed to go see my father, my sister, and my brother at least twice a week. There's always time for other people if they matter to you.

A baseball team is a kind of family. The team I played with when I was growing up—we kids stayed together as ball players till we stopped playing. And we were a family. *We were a family.* We did everything together. We shopped together. We went downtown together. When one guy was getting a new pair of shoes the other guy went down to Market Street and paraded around with him. We were best man at each other's weddings. And now, sixty years later, we still meet every Friday night at a bar across town. There are only four of us left from the original team, but of the ten guys that come, nine of us went to the same grade school. And we're still a family. We take care of each other like a family.

When I was younger I used to think of the pro teams as families—I thought of the A's as a family—but I don't think that now. I think—and I guess we all think the same thing—that money stopped them from being family. You talk about Connie Mack. I have an article at home, written back in the Depression by one of the great writers in Philadelphia. This article says that Connie Mack had a special fund that reached six figures and that took care of ball players who fell on hard times. People say he was a cheapskate. But here's a guy whose wife and father died in 1892 and who took care of his three children and his took his mother in to live with them for the next 18 years. He also took care of all his relatives. You don't hear about these things. And he was good to the fans. The A's, I think, are the only team that gave out scorecards for nothing, and when we were kids working the ball park we got a bonus at Christmas time. All clergy just walked into Shibe Park, till the Phillies came over. They'd just walk into the ball park. No ticket, nothing. Just walk through the press entrance. Rabbis, ministers, priests, people studying to be a minister, rabbi, priest—they just walked in. As long as you had a black suit on. If it was a priest it was a collar. If it was a guy studying for the clergy it was a black tie. They walked into the ball park free because those were Connie Mack's instructions.

A ball team used to be a family, but it isn't anymore. Money killed it. I just can't stand the fact that there's not one guy playing who's willing to come along and say, "Listen, you write my contract and I'll sign it." Or that the players' union can't finally say, "Well, we're making enough. We're not gonna ask for an increase if you'll lower the ticket prices for the fans." Same with the owners. If you're making so much money that you can pay Bonilla or Bonds 30 million dollars for four or five seasons that means you can lower the ticket prices so other people can come to the games. But it's not gonna happen. It can't be a family. It just can't.

I don't think they take care of ball players like they did years ago. All the guys that played with the A's in the late '40s, when they became a fairly good team for about four years, made two runs at the pennant before they folded—all those guys got jobs with the organization. Connie Mack or the Mack family saw to it. They felt an obligation to take care of them.

I think back to the 1942 Cardinals, who were a bunch of young kids. They were a family. They did everything together. They went out together, they raised Cain together. I've just been in St. Louis, at a hotel where the players stay. I saw the players come out of the hotel, going this way and that way, each one in a different direction. In a strange city you'd think they'd go out together, four or five of them, just to be together or to take care of each other in case they get in trouble. But they don't. They get tied up with girls and bad things, and they've got tied up with history. They're thinking only about themselves. The other guy doesn't count for much anymore. The old feeling that we're a family, that we're here to take care of each other—it's gone. It's gone.

Something I Cared About, Something to Defend

Erik B. Born 1973. University student. Raised in southern New Jersey. Philadelphia Phillies.

My first recollection of baseball is when I was 6 years old and started to play in the T-ball leagues. We practiced after school three days a week, and every Saturday we had a game, and that was my first introduction to organized sports. It was a lot of fun, and it took up a lot of my free time after school which was good. It kept me from watching too much television and from other unproductive things.

My first recollection of big league baseball is when I was 8 or 9 years old and my dad took me and my twin brother to a Phillies game as a birthday present. It was a Sunday afternoon game, and I think they were playing the Pirates. I don't remember too much about the game, but I do remember how I felt when I first walked into the ball park. I was really amazed. I had only seen baseball on television, and I never knew how big the parks were, how huge the fields were. I could never imagine 400 feet to the center field wall, it was just amazing. We had really good seats where you could see the whole field and all the players on it, and you got a sense of the enormous size and dimensions of the field. We played in a T-ball league, which didn't have regulation bases or distances. I think our lines were either 30 feet or so between home plate and first base, and of course it's 90 feet in a big league park. It was three times the size of the field I was used to, and it was just amazing. I was 8 or 9 years old, and a kid that age isn't prepared for that kind of shock when he sees a baseball field like that 60,000 seat stadium, Veterans Stadium in South Philadelphia. I was in awe.

Of the players, too. To me, the players were superstars. Steve Carlton was in a race at the time with Nolan Ryan for the most strikeouts, and Mike Schmidt was the home run king. Watching them on television day in and day out made you feel you were a part of something. Something special, something bigger than life.

It was important to me to feel like I was a part of it. I felt that by watching them on TV and cheering them on I had become part of the team. I wasn't part of the team, of course, but it seemed that by watching them, by cheering them at the game or on TV, you somehow influenced the play. By cheering them on you thought they would perform better, even if you were cheering from your living room. It doesn't make much sense, but that's what I thought, and it gave me a feeling of pride, a feeling of being special. You watched them come back from blowing a three-run lead or whatever to win the game, and you felt like you were a part of that. You felt they won because you never gave up on them. Everyone else gave up on them in the eighth inning, but you were there standing by for the Phillies, believing in them, waiting for them to win it in the tenth or the eleventh and feeling that if they did, maybe it was because you hadn't given up. You'd kept on believing.

You'd hear people on TV or even in school, all kinds of people saying "Oh the Phillies lost the game this past weekend to the Cubs, who really stink, so the Phillies are never going to make the playoffs." But I would never give up on the Phillies. I was loyal, and I was proud of that. I'm the guy who sticks with them no matter what's happening.

At a certain age, about 11 or 12 maybe, I realized that by rooting for the Phillies every day I wasn't really having too much of an effect on them or the way they played. I couldn't help them win, but I could be out there cheering for them, defending them. When other people are saying bad things about them, you can be there to defend them.

Most of the arguments I got into were with my twin brother. He was also a Phillies fan, but he's like most of the fans in Philadelphia. He was a fair-weather fan, so if they lost a few games he'd give up on them and look for another team he thought would beat them out. We got into a lot of heated arguments about that. I don't like fair-weather fans. They're not real fans. A real fan won't forget his team, won't turn his back on them. He's with them for the good times and the bad.

That's loyalty, and loyalty is very important to me. It always has been. With friends I'm very loyal. With friends, classmates, parents, even professors. It's a very important thing to me. Having a twin brother probably had a lot to do with how I feel about loyalty. We both went to the same schools, played for the same baseball teams, and encouraged each other and supported each other through it all. We still do. We both go to the University of Pennsylvania, and we continue to support each other. Our parents haven't supported us on certain issues, but we've been there to support each other and defend each other.

Being a twin means you're around this one person your whole life. When you're young he's the one person you can always depend on to have time for you, to play with you or whatever. He's the loyal friend you have and come to depend on, and it goes both ways. You feel a stronger obligation towards him because he's your twin. It's sort of expected of you. People expect you to stick up for him, and you want to anyway. So loyalty becomes very important to you, and it affects all your relationships.

But in order to stay loyal, you've got to feel the person or team you're being loyal to needs your loyalty and deserves it. And when baseball became big business, when the players began to sound like corporate executives, it was hard to feel that way. I think I stopped feeling this need to defend the Phillies around '87 or '88 when I started reading in the papers and in *Sports Illustrated* about the kinds of salaries these guys were making. I think Mike Schmidt was the first player to make over three million dollars a year, and I thought it was ridiculous. It's just crazy. I know they only play for 10 or 15 years, but I still don't think they're worthy of that kind of money.

Gradually it affected my feelings about the team. I became less loyal towards the Phillies and the players because I saw they weren't there to work together as a team. A lot of them were there as individuals, doing their own advertisements and stuff and worrying mainly about themselves. They had their own agendas, and it seemed making big money was more important to them than making the playoffs.

I had defended them because I thought they were something special. As people, as a team, as players. But it became harder and harder to hang onto that feeling. They were at their best as a team, working together, in 1983. They were in the playoffs that year, and they had all the veterans. They had Joe Morgan, they had Tony Perez, they had Mike Schmidt, they had Steve Carlton. They had all these older guys, and it seemed they still enjoyed the game, played because they loved to play. I cared for them because they cared about the team. They were like an extended family. They cared about each other, and they supported each other through the good times and the bad. And they also cared about Philadelphia and the towns around it. They did all kinds of things. They donated a lot of time and money to organizations in the area. They really cared about Philadelphia. They loved the city and they loved the game.

And then, as the years went by, these guys grew tired and it seemed the new players that came in didn't really love the game of baseball. They were playing it for the money and for the fame, and that made my loyalty look a little foolish. They let me down. All of baseball has pretty much let me down. All organized sports these days have let you down, and this is a real loss for me, a tremendous loss. Baseball can't give me that feeling any more, that sense of dedication, the sense that I was helping my team by rooting for them and that I would stay loyal no matter what. But no one can take it away from me either. What baseball gave me as a little kid became a part of me. That feeling that I was part of the team, helping them out by cheering for them, it gave me a sense of pride, maybe even a sense of meaning. It was my first encounter with something outside my family or school, and the way I related to it distinguished me as a person.

As a young kid you're out there having all kinds of fun, no responsibilities. Nothing is really important to you besides having fun, but with baseball I felt a small obligation. Something that had meaning to it, something I cared about enough to invest time in. Baseball wasn't going to spoil me and take care of me and nurse me like a little boy. Playing baseball meant the responsibility of baseball practice three times a week and a game every Saturday. There was a time commitment involved. And being a fan also had its obligations. The responsibility was to look at the Sunday papers, to see how they're doing, to watch the game on television, to go to some baseball games, and to defend them. You had to be the one watching what other people said. You had to know enough to argue them down, and you had to take a stand. I was the public defender of the Phillies, and I'd read the box scores with that in mind. I'm picking up material here that I'm going to use to defend them next time they come under attack.

Rooting for the Phillies made me feel special because there was something I could do. You know, I was a little kid. A little kid doesn't have much responsibility or much to do, and by rooting for the Phillies and watching every one of their games on television or reading the box scores, I felt a sense of purpose. I spent a lot of time caring about the team. And you know, it just seemed like I was someone who really cared for the Phillies. Other people, like my brother and my father who really enjoyed baseball, didn't really follow the Phillies that closely and didn't really care how they were doing. So it distinguished me from my twin brother and my father and also from other students in my school. I was the one who devoted himself to the Phillies, the one who defended them, the one who cared. Baseball was the world to me at the time and that's how I identified myself: as a baseball player and as a fan who cared about the Phillies.

Baseball was probably my first introduction to the outside world. It gave me my first real sense of responsibility, and from there it seemed to spread. As I got older I realized there were other things out there bigger than myself and my friends and family. There are social concerns also. As a high school student I volunteered a lot in homeless shelters and soup kitchens, and I really got to see what society was all about and what was wrong with society and how you should go about helping others, and all that was very important to me. My first job was in a nursing home, in the cafeteria. We'd serve lunches and dinners and prepare food for the elderly people, and I saw that as a way to get involved in helping others and gaining some sort of understanding.

Once baseball let me down I had to find other places to apply that sense of loyalty and responsibility, that desire to help. If I'm going to help, somebody has to need my help, and these guys are a bunch of selfish millionaires. They aren't underdogs anymore, and they don't need my help. You always want to cheer for the underdog, the Cinderella team. The other teams, the teams that have all those fans—for them the value of gaining one more fan is not so great. If you really want to have an effect on other people or other teams or organizations you need to get involved with those organizations that don't have very much support.

I think it all goes back to the sense of purpose. Baseball was the first organized sport I played or cared about, and it gave me a sense of responsibility I've never lost. I owe that to baseball. It gave me that sense of responsibility.

"Go and Talk to the Kids: It Had a Lot of Meaning"

Dan J. Born 1947. School psychologist. Born and raised in Buffalo, New York. Milwaukee Braves.

When you ask for my first recollections of baseball, what it meant to me, I get emotional, partly because I love the game so much, but mostly because I think of my father, who always talked about the DiMaggio days. My father left Italy during World War I, at 17. He actually snuck out on a freighter, trying to avoid serving in the Italian army and being part of the Axis. He was a laborer, and he always talked to us about Italians that made it from humble beginnings, and the DiMaggio boys were at the top of his list. My father died when I was 8, a time when my interest in baseball was real, real intense, and he had a powerful impact on how I felt about the game.

I was interested in the Milwaukee Braves and a couple of players on the Braves who were my heroes. One was Warren Spahn. He was from my hometown, and I used to see him around the neighborhood. But the player who stood out for me was Hank Aaron. He was probably my all-time favorite player because he wasn't very big; he was black; he was a poor kid; and he was a rock of sheer consistency. He always played very, very hard, and he did a good job. The fact that he was black mattered to me. I lived in an Irish neighborhood where everyone was identified by his race or color. This guy was the Nigger, that one was the Polack, and we were the Guineas and the Wops and the Dagos. Those names were always being thrown around. I remember once, when I was

6 years old, some of the older boys in the neighborhood were playing cowboys and Indians or some kind of game, and I remember the police showing up because these guys were gonna hang me. They were playing Lynching, and they must have picked me out because I was the little Dago. I remember my mother, who was about four foot ten, fighting with these big Irish kids, shouting, "What are you doing to my boy?!" I think my family moved to this Irish neighborhood because the old Italian neighborhood was starting to deteriorate and they thought things would be better for us there, but it didn't work out.

I was very conscious of prejudice against blacks, even as a little boy. And I was aware of Hank Aaron more than I was of Jackie Robinson. There was something about Hank Aaron. He wasn't on one of those big city teams, he wasn't in the glitz of Yankee Stadium, and what I liked about him was the understatement. I always found the Broadway Joes, the big mouths, the Hendersons and the Deions, repulsive. One of my dad's values was that you understate. You don't call attention to yourself. You just do what you do quietly and efficiently. I learned to appreciate that, and some of what I saw in my dad I saw in players that I liked. I liked extremely competent, driven, but understated players. They seemed to stand for what my dad stood for, and since he was dead by this time I guess you can say that in a way they were his replacements. They were carrying on his values.

My dad worked lots of jobs. I didn't see much of him, but the legend of my father was alive and well in my family, because my brothers would talk about him. He was gone physically, but I'd hear how Dad would do this or Dad would do that, and you know, strange little things. My dad did some work as a longshoreman, and he loved peaches. So when there was damage to a crate of peaches, they'd give it to him to bring home because they knew we didn't have a lot of money. When he got home he'd give them all away. He'd offer them to us, but we knew how much he loved them so we'd say, "No, you have them, Dad." And there would be some peaches left, and all of us would want them, but no one would eat them because we would wait it out until my dad would eat them. If he didn't give in, they'd be left in a little cup in the refrigerator for him to eat, finally, whenever he got around to it … or forever. It was that sort of thing. He was giving up what he loved for us, and we learned to do the same for him.

That kind of sacrifice is something I looked for in teams and players. You play to win, but when you play ball you have to sacrifice. You do lots of things to make it happen for the team. You don't try to hit it out when you're down by five just to inflate your statistics. You try to get something going. You have to be willing to give of yourself. What really matters is, who are you in the foxhole? That's it, that's real important. A lot of people may be good, you know. They may have tremendous natural ability. But what you really want to know is who they are in the foxhole. It's intangible, but it's what counts.

What I learned to look for in baseball, in a team, in the players, is their values. The way I remember the game when I played it as a kid, there was a lot of talk and interaction and trying to support each other. A lot of the focus was on collaboration. Today most people don't realize how important collaboration is in baseball. They see basketball as that kind of a game because it's obvious that they're collaborating. It's subtler in baseball, harder to see, maybe, but I believe it's there. If you were well-coached when you were a kid you picked it up. That's what they'd teach you, and I appreciated it, first as a kid playing ball, then as a fan watching the pros. What mattered to me was collaboration, and that meant the willingness to sacrifice and doing your best in a quiet understated way.

Doing your best, personal achievement—that was also important, because people should reach for the stars. Sometimes these two values—individual achievement and sacrifice, cooperation—conflict with one another, and when they do a tremendous tension is created. I was very excited by the Great Society programs. I believe they were necessary at the time, but I also came to realize they weren't effective, and that was a major disappointment. It seemed the right thing to do, but it didn't work out. It discouraged personal ambition and rewarded mediocrity. You have to have cooperation and sacrifice. You have to think of the larger group and not just yourself, but you have to push yourself as well. You have to reach for the stars. There were times when I did not do my best. I felt I could do more than I was doing, but I felt that if I pushed myself too hard and stood out too much, it wouldn't look right and it might not be good for the others, who had less ability. Even as a kid that tension made me crazy and neurotic at times. But it also made me feel like I was growing. I didn't know how to resolve it, and I'd be pulled back and forth between these two sets of values. When I was signed by a minor league team, I was excited, I felt I could get somewhere. But I also felt like I was selling myself for 30 pieces of silver. There were times when I did what was best for me as a player, when I really got into it in a personal way and felt I was doing great. But right after this flush of success I'd be bummed out. There was the Catholic stuff to deal with. I used to feel, Hell, I'm gonna be punished for this, and this would put all sorts of superstitions into play. You do weird things to ward off the punishment, to drive away the demons.

Even when there's this war in you between the individual wanting to make it and the obligation to sacrifice for the team, the bottom line is victory. The idea is never to have grace and lose; you want to win, and if you decide that your individual efforts have more chance of bringing your team home to victory while your coach is telling you something else, that dynamic tension becomes the most important part of the game and the most painful part. I know that whenever I'd let loose and do my own thing I'd get into the craziness of superstitions. God's gonna punish me for doing this. I'm gonna get into a slump; I'll drop pop flies; I'll get beaned. In the end I think these fears had a lot to do with getting me out of baseball. They tired me out, they exhausted me.

As a fan I've always admired players who felt that tension and seemed to be made better by it. Players who weren't so preoccupied with personal achievement that they didn't feel the obligation to sacrifice. I saw that in Hank Aaron. There were some years when he let his pursuit of Ruth's home run record take over, but I remember years when he wasn't trying to knock the cover off the ball. He was just trying to place it; he was trying to push some people up, and I appreciated that. At the same time, he disappointed me a little on the issue of civil rights. I read his book, *If I Had a Hammer*, where he talks about his part in the struggle for civil rights. When I was a kid I was looking for that, and I remember other ball players who were much more outspoken than he was. So in terms of my hero worship I was a little disappointed, and I have a feeling he's rewriting history, trying to make himself look a little better than he was. As I remember, he didn't do all this talking against discrimination he claims he did, though I do remember that he tried to let his actions speak for him. He agreed to sleep in less than adequate housing because he wanted to play the game. He was going to make a contribution as a player, and that would show them. But his claim that he was involved in all that dialogue and rhetoric over civil rights— I don't think it's true, though I wish it was. I would have liked for him to be as noble off the field as he seemed to be on it. That would have mattered to me.

What I was looking for was someone who was not physically exceptional, but who had extraordinary ability he didn't need to make a show of and who could quiet it down sometimes for the sake of the team. Mickey Mantle was the quintessential American: blond hair and blue eyes, six foot ... like a diamond. He was the American stereotype, but that's exactly what I didn't like. That has something to do with why I liked the Braves. I was from Buffalo, and when you think of Milwaukee, Detroit, Cleveland and Buffalo—not Chicago— you're thinking about cities that are a lot alike. They're blue collar industrial towns with working people and a lot of immigrants, like my dad. I tended to go for the smaller markets. I've always hated the Dodgers. I hated them when they were in Brooklyn, but I certainly don't like them in Los Angeles. I never have. You know: the glitz, the Hollywood glamor, the show. And I never liked the Yankees because they had a couple of farm teams that were in the major leagues and that seemed to be there just to feed the Yankees the players they needed to keep them on top. I didn't appreciate that. It wasn't a level playing field. It was win at any cost, and the Yankees had the silver; they could pay the price.

I admired the ordinary guys, guys my own size who didn't have everything going for them, but who did great things with what they had. I admired that dedication and the other things you had to have to make it when God hadn't dunked you in a perfect gene pool: the acts of heroism and sacrifice, the ability to stick to it. Al Kaline started at 19 years old and he just worked and worked and worked till he made something of himself. And yet he was humble throughout. These were people who established themselves, who showed that if you work hard, if you give, if you do the right things, if you take care of your body, you will succeed. Some of the players I'm speaking of weren't saints, no more than Mickey Mantle was. But they made it with half his natural endowments because they didn't abuse themselves the way he did. Mantle disgraced himself with all that boozing, coming to games smashed. All that talent, a quintessential American, and look what he did to himself. If he'd have been more careful, more dedicated to his team and to baseball, he could have lasted a lot longer and he could have been among the greatest.

I was always a judgmental fan. These kinds of things always mattered to me, and I guess in a way I was judging the great American pastime from an immigrant and working class point of view. If you work and work and work, even though you're at a disadvantage, you can make it. And baseball was the metaphor for that, and the proof. I believed that as a kid, without a doubt. I saw a lot of them make it. The Latin explosion happened then, too, and there were a fair number of Italians as well, like Carl Furillo. It was a level playing field. There were opportunities for blacks, for immigrants, for anyone who had the talent. Or so it seemed to me at the time. As an adult I learned that there were lots of players who were held back for racial or other reasons through the '60s. But I didn't know it then. It looked like the world of equal opportunity, and at least to an extent it was. It was a metaphor for making it in America.

Baseball was a wonderful distraction, but it had more meaning than that. You go and talk to the kids. It had a lot of meaning. There were these values, and they were important. I was also an altar boy, and even when I got older and was planning to go into preseminary, baseball was still big in my life. I didn't have very positive experiences with the church. I was coming to the realization that there was hypocrisy, phoniness in the church. Things were coming out, and they cut me pretty deep. We have some relatives who are priests in the Vatican, so this touched me personally. I was discovering cracks in this core institution and in religion itself. During the war, the church failed to show the understated courage I was looking for. You know, Pope Pius and some of the things that came out about his activities during the war, the wheeling and dealing that was going on to protect the position of the church while people were being murdered in droves—learning these things undermined my interest in a vocation in the church, which I'd been considering.

The church, it turned out, didn't live up to the values it preached. The values I picked up on the baseball field and that I saw played out over the long haul, over the 154-game season—they should prevail everywhere, but they don't. In the '60s it seemed that all the institutions you depended on and believed in were crashing, and you looked for something that could revive your faith. You had to find something, some activity, that held up under scrutiny, some place where values were still alive and still important. This was a painful period in my life. I lived it like most people; I did lots of experimenting, tried out lots of gurus and strange beliefs, Carlos Castaneda and all that stuff. This was the late '60s, when I was 21, 22 years old, I was looking for a new religion, and even baseball disappointed me. Baseball is also a religion, you know. It was much less abstract than the other religions, but it also began to show some cracks, though not as many as religion had.

Baseball is a religion because it's a playing field for values, and it has an orthodoxy, an ancient tradition and an ancient book of rules that hardly changes. Of course there are a thousand differences between baseball and Catholicism, but they're alike in important ways. There are the rituals these guys go through when they're warming up, preparing for a game, and the superstitions some of them have. There's the need to confront your prejudices, to accept all people as equal and to focus on their quality as people. There's the idea of sacrifice which, as I said, was so important to me, and the idea that virtue is rewarded, the belief that more often than not, in some actuarial, probabilistic sense, you will be rewarded for the good you do. That's also religious, though more in a humanistic sense than in terms of a chosen faith. I still believe that if you perform virtuously and well, if you somehow strike the right balance between personal excellence and cooperation, the odds will be with you. This is natural justice. God wants ability and dedication to pay off. He wants the universe to speak through baseball, because in a way baseball is an embodiment of natural justice.

I believe that very strongly. I know I've felt it. It shows itself in many places, of course, but nowhere more clearly or more consistently—day after day, season after season—than in baseball. Look, it's right here in the paper. The Tigers beat the Yankees 6–4 with three in the ninth. The Yankees are being punished! I mean, how did Detroit beat them? They're not that good. I know this sounds nuts, but that's where I was at when I was a kid. I really believed it. I'm laughing now, but I was deadly serious about it then. That's really what I thought.

My mother was an epileptic, and I was always afraid she'd go into one of her seizures. I was always worried as a kid. Then my Dad died. I don't know why he died so young. He was a healthy guy, and then he was gone. There was so much that was unsettled in the universe for me, so much early tragedy. I needed something to hang onto. I needed the constancy of baseball. Religion, the Catholic faith, didn't suffice. It had sprung too many leaks. I wanted something to show me in some tangible way that there was an order to things. The laws of the universe seemed not to be working for me, and I needed something to restore my faith in them, to put things in order. Baseball did that for me.

Life is so varied, so confusing; there's so much to deal with, and it all seems unconnected. But the baseball season has a constancy to it, and it made perfect sense. You knew exactly what was going on and why. There was almost a Zen quality to it. There was an order and a beauty that I appreciated, a certain rightness. The fact that the Yankees came back from three games to one to win the '58 Series, and the way they won it—even though I smashed the radio when it happened—there was a heroism about their accomplishment that I appreciated. There was a beauty. It was a symphony in its own right, even though I hated the Yankees. This isn't just something concocted by a middle-aged guy. I remember feeling that way as a kid, appreciating this event that made me miserable, simply because it closed the long season in this beautiful and heroic way. It showed that events were not meaningless or random. What happened seemed to make sense, and it gave a sense to things.

II. Striving for Excellence and Perfection

More than one effort to explain the powerful appeal of baseball fixes on the pursuit or achievement of perfection. Athletic achievement, as theologian Michael Novak puts it, is "the momentary attainment of perfect form." The athlete, writes Paul Weiss, "is an outstanding instance of what man might do and be; he shows us what we ideally are as bodies." And William Saroyan, whose admiration for baseball shines radiantly from his language, praises it as a "pure demonstration of the unaccountable way by which the human spirit achieves stunning, unbelievable grandeur." As in all these examples, the focus of such explanations is typically on the athlete: his body, his prowess, his mastery, his gift for bringing the human body, known for its frustrating limitations, to the fullest expression of its capabilities. The account is appealing; it rings with a certain logic and probability. But in fact remarkably few of the more than 100 fans I interviewed mentioned this as a primary reason for their attraction to the game. A number spoke of their admiration for the performance of particular players: DiMaggio's regal dignity and ease, Williams' uncanny hitting eye, Mantle's speed and power, Mays' grace, flare, and style. But none praised these talents as manifestations of human perfection or perfectability, and even among the many who as children perceived their favorite players as supermen or minor deities, none cited this all but divine bestowal as the principal source of the game's attraction. One may claim, of course, that these fans are not aware of what draws them on, that the subtler or more primitive forces at work on their responses are lost on them when they attempt to articulate their love for the game or what it meant to them as children. But so many of these fans are so probingly insightful when they speak, so trenchant and eloquent in their accounts of what moved them, that appeals to causes beyond their own understanding seem somewhat strained.

A number of these fans do emphasize the pursuit or attainment of excellence as the principal source of the game's early hold on their imaginations. This should not surprise us. We are all quite taken with, if not always dedicated to, the ideal of excellence, smitten by, if not always driven toward, the images of our own best selves. But the drive and appeal are perhaps most powerful during the periods of middle childhood and adolescence (from 8 or 9 to 17), the time of the fan's most intense, often obsessive, involvement with the game. During these years the child or adolescent is typically preoccupied with the acquisition, testing, and demonstration of his competency and skills. He is ready, as Erikson puts it, "to apply himself to given skills and tasks," hoping "to win recognition by producing things"—or, one might add, by doing things, ideally the way Ozzie Smith or Ken Griffey, Jr., do them. It is also the time when the child looks beyond parental models to the often idealized images of the larger world around him and enhances his often shaky self-esteem by attaching himself, first from an admiring distance, later perhaps by active affiliation, to heroes, gurus, and inflated gods. Perhaps because late childhood and early adolescence are more given to struggle than achievement, centered on struggle even when there is achievement, the excellence or perfection fans speak of is a subtler and more complex thing than the athletic prowess theorists point to. It is more typically attached to the achievements of a team than to the genius of a given player. And it is often more grittily and heroically connected with the ideas of hard work and struggle than with the notion of mastery; it has more to do with striving than with perfection.

Paul K., for whom the Yankees of the glorious '50s were indeed perfection, suggests the complexity of the fan's attraction to this ideal by describing it from a number of different perspectives. For Paul, the Yankees were excellence incarnate or in uniform, symbols of perfection. To be the fan and admirer of such a team is, therefore, to absorb at least a glimmer of their splendor, to experience a kind of elevation by association. In their roles as models of perfection and bestowers of grace, however, the Yankees were a stimulating but ultimately deceptive illusion. Misleadingly, yet drivingly, they held out the illusion that what they had achieved, we could achieve, that their greatness, as Paul puts it, was "up for grabs." They drew us on and, it seems, rather harmlessly fooled us at the same time. But there is also a strong personal cast to Paul's response. As a victim of scarlet fever, confined for many months to his room and bed, the Yankees, as brought to him on a magic carpet of sound by the voice of Mel Allen, were his company and salvation. Their immediate message was, we are here, you are not alone. Their implicit message was, if we can do it, so can you, and the gift entailed a debt, the desire to excel in later life as a kind of magical payback. What you have done for me I will now, in my own more modest way, attempt for you. The Yankees, in other words, were simultaneously or serially a symbol and source of excellence, a somewhat delusive proof of its attainability, and an implicit summons to this virtue that inspired. What one sees also in this interview is that the appeal of excellence or perfection is not intrinsic. What is sought here is not the full expression of capability for its own sake, but as a road to "the top." The summons to this once enfeebled bedridden boy was not to self-fulfillment, but to supremacy and dominance.

II. Striving for Excellence and Perfection

The emphasis of the interviews with Walter S. and Clive C. is on striving and overcoming rather than achievement, on the pursuit of excellence rather than its attainment. The key words are work, struggle, adversity, and reward. Walter's beloved Red Sox are as central to his preoccupation as Paul's Yankees are to his. So powerful are the influences of these teams on the forming values and thought patterns of their young fans that one is tempted to assume that had Paul grown up in Boston rather than in Newark, New Jersey, the central theme of his life would have been not the striving toward an elusive perfection, but the triumph over limitation or adversity. That, at any rate, is Walter's theme, and while the message echoed in his home as well as from the notoriously short walls of Fenway Park, it is difficult to separate his passion for the Red Sox from his tragic and heroic view of life. Tragedy, he half mournfully admits, "is an important theme in my involvement with baseball." But "setting off the tragedy is a wonderful excitement." When players perform heroically, overcoming injury or natural limitation in a moment of self-transcendence, "it's a wonderful triumph of the human spirit," and that, he insists, is baseball's "great message."

As Paul was ill and house-bound, Walter was small and skinny. In that unprepossessing frame, what he learned from such performers and such performances is that life is a wonderful gift, that we can achieve excellence with much less than maximum endowment—if we're willing "to go for it." And when one, beset by such limitations, does go for it and, miraculously, finds it, his pleasures are greater than those whose obstacles are too easily surmounted, whose treasures are too readily at hand. All 33 Yankee pennants and 22 World Series will pale beside that one thirstily-panted-after Red Sox world championship ... if it ever comes.

"Going for it" is also the dominant melody in Clive C.'s overtly religious hymn to baseball and to those who "give it 110 percent" every time they play. Like Walter, Clive is especially taken with those whose extra effort achieves a victory over natural limitations. But where Walter hopes and waits and hungers, Clive insists on an inherent connection between striving and success. In his God-centered universe, effort and goodness are rewarded, and so central was baseball to his early development that it is not clear which was causal, which the mere extension of a belief formulated in the other sphere. If anything, despite his profound and obviously earnest religiosity, Clive is inclined to give precedence to baseball. "Now I see," he exclaims, delighted with the discovery, "that doing the extra work [produces] success, and I learned that from the Mets that first year." That first year was 1986, the year Clive, then 9 years old, first took an interest in baseball and the year, of course, when the striving Mets defeated the tragic Red Sox in the Series. Being a devout Catholic, Clive believes in the idea of just reward. He believes that the reward for the good life is eternity in Heaven. But he recognizes that the seed of this belief might first have taken root in his earliest attachment to baseball. It was the Mets' victorious season that taught him what has become the guiding principle of his ambitions: "In baseball you put in the hard work, you do your best, and you win the championship."

What one notices in all of these interviews is the prominence of subthemes. While striving for excellence and reward is the dominant theme in each of these conversations, other, almost equally compelling explanations for the appeal of the game repeatedly assert themselves: Paul's and Walter's baseball-centered bond with their fathers; Walter's and Clive's feelings of empowerment, the sense of equality achieved with one's father or other significant adults when baseball is the subject of conversation; Clive's fertile analysis of the analogousness of religion and baseball; Paul's and Clive's warm receptivity to the camaraderie of baseball: the team as a kind of family or group of friends, players as caring members of the community, the bonding of fans around the game, their friendship revolving around and feeding on it like hummingbirds on nectar. Many of these subthemes will assume dominance in other interviews. What is important but secondary for these fans becomes central to others, for whom the theme of striving might drop to a ground bass, played beneath the melodies of father-bonding, religion, or empowerment. What this confirms, of course, is that one's response to baseball is rich and multifaceted. Baseball is not only many things to many people; it is many things to each of us.

Greatness Up for Grabs

Paul K. Born 1934. Advertising manager. Raised in Newark, New Jersey. New York Yankees.

My interest in baseball began with the onset of a sickness I had. I had scarlet fever at age 7, and it rendered me incapable of doing anything for the springtime of 1941. So I had nothing to do, and I used to listen to the baseball games. You might say it was Mel Allen, the Yankee announcer, who inspired my interest in baseball. And it was Mel Allen and the Yankees who helped me to get through my sickness and my isolation. In those days, scarlet fever was sometimes fatal. I was very sick, and I fought it, and I felt I was helped through it by the Yankees. This wonderful feeling that I knew there would be a baseball game every day helped me fight it. Mel Allen seemed almost like a friend. He was talking to me only, and it seemed he was the only friend I had. I was an only child, scarlet fever was a communicable disease, so no one could visit me, and it was like I was on an island. But I wasn't because I had the Yankees. They were all mine, in my room, in my house, on my radio, for me. It's amazing that I remember this, but this is the way it was for me.

I became a fan during the time when the Yankees were not the Yankees, not the Yankees who were or the ones who were to be. It was wartime, and since most of the first-string players were drafted, they had ballplayers that were marginal, ballplayers like Snuffy Sternweiss and Johnny Lindell—guys who were probably not that good, but who were filling in for the guys who were at war: for DiMaggio, Keller, and the others.

When I got better my father took me to the games, and as the war came to an end the Yankees began to be a lot more exciting. I remember the first baseman—I think his first name was Nick [Etten, who played for the Yankees from 1943–1946.]—I remember Joe Gordon, and then they got Billy Johnson. In left was Charley Keller, in center field was DiMaggio, and in right they had Henrich. And I remember the last years of Bill Dickie, and when he faded out Yogi came up. Some of the pitchers I remember were Allie Reynolds, Vic Raschi, Eddie Lopat, and a little later Whitey Ford. That's when the dynasty began. Casey Stengel came aboard after Joe McCarthy left, and then came that flurry of pennants.

You got a feeling when you went to Yankee Stadium that something special was going on. The walls, the stands, the people, they were class people, they were different people, they were Yankee people. Through and through Yankee people. You couldn't be a Yankee fan and a Giant fan. You couldn't be a Yankee fan and a Dodger fan. You couldn't divide your commitment to the Yankees. They were all for you, you alone, and you had to be for them in the same complete way. They were important to you.

As a kid I lived in the time of the Yankees. When I played stickball with my friend Sammy, we used to stand like the Yankees. If we stood a certain way, we said, this is the way Henrich or Rizzuto or DiMaggio stands. We used the numbers of the Yankees: Rizzuto was number 10 and DiMaggio was number 5. OK, this is who we want to be like, but whoever we picked, we were Yankees through and through.

I remember going to Giant games with my father. It was wonderful, but nowhere near as wonderful as seeing the Yankees. The Polo Grounds was very nice, but it was not Yankee Stadium. The lawn at the stadium was manicured, it just seemed to sparkle, and the scoreboard was elegant for those days. It wasn't an electric scoreboard till later on, but it was just perfect. Everything was perfect, and the Yankees became part of you. It was their perfection that appealed to you, the quest for excellence, because that's what they were: excellence.

I loved the Yankees, and it was important to me that they were winners, because it made me feel that I was a winner. You just felt that you were a little piece of them because you were a fan. Whenever I'd play a game I'd think I was one of them and that I had to make good. I had to do it for them just like they did it for me. It was a strange thing. I was paying them back for taking me through my illness. It was crazy, it really was. I don't have that feeling now, because what I see today is a business, a business instead of a quest for excellence. Years ago they played every game like it was their last. Those guys really tried.

I remember Enos Slaughter in the twilight of his career. He came to the Yankees at the age of 38, I think, and he ran and he gave it everything he had. I think part of it was because he realized what stadium he was playing in. After all, he had played with the Gas House Gang. He played with the very best. But when he came to the stadium, I think he felt the tradition, and I think it helped him last another year or two. That may have been true for a lot of players, Johnny Mize, for example. Every year a different player in the twilight of his career came to the Yankees to help them win.

The team was a kind of family or group of friends. They all pulled together, and a lot of close friendships were developed, intrateam. They cared about each other, and that appealed to me. Everybody was more family-oriented in those days. Today, families are separated, spread over the whole United States and beyond. Years ago, you and your family lived within a certain area, and the Yankees were part of you, strange as that may seem. You felt you were part of their family and part of their greatness. Lots of people wouldn't agree with this. They have that image of the Yankees as a business, a corporation. But that was just because the Yankees were all standouts, not because there was something really impersonal about the team. If you became the shortstop for the Yankees, you'd own that job for ten or fifteen years, and nobody could touch it. You became part of the family. The ball players felt loyalty to the fans. They gave the fans what they wanted; they gave them their money's worth; they played their hearts out; and the fans gave them loyalty in return.

The Dodgers were the same way. The Dodgers were a family. They were very close-knit, and you always felt that in that little town of Brooklyn they were all in it together. In my mind the Dodgers were one of the most respected and interesting teams in baseball, and of course they gave Jackie Robinson a chance. But they were the team of the underdog. If you felt you were an underdog, the type of guy who's scratching and scratching to make it up there, the Dodgers were your team. If you felt you belonged on top, that you were quality, you wanted to associate with the Yankees. I wanted to be a winner, and I felt like a winner with the Yankees. Definitely.

My father had been a catcher on his high school team, and he'd seen all the old players, the best of them. He would say to me that some of the ball players he'd seen were better than the ones I saw and that they didn't compare to the players of his time. That's just how I feel about the players of my day in comparison to the guys playing today. The ball players of today are probably in better condition, their bodies are better, and they're probably better athletes than some of the oldtimers. But I still hang onto the idea that the ones I saw were better. Maybe that's because I lived it and enjoyed it more than I do now, but I think it's because the players felt a greater commitment to the game. It meant more to them than it does now. They had that old mentality, and they played slap down drag out baseball.

It's different now. The Yankees are different, and I'm different. I lost interest in baseball; it became a little boring. I couldn't attend as many games as I used to, the stadium became a pretty unsafe place as time went by, I grew older, and I got married. I took the kids to some games, but being daughters they weren't into baseball as much as I was. I couldn't share my knowledge with my daughters and my wife. It isn't like going out with a friend, where you go down the lineups and say, remember this, remember that. There's no way you can do this with children, not with daughters.

But to the day he died, I was able to share it with my father. It was part of the bond between us right to the end. We had to share the Yankees and Giants because he was a Giants fan, but I learned it all from him. I remember—it must have been two or three weeks before he died—he wasn't feeling too good and he would ask me how the Mets were doing because the Mets had become his team, and he would name the teams, the lineups from top to bottom. But then, a day or two before he died, I saw his mind begin to slip away, and I asked him: "Hey Dad, can you still name the Giants?" No, he'd lost it completely. He couldn't do it.

It's different now; it's just different. Your job isn't your life anymore; it's just your job. These guys trained and worked, did what a guy had to do to get into professional baseball years ago, and it was a hell of a lot different than it is today. Today they don't pay their dues. They come up a lot faster, and the league is a lot larger. That's why there's so much mediocrity. There are so many more teams that the talent has been spread out thin. The old Newark Bears of the International League were probably as good as some of the major league teams today. The work ethic has changed, and therefore the athletic work ethic has changed.

But we also change. You get older, and other things in life take the place of baseball. When you're a youngster you don't have responsibilities. When you're a kid you're baseball, you're schoolwork, you have a girlfriend, you have a car, and you play ball. Mainly you watch and listen to the games, you study the box scores and the stats, and you learn everything you can about the players. In those days I could tell you what they ate for breakfast. I knew every Yankee and everything I could about them because it was important to me. Our parents used to say: "Why do you worry about them? Do they worry about you? Do you think Joe DiMaggio cares if you fail Spanish? They don't give a damn."

But that didn't matter. We cared about them, and when they lost I took it personally. It ruined my day, my evening. If the Yankees lost I didn't feel hungry, I didn't want to eat. It was stupid, but we couldn't help it. It was part of our skin. We thought about the Yankees as personal relatives or friends, and we wanted our friends to be winners. Somehow we felt that all our dreams would come true if the Yankees won. The Yankees win and everything will be great. It couldn't help me with my Latin, couldn't help me with Spanish, but I thought it might. Wouldn't hurt. So they were a symbol of the possibilities of achieving my own personal greatness, so to speak. Somehow I would do a little better in school because of the Yankees. It never worked out that way. The more I listened to them the worse I did, but I kept on feeling what I felt when I was in bed with scarlet fever: If the Yankees can do it, I can do it; if things go well for them, things will go well for me.

If you talk to people our age, in this part of the country, I'd say the key issue would be the quest for excellence, that longing to be on top. When we were younger, naturally we wanted to achieve greatness, to be the best. And as

Yankee fans what we all shared was that quest for excellence, the quest for respect and acceptance, the desire to be as loved and adored as the Yankees were. What we loved and admired in them was something we can never touch and never hope to be a part of, because it was unreachable, untouchable. And yet, in our minds, we thought it was up for grabs.

Tragedy and Triumph
Up from Depot Street

Walter S. Born 1928. Professor of mathematics education, retired. Raised in Chicopee, Massachusetts. Boston Red Sox.

Now that I'm retired I'm taking the opportunity to fulfill my lifelong desire, which is to read everything there is to read about baseball. So much is available now which wasn't available when I was a young child. When I was growing up, times were so different. Kids used to stand around on street corners, and we'd argue baseball all the time. There were the Yankee fans and the Red Sox fans, and of course we'd argue about who was better: Lou Gehrig of the Yankees or Jimmie Foxx of the Red Sox. We didn't have the stats that you have today, but we were so deeply involved with our baseball heroes and idolized them so adoringly that we would argue heatedly with one another, though we were the best of friends.

But what affected me most was my father's interest in baseball. I really believe he instilled in me a love of baseball when I was still in the womb. I remember as a kid how we'd listen to the ball games together and how he used to keep score. He would keep these great detailed results and the scores of the ball games while we listened on long-distance radio from Philadelphia, which was staticky. Of course there was no television then. We'd be glued to the radio, because we'd want to know how the Red Sox were doing in Philadelphia. I vividly remember, when I was 9 years old in 1937, in the days when travel wasn't so easy and going to Boston was a really big trip, we went in my father's old 1932 whatever-it-was ninety miles to Boston to see a doubleheader against the Cleveland Indians. It was such a fantastic thing for me to go to Boston, and on that day everything was just absolutely wonderful.

There was my great hero—the first one—Jimmie Foxx, the one I always said was better than Gehrig. And Foxx didn't disappoint me. In the first game he hit a home run way over the fence, over the net in Fenway Park, and my father said to me, "See that, it didn't even hit the screen. It went over the net!" And I saw that from my left-field seat. There was a feeling of awe about the whole thing. Being with my father, who loved the game so much and who instilled that love in me, was a deeply personal, emotional experience for me, a kind of high. Young people are trying to experience that today with drugs and sex, but all I needed was baseball.

It was so exciting to see this green wall at Fenway Park and the crowd cheering and Lefty Grove, who won 300 ball games, in the twilight of his career. He won that game 5–2; it was an awesome experience. And yet, as they say, baseball imitates life. Like life it has its thrills and its sadness and frustrations, and in the second game I experienced some of that because the Red Sox were losing 8–7 in the bottom of the ninth inning. They got two men on in the ninth with two out, and Jimmie Foxx came up. The stage was set. He'd hit a home run in the first game already, but this time he did what Foxx did often: he struck out. He ended the ball game with a strikeout. It was such a tragic experience for me as a 9-year-old that I actually wept.

For so many years now I've lived through disappointment with the Red Sox, their habit of losing the seventh game—they've done it four times in my lifetime and they've lost two playoff games at the end of the season. They lose in the most tragic ways, and I've taken it to heart and suffered with it.

Still, I loved the game. I grew up in a slum area where the kids loved baseball. We didn't know we were poor, really, and we would play forever on a vacant lot. When 5 o'clock came some kids would say, "We've got to go now; we have to listen to the radio. *Dick Tracy* was on for fifteen minutes, and *Jack Armstrong*, and they would go for that. I couldn't understand it. I couldn't understand why they'd stop the game to listen to a program, and I would say, "We've got to continue playing." Nothing was more fun to me than being involved in any way at all with baseball.

Everything seemed so spontaneous, so natural, and it was all connected to my father, who had those wonderful scorebooks full of ball games. I did a terrible thing when I moved to Vancouver twenty-some years ago. I had to make a decision what to do with all those scorebooks, which went back to the '30's. We had so much weight, so much to ship, that I decided to throw away the scorebooks. But now, when I think about it, how I'd love to go back and look at the scorebooks he kept in such beautiful detail, the way he did. And to see pictures of those ball players that I would recognize.

I had so much respect for my father, because he was a father, and we had this one channel, baseball, where we could communicate, so evenly, with such understanding, where we could appreciate what we gave to each other. Baseball seemed to smooth or break down the hostility that might exist between father and son. Not so much hostility as awe. He wasn't an awesome figure to me, but he might have been if it weren't for baseball. Baseball humanized him, brought us to the same level. In baseball he was my dad, and we were two great baseball fans communicating as equals through this one thing we knew so well.

Having baseball, for me, is almost like having a love, something very personal and intimate. Not sexual necessarily, but in a sense baseball did rise to that level of intensity. Because I felt so deeply about baseball, I would lose sleep over a loss, and I would have great joy over a win. I can still remember calling my wife on the telephone to get a report on the playoff game in 1978 between the Red Sox and the Yankees. The Red Sox won the last game of the season and the Yankees lost theirs, so they finished in a tie, and they were playing the playoff game in Fenway Park. I had a class that afternoon, and after the class I called my wife. The game was still on, and my wife was telling me what was happening as she watched it on television. There were two men on and one out, and the Red Sox had a chance to score with Jim Rice at bat. Then I hear my wife say, "Oh, it's a hit!" and I think, Oh, it's a hit, and the Red Sox will tie the game. But then she says, "Oh, he caught it," and I realize that my wife, although she's lived with me all these years, still thinks it's a hit when a batter makes contact with the ball. It brought me from up here to way down here. And there I am, a mature professor at my desk, feeling so terribly awful and angry at my wife. There's still a chance, though, because Yaz is the next batter, although there are two outs. And then she tells me that he lifts a foul pop up, and Nettles gets under it and catches it for the third out, and I am totally distraught, devastated—over a ball game. It remained with me. It will never go away.

It's hard for me to identify the source of that feeling. For one of my daughters it's a personal thing. She identifies with the pain of the players in situations like that. I remember watching the sixth game of the 1986 World Series on television with her, the game the Red Sox lost when the ball went through Bill Buckner's legs. We couldn't believe it. I later found out, when I went into her room and saw the picture, that she had cut from the newspaper a picture of Wade Boggs, sitting on the bench, slumped over, in great agony over having lost the Series. I felt she saw the pain of Boggs, that she had experienced his pain. It meant something to her, even though she isn't much of a baseball fan. The picture is still there, in her room, although she's in Tennessee, a graduate student at the university down there.

For her it was personal identification, empathy, but for me it was selfish. I wasn't concerned about Boggs feeling bad. I was concerned about me feeling bad. I just have to admit that. If I try to say why, I'd say there's a kind of fever that exists, among men especially, a competitive spirit that makes winning important and losing in a sense tragic. You personalize these things, you allow them to come into you and you feel they have meaning.

Tragedy is an important theme in my involvement with baseball. It seems to come up over and over again. I've written a poem, a three-page poem, which is a historical memoir of the tragedies of the Red Sox. Their four losses of World Series, always in seven games, their two playoff game losses, and their one end-of-the-season last day loss to the Yankees in 1949. So seven times they have lost faithfully. Zero times they have won faithfully. You might call winning on the last day of the season in 1978 to tie for the pennant a kind of triumph, but in the final analysis the pennant was gone in the playoff game.

Setting off the tragedy is a wonderful excitement. I still love reading about baseball. I've bought a dozen books to add to my already huge collection. My wife says, "You've got enough baseball books," but she's wrong. Everything you read about it is a new wonder. The fact that Hank Aaron wore 44 on his uniform and tied for the home run title with Willie McCovey one year with 44, and that he hit 44 home runs 4 different times. What a coincidence to uplift you! It's things like that that compensate for some of the deep depressions I've experienced.

When Kirk Gibson hits a World Series home run, even though I don't care about either team, the fact that he hits a pinch-hit home run to win the ball game though he's practically hobbling around on one leg—it's a wonderful triumph of the human spirit. So good things can happen, as Gibson showed. And the 1991 World Series, with two teams rising from the depths, from last place to first place, and meeting each other in a titanic struggle—how can you not admire that? So when they talk about baseball imitating life, which has many ups and downs, well, baseball surely does that. And you never lose that excitement. You feel it in the atmosphere when baseball people get together. And you hear it from the fans you talk to, the stories they have to tell. Here we are, from bus drivers to accountants to lawyers to professors; whatever the occupation, they have this deep love for the game. And even today's prima donnas with their massive salaries haven't spoiled it for us, because it's too deep.

The triumph of the human spirit—it's a great message. I always think about the underdog who works harder than the next person, who doesn't have as much natural talent, who's willing to go for it, who doesn't say, "I don't think I can do that" or "I don't think I have the chance to do this," but who says, "Even if there's just one chance in ten or one chance in a hundred, go for it." When you do that, sometimes you win, and those triumphs are glorious. So no matter what I read, when it's about somebody who has overcome some sort of weakness or handicap and who has not only overcome that handicap by doing something great, but has shown that he can also be happy, that thrills me. People today equate happiness with quality of life, and quality of life has come to mean material quality. But there's much more to life than that. In fact materialism is a way to eliminate happiness, because you become so conscious of how much more you can get that you lose sight of the deep feelings that arise out of intimate relationships. You lose the ability to feel what the other person is experiencing, to understand if there is joy or tragedy in that person's life and what it means.

So when I hear somebody speaking about how exhilarated he felt when he spoke with a great baseball player or writer I can put myself in his shoes and feel the same joy. But it doesn't have to be baseball. I see more examples of human tragedy today than I ever did before. I feel sorrow in those cases, but in those instances where people have risen above those tragedies it's exhilarating. And you know that humans can rise above difficult conditions. They can do it if they put their minds to it and if they put their force to it. It's a matter of giving a lot of effort, and I think there's less and less of that. We have begun to think about how much we can get and how little we can give, a very sad state.

When I read these things about people and personal tragedies and personal victories, they help me appreciate that life is a wonderful gift. And you don't have to be rich. You don't have to be strong. I think of myself; I've grown up skinny. I was a very skinny kid when I grew up, and I grew up in the Depression. My mother, being very poor, didn't have the nutrition that mothers have today, so I was probably born a scrawny little baby. But just because I wasn't six-foot-four doesn't mean I couldn't do things. And I made my parents proud, because I did many things by working harder and going for it. I learned I didn't have to be big and healthy, that there's more to life than great physical talent or great intellectual talent. You can be good and successful with lots less, but you've got to be willing to go for it.

You can see all this very clearly in baseball. You have people who are called hot dogs. You know, they're great ball players and they do well, but they can do still better. The real competitors are different. Instead of running when they feel like running, they run all the time. Like Eddie Stanky of the Dodgers. He couldn't hit much, he got a lot of walks, but that guy was a competitor. He could kill you. Like Billy Martin. Sure, Billy Martin was a drinker and he used hard language. He was a human being and he had his weaknesses, but nobody could get in Billy Martin's way, because he'd go all out. He would go in front of a 300-pounder. He wasn't afraid of anything, and though he didn't have Joe DiMaggio's talent he played the game 100 percent. As much as I hated the Yankees, I admired Billy Martin. He epitomized human nature itself in that he had that drive. He was morally, let's say, not the best sort of person, but he had guts. Nobody is perfect. I would take Billy Martin over a Rickey Henderson any day, although Henderson has far more natural talent.

I guess I got at least some of this from my parents. My parents wanted me to do better than they did. They were only eighth-grade educated. My grandparents came from Poland, and they knew that life was hard. My parents struggled through the Depression, and they didn't want a life like that for me. They were very happy that I was able to go to higher schooling and succeed, and they were proud of that. Somehow or other they must have instilled in me this drive, the quest for excellence, the drive to do more than you might ordinarily be capable of.

When I tell my wife that I'm retired and haven't done very much with my life, I don't really mean it. Still, it's nice to hear her say, "What are you talking about? You grew up on Depot Street"—you know what typical old city slum areas were like—"and here you are now, and look at the house you have." And I look at that and think, what a long way this is from Depot Street and boy, yeah, I've come a long, long way, and I'm sure that my parents, if they were still living, would be happy. And my own children, I'm sure they're very happy too, and they seem to have developed very similar outlooks toward life. With four children, all of whom have done nothing to disgrace us—and you know that's pretty rare today—it's really a wonderful feeling.

So I think my mother and father must have passed something along to me, and my wife and I have passed something on to our children. The things they have done, while not related exactly to baseball, in some ways may typify baseball, which is a game in which you'll do better if you try harder. And that's what all life is about—trying harder. I think baseball has probably done a lot for me in that sense, besides all the thrill and agonies it's given me. Without agonies you can't have thrills. Because if you care about something then you don't have apathy. And you do more. So every time you care about something and you fail, while there may be a sense of loss, it magnifies the sense of victory when the victory comes. If you win 4-to-3 in the last of the ninth, just barely, by the narrowest of margins, you feel a tremendous kind of ecstasy, whereas if it's too easy, 10-to-0, there's no challenge, there's no fun in it. Maybe that's why I never intentionally let my children win a game, whether it be checkers or tennis, when they were growing up. If you let them win a game, how will you know how good they are? And what fun will there be for them when they finally win the game honestly? So when my sons, at age 16 or 17, finally beat me at tennis, I didn't feel a sense of "Oh gosh, I lost." I was proud because they'd been victorious in an honest way. And my victories when they were younger didn't ruin them. They enjoyed those experiences as well; they saw where I was coming from, and they kept fighting away.

The great thing about baseball is that this triumph over difficulty repeats itself over and over. In every game there will be an eighth and a ninth inning, and with two outs and two strikes it's still possible. Even though it's worked the wrong way much of the time, you know it is still possible for you to win. I was just reading an article titled, "Red Sox Fans: There Still Is a Chance." It said there's a 45 percent chance that the Red Sox will win a World Series during the lifetime of a fan now 65 years old. Well, it's not 50-50, but there's still a non-zero chance it'll happen. And my wife and children have a greater chance of seeing the Sox finally win it all.

When that triumph finally does come, there'll be nothing like it. It'll be a Mount Olympus and beyond. It'll be the ionosphere, the next universe. Once again, to experience happiness you've got to experience tragedy or disappointment. Because I've experienced the negative so often I'm able to enjoy joy and happiness at a higher level, I think, than many other people. If I didn't have as much ice cream when I was growing up during the Depression, and if I have it every day now, I appreciate it more than my children, who have always had ice cream. I remember when it was a rare thing, and I'll never forget it. My capacity for being elevated, I think, has increased, and in baseball it's increased even more because of the long-term downs and depressions of the Red Sox. But I can still find the great positives. I see that Ted Williams has the highest on-base average of any ball player, and when I see all the records he established and how Yastrzemski did such wonderful things in 1967—you can't take away the joy of all that.

In a way you might say it was good to have grown up on Depot Street, just as it was a good thing to have grown up with the Red Sox. We often say that everyone should live in a nice house with a well-tended lawn and three good meals every day, with a video player and all there is to buy nowadays. But growing up on Depot Street I didn't realize I was growing up underprivileged. We lived in a tenement, and I walked to an old-fashioned four-room school. But my experience was common; it seemed everybody was in pretty much the same boat in those days. I could play baseball or listen to the radio and derive enjoyment which, relative to my knowledge of the world then, seemed quite enormous. Since kids today experience so many more thrills and get used to them, they get blasé about it. Well, if this weakens their capacity to enjoy the things they have, then they're the ones who are disadvantaged.

Depot Street was something for me to relate to as a marginal point, a liftoff point from zero, where things would get better and better as I went along while I retained these deep visual images and remembrances of the tenement building and the vacant lot nearby and how much fun it was to play those games there. Even though at 5 o'clock the kids ran off to listen to *Little Orphan Annie*.

Baseball and Christianity
Going All Out for That Great Reward

Clive C. Born 1977. University student. Born and raised in Hillside, New Jersey. New York Mets.

My first recollection of baseball is 1986. Everyone in north Jersey was in a craze over the Mets at the time, because they were in the drive for the pennant. I remember parties at my house, gatherings of friends and that type of thing, and it somehow ended up that everyone managed to get into the TV room, where they'd gather around and watch the Mets game. There were people who were baseball fans and people who had no clue. They just knew the Mets were some kind of a team from around here that was doing really well and that everyone was going crazy over. Everybody really went bananas over the Mets in 1986. I was 9 at the time and I got into it. I started watching the Mets games with the older people and learning the names and stats of all the players.

It's clear to me that I followed the Mets because everyone else liked them at the time, because it was the in thing. It was what the crowd was doing and I was drawn in. I remember staying up way past my bedtime to watch the ends of the games, and I'd watch all of them. I'd feel terrible if the Mets lost because after all the work they put in it almost hurt to know they might not get anything from it. They might be left with nothing. I'd be concerned that they would be eliminated from the playoffs and then all that work would be in vain. They could end up with the best record and just lose a couple of games, and they'd get nothing for all their work. And you know, even if they came in second, second is nothing. Basically, if you don't get the championship you may as well have been last.

I felt a close association with the players. I would read about them in the paper and I would look at the statistics. I felt like I almost knew them. I really loved Lenny Dykstra. He was my favorite player and still is. He really plays hard. It's one hundred and ten percent dedication every time he plays. Whether he plays well or not up to par he always plays well above and beyond normal expectations. You know you're going to get the best he can give every time he gets on the field. You know he's going to have total drive and total dedication.

I like players who put in that extra effort, especially those who don't have all the natural ability and have to overcome that limitation. With them it's even more obvious that putting in the work is what brought them success. Take Mookie Wilson. He's not a really big guy, but he put in a lot of effort. He did weight training and pumped himself up and improved himself tremendously. Back in '86 he didn't even play a lot, but he turned himself into a great player by putting in the effort. He put in the work and he got the reward. I like to see that.

When people do the best they can you can't complain. What can you say? You can criticize them for not being completely successful, maybe, but that's not a fair criticism if they've put in a hundred and ten percent, if they've done the absolute best they can. When I watch I ball game I see people trying their best to succeed. It's for bragging rights, it's for pride, but it's also for the championship. It's to be the best of the best. I love to see a team work, to see them give it all they've got, and I love it when they get the reward that they deserve. I believe people get pretty much what they deserve. I really can't imagine what would have happened had the Mets lost in 1986. It was the first year I watched baseball, and it would have been very hard for me if they'd put in all that work and not been rewarded.

I think I used baseball to further my drive. I'd say, "You've got to keep pushing, you've got to keep going and you can be the best." Had the Mets lost in '86 after pushing that hard, who knows? Maybe I'd be saying to myself, "Forget work. Why should I do this paper if it's not going to get me a really good grade? Why should I bother?" Now I see that doing the extra work is driving for success, and I learned that from the Mets that first year. I took it very seriously. I was only 9 years old and it made a big impression on me. I don't know if I'm like I am specifically because of that, but I think it's a key point in why I've always associated success with drive. It taught me that if you have the drive you'll have the success.

It's a matter of fairness. If you put in that much effort you should be rewarded, just as other people who don't put in as much effort should be dealt with accordingly.

I'm pretty annoyed with baseball right now. I still see ball players putting in the work, but there's a difference. Back then they'd work for the reward of the championship, just to be number one, just to be the best. Now it seems they're overly focused on monetary gain, and that sickens me because I always thought of baseball as a very pure thing, the American sport that means something to everyone.

One reason I like Ken Griffey, Jr., is that he seems to be out there to play and not for the money. Griffey has the drive. That's why I like to see him succeed. He's not like Darryl Strawberry who complains he can't play because of some spasm or other, because he was injured or in pain. I've played baseball when I've had serious ailments and pain. You've got an obligation to the team. It's your family, those are your brothers. You do your best because you expect them to do their best, and you expect that to bring success.

I'm very religious. I'm a Roman Catholic, and I'm very, very religious. I believe in the idea of just reward. I believe if you work hard in school you're going to have success. I believe if you live a good life you're going to go to Heaven. That's your ultimate reward. In a way I think baseball might have set the stage for this belief. In baseball you put in the hard work, you do your best, and you win the championship. I saw people putting a lot of work into it; I saw their dedication; and I thought they'd have to be rewarded for it. I've got quite a bit of drive myself. I party a little too much sometimes, but mainly I think you've got to keep going. You've got to keep working. Don't let anything go; don't just blow off a paper or an assignment. I work hard in school because I realize that if I put in the work I'll be rewarded with a good grade. If you keep going you'll have success. If you get your bachelor's degree you can get a job, but if you have the drive you can go to law school and get a law degree and you can get a much better job. I think I learned that lesson from baseball. At the time I didn't realize what I realize now, but I can look back and say, "Wow, baseball was really great. It had a really good influence on me." I think it played a key role in forming my personality, my values. To find out for sure I guess I'd have to have some psychologist analyze me. But I can analyze myself to a point, and I think it definitely had a key effect.

It's connected to my Roman Catholic upbringing. Since I've been here [at the University of Pennsylvania] I've been to church five times, whereas I notice other people don't go at all. I make that effort because I want to go to Heaven someday. If you care about something you should put in the effort because you'll get more out of it. Going to church is putting in the effort for your salvation. There was one weekend when I went to bed around six in the morning. It was the third weekend I was here, and I'd gone to church the first two weekends with this one girl. I usually drag a couple of people to church with me, just like to a baseball game. If I hadn't been dragged into watching it while everyone else was watching it I wouldn't love baseball right now. So I drag people to church, because I figure, who knows, maybe they'll like it and maybe they'll become Catholic converts. I remember I went to bed the third week at six in the morning. Pretty nearly everyone did, and the two people who were supposed to go to church with me didn't go. Yet I got up and went to church. With only a couple of hours' sleep I got up and went to church. I have a drive towards religion, even more than towards doing well in school.

I seem to associate baseball with religion, don't I? They're alike in many ways. The purity, the drive, the sacrifice, and the reward in the end resulting from the drive. Also, religion is based on a series of key events: birth, baptism, communion, confirmation, then the rites of marriage and finally the death rites, the last rites before you die. It's a whole process, an entire lifespan, like the one I've gone through with the Mets. I saw the birth of a great Mets team and now they're pretty close to last. I went through that whole life span with them, back to the beginning when they first got Strawberry and Gooden. I missed some of those things, but I was there for the crucial events that you can liken to a graduation, a marriage, the peak of success. And then, when the players started getting old, when Keith Hernandez and Gary Carter retired and Darryl Strawberry and Lenny Dykstra were traded, I was with them through the decline. They were heading towards their last rites, you might say, and they pretty much got there when they finished last last season, behind two expansion teams. It doesn't get worse than that.

Baseball and religion share these basic principles. Not the physical, but the mental or spiritual principles, like the drive. You have to go all out for your reward, and you have to sacrifice in order to deserve it. Religion and baseball emphasize, more than anything else, the qualities I value. They both represent my values, and they give me a lot of the same kinds of feelings. After we win a baseball game I feel great. I feel like I'm on top of the world, and that's how I feel after I go to church. I feel great, I feel like I've just received communion and I've got Jesus in me. After we win a baseball game I have this feeling like "yes, we won, we're the better team. We put in the work, we did better, we won, and we deserved it."

Being the best is a little like taking communion—it's a kind of high. It's almost like an adrenaline rush, being the best. The fact that Jesus is in your body, the fact that you're number one—it's like an adrenaline rush. After watching a baseball game I feel great, especially if my team wins. And if it was a good game I can still appreciate it like I appreciate scripture. If it's a scripture that I particularly like I'll come out feeling really good, as if the team had won. But if it's something I didn't relate to, I can still say, well, the team didn't win but at least I got to say some prayers. I got to watch a good game, and it was fun just being there. You see, when I was young I didn't always like going to church, but now I go just to go. I'm really into it. When I'm in church I'm around likeminded people, people that have the same general feelings I have. The people in church and the people at a ball game—they have the desire to be there; they've come to pray and they've come to cheer.

You can even compare the wave to singing or chanting in church. Everyone at church gets into that. The choir starts the singing and the next thing you know the whole church has broken into song, all together. I don't even have to be a part of it. I can just stand at the doorway and say, "Wow, this is great, just to hear this," and I feel the same way at the stadium. I love getting into it when my section goes into the wave. This happened at a Phillies game a little while ago. The wave went around the whole stadium again and again. We just kept it going. It went around continuously, and when it hit the other side of the stadium the people on our side would start clapping, like yes, it's on the other side of the stadium and it's coming back. Wow!

It's a sense of community. Everyone participates. If any one section had let it die off you would have nothing. But when everyone puts in his little effort, you have this one huge victory. Which gets into the drive again. Someone might think to himself, if I don't get up who's going to notice? But if everyone thinks like that then no one will get up and nothing will happen. But if I have the drive I think that if I get up maybe the person next to me will get up. Maybe he'll think, "Well, if that guy can make an idiot of himself so can I." He'll realize it's not really that big of a deal and maybe he'll participate. It's like going to church. I notice a lot of people there don't want to sing. They don't want to say the prayers out loud because maybe they're afraid they'll say the wrong word and sound stupid. But I think, who cares. I'm not here to please the others; I'm here to please God and myself, and if I say the prayers out loud so everyone can hear me, other people who weren't going to say them because they were shy or afraid of making a mistake will hear me and they'll join in. And we'll all be singing together for what we love.

III. Empowerment

In her essay on "Fandom as Pathology," the principal purpose of which is to unlink these two terms, Jolil Jenson recites the pitying or dismissive litany of charges against fans of every fanatical or "excessive" stripe. The fan, in the view of his or her critics, is a weak or incomplete individual, seeking power or self-enhancement through fantasy or allegiance. Fandom, therefore, is a "chronic attempt to compensate for a perceived lack of autonomy, absence of community, incomplete identity, lack of power and lack of recognition." Baseball fanatics will be pleased to know that Ms. Jenson rejects this definition as misguided, muddleheaded, and insulting. We are inclined to agree—we certainly want to agree—with Lawrence Grossberg's far more sympathetic assertion that the object of devotion and loyalty provides fans with a degree of control over their social and emotional lives and helps them cope with forms of pain, frustration, and alienation felt, perhaps, with increasing frequency and intensity in modern life. But even if one recoils at some of the more extreme forms of fandom and shakes his head at the ability of "grown men" to sustain what seems a basically adolescent enthusiasm, it is well to bear in mind that what may be extreme, even pathological in the behavior of adults is often quite normal, even healthy and desirable in children and adolescents. At this age the young fan, even the healthiest, may indeed suffer from a perceived lack of independence, a dearth of community, an incompletely formed identity, a lack of power and recognition. Battling with siblings for his place in the family, testing himself against his peers, or moving out into the adult world and measuring himself against what he can as yet only strive and hope to be, the pre- or early teenage child does indeed feel a lack of power he unashamedly craves.

We have spoken already of the themes of morality and striving for betterment in the experience of young fans. Both may be of assistance in satisfying the more immediate and deeply felt need for power and acceptance that defines this period of development. Like a knight on the perilous road to the palace of adulthood, the adolescent cannot hope to subdue the dragon (who often looks strangely like one or both parents) unless he is equipped with moral probity and a degree of mastery. But power, inherent in both and the third member of this youthful triumvirate, is his most pressing need. There is power in moral rectitude, power too in the acquisition and mastery of skills. But empowerment, perhaps the central theme and attainment of this critical stage of the young person's development, is larger than either. Expressing itself through them and a variety of other vehicles—physical attractiveness or strength, popularity, athletic ability, independence, distinctiveness, and knowledge, to name a few—the sense of power is typically the end to which skill, morality, and these other instruments are the means. What one seeks as a young adolescent is, above all else, power, a gift he feels he will need if he is to forfeit his earlier dependencies, turn away from those who encouraged them, and take his first, often brazen and chest-thumping steps along the darkened path toward adult responsibility. He or she is whistling in the dark, perhaps, but he holds a steadier note if he is wearing his Dodger uniform, carries his Ted Williams bat, or struts into the street flashing his team's first-place standing like a sheriff's badge.

Baseball as a source of empowerment takes a variety of forms in these interviews. One is stricken first by the richness of that variety, then by the importance of the game as a supplier of that crucial sense of power, finally by the persistent recurrence of identifiable empowerment themes in the reports of otherwise very different fans. While there are substantive differences of emphasis and angle in these interviews, differences I hope to clarify in the discussion that follows, the similarities and recurrences enable us to introduce these tales of empowerment in terms of the repeated forms that communalize their experience. In both of its uses, in its service of both common and highly individualized needs, one finds striking testimony of the game's quite remarkable adaptability to the needs the child brings to it. While baseball may be the origin as well as a later expression of a child's moral sensibility and his quest for excellence, as empowerment baseball is less mother than indispensable helpmate. The need is already there; baseball, in direct and surrogate ways, meets and answers it.

Identification with winners, with baseball heroes, or with a team's excellence and fame is of course a recurrent theme in all the interviews. And in its most blatant form, this alignment is empowerment itself, substantially determining, as for Michael K., his status in the neighborhood. But there are more surprising similarities. Sibling rivalry is a significant factor for three of these four fans. For Mel P. and Bernie O. knowledge of baseball and an ability to play it were ways of evening the score with brothers who were more successful than they in ways their parents were more likely to approve. The brother may be the "good" boy or the one who excels in school, getting all A's, but an intimidated sibling may pull himself out of the shadows by spouting statistics at the dinner table or by regaling the family, however uninterested they may be, with tales of his ball field heroism. For Carol T. it was the same. Only the gender was altered. For her it was a straight-A sister who had to be brought within reach, and for her too, baseball as both expertise and activity provided the ladder. For Michael K., the "rivals" to be outdone are on the street corner rather than at the table, extended siblings if you like, but the motive and the weapons are the same.

For three of these fans—Mel P., Carol T., and Brandon M.—there was tremendous satisfaction in the triumph of the underdog, with whom they were stickily identified. For Mel and Carol, despite their shaky position in the family hierarchy, this is a relatively minor theme. For 10-year-old Brandon, apparently because, as he admits, he is overweight and thought an unlikely athlete, it is central. There is nothing he likes better or derives richer satisfaction from than "surprising them," showing them what he is made of, what he can do if he puts mind and will to the gratifying task. That, after all, is what the Atlanta Braves did, pulling themselves up from last place to first in 1991 and nearly winning the World Series. And that, as Brandon precociously perceives it, is what baseball, like life itself, is finally about.

For Carol and Mel baseball provides an opportunity for rebellion, in both instances against the mother, though in different ways and for different reasons. For Carol it is a direct uprising, a revolt against the prohibitions and restrictions she felt as a defining feature of her youth. Baseball was of primary importance to her as an incorporation of the male power she envied and longed for. But it was also a form of escape from an otherwise confining youth and a release from an otherwise suppressed exuberance. Baseball, as she puts it, "gave me a chance to let myself go emotionally." "That's what sports do for people," she muses. "They give them a chance to get all excited about something." For Mel, the struggle against the mother is a surrogate rebellion. It is enacted on behalf of the father who, he feels, derived unspoken satisfaction from his son's small rebellions, since they represented what he would have liked to have done but lacked the courage for.

What Mel is doing, in other words, is filling a void left by his father's meekness, and he fills this void largely with the empowerment he absorbs from baseball. He will take risks, as his father would not, and baseball provides him with a treasuretrove of opportunities. Identifying with the Dodgers he is identified with "Da Bums," a collection of risk-taking eccentrics who, among other things, brought the first black player into major league baseball. Making the Dodgers his team, when all around him were choosing Yankees, is another sign of his risk-taking difference. And to be a Dodger fan is to be associated with all those strange exotic creatures howling and hooting from the bleachers of Ebbets Field.

Filling a void is a task to which both Carol and Bernie also set the game of baseball. For Carol, whose father was successful but not powerful, baseball players, whom she regarded as "powerful friends," filled the void he left. For Bernie, it was the Red Sox who invitingly left a hollow he felt obligated to fill with his own superior achievement. As the child of immigrants, Bernie's beloved Red Sox were chiefly an entrée into America and an instantiation of raw American might and power. They represented a native, majoritarian refusal to compromise, an inflexible integrity of self that, even at the price of defeat, would not bend. But they were also the Red Sox, which is to say that partly because of this very inflexibility, they failed in the clutch; they didn't win the big ones.

Bernie's obligation, as he understood it, and one, empowered by the otherwise awesomely potent Red Sox of the '40s and '50s, he knew he could meet, was to succeed where they had failed. When it came to the crunch he, unlike the folding Sox, would come through.

To all of them—to the outgunned sibling, to the girl in a boy's and man's world, to the bright boy in the neighborhood, to the overweight child, to the child of immigrants in the New World—to all of them baseball offers, in addition to its many pleasures, status, power, and acceptance.

"Taking Risks and Chances— The Way the Dodgers Did"

Mel P. Born 1937. Psychiatrist. Raised in Winnipeg, Canada. Brooklyn Dodgers.

I grew up in Winnipeg, Canada, and lived there till my early twenties. I've had a long interest in baseball starting when I was about 7 or 8. I remember being in the hospital to have my tonsils out. A favorite cousin of mine, Willy, visited me in the hospital and, sensing that I was starting to develop some interest in sports, bought me a subscription to *Sport* magazine, which was very popular then. The thing I remember about *Sport* was these lovely full-page photographs of ball players. I'm not sure how I got interested in the Brooklyn Dodgers, but very quickly they became a kind of obsession.

Part of the reason, I think, was that Brooklyn was part of New York. I had an aunt and uncle who lived in New York, and I desperately wanted to visit them there. We were a rather poor family, and this uncle, a traveling salesman, used to come every summer from New York and talk about New York. He would bring us toys and other presents—he was a very beloved uncle—and his descriptions of New York excited me. I had great images of the city: huge buildings, exciting things to do—theater, movies, restaurants—none of which I'd ever experienced myself. I'd never been out of Winnipeg, which was a rather small western Canadian city of about 300,000 at that time. I had longings to go to the States and see these big, big huge buildings, these skyscrapers. I remember being captivated by pictures and descriptions of the Empire State Building, images like that, and I knew there was a connection between Brooklyn and New York.

I think my serious interest in the Dodgers began when Jackie Robinson broke into baseball. There was something about the Dodgers getting Robinson, who at that time had been playing for Montreal, a Canadian team, that excited me tremendously. It was made clear to me that Robinson had broken the color barrier and that the Dodgers had done something very special by signing him.

III. Empowerment

From that point on this team became for me a symbol of goodness and courage and the willingness to take chances.

I was infatuated with the Dodgers. I've always felt an identification with the oppressed and the underdog, and I think I owe that to growing up in a pretty liberal family with a father who was very much concerned about fairness and equality and the underprivileged. I think it was also related to my being a very small boy, short and terrified that I would never get bigger, feeling sort of downtrodden myself.

On top of that, I also had an older brother who was a kind of perfect son who did everything my parents wanted. He was a very, very serious student and a very good one, and I think I believed he was a genius. Since I felt much less than his intellectual equal, I sought out other areas that I could both enjoy and become expert in, where my knowledge would exceed his. Baseball served that purpose perfectly. It was something one could acquire a tremendous amount of information about; you could become an expert and demonstrate your expertise. Knowing a lot about baseball gave me something to compete with, something I could use to raise me to my brother's level. I remember memorizing statistics and quoting them at the dinner table, trying to enlist the interest of my father and brother. It didn't work, but that wouldn't stop me from letting them know how much I knew about baseball.

Sometimes I'd play a little fast and loose to make an impression. I had pictures of the Dodgers, that I'd cut out of newspapers and magazines, all over my walls, and I used to forge their signatures and pretend I'd received these personal autographs. I got away with it too, until my dearest friend, who is my friend to this day, caught me out. Sammy was a fantastic guy with a wonderful family which I adopted as my own. His parents were wonderful people, and I spent many hours at their home. Anyway, he came over one day, and we were looking through my collection of autographed pictures, being particularly proud that I'd just gotten a few new ones, when Sammy notices that Campanella's name is spelled wrong. I'd spelled it with only one "l", and I remember this incredible fear and panic I felt at being found out. We were able to laugh about it much later, but at the time he was very angry at what I'd done, because having all those great autographs had made him and my other friends very envious of me. That was the idea, of course, to make me feel important, to make my friends envious.

One Dodger who was very important to me, because of my shortness of stature and my concerns about my adequacy, was Pee Wee Reese, the shortstop, who I adored. But I adored all of them: Duke Snider, Carl Furillo, Gil Hodges, and most of the pitching staff. They had some eccentric pitchers. Preacher Roe was a weird guy, and I think that attracted me. As I remember, he was a nonconformist. He was aloof. He kept to himself. He wouldn't sign autographs; he dressed the way he wanted to dress; and all that appealed to me. I admired that eccentricity and independence. He seemed to know who he was and what he was worth. He didn't need to impress anybody or make himself loved. The other guy I thought the world of and who I watched very closely was Duke Snider, the center fielder. To me he was a superstar and an obviously outgoing, personable character. I remember seeing Snider interviewed on television back then and being impressed with the way he handled himself—so gracefully, and with a sense of humor.

It's funny. I was attracted to Roe because he was aloof and to Snider because he was personable and friendly. I don't really understand why these two very opposite characters appealed to me so, though maybe it's because they're reflections of two sides of myself. I consider myself very outgoing and gregarious, very warm and sensitive. But there's a side of me that's shy and retiring, and certainly a side of me that is very nonconformist. Very. If I feel pressure to do something because it looks good or is the right thing to do, I simply won't do it, even if it's to my own disadvantage not to do it. I think that goes back to the fact that I was raised by a very obsessional, controlling mother who couldn't control me, despite all her efforts, and by a father who somehow got great pleasure out of my rebelling against my mother because I was doing what he would've liked to have done and couldn't. But that wasn't all. I was also rebelling against having this older brother who could do no wrong.

It's interesting how our lives have turned out. We're both in the same field and, I think, fairly well regarded. But I do feel that in some ways I've surpassed him in the field, grown beyond him. He's much more the administrator, the political animal, while I'm more interested in teaching and in radical ideas and the possibilities of integrating them. That I should surpass him seemed incongruous, and it was difficult for me, later in life, to see it clearly. On the one hand I felt good that I had much more ability than I assumed or thought or realized. And it was a relief, too, not to see my brother as the intellectual giant I'd thought he was. But to see him as someone who was quite limited in ways—though he's a wonderful person and has done well—that required a readjustment. Sibling rivalry has been our theme throughout our lives.

When we were kids he was the accomplished one, the Yankees maybe, and I was the rebel, the Dodgers. That was the image they projected by hiring Jackie Robinson and a number of other black players and by being in Brooklyn, a fascinating place as I imagined it, full of fascinating people of all types. I got a lot of vicarious pleasure out the success of the Dodgers. It was as though if the Dodgers did well, I would be okay. I would manage somehow. I'd become better known, better liked. I remember not being able to sleep at nights if the Dodgers lost. When that happened I'd fantasize that I was either Pee Wee Reese or Duke Snider, and somehow that would settle me down, and I'd fall asleep.

When they lost over and over to the Yankees, I was furious. It was as though one of those dreams had been stolen from me. I had been deprived of the chance to climb higher on the Dodgers' backs. When they finally won in 1955, I was in seventh heaven for a long, long time. It really sustained me. The Dodgers were like a tonic for me. I think I was probably a frightened youngster, and there was something about the Dodgers that made me feel empowered, made me feel stronger. I felt some kind of union with them, some kind of connection.

To me the Dodgers weren't the Bums. They were winners. I never saw them as bums, but there was something about the fact that they were called the Bums that pleased me a great deal. The name confirmed them as rebels. It pointed to the fact that they weren't your customary ball team that does everything according to the book. They were willing to take chances, do things differently. I'm not sure whether they valued that in themselves or whether they really were that way or not, but that's how I chose to see them, or maybe how I needed to see them.

There was something else about the Dodgers. The players seemed very loving amongst themselves. Whether they were or not, I saw them as this big family that got along despite their differences and excelled as a team. I remember being very excited when double plays were well-executed. That meant to me that they were working well as a group and gelling as a group, and to me it symbolized some kind of unity and mutual concern, a respect for each other that was obviously very important to me.

It had to do, I think, with my own family. There were lots of problems in my family in those days and not much of the harmony I saw among the Dodgers. I wanted my father very much to … he was really a great guy … but something wasn't right in the family. The problem, as I saw it, was that my father should have done more. He was a house painter. He was well-liked in the community, a good craftsman, and in order to expand his business, he'd take on a partner from time to time. My mother, who had fled the Nazis at a very early age and who was a product of the Depression, would get very frightened at that. She was a very cautious, frightened woman, and I would watch this go on all the time, where my father would want to do more, to expand, to take chances of one kind or another, and she would threaten that if he did that, she would pick up the children and leave. And that would stop him. I remember being terribly disappointed that he didn't take a stand with her.

To make things worse, I had an aunt and uncle who lived near us. He was a very prominent manufacturer in Winnipeg, and I adored his sons. He had three wonderful sons: Leo, Frank, and Willy. But my father and my uncle didn't get along. I remember once overhearing my uncle saying to my father, "Your sons will never amount to anything." His sons were very precocious; one in particular, who was probably a genius, a mathematician, and there was this constant rivalry. My mother also had this constant rivalry with my aunt, so I was in a bind because I adored their sons and wanted to spend time with them. My cousins were extremely kind to me. They had an automobile, and they would take me for rides. I just adored them, but I felt trapped. I felt that if I paid too much homage to them it would be threatening to my father, who I also adored but resented because I wanted him to be more than he was. So there was a family conflict, and I was caught in the middle. I hated the animosity between them, the way they'd badmouth each other. They were all really good people, nice people, but their relationship was terribly destructive.

And then, set against all this, as a kind of glowing harmonious family, there were the Dodgers, the family that took in this black guy when you didn't do such things and made it work. And they didn't just make it work. They also seemed to be enjoying themselves. They seemed to be having a good time doing what they were doing. That was terribly important to me because I didn't see enough of that in my family. My father was a very hard worker. I remember him leaving early in the morning and coming home late at night. I think in his best year he made maybe $5,000, and he often paid a price for putting too much trust in people. He'd often neglect to get a written agreement on a price from his customers, and then he'd come home claiming he'd been screwed out of several hundred dollars. I would say, "Pa, why didn't you get it in writing?" And he would say, "Well, not everybody is dishonest." He never learned. He worked extremely hard for very little money, though he did get a certain satisfaction out of his work. He took great pride in his craftsmanship as a wall-paperer. I remember working with him during the summers and looking at the walls to see if I could find where the seams were and not being able to find them. That made me very proud of him. But I was always a little sad that he didn't seem to enjoy his work more, and a little disappointed in him for not taking risks and chances ... the way the Dodgers did.

"Part of This Masculine Thing"

Carol T. Born 1950. Health care administrator. Raised in Camden, New Jersey. Brooklyn Dodgers.

My first memories of baseball are watching Dodger games on TV. I was a very avid Dodger fan, probably because of my father who grew up in Brooklyn. When I try to think of the year I think it must have been after the Dodgers moved to California, because I'd see them only when they came out East to play in Connie Mack Stadium against the Phillies. I remember being very, very excited the first time I went to a game. I don't remember who took me—if it was my father or my friend's father—but I was most certainly with my friend, a girlfriend of mine who was as avid a fan as I was. Baseball was a significant part of my friendship with Dana. We had baseball cards, and we knew all the statistics, and we could keep them on the scorecard while we were watching the game.

I didn't attend many games, maybe ten games altogether. It wasn't one of the things we did in our family, but baseball was something I shared with my father. It was rare in that way, almost unique. There weren't many experiences I shared with my father. I was his daughter temperament-wise, and we really had a lot in common. But I don't remember him being very much in the picture, very much a part of my life, and maybe baseball was a way to have one of those rare shared experiences with my father. He was definitely the reason I chose that team. He was from Brooklyn and he was a Dodger fan, and I was probably looking for an interest we could share, something we could do and care about together. He had almost no relationship with my sisters, but he was politically active, and sometimes he'd take me to political luncheons. Also, he was a pharmacist—still is—and I worked for him every holiday break. We also raked leaves together. I was the little boy. Actually, I was the middle of three girls, but I was tomboyish, and I think I was the replacement for the boy my parents never had but always wanted. I provided my father with the experiences he otherwise wouldn't have had. That was my role with my father, all the way into adolescence.

I was an expert, mainly on the Dodgers. I knew everything, everyone, how old they were, where they were from, what their batting averages were, and I also knew a lot about players on other teams. This kind of knowledge gave me a sense of expertise, status among people who respected that sort of knowledge. My father was also into statistics, but I think I knew more than he did. That wasn't why I knew what I knew—to impress him—I was just interested in it for me. At least I thought at that time that I was doing it for me, though now I wonder. Perhaps it was a way of impressing him, getting closer to him somehow. I used to play baseball, and I was very good. Better than all the boys on the block.

My first real memory of the game, though, was when I was sitting in the bleachers at the Phillies' stadium, the first time I'd ever seen a real ball park, and it struck me how far a home run had to go to be a home run. It really struck me. I mean, it was far. That's a very long distance to hit a ball. I always wanted to catch one, but I was a choker. I used to choke in sports, and I always figured, well, even if it came to me I'd probably drop it. But that was really what struck me: how far that ball had to go. How powerful these guys had to be. And that power was awesome to me—you know, as a girl—and I wanted it for myself. At that time there was really no difference between my interests and those of the boys in my class or neighborhood. I was better at athletics than many of them, and I was accepted by them, largely for that reason. It was important to be better than the boys, and I was conscious of it. The fact that I was a girl among boys was something I was always aware of.

Little girls grow up looking at little boys. You know, little boys grow up doing things, and little girls grow up looking at little boys. That's how it is. Well, that's how it was when I was growing up, and I think it's true even now. I see the difference. I see it in other girls. It's the boys who do and the girls who watch. That was my experience from a very early age, and I was very conscious of it. Baseball was part of this masculine thing, this active approach to life. It's the men who do and have the power, and I ate my heart out for many, many years because I was born the wrong sex. I still feel it. I definitely should have been a man. It's all based on my parents' having wanted a boy. They wanted a boy, and I wanted to be what they wanted. It was easy for me to step into the man's or boy's shoes, easier than it was to identify with my older sister or my mother. I felt very strongly my father's desire that I be a boy, and though it was only much later that I learned my mother also wanted me to be one, I think I must have sensed it.

I was much better at the realistic subjects than I was at the humanities in school. Siblings grow up in competition with each other, and I had a sister who was an all "A" student. She never got a "B" in her life. She graduated high school number one out of a thousand pupils. I couldn't possibly compete with her, and I grew up in her shadow, academically at least. Baseball was something I did better than she did and something my father approved of. It gave me an identity, at least for a while, but it was a male identity and of course it couldn't last.

The girl I shared my passion for baseball with felt the same way I did about baseball, but she didn't have the same hangups about being a woman. Eventually she became a home economist. It was terribly popular in our day for women to become home economists. I would have, could have, and should have gone into the computer field, and I almost did. But I was scared out of it because I was a woman. Women didn't go into computers. I also have a woman friend, a childhood friend, who became a doctor. It never occurred to me that I could become a doctor. I wanted to be a doctor, but I grew up feeling that the only realistic profession, medical profession, that I could go into would be nursing, and I hated that, hated it. Obviously there was something very, very sexist about the way we grew up, and I paid a price for it, a very high price.

I felt defined and confined by my sex, and I loved getting out of it. I loved annoying my mother with my tomboyishness. In the beginning she liked it—she wanted a boy—but I went too far. Basically I did it to get closer to my father. I was much more identified with him than with her. I had an identity problem, and I probably still have it. To this day I hate the role of housewife, I just hate it. If I'm home for a long period of time I just go nuts. I cannot fully take on women's roles. I'm glad that things are different today, but I don't feel the change in my life. Women still have the heavier burden at home. Anyway, this identity thing was an issue with me, and baseball was a way of identifying with men, a convenient and important way of identifying with the male sex.

Above all, I think, I identified with male power. I saw that women were not powerful, not movers. They were laid back, quiet, and they choked things back. They were the ones who kept it all in. It's really my mother I'm describing, though many other women were just like her. Let's say this: I had a negative identification with my mother, and I projected it onto other women. I didn't want to be with her. I couldn't relate to her or to her role. She was a very traditional woman, though it's hard to see my mother as traditional. She was self-negating, and she definitely couldn't handle me or the way I wanted to grow up. So our whole relationship became cat and mouse. Not that exactly, but I just didn't fit into her mold. I was defined, but I didn't fit the definition, and she didn't know what to do with me. I loved that: adding salt to her wounds by breaking out of the boxes she put me in.

Now, for the first time, I'm beginning to see power in women. I'd say it's only in the last five years. Before that I just couldn't stand being a woman. I hadn't worked out the problem of female identity, and I was basically very unhappy because of it through most of my childhood. And through all that, baseball was a way to, well ... baseball was happiness. For the time that I was avid about it baseball was very much happiness. Every game was happiness.

Part of that happiness is associated with the physical beauty of the ball park. The first thing I think of when I think of baseball is the green, the amazing green color of the field. When you went to a baseball game for the first time you saw how green it was. I think it had to do with the fact that we had no color TV at that time; it was all black and white. And then the first time you went to the ball park you discovered how green it was and how vast! You noticed the large numbers of people around; you felt extremely small. Today I have that feeling when I go to the sea: a sense of the insignificance of the individual, of myself. I like that feeling, that anonymity, and I remember feeling very, very tiny in a crowd of so many thousands of people.

I lived and breathed the game when I was there. I was always looking for an area of identification, and I felt that at the park. I felt very good there. Wow, look at all those people who are in this with me! I felt that strongly because when the Dodgers came to Connie Mack Stadium many of the people at the game were Dodger fans. The Phillies weren't much good in those days. I remember being shocked when the Phillies finally got into the Series. I felt the same about the Mets when they finally won in '69. It was as though the underdogs, the people like us, had finally made it, and even though I wasn't a Phillies or a Mets fan, that meant something to me.

You didn't have that sense of anonymity, of mass identification, and you didn't have that green sensation watching a game on TV. But even then the game was colorful in a way. Emotionally colorful. Exuberant. We sat there, my friend and I, with our popcorn and whatever, and we just got all into it. We rooted and hollered and cheered, and you name it. I don't know if we watched entire games together; we were young kids. But we were close friends, and we were together at one of our houses. I was very, very happy doing that.

That's what sports do for people, you know. They give us a chance to get all excited about something. I don't remember having anything else at the time, anything else that would excite me like that. Baseball gave me a chance to let myself go emotionally. It did. It really did. It was seeing all that ... it was being a part of the team. If they lost, we were miserable, very miserable. But if they won, we were ecstatic. There weren't that many activities you could get excited about. School took up a large part of our day, and you couldn't just go running in the streets being exuberant over nothing. You had to have something to be exuberant about. Baseball provided that. Baseball was definitely happiness.

Were there other happinesses then? Probably not. If I turned out all right, baseball had a lot to do with it. And so did the Dodgers. I liked the Dodgers. I liked every one of them. I liked his background, I liked his hometown, I liked the fact that he had a good average. I loved that. I identified with these players, both for being famous and for being the best, for being on a major league team. And I felt that they were my friends. It was as if they were a part of me, and I felt I knew them personally. I don't know if I got all this information about them just from baseball cards or whether I knew about them mainly from the newspapers and other literature, like the scorecards and yearbooks they sold at the games. I used to read all that. Oh wow, yeah, I incorporated them into my being!

It's interesting how one unincorporates afterwards. After I stopped being such an avid baseball fan, what happened to that? I don't know. Maybe there were other stars who took over, like the Beatles. They were very powerful figures for me, but there was a difference. I felt I knew the Beatles very well, but I didn't feel they were my friends. Baseball is somehow a friendly sport. Afterwards I found out all the ugly and shady things that go on, but it was decent and honest at that time, and it smacked of power and success. I guess I needed friends like that, so I'd read about them and believe what I read. Somehow I needed it. I needed them to be a part of me. They were my friends, powerful friends, and I didn't have people like that in my life. I didn't admire enough people at the time, so I admired them, and they became incorporated. Maybe that's it. I guess I admired my father, and if I did, that enabled me to admire these players even more. I was admiring them for the same reason, for their success. I think I saw my father as successful, but not as powerful. I think the power was lacking, and the ballplayers filled the void he left. The players were real to me. Powerful, successful, and part of me, and I needed them. I was not a successful child, but in baseball, in the Dodgers, I had powerful friends. Maybe they could get me out of it.

Of course the most powerful and successful team was the Yankees, but I didn't like the Yankees. Partly, I think, because my father was anti-Yankee, but more because they were too successful, and I usually preferred the underdogs. I've always identified with people who were in trouble, who need a hand. Hence my profession. That's why I went into health care. Most of us in the field are like that. It's pretty directly linked. The Dodgers were just the right combination for me. They were the underdogs who proved themselves, who achieved enough success to lift me up.

I didn't see the Dodgers as being as down and out as I was, but when they went against the Yankees in all those Series they were the underdogs. They were the down and outers. I was at one of those games, one of Koufax's victories in '63. At least I think I was there, though it doesn't really matter. What matters is that we had to fight this really good team—like I had to fight an older sister who was really good at everything and whom I could never equal. I can see the parallel. What the Dodgers were to the Yankees I was to my sister, though in '63 the Dodgers beat them. All of life goes back to our earliest relationships, doesn't it? How we see people and the things we do.

Baseball reflects my life, I guess, but more than that it added to my life. It was something very good that I had at one time, growing up. It was probably one of the best things in my life at that time. That's pretty terrific. It has a high place. There were other things, but none compared to baseball. Baseball was the main, the most wonderful thing I had: a source of power, even if it was second-hand, and the greatest source of pleasure. It wasn't a source of happiness. Baseball *was* happiness.

Status in the Neighborhood
Michael K. Born 1961. New York Yankees radio broadcaster. Raised in the Bronx, New York. New York Yankees.

I became a Yankee fan around the age of 8 or 9, and I did the whole bit: collected baseball cards, bought the yearbooks, all of it. The real love affair, though, began a few years later when my fifth-grade teacher took me and a couple of other kids—it was a present for getting good grades—to the Hall of Fame in Cooperstown. That was the start of the passion, when I felt that baseball was what I loved. I always loved to play it, played it almost every day in the summer, but I wasn't very good. I was always afraid of getting hit by the pitch. And the fact that I wasn't very good at it made me marvel all the more at what an incredible thing it is to hit a baseball. The thing's coming in at 95 miles an hour; you have only the splittest of seconds to make a decision whether to swing or not, and you've got to meet it with a bat hardly wider than the ball.

As a kid you latch onto one team, and that team becomes your representative, your knight wearing your colors. In a sense they're playing for what you're worth in the neighborhood. If you're a fan of a winning team you get to carry yourself a little bit differently, a little taller, a little prouder, and your word carries a little more weight on the street corner. You live and die with each win and loss because you know that if your team loses, when you go out on the corner you're gonna get most of the crap in the arguments. They're gonna rag you as if you're the Yankees, as if you're the team ambassador or messenger and their loss is your shame.

Your team has a lot to do with fixing your status in the neighborhood. You're not so much what you eat, you're who you root for and how they do. When the Yankees did well, you could carry your head a little bit higher. And when they didn't, when they did crappy, you took the brunt of the abuse in the neighborhood. That's especially true, I think, in a two-team city like New York. I wonder how it is in a place like Minnesota where there's no other team. If the Twins do well, does everybody feel good? Is there no one around you can get on and no one who'll rag you when the Twins lose? I grew up in New York, where it was the Yankees and the Mets. The Yankee fans ragged the Met fans and the Met fans ragged the Yankee fans. And if you had a good year, if the Yankees had a good year, you could ride them all winter long. So it was a sort of status thing.

Knowledge was also a source of status. In those arguments on the corner you could ward off a few blows if you knew a lot, and I did. I don't think there was ever a bigger fan than I was. Maybe some who were as big, but none bigger. I mean, I knew every single stat. I knew every single thing about every player. I also knew the history of the team, which I think is what separates a lot of today's fans from fans back in the '70s. Even some of the players don't know Yankee history. When Don Mattingly first became a star he really didn't know who Lou Gehrig was, and though he'd heard of Babe Ruth he didn't know much about him either. A lot of young fans today are like that. They don't read. This is a society that doesn't read a lot, and the fans just don't know the history.

I don't want this to sound egotistical—it really isn't—but I was an excellent student in school. Usually it's one or the other: you're either a sports fan and you're not that great in school, or you're really good in school and you're just a bookworm who doesn't care about sports. But I combined the two; I was a sports fan and I did a lot of reading. When I like something I really research it and look into it; I want to know exactly what I like. So I read a lot when I was a kid, and I could read pretty complicated stuff and retain it. When I was in fourth grade I had a twelfth grade reading level, so I was able to comprehend. I was a voracious reader, I knew a little bit more than other kids my age, and that helped me out. That gave me a little status even when the Yankees were losing.

I liked lots of sports, but baseball suited me best. It fit my personality. I was a bright kid, and I think that of all the sports baseball is the most intellectual. A lot of people say baseball's boring because there's so little going on. But I think baseball is boring to boring people. If you have an active mind, if you can keep lots of different things running around in your head, you're aware that there are 15 to 20 things going on between any two pitches. That's what makes baseball such a great game. It's a thinking man's sport, and it caught hold of me. It's not just the action that's going on. It's the thought, all the what-ifs that are happening as well. Every single pitch has dozens of implications shooting off in all directions, and as a kid I was able to absorb them. I was able to grasp some of the nuances that others didn't. Don't get me wrong. A kid can be a great baseball fan and not be the brightest kid in the world. But I grasped nuances at a young age that other kids missed. I would discuss thing with friends when I was 11 or 12 that they just weren't getting.

When I started rooting for the Yankees they were absolutely awful! I don't know why I did it, but I grabbed onto the Yankees and the Giants, two terrible teams at that time, and I lived and died with them. Mostly I died, and if I didn't do enough dying on my own, the kids on the corner were always willing to help me out. When the Yankees finally got to the playoffs in 1976, after so many years, when Chris Chambliss hit that home run and they got into the World Series for the first time in twelve years, I felt this sense of euphoria. I see all the players jumping around on the field, hugging and falling over one another, and I'm just ecstatic. Then, moments later, I feel a letdown. Something hits me. Something that never occurred to me while the Yankees were losing dawns on me. All of a sudden I hear myself asking, "What does this mean to me? What do I get out of it? Does this really make me better, stronger, more important? OK, they won. But now what? Does this really make me better, stronger, more important? I don't get the $70,000 World Series bonus. I don't get to parade around in an open car. I won't be interviewed on television or asked to endorse soft drinks. I get nothing! I've been living and dying with these guys, and I get that moment of euphoria when Chris Chambliss hits the home run, and that's it! There's no more after that!" It was jarring! Suddenly I'm asking myself: if this is all it means to win, what have I been rooting for? Maybe I'm weird, but that's what I felt, at least initially.

I continued to root for the Yankees, but it was different after that. I never found the answers to those questions, and I don't think there are answers. As a kid, when the Yankees won, you got to go out on the corner and say, "Heyyyyy! The Yankees are in the Series and the Mets aren't," and you feel a little taller. But I was 15 in 1976, and that wasn't enough anymore. I was old enough to realize it was the players who were making the money, and it made a difference. For the fan, when you come right down to it, it's no big deal. And when your status is measured in other ways, when it's determined by things other than who you root for and how they do, something goes out of it. Once I started covering the Yankees, first with the *Daily News*, then as a radio broadcaster, I couldn't be a strictly partisan fan. But even if I were allowed to be partisan, I don't know if I'd have sustained that feeling and that allegiance

Covering the team you see that these guys you idolized have just as many human frailties and failings as any of us, maybe more. If I had a child I don't think I'd want him to idolize a sports star. They're not gods, and they shouldn't be looked at as such. I wouldn't want my kid to be devastated if the guy he idolizes becomes a drug addict. I know the lifestyle and I know what the players go through, so I know there's a good chance that can happen, and I wouldn't want my kid taking that kind of fall. I'd want him to be a fan of sports, but not a fanatic. Fans have to watch out about becoming fanatics because they can really be crushed by these people. There are very few ball players who take into consideration what a fan thinks when they do what they do off field.

Most fans aren't up this close, though, and for them baseball is a release. More than a release, if I think about it. The big question is, why do we get so excited about a sport or about one team? And I think most fans live out their dreams, and possibly their frustrations, through the players. That's why they're so vitriolic when a player fails and so euphoric when he does well. It's as though it's happening to them, as though it makes sense to rag a fan when his team loses because it really *is* him. He really *is* a loser when they lose, just as he's a winner when they win. His status and his sense of his own worth seem to rise when they win. I think almost every fan in the stands wants to be out on that field. He feels a sense of frustration that he isn't, and he uses the players to compensate for that failure. That's why fans sometimes get overzealous. Maybe that's the answer: we're living out our fantasies or trying to, and it's the player's job to be what we can only dream of. But in 1976 I had that revelation. Yeah, they lived out my fantasy, but it's not me out there. It's just not me. If someone's going to live out my dream it will have to be me. They can't do it for me.

Showing Them You Have It in You

Brandon M. Born 1982.* Raised, so far, in Philadelphia, Pennsylvania. Vice President, he claims, of H & R Block. Atlanta Braves.

When I was around seven years old, my dad took me to Veterans Stadium to watch the Phillies versus the New York Mets. At first it was really boring because it was just balls and strikes, but all of a sudden somebody hit a home run. It was something that felt like, "Wow, how did he do that?" And I wished I could do that, and I jumped up in my seat and started going nuts because this little guy hit a home run. At first I wasn't really interested in the game, and it's weird how I changed. It was the home run that did it. But now it's a lot more. It's how the pitchers pitch fast to 'em, and how the batters hit it, and the great plays in the outfield, and the shortstops fielding those grounders. It's Rickey Henderson stealing a base and Mark McGwire hitting a grand slam. You gotta love baseball. It's weird how people say it's boring, 'cause it is and it isn't. If you're really interested in the game, nothing's boring. Even though it gets a little sleepy and tiring at times, you just gotta love the game.

Take the World Series last year—the Twins winning the last two games with runs in the tenth. It was weird how everything happened. The last game started out at a slow tempo, and then people were getting hits and finally the Twins win it. What you have to love is the way a game builds and the way it just explodes. It's the bases loaded and it's the bottom of the ninth, and it's tied and the home team hits a home run and everyone gets so excited. You gotta love that, even if you hate baseball. An inning or a game like that would make a fan of anybody. It's like a screenplay. The movie starts out real boring and all of a sudden the action comes and the cowboy shoots an Indian and somebody dies and they fall off the horses and they get in a fight. It's the same thing in baseball. It's the same feeling, how you jump in your seat and say, "Go get 'em, throw a fastball down the middle, come on, you can strike him out." That's how the drama is.

I love the surprise. Say it's the Phillies. They're an OK team, but really nobody likes 'em, because they have good players but they don't really play

---

This interview was held in 1992, when Brandon was a remarkably articulate and self-aware ten-year-old.

good. Say John Kruk is up. This guy is overweight and he looks like he can't play baseball for nothing, but he's sitting there batting .342, and you can't help hoping he wins the batting title. Anyway, Kruk hits a single and Darren Daulton comes home and the Phillies win it, and if they beat the best teams like the Braves or the Reds it's just the best feeling. Everybody says they stink, when all of a sudden somebody gets the winning hit or makes an incredible play, and the crowd goes crazy.

Look at the Atlanta Braves, my favorite team. Last year they were supposed to be very terrible, but all of a sudden, in the middle of the season, they're in first place. When they went into the World Series, everybody expected the Twins to win. It wasn't even supposed to be close, but the Braves gave them a good fight. Every game was close [except Atlanta's 14–5 victory in game five], and it went down to the last inning of the last game, when Gene Larkin knocked in the winning run. The Braves didn't go all the way, but they showed what they could do.

If the Phillies did what the Braves did I'd like them, too. But I stick with Atlanta 'cause my heart's with them. Like Milwaukee this year. They were last, and now they're in third place and everybody says, "Wow, look at Milwaukee!" But if they go into a slump everybody's gonna throw their new Milwaukee hats in the trash and say they wasted money. That's ridiculous. I never liked Milwaukee, but now I'm starting to think they really might do it. It shows that people can do whatever they want to if they put their minds to it. Milwaukee always had the talent, and now they're showing that they have it.

That's what I try to do. Early last year, I was in a really bad slump, and with the bases loaded, we needed two runs, and I hit a key double. I won the game for my team. The next game, I had two errors in the opening inning, and my coach pulled me out of the one inning so that I could rest a little. The next inning I make a wonderful catch and everybody likes me again. It's totally weird how baseball works. You love him, you hate him. You stink, you're the greatest. You can't count on anything. First they love you, then they hate you, but you got to keep trying. You got to show 'em you can do it.

It's not just baseball. It's like that everywhere, definitely in school. Last year—this is a true story—last year in math I did terrible. This year, though, I was one of the smartest kids in my class, and everybody was like, "Wow, brand-new Brandon, he got A's on his test again." I was surprised and shocked. The year before I was copying off of papers. Now I don't have to. My teacher was shocked, too. She thought I was doing borderline, but all of a sudden I'm getting A's and B's. It was just like baseball. When a guy who stinks hits a home run, he shows them that he really has it inside of him, that he can do anything he wants to. He can do it if he puts his mind to it.

That was the great thing about the Braves and the Twins. It was so amazing how they both won their pennants and went to the World Series. They were the worst teams in their leagues the year before that, and now they were the best. It was shocking. That's every kid's dream, coming from last to first. Everyone wants to be the best, but it's O.K. to come in second or lose. As long as you came a long way. Say I was in the Olympics and some other athlete did better than me and won the gold and I won the silver. Most people would say, blame it on the judges. They don't like my country and stuff like that. I would say, just look how far I came. I was a little kid growing up in Philadelphia and I came all the way up. My dream was to go to the Olympics, and I came here and I got a medal. I would be happy just to go to the Olympics, but most people aren't like that. They have to win. If they don't win, they go nuts.

One of the things you learn from baseball is that you can't always win. Nobody's perfect. Everybody knows that. Maybe you're great sportswise, but you may not be a good person inside. Even though you're like a Barry Bonds or a Mark McGwire and everybody admires you, it doesn't mean you can go crazy just because you lose a game. If you do that all the fans think it's O.K., and when they go to Little League maybe they'll chew tobacco and go crazy throwing their hats and everything. If the pros do it, and they get paid six million a year to do it, well why can't I?

But most players aren't like that, so a kid learns the right way to be. Your heroes teach you what to do. Your parents do it sometimes, but most of the time it's your heroes. I really look up to my heroes, like Mark McGwire and Ron Gant. If they do bad then they do bad. They just come back the next night and hit a home run. They're doing what I would like to do. Maybe I can't hit a 450-foot shot out of Vets Stadium, but if I try my hardest maybe when I'm around eighteen I'll be able to. Maybe I can do it if I try.

I'm a little overweight, and because of that everybody thinks I can't play baseball. But I'm one of the best kids on the team. Everybody's shocked to see me hit. All my friends know I'm real good, but people who never saw me before think I stink. I have to prove myself to them, and I think I do a good job of it. I get a special boost out of the fact that they're surprised.

Enfranchised in America
We Are Who We Are

Bernie O. Born 1934. Director of campus Hillel Foundation. Born and raised in Boston, Massachusetts. Boston Red Sox.

For me baseball wasn't just the professional game, but a sport we played ourselves. When we were kids it was the major sport; we grew up with a bat and ball. It wasn't always hard ball. We'd often play with one of those soft rubber balls, and we used a stick rather than a bat. We called it stick ball. Right behind our house there was a baseball field, and in the evenings we'd go and watch the games that were played there. Each street had its own baseball team. We were the Lawrence Avenue Reds. We had special team shirts, and I can remember the colors: yellow and red, with long sleeves. And we had caps with an "R" on them. We raised money to support the team, buy equipment, by selling raffles in the neighborhood. We couldn't turn to our folks for money to buy uniforms, and each of us was responsible for getting his own glove.

Our enemy was the Intervale Indians. In fact they were the only team we played against. They were good Jewish boys and we were good Jewish boys. They lived just one street away from us, but we were worlds apart. We went to school with them, we were friends with them, but when it came to sports we were at each others' throats. We were identified intensely with our own street. So much so that the kids who lived on the cross streets had to choose. Some would go with them and some with us. As fans we were identified with our city, with the Red Sox or the Braves. But as players it was more localized. The lines were drawn from street to street, and the loyalties were fierce.

My father was an immigrant who came to the States when he was in his early twenties. He never went to school in the States, so baseball for him meant foolishness, foolishness at best. At worst it was, "If you have time to play baseball, then you can go to work in the store," or something of that sort. But for us baseball was a way out of the store and into America. As the sons of immigrants baseball was one of the things that made us Americans. We were able to play this game that was played by everyone and that was of course the American pastime, so if we played it it meant we too were Americans. And this process of assimilation involved certain rituals, less in the playing of the game than in the preparation for it. The games we played were really very boring. It was getting your baseball glove and rubbing it with Vaseline every night and putting the baseball inside and tying it up and taking it out again—this is where the real excitement was. There was so much ritual involved in this it could keep you busy for hours. And then of course there were the rituals of imitation. You'd stand in your room for hours, swinging the bat, more likely a stick, imitating your favorite player's stance and swing.

It was all part of our entree into mainstream American life. In those days Boston had a basketball team and a football team, but these really meant nothing to us. We did play football, but hockey was out, and tennis and golf we hadn't even heard of. Baseball you could play by yourself, fantasize with one other friend, or play with ten or twenty other people. It really didn't matter how many people you had, you could always play, you could always get a baseball game together.

The kick I got out of playing baseball had something to do with my brother. My brother was not a baseball fan. He wasn't into sports, and I think that had something to do with it. We were very close in age, he was good at everything else, and yet here I was playing sports, which he wasn't good at all. I sort of accepted the fact that Michael was going to be my parents' favorite, the admired one. It's not that they loved him more. He was just more competent doing things that were more important to them. The things I was good in, like sports, gave me acceptance among friends—a kind of compensation.

I was always good in sports, and this was very important to me, though it was totally foreign to my parents. They had no appreciation for sports whatsoever, and the players meant nothing to them. But to me they were heroes. They were the people I identified with, and I'd spend hours fantasizing about myself as a great American baseball hero. It was amazing how we could always identify with these baseball players who were so far removed from the ideals of our parents and everything that mattered to them. Maybe that was part of the attraction: that these apparently uneducated people were so totally different and that being different they were a part of the American experience we wanted to be part of.

Baseball, in other words, represents America, nonimmigrant America, mainstream America. It was a way of rebelling against your immigrant background and establishing yourself as a full-fledged citizen of this new country. O'Donnell might bomb us with snowballs when we're headed for the library, but he lived on Lawrence Avenue. He was a Red. So we had this feeling of being together, at least while the game was on.

As a fan I was for the Red Sox. They had a great team right after the war. In Boston in those days you could choose your team, and you couldn't change without being called a traitor. I can't remember any of my friends being Braves fans. It always seemed to us that in Boston there was only one team. Only losers were Braves fans. We didn't go to Fenway Park often—it was too far away—but we were powerfully attracted to it in some way. It represented something so American.

My favorite player was Bobby Doerr. He was the leader who kept the team together. He was disciplined, he was in control, and he was steady. He wasn't going to hit .350. He was going to do about .280, .290, but he was dependable. Especially in the clutch you could depend on Bobby Doerr. The story went around that he was the one who beat the shit out of Ted Williams when he came in drunk or when he thought Williams wasn't playing for the team. He put down the law; he was the sheriff; he was the closest thing to being the Jewish father that I could identify with. So there was a bridge through Doerr (the name seems symbolic) from the Old World to the New. Williams was all New World. He was beyond one's imagination, magnificent, the greatest hitter of all time. This is what I believed then and still believe today, no question about it. This is not a belief, it's a fact. He had the eyesight, he had the wrists, he lived for his craft in a way the others didn't. He was a perfectionist.

Nineteen forty-six was the dream year. They seemed unbeatable, but they weren't ready to do whatever it took to win. Who scored the winning run for the Cardinals? I think it was Enos Slaughter. Boston could never do cheap things like that, scoring from first on a single. You don't score that way. You score when you hit the ball out of the park, or when you clear the bases with a double off the wall, or with a triple that rolls to the wall. You know, Boston was never capable of bunting. I mean, you don't bunt a run home. This was not our vision of how Boston should win. There was something large scale about the Red Sox, something hugely and clumsily grand. They'd either do it with power or they wouldn't do it at all. They wouldn't get down in the dirt. They wouldn't lower themselves to adjust, to adapt, to do the smaller less majestic things you sometimes had to do.

Ted Williams epitomized this. When they went into the Boudreau shift, where everyone but the third baseman played on the right side of the infield, Williams ignored it. He acted as though to take notice of this shift and to alter his stance or accommodate it in some other way would have been beneath him. He wasn't going to stoop to that. He was going to say, "Throw your best at me because I'm going to beat whatever strategy you can think up, not by going around it, but by crashing right through it. I'm going to beat you at your game by playing my game better." He was Boston in a sense, projecting the image of the roughness behind the game, the brute power behind baseball, rather than the finesse.

The Red Sox seemed to embody one aspect of the American success story at the expense of the other. They represented the raw power of America, its supreme confidence and industrial might, but not its ingenuity, its shrewdness. Nobody stole bases in Boston, nobody was an outstanding fielder, nobody made the doubleplay with any finesse, and if they had one or two decent pitchers they'd overwork them so that by the end of the season they were worn out. There was Ellis Kinder whose arm just wore out. There was Mel Parnell whose arm just wore out. When they came up against a team for a three-or four-game series, what they did today had no relation to tomorrow. There seemed to be no planning, no sense of the need for an overall strategy. When other teams were turning to specialization and to more and more complicated strategies, Boston stayed Neanderthal, and it's only because they had so much raw power that they were able to survive.

I was of two minds about this "we are who we are and we don't budge" attitude. I hated the fact that it consistently cost us big ball games, that we seemed ready and willing to lose rather than adapt. But the fact that we are who we are also filled me with pride. Maybe in a way they were the citizens, the established residents I wanted to be. They didn't have to prove anything to anyone, didn't have to adjust or assimilate. We were the immigrants. We had to learn how to play someone else's game. But not the Red Sox. They were brazen enough to play their own game whatever it might cost them. The implication was that if you really played the game fairly, we would knock the shit out of you. But if you don't play fairly, well, you'll probably beat us, though we'll go down swinging.

It's interesting. None of them had nicknames. Bobby Doerr was Bobby Doerr; Vernon Stephens was Vernon Stephens. Johnny Pesky was Johnny Pesky. In New York you had nicknames: Joltin' Joe, Ole Reliable, King Kong, Scooter. In Boston none of them did. Ted Williams was Ted Williams, with no frills around it. This is how the game should be played, reduced to basics. It was really just a guy with a ball trying to get it past you, and it was your job to see to it that he didn't. It was your job to knock it down his throat or over the fence and into the next town. This spoke to me. Something in me responded to this bat-cracking attitude. If I hadn't been a Red Sox fan or if I'd grown up in New York, I'd probably have liked the Giants. The Giants also had these big burly guys who were always chewing wads of tobacco and spitting it in all directions.

But in the end you can't win enough games with a heavy bat and a wad of tobacco. In the end shrewdness defeats raw power. Bre'er Rabbit gets the best of Bre'er Bear, and Bre'er Rabbit was the Yankees. We were more or less the perennial losers, and the Yankees, well, they were simply winners. It was my feeling that if it came to scratch, if push came to shove the Yankees would shove last. If you were in the ninth inning with Boston a run ahead and there was one man on base and Joe DiMaggio striding to the plate ... oh no, I want to turn off the set 'cause the game is lost already. Whereas if the situation was reversed it was inevitable that the Red Sox would lose. It's the small town boys against the city slickers, and we didn't have a chance.

Joe DiMaggio was the ultimate city slicker. Joe was cool, unemotional. There was a coldness about him that Ted Williams did not have. Ted Williams always reacted to the fans, overreacted in fact, while Joe DiMaggio did not react at all. He may have reacted inside, but he showed no emotion. He was all steel and glass, like one of those sky scrapers in New York City. Williams would swear and make obscene gestures at the crowd, and when he was up at bat he would be facing the enemy; nothing else existed. It was one on one and it was more than a game. If the pitch came in and it wasn't where he wanted it, he wasn't going to swing at it. He might have been able to hit it if he'd gone with the pitch, but he wasn't going to lower his standards. He'd wait for the pitch he wanted and take his cut with that perfect swing of his. That's something I could identify with. You don't lower your standards. Not for the fans, not even for your teammates, not even if it means losing the game. We suffered for those losses, but we admired Williams for what he stood for. I think the whole team was like that. You don't lower your standards; you don't play their game.

When the Red Sox won, it was my personal triumph because I identified so much with the team. If they lost I wasn't really depressed because you sort of accepted it. If Boston was leading by 15 games going into September, if they would win the pennant by one game you thanked God. To go beyond that, the World Series, who knew what the hell was going to happen. I say who knew, but we knew. They'd lose it in the clutch. You see, the team was a great team. They would win more games than they'd lose, but they wouldn't have the pitcher who would come in and win that close game. I guess it should have made me mad, but I sort of accepted it, because there was so much that was positive about the team. And there was also some basking in defeat. These guys populated a different world than I did, and their world was so much more exciting than mine that I was able to enjoy the fantasy, even of defeat. Even if they lost, these guys were up there. They were on a different plane. You admired them for what they did. It gave you the feeling that you yourself could match that. Once you reach the age when you don't have these fantasies you're getting old.

I remember, I can picture ... we were living in a house with a family room, a porch in back. To get from the living room to the kitchen you went through the bedroom my brother and I slept in. There was no privacy. We had a bathroom that had no lock on it. My mother didn't see why you had to lock a bathroom. Dad would leave the house early in the morning and come home at night after working hard six days a week, Saturday included, not Sunday. Mom would be reading the Yiddish newspaper, and they would never take you any place. My mother was 42 when she had her first child, so I always had a vision of my parents as old. So my parents are old, my father's always working, my mother's reading the paper, and we're not going anyplace. But with a little ball and a stick I was able to create a fantasy world where I was good. What else did you do? Go to a movie once a week maybe, or listen to the radio. I didn't have a bike, didn't have skates, didn't even have a sled. Well, I did, but my dad took it away. So what did you do? You played these games. You could be by yourself for hours, fantasizing. You played and you fantasized: It's the last of the ninth, the bases are loaded, you're down by four, it's a 3-2 pitch and you're up at bat and ... it's outa the park! You win the game! You win the big game, and that's how it's gonna be in your life. You're gonna win the big game. For me it was a positive thing. Despite the fact that I was identifying with a team that was not a clutch team, baseball gave me this feeling of being able to succeed. People were going to depend on me and I was going to come through. I would make up for what Boston didn't do. That may be why you can identify more strongly with a losing team than with a winning team. It can mean much more to you because you were going to add the missing ingredient they didn't have. It was all right that they didn't have it, and you knew it was a fantasy, but it was a fantasy that worked. So even if they were going to lose the big game, in your mind, when you replayed it, when Big Bernie stepped in, look out!

Thanks for helping me remember these things. I feel good being taken back this way. When I think about my childhood I think back fondly despite the problems. Those were nice years, good years, and baseball was a part of it. No question about it. As I said, it wasn't just a spectator sport. We played it and we lived it. I was on winning teams. I made my contribution. At baseball and basketball we were the best. Not football, 'cause they roughed us up. If it was a game with rules we beat them. I think that's what my parents taught us. There are certain rules, and if you play by the rules you'll beat them if you're better. Of course they didn't know about the Red Sox. The Red Sox played by the rules and always folded when it counted. But we'd make up for that. We'd come through.

IV. The Contained Aesthetic Object, the Mirroring Work of Art

For George Will, as the subtitle of his book announces, baseball is a craft, the complex craft of gifted, diligent, and thoughtful men at work. For others, however, to portray baseball even in these exalted terms would be insufficient praise. "The thing that depresses me," complained Tom Seaver in 1982,

> is that so many of the owners think of me and all the other players essentially as laborers. They have no appreciation of the artistic value of what I do ... Pitching is a beautiful thing. It's an art—it's a work of art when it's done right. It's like a ballet or the theatre. And, like any work of art, you have to have it in your head first—the idea of it, a vision of what it should be like. And then you have to perform. You have to make your hand and body come up to that vision.[1]

It is an eloquent plea and one, Seaver will be happy to know, that resonates deeply with fans as well as artists. In his elegant tribute to baseball, "At the Ball Game," the poet William Carlos Williams tells us that in baseball, delightful uselessness and a beauty that touches the eternal are the defining marks and accoutrements of the work of art as poets and philosophers have defined it. Poetry, as another poet, W.H. Auden, ambiguously praised it, "makes nothing happen," and Williams, speaking of the game's enjoyable uselessness, seems to agree.

The claim, however, for all its appeal and partial rightness, insulates both of these art forms more hermetically than seems warranted. Like the poetry, drama, or fiction to which the fans in this section repeatedly analogize the sport, baseball provides, alternately or at once, a protective or exalting refuge and a mirror of experience. Different fans have different emphases, some stressing the game's gift of sanctuary and purified isolation, others its at times even causal interaction with the world around it. But for all of them, baseball makes (or made) a good deal happen, if not deliberately or propagandistically, then, like the purest art, by dint of its enhancing purity. And if not to the social setting, as it almost certainly did when Robinson broke the color barrier, then to them, the young and older fans who were so profoundly moved and changed by it.

I have already expressed, in the general introduction to this collection, my own view of baseball as a somewhat worldly work of art, my sense of the game's rather special blend of separateness and relevance. I will not repeat myself here. This is the place for the fans to speak, or rather other fans, and what one hears when listening is what always raps for our attention: how wide a berth the game allows for varying perceptions and responses, even within a given, perhaps arbitrarily defined, category of response. Almost certainly because, as one of these fans wisely put it, what we seek and discover in the game is largely "a reflection of who we are as individuals," aesthetic responses to the game—like all others— vary with the fan's background, biases, and needs. Art and aesthetics is an encompassing category, and baseball, always a generous game, is equal to its size.

Aesthetic views of baseball, it should be noted, seem less team-oriented than other categories of perception and response. Fans who regard baseball morally or as an instrument or object of their drive for excellence or empowerment, typically respond to messages their teams seem quite uniquely or characteristically to send. The Yankees are a symbol and vicarious source of excellence, their relentless dominance from 1947–64 a proof of cosmic rightness or an empowering weapon. The Dodgers, though less successful, inhabit the higher moral ground. They are gentlemen, flakey risktakers, social crusaders above all else, and the proper object of proletarian love. The Red Sox, teaching a different set of lessons, provide a broken ladder that must nevertheless be climbed. They are raw, unbending, if often inefficient power, emblems of tragic failure, awkward knights whose floundering at the chapel door is a ringing reminder of imperfection and an implicit summons to do better.

Fans who read the game aesthetically point to DiMaggio's otherworldly grace, the beauty of Will Clark's swing, the flare and style of Willie Mays. But the teams they are attached to need not carry the aesthetic message or embody to an extraordinary degree the beauty and balletic grace, the completeness, mirroring imagery, or purified isolation they respond to. Some of these virtues belong to individuals and can be appreciated even by fans of other teams. Others inhere in the sport itself: in the shape of the game or season, in the fullness, transcendence, or reflectiveness of the universe it creates.

All three of the fans in this section are sensitive to the beauty of the game or its environs. Andy speaks of Joe DiMaggio as a "beautiful athlete" and finds Dennis Eckersly "beautiful to watch." John remarks on the beauty of Will Clark's swing and, like Sanford, is responsive to the astonishing magnitude and fairy tale splendor of the stadium and field. All three likewise dot their conversations with analogies to, dare I say it, other forms of art. Andy compares a well-caught ball to a well-turned phrase and perceives the game as a drama of redemption, a "social drama, often involving race." John compares baseball to a poem, while Sanford, the most prolific in his recognition of analogues, sees the game as a play and an unfolding drama, a story with narrative shape, even a ballet.

IV. The Contained Aesthetic Object, the Mirroring Work of Art

But the aesthetic focus is markedly different in each instance. For Andy, the game of baseball is an Olympian playground on which mythical heroes enact a noble drama of redemption. What excited Andy about the game was the style and flair of certain players, almost all of them, not incidentally, black. What he looked for and appreciated in a player's presence and performance was an integration of grace and function, the special blend of "the aesthetic and the spiritual" that charges the game with the sacred force it needs to elevate the unannointed world around it.

For John and Sanford, the other two fans interviewed in this section, the emphasis is less on the style and performance of special players than on the coherence, completeness, or girdled self-sufficiency of the game and the world it comes from. Sanford, who began his attachment to baseball in a state of aesthetic wonder at the magnitude of the park and the sparkling cleanliness of the field, shifted his attentions as an older fan. What he came to admire instead was the purity of the game that frees it from the corruption of the sullied world of ordinary experience; still more, the sealing completeness of the game. An habitual procrastinator and noncompleter as a child and young man, Sanford developed a self-correcting affection for the completed process. The nine-inning game, with its classically narrative provision of a neatly packaged beginning, middle and end, its detective-story unpredictability, and its eternal promise of the happy end, is a flawless and richly satisfying enactment of that process.

Part of the attraction of that completeness for this fan is its capacity to draw him into its self-contained world and release him from the worries and problems of ordinary life. But if that is an added attraction for Sanford, a delectable supplement to the satisfying completeness that was his main course, for John the promise of securing refuge is the main attraction. Often unhappy as a child, John sought escape first in the imaginary games in which he was the unfailing hero, then in the wider world of an entirely imaginary league. When the unreality of that world became too strident, defeating the escapist purpose, he turned to real baseball which, he savingly discovered, "Is also a kind of fiction, a separate world." Unlike the purely fictive world of imaginary baseball, however, the real game was at once self-contained and a reflection of the real world that alternately mirrors and affects it. Like both Andy and Sanford, in other words, John mediates, through baseball, his place in and just outside the world. He finds in it a closed room to escape to and, when he is ready to reemerge, a door or window to the real.

Like the work of art, the game of baseball serves its fans as a kind of transitional space or object, a middle ground between fantasy and reality on which the young fan may situate himself according to his changing needs. When he is susceptible to fantasy and wonder, baseball is fairyland. When he requires a purified sanctuary from a contaminated world, baseball is a monastery. If he would heroize either himself or others, real and imagined baseball is the playground or battlefield of the gods. And when he grows a little older and finds himself better prepared to face the real world, the game is a transparent or refracting lens to hold its shifting images. While contemporary players, in Andy's view, cannot provide the magic that presences like Mays, Clemente, and DiMaggio once provided, the game itself still may. At times, an extraordinary game may exhibit a blend of grace and spirit and prove "completely magical."

Notes
1. Quoted in Roger Angell, *Late Innings*, p. 30.

Style, Flair, Transcendence
The Gods of Baseball

Andy C. Born 1953. Freelance editor and writer. Raised in White Plains, New York, now lives in Berkeley, California. New York Giants and San Francisco Giants.

You wanted me to begin with an early recollection of baseball coming into my life. One of my earliest recollections is of me and my older brother Dan, who's two years older than me, being introduced to the game and its heroes by our parents. I was already familiar with baseball. I must have been. It was when the Giants were still in New York, and since they moved in '58 I must have been 4 or 5 at the time. I remember my brother and I going first to my father, and then to my mother, and asking them who their favorite team was and who their favorite player was. We went to my dad, and he said his favorite team was the Giants, his favorite player Willie Mays, and I still remember it. There was something about the way he talked of Willie Mays that made a tremendous impression on me. For some reason I felt an absolute certainty that he was also my favorite player, and since that moment Willie Mays has been my hero. From then on I had a very positive feeling towards Willie Mays and the New York Giants.

A mystical explanation would be that it connected to some sort of intuitive, deep knowing within myself. It was as though something in me was waiting to be told about Willie Mays. There was something magical, transcendent, or in more mundane terms, something altogether amazing about him as a ball player. He was—he still is—the standard. I still think of him—and many people do—as the finest baseball player ever.

There are certain athletes—Willie Mays is one, Babe Ruth and Joe DiMaggio are others in baseball, Magic Johnson, Larry Bird, Bill Russell in basketball—there's something about them. The whole is greater than the sum of their skills and abilities. There was something about Willie Mays. If you took all his abilities and added them up, it still wouldn't capture his greatness. There's still a whole other level to it. I was too young to see Joe DiMaggio, but to my father's generation he seemed to be the epitome of that quality. You know, you compare DiMaggio with Ted Williams, say, and Williams was a far better hitter. Not nearly the fielder DiMaggio was, but if you weighed their various skills I think they'd come out more or less equal. But DiMaggio had a whole other aspect to him, a quality that can't be weighed. Whether we take the psychological or mystical explanation, that "something" is part of what I picked up about Willie Mays from the first moment I heard about him.

I became a huge Willie Mays and Giants fan, and the next year, or soon after that conversation with my parents, the Giants moved to San Francisco. I had no notion of distance at the time, but I do remember that San Francisco, the whole city, assumed a certain magic. There was a certain glow about the name San Francisco. It became my favorite city simply because that's where Willie Mays and the Giants were. They were hardly ever on TV, but occasionally they were, and I followed the statistics, the baseball cards, everything I could. I knew the batting average of almost every player in the league, but I knew all of Mays' statistics, and through him I became a fan of other Giants as well: Orlando Cepeda, Felipe Alou, and Juan Marichal, the great pitcher.

None of these players was white. That was a major thing. The American League at that time was still almost all white. The Yankees had Elston Howard, but I think that was the only black player they had. I guess I was hooked on black and minority players, though it started as a coincidence. Hearing the name of Willie Mays from my father I didn't know what he looked like. I didn't know whether he was white or black, and I don't know if I even understood anything about race. It's hard to explain. I was pretty young at the time. People can have certain dispositions that, given certain circumstances, develop in certain ways. Maybe I had such a disposition toward black players and black people. It's hard for me to say. There was something, though—a matter of flair or style—that attracted me. Even the white players I liked were generally players with a lot of grace and style, but that's a style of play more characteristic of blacks than whites.

DiMaggio was before my time. I've seen film clips of him, and he's as beautiful an athlete to watch as you could hope for. Sometimes he had almost a supernatural grace. But Mays—he was my man. His style, the basket catch—he was the only person who did that—the stories about his extraordinary plays on the field, it all got to me.

I've got a picture of one of them on the refrigerator, and I remember my father telling me of the greatest play he'd ever seen. It was against the Dodgers in Mays' rookie year, and it's a very famous play. Mays went running into right field to catch a long drive. Furillo, who was on third, tagged up, and Mays threw him out. It was a sure run scored, but Mays got him. Mays is right-handed, and he was going to right field. He caught the ball on the run and somehow stepped, pivoted, and threw in one motion, and he threw Furillo out. That sort of established him, though people said it was just a freak play, that that sort of thing just doesn't happen. So I'd hear these stories, and when people tell them, just as with DiMaggio, there's a sense of awe about it. That was a part of what I first picked up from my father, and it stuck with me.

Psychologically, I think archetypes and mythic structures account better for how I felt than an explanation that reduces it to Willie Mays and my dad. Not that those things might not be a part of it, but the way I responded to Mays and the Giants was on a par with the way the Greeks must have responded to the stories of Achilles and Odysseus and the great battles. It was hero worship or just a sense of being deeply touched by some sort of heroism. Whatever you call it there was something definitely heroic about it. Baseball was some sort of mythic or heroic struggle for me. It touched places in myself, touched me in very deep ways. It was as though the players were fighting for great and noble causes, and Mays, he was the noblest of them all. Off the field he certainly wasn't a bad man, but neither was he a person of stature. But on the field...

The non–Giant I had that feeling for was Roberto Clemente. Again black, Latin, a National League player who, by the way, is a national hero in Nicaragua. He died bringing relief to that country, so he's considered a hero of the Revolution. Next to Mays he was my favorite player. He also had a supernatural or charismatic quality to him. He had the style I was speaking of, and I want to say a little more about it.

Style is often thought of in contrast to getting the job done. But when I think of style I don't think of it as something different, something in contrast to other abilities, but of a piece with them. There's something so appealing and compelling about an athlete who brings a certain eloquence and grace to his sport. These things are not frosting on the cake, they're the cake itself. For that reason I'm not a big fan of Michael Jordan. To some people, Michael Jordan is the classic magical, charismatic ball player. One of the plays they always show of him when they show great plays—I was furious when he did it—is one of the most spectacular athletic feats I've ever seen, but it was completely unnecessary. It was showing off. Willie Mays didn't do that. Roberto Clemente didn't do that. Magic Johnson doesn't do it. They're aware that they're interacting with the crowd, that the people are there, and they can have fun with that. It's not that I think you can't have fun with pizzazz. But for me, at its best, style isn't showing off. It's not something in addition to getting the peak effort. It's part of that peak effort. Or it's a complete integration of grace and function. They're entwined and together. To me that's much more appealing than an athlete whose performance is empty style or graceless function.

It's hard to think of a great athlete for whom that doesn't hold. Ted Williams was not DiMaggio as a fielder or on the base paths, but his swing was pleasing to look at. No one would accuse Will Clark of being a man of grace, but when he swings the bat he is. That's what he's great at. But with Mays or Clemente that grace seemed to be a part of everything they did.

I don't know why I respond to that special quality the way I do. I know it's not confined to sports. I also appreciate and identify with particular elements of form and style in African American culture. The music I listen to is almost entirely black music, whether jazz or rhythm and blues. There is, apart from the particular relation to black culture, an aesthetic resonance. There's something appealing to me about a writer who writes with grace. In psychology, I have a hard time reading most of the things that are written, because the writing is so purely functional. Writing is a way of making points, but these writers have no sense that how you write is making the point itself. Although occasionally you do have that. Freud is a good example.

So this is part of my outlook on various things, not just sports. Why that is I don't know, except to say that it enthralls me. Whether it's a well-caught ball or a well-turned phrase, there's something deeply satisfying about it. It's a blend of the aesthetic and the spiritual. Spirituality can be merely functional, and content can be divorced from form, but at their best they're blended. In many cultures—East Asian cultures, Middle Eastern cultures—the expression of many of the greatest poets and artists was and is aesthetically pleasing, but it's very much merged with the content. In those special works and moments grace and function and ability all come together in a whole. Aesthetics is part of it, but there's also something spiritual about it. There's a sense of being right there in the center of life, or something like that.

Baseball does that, and when a game produces that feeling it's a special experience for me. Throughout last year's World Series and playoffs, for example, and of course in the '86 Series between the Mets and the Red Sox. '86 wasn't a greatly played series, but as a kind of archetypal drama and romance—the battle and tension and resonance with the ghosts of the past—it was altogether extraordinary. When you've got a great sports drama taking place, there's often tremendous symbolism, and the ghosts of the past are always there whenever the Red Sox are involved. The whole history of the Red Sox followed them into the Series, the fact that they hadn't won a Series since 1918 and the way they lost, which they did again. All that's in the air. It was there then, and it adds a whole other dimension to the drama.

Baseball is not as appealing a game to me now as it was then. I know there are great players now. Rickey Henderson is one of the greatest players ever. Wade Boggs is a great player. So are George Brett and Roger Clemens. Somebody could say I downgrade these players because of my age, and that when I was a kid the players were no better. But I don't think so. The players today are not the same, they just don't have the grace. I can't think of any who do. Rickey Henderson at times, but he doesn't know how to understate. There are times to show flair, and there are times to understate, and by doing so you show more flair. Also, Henderson's just childish. Keith Hernandez wasn't as great a player as Mays or Clemente, not nearly. But he had a certain style and knowledge of the game and leadership that made him special. Eckersley might belong up there. He's got tremendous style. He's beautiful to watch. There's not a wasted movement, and when he walks out onto the field there's an excitement that builds. So it's not totally gone from the game, but it's not like the mid '60s with

Mays and Clemente, Brooks Robinson, Sandy Koufax, and Mickey Mantle. These were all players who had something, whatever you want to call it—charisma, transcendence—this ability to come out on the field and make the game matter. When they played the game meant more. These days the game itself has to do it for me rather than the players, and on occasion it does. The game can still produce that sense of magical grace and archetypal drama. When it happens it's the situation that does it. Everything comes together. Like 1991, when two last-place teams made it all the way to the World Series and had this astounding Series. At times like that the game is completely magical. But for me, there are no longer the players who, just by their presence, create that magic.

My father's favorite ball player when I became a fan was Willie Mays. But his all-time favorite player was DiMaggio. Although now it's good-natured, we still argue whether DiMaggio or Mays was the greatest player ever. I'll tell you one last anecdote. DiMaggio, you know, lives in San Francisco. Well, after the earthquake in '89 everybody here went through a process of emotional and psychological healing in their own way. I think my experience was pretty common, because over the course of days, different aspects of it would sink in. At first it was mainly shock. A few days later, in the newspaper, there was a picture of DiMaggio, who lives in San Francisco, standing in a relief line. He lives in the Marina, which was the area most completely destroyed by the earthquake, and the picture struck me. It's not that I felt bad for him, but suddenly I realized just how serious this disaster was. Even Joe DiMaggio was affected by it. Even DiMaggio had to wait for relief aid. If ever there was a mythic ball player, it's DiMaggio. But the earthquake was bigger still, bigger than the god of baseball.

From Wonder to Completion

Sanford F. Born 1916. Retired from auto salvage business. Raised in Philadelphia, Pennsylvania. Philadelphia Athletics.

I grew up in a neighborhood that was about four blocks from what used to be Shibe Park, which later became Connie Mack Stadium and which is now a big empty lot. I first became interested in baseball because we were just three or four blocks from the park, and many of the people in the neighborhood, whom I knew, worked there at Shibe Park, parking cars, cleaning the field and the stands, or doing who knows what. This goes back to 1927 or '28 at which time I was 10 or 12 years old. One of the most vivid images, as I look back, was standing outside our store as the fans came from the park. We lived on a main street and after the game many of the fans would walk down that street, either to get the train which was not too far away or because they had parked not far from the store, and I would get the scores from them.

But this goes back to the A's. You see, my first love was the Philadelphia

Athletics. The Phillies played at that ridiculous field called Baker Bowl, which was about six blocks from Shibe Park. The Phillies were always a losing team, always in last place. We were A's fans, and for us the most exciting time was in 1927-'28-'29 maybe even into '30, when the A's were contenders battling the New York Yankees for the pennant. There were many crucial—spelt c-r-o-o-s-h-u-l—series between the two teams, most of which we lost, and that's when I learned to hate the Yankees.

I loved the A's. In those days they could do no wrong. Even when I learned that guys like Al Simmons and Mickey Cochrane and Mule Haas and Max Bishop were not the heroes that I imagined them to be, I still idolized them. They were beer guzzlers; they were mere drunks; they were known for womanizing. As a matter of fact I can recall my first great disillusionment. Somebody said to me, "Al Simmons? You never met Al Simmons? Well, go up the street here (he named the street; I think it was around Fox St. someplace) some afternoon or evening after dark. Look in the back seat of a big car parked there, and you'll find him screwing a woman there any day of the week." But even that didn't deter me. I still loved Al Simmons. I was only about 12, after all, and sex didn't matter to me. If he wanted to have sex with some woman in the back seat of his car, that was his business. As long as he could get that hit and make that catch—that was the important thing.

What mattered was victory for the A's. They were us. They were a Philadelphia team, and it was as though their victories were personal triumphs. This was Philadelphia, I was a Philadelphian, and I lived virtually on the same street where the players played. They were my idols, and if they won, in a way I won, and when they lost I was very unhappy. When they lost it was as though the United States had lost, Pennsylvania had lost, Philadelphia had lost, my street had lost. I was miserable.

The most exciting thing was being at the ballpark when I was lucky enough to get in. Very often—not as often as I would have liked, but very often—one of the policemen my father would befriend in small ways would get me in for the second game of an afternoon doubleheader. Well, getting in for the second game, sitting out there and actually seeing it as it happened, not listening to it on the radio while somebody described it, but actually seeing it: that was sheer magic. As you came out of the runway and you first saw the field, it was fairyland, it was unbelievable, and yet you were here. Everything looked just the way you wanted it to. The field looked so big. I remember being astonished at the pitcher's mound. I never knew that the pitcher's mound was actually a mound. I always thought it was at the same level with home plate. Oh, I also remember the sharp clean colors. I must have come in at the beginning of the game, because they were marking the foul lines, and I was astonished at how clear and white these foul lines were. And how green the grass was. And how the dirt at the baseline going from first to second was so neatly packed down, and how they were drawing a perfect line between the grass and the dirt. These things were a wonderment for me, a source of amazement.

Wonder is the word for it, sheer wonder: sounds coming through in sights, if you could put it that way. I always imagined the greatest thing in the world would be to get a ball. If I got a ball I could take it home, and I'd have a real live baseball that one of these men had hit. They were never boys; they were too big to be boys. The announcer would sometimes describe a player as short, but I don't remember as a kid ever seeing a short player. I don't remember ever seeing a fat player either; they were all supermen.

This was fairyland, these were special creatures, and they were playing for me. They were doing this for me, and in a way it was as though I was doing it myself. It was as though I was accomplishing something through them. I don't want to be psychoanalytical or anything but that's how it seemed. One of the most satisfying things about all this was that when I listened to a game or watched it, my own lack of athletic prowess didn't matter. I couldn't play very well. I couldn't bat very well when we played in the park; I couldn't throw very far; and when the ball was coming towards me it was always an adventure as to whether or not I would catch it. So while I would get angry at a miscue, a player's error, I had a lot of empathy down deep because I knew that was the kind of thing I might have done myself. On the other hand, when someone made a sensational catch or stole second or hit one into the center field stands, it was as if that was something I did indirectly. In a way it made up for my own lack of ability. I could fantasize; I could put myself in their place. There was a sense of identification that made it great when they won, but especially painful when they lost.

When they lost, I felt it deeply. It was a sad thing, it hurt; I had a sense of personal defeat when they lost. I would remember the loss throughout the rest of the day, and I'd take it with me when I went to bed. When they lost a crucial game or series, I'd look for friends who felt as crushed and defeated as I did. We'd commiserate with one another and ask the painful questions. Why didn't he run? Why didn't he strike out Lazzeri when he should have? All they had to do was get one more out. In these sessions there was a contact with the outside world that I didn't have in any other area and that wasn't characteristic. Baseball was mainly a private experience. We were a close family with a family business which my brother and I participated in even though we were very young. Baseball was not something our parents thought we should be involved with. We should be working and paying attention to our school work. I was forced to keep these feelings to myself because I couldn't share them with anybody at home. It wasn't something my parents could appreciate in any way. I couldn't even share it with my brother, though he was also a baseball fan. For some reason I didn't share it with him either. It was a completely private thing. I lived alone in this world of heroes and excitement. I would have appreciated more company, but there was enough going on in there to satisfy me.

That's how it was for me then, but it was different when I grew up. I'd like to say this. I hope I'm not going to sound like I'm pontificating, but I seriously feel that one of the great things about baseball is that it has something different for you at every age or period of your life. As an adult it's a different experience than when you're a kid. I don't worship these guys. I see the Phillies players chewing tobacco and I feel like reaching out there and kicking them in the behind because it's so disgusting.

What I most appreciate about baseball now is that it's something that begins and ends. It's a complete thing. There are skills in the game that, for want of a more accurate word, have "character." The ability of a pitcher to perform in a stressful situation, or of a batter who comes up in a situation where he has to hit the ball to a certain place, get a hit or get a fly ball or advance a player—these things impress me. There's a quality about that athletic act that I can't find in many other sports. Look, there are skillful runners, there are skillful pole vaulters, and I suppose in their way bike riding and tennis and all the other sports have certain qualities of their own. But in baseball you have a nine-inning situation which begins with a pitcher and hitter and two teams on an equal plane, assuming that they're all big league players and in the same class. There's no telling what will happen in the next nine innings. And what happens in the next nine innings is similar to a bridge hand, because no two games are the same. There's a sense of wonder about the fact that this pitcher can make that ball do what he wants it to and fool an equally talented batter. And it's just as amazing that a batter can judge the trajectory of the ball skillfully enough to make contact with it and make it go where he wants it to go. And from the top of the first inning to the end of the game, no two games are alike.

There's a whole story that's going to take place and that's different from every other story, in baseball and outside it. There's a purity about those nine innings that transcends what we see around us, and there's a quality, an aesthetic quality, about almost everything that happens during the course of those eighteen situations, those eighteen half innings. Sometimes they're routine, sometimes they're drawn out, sometimes you can fall asleep while watching if you're watching on television. But somewhere along the way, in several places during the course of the game, there's going to be a kind of drama, a kind of excitement that stems from the ability of the players that is not the same as any other human experience.

Don't misunderstand me. I'm not saying this is Hercules and the Amazons here, or some classical Greek event. But there's a certain quality about baseball, something very restful that appeals to me. Restful in the sense that if I were to have a bad day for some reason, or have a problem—someone is seriously ill, for example—if I listen to music I'm going to think about that problem. If I'm reading a book there are things that may occur in the lines of the book that are going to remind me of my sorrows or what's troubling me. And the same goes for a play or even an opera. But if I'm at a baseball game, where every inning will present a different scenario, where there are so many possibilities, and where everything that happens is an expression of athletic talent, well, I'm going to be drawn into that world and be carried along by it. I'm going to forget whatever's on my mind and what a lousy day I'd had.

In a way it's like a ballet. The runner is trying to get to the base, and the infielder is trying to field the ball and at the same time tag the runner or catch the ball and make sure he touches the bag. There's a certain pattern of grace and response you can't help but admire. Look, the ability to get a three-pointer from far out, that's a tremendous thing, there's no question about it. And the ability to pass behind your back or make a driving layup is a big thing in basketball. But there's something in the sport of baseball that's farther removed from everyday. It's a complete event that occurs within itself. During the time of the game baseball is a sanctuary. There's a sense of isolation from the outside world. I'm at peace and at one with the game I'm watching.

As I said, this is different from the feelings I had when I was a child. Then the ballfield was a fairyland, a wonderland, an awesome place peopled with supermen. Now it's this ballet, this play, this story, this beautiful, complex world, complete in itself. When the game is over, they've finished nine innings. There's something good about starting a project and seeing it completed satisfactorily. Maybe it goes back to my habit of putting things off: having to write a paper in college and never completing it, or having to write a letter and postponing it until it's too late. Unlike me, these guys have finished the game, so I'm a little envious.

In later life we were in the automobile salvage business, and I would take great pleasure in the completion of a deal. I would get a call from the insurance company or the dealer to come and look at a car, and there were various steps to the procedure. I would look at the car, I would analyze it and put a price on it. Then if the price was satisfactory I would buy the car. I would remove it from its location and take it to our location, where the car would be processed. So the entire procedure, beginning with the phone call and continuing through the inspection to the end, would be like a story. It started off with a phone call and it ended up with me making a buck, but the making of the buck wasn't as important as the story that had taken place. There was a certain narrative shape, in a classic sense, and so there is in baseball. The game takes place inside of three hours. The guys come out on the field and they perform for nine innings; then it's over and it's done. There was a certain excitement, drama, workmanship, during the course of the game which paralleled what I was doing. In both there was the joy of completion from one end to the other.

You can probably get that sense of completion from other things as well, but baseball is unlike any other experience. If you go to a concert and listen to a piece of music, every bar is gone almost as soon as it's played. Unless you have a very good ear, you can't remember the individual melodies or the combinations of sound. They occur and they're gone, and you're on to the next one. But you can remember what happened in the second inning because something clear and sharply defined took place there; you can pinpoint it. A baseball game is a story that can stay in your mind, and if you lose parts of it, the next day you pick up the paper and you're reminded. The images come back to you again; the story retells itself.

When I was a kid I didn't appreciate that aspect of the game. I didn't think of the game as a whole. I didn't fully enjoy the process of its happening, the unfolding drama, the way I do now. Then too, if I can add this one more dimension, in baseball as in a good play or story, things can work out right. The good guys can win. We never seem to win in politics. The good guys don't win. The other side always seems to win, whether it's the conservatives or the ultra right or the out and out fascists. There are always bad guys and good guys, and the bad guys always seem to come out ahead. But in baseball the good guys can win. Not always, but even if you're rooting for a very poor team there's always the possibility that at any one time the ball will do what the pitcher wants it to do and the batter will do just what you hoped he would.

Maybe it's just luck, but it's a victory all the same, and as I said before, there's a purity and an honesty about the nine innings of a ball game that distinguish it from other events around us. The ball game is a place where things go right, or can go right. There's a greater chance of good things happening to your team. Even in a game your team eventually loses there was always the chance that it might have gone right. You didn't know from the outset that you would get beaten, and no matter how far down you were, there was always the possibility that your guy might hit a home run and turn things around. And if it doesn't work out that way, well, there's always the sense of completion, the last out that gives the game its final shape and puts it neatly away.

Baseball as Poem
The Self-Sufficient Mirror

John S. Born 1942. Poet and school teacher. Raised in Manhattan, now living in Oakland, California. Brooklyn Dodgers and San Francisco Giants.

My family were all Brooklyn Dodger fans. I remember, when I was about 5 years old, my father running down the three New York teams and asking which one I wanted to root for. I said the Dodgers. I knew they rooted for the Dodgers already, so I don't know if it was a really free decision. The historical irony is that I've come to be a Giants fan in my adult life in San Francisco, and I'm faced, for the second time in my life, with having to watch my team move across country.

I don't know if I remember specifically when I first went to a ball game. I do remember the feeling of entering Ebbets Field very well. It seems to me that you entered from the street into a kind of rotunda-like entranceway, but I may be mistaken. It seemed very large, but of course I was very small, and it seemed to me very much like a huge echoing shrine, like a mosque. You'd pass through this dome-like entranceway and come out into the field area, and though it was like a bandbox compared to later fields, it seemed enormous. I remember the right field wall that players would occasionally hit balls over. Duke Snider often hit them over that wall. "Into Bedford Avenue" was the phrase.

I'd go to games with my friends, five, maybe six times a year. But I listened to games on the radio a lot more often than I attended them. My audial imagination was the receiving instrument for baseball when I was a little kid, and my imagination itself was a generating instrument. I used to make up ball games in the back yard. I would bounce a rubber ball off a wall and play all the positions on both teams, while at the same time announcing what was happening at the top of my voice. When I didn't have a game on the radio, I'd have one in my head. I remember being told that our next-door neighbor was a friend of Dwayne Brecker, a popular juvenile baseball author at that time. He wrote *The Catcher from Double A* and some other baseball books, and I was told that while visiting our neighbor he had observed me playing these imaginary games and was tempted to write a short story about a kid who makes up ball games. I wonder if he ever wrote it.

In my own games I was always the star. "And now, ladies and gentlemen, stepping up to the plate, batting .328 and playing center field...." A kind of "Casey at the Bat," but with a better ending. Naturally, when I came up I'd always make a grand effort to slam the ball against the wall. It would go way over my head and win the crucial game. In fact I was a pretty mediocre ball player as a kid. I had a lot more experience playing against myself than I had playing actual games.

I played those games in the yard until the age of about 11. Then I became a stats freak and had an imaginary baseball league going on, for which I kept the stats. Here too I was a star. It was an imaginary league, a kind of precomputer version of Earl Weaver's "Baseball." I put a plywood sheet in my room and put books around it for the stands, and I pitched with a marble and hit with a pen. If you spin the marble it makes a sort of curve, or if you just snap it, it makes a fastball. Of course if you're playing against yourself there's no deception involved. I would play out entire games like this and spent enormous amounts of time at it.

Everything was imaginary. I even made up players and some of the teams. I put San Francisco in the league years before Horace Stoneham did because I had family around here. It was a point in my personal geography. I did this for a couple of seasons and kept complete records for those seasons: RBI's, ERA's, runs scored, hits, everything. What I liked about it was the coherence. There was a coherence to a baseball season, to a baseball league. Whether it's real or imaginary, we watch it develop. Every year we take notice of who stands out and who fails, and there's a kind of ecology to it, a predictable form. It was an imaginary world in which I belonged, and I placed myself there as a star of my own imagination.

At the same time, I was trying out for the Babe Ruth League and not doing very well. The real world was harder to compete in. I was also paying attention to real baseball, and I became aware, particularly as I got a little older, that my fictional baseball league was insufficient. It was a whole universe, as any baseball league is, but I could no longer lose myself in that delusion. I was uncomfortably aware that it was a fiction. Then again, real baseball is also a kind of fiction, a separate world. The stats and anecdotes seem to have a rhythm from generation to generation.

Baseball is a self-sufficient universe, but it's not sealed off. Like a poem or work of art, it's self-contained, yet it keeps on referring to the outside world. In a way, that's what's interesting about having followed baseball for 40 years or so. You notice the ways baseball changes as the society changes, as you change. I think we American men measure ourselves in relation to the age of sports heroes. When I was a kid, it seemed that the golden age of a man was somewhere between 25 and 35. That's how old ball players were, and it seemed to me an immeasurable distance from where I stood. Then there was a period when they were my contemporaries—that was in the '60s and '70s—and now of course, they're all really young from where I sit. It's a universe in a way. It's relatively changeless, though it reflects changes from outside. We pass through it. We go from being batboy size to being the oldest living player in the Federal League, or some such. And as the relationship between ourselves and baseball changes, so does the connection between baseball and the world outside it.

To me, there was also something mystical about the Dodgers. I loved them; I lived and died for them. Certain teams have an aura about them, though in part at least it's an aura we create. Major league baseball is real. It's not a fictional league like the one I created, but to an extent it's also a reflection of ourselves, an imaginative creation. I think we endow the teams and players we love with a special aura, and I don't know how much it reflects reality. That's a question for me. A lot of it, I think, is a projection of who we are as individuals, or perhaps rather there's a mesh between the individual and the team. In part we recreate teams and players in our own image; in part the teams and players we attach ourselves to are chosen because there's something in them that mirrors us or answers to our needs. My girlfriend, for example: I can practically sketch her character for you by telling you she's a fan of the Red Sox and the Cubs. She's given her heart to two teams which, between them, haven't won a World Series in over a century and a half. That tells you a lot about her.

It's hard to look at a team like the Red Sox or the Cubs and not see some sort of presence hovering over Fenway or Wrigley, a certain kind of spirit. I think the Brooklyn Dodgers had that sort of magic. It's hard for me to see it in the Seattle Mariners, say. But some 10-year-old kid in Seattle, living and dying with his team, has endowed them with something like that. And the spirit he perceives, which is valid for that kid, may acquire the quality of legend as time goes on; it becomes a part of the team and its mythology. And like any great myth or story, it's sustained by the beauty of its images. These young men with multi-million dollar incomes—their values are not the same as mine. And yet there's a quality of belief that adheres to Will Clark's swing that I don't want to have to give up. It's a beautiful swing. The last game I went to, about two weeks ago, I saw him park one on the right field pavilion. It's a beautiful swing, even when he strikes out or fouls one straight back. I sense some kind of anticipation when Will Clark comes up to bat, some sense that this is what we came for, that this is worth watching. Something's going to happen. Maybe he'll strike out, maybe he'll hit a home run. But either way, this is the man. So there's a spirit hovering over Will Clark when he comes to bat. Yet Will Clark the human being, the personality, is probably pretty ordinary, except in so far as he may be uneasily conscious that there's something hovering over him.

The Dodgers emanated a spirit of their own. They were a very hard-bitten bunch of ball players. They introduced a new kind of baserunning to the game. Jackie wasn't the only one who ran the bases; Pee Wee Reese was also a tough base runner. They would slide hard and break up double plays. And Preacher Roe had his spitter. There was a grittiness and a toughness to the Dodgers. If you were defining their "geist," you'd have to define it in those terms. Some of the players were real blue-collar types, and Billy Cox on third base, it seemed to me, always had his glove dirty. He was down in the dirt fielding balls.

It's a double thing. The Dodgers were a self-contained world guarded or inhabited by a certain spirit. But at the same time, through the grittiness of that spirit, they reflected part of the world around them. It's this doubleness that makes the real world of baseball ultimately more satisfying than the fictional world in which you're the star or captain of the winning team every time. It's more dramatic. Every real team has weaknesses. Even the spirit of a very, very good team has holes in it. There are Achilles' heels which, in the Dodgers' case, were ruthlessly exposed when they came up against the Yankees in the fall.

When they lost I felt really down, teary. The universe was a gloomy place for a while. It wasn't just the defeat of a baseball team. It was a personal defeat and the defeat of an idea. The Dodgers were carrying the banner for us. They were carrying our standard out into the world, fighting the good fight. They had that spirit. It was as if they were reaching into some sort of legendary realm, where their winning would justify us, assure us everything was OK, and their losing proved we were no good. Our self-worth was riding on their performance. We handed them that self-worth, passed it on to them like a fragile treasure they agreed to guard, and for the most part they kept their word. When the season ended we were thrown back toward a reality that might not have been very pleasant. But until that happened, the Dodgers offered a kind of sanctuary. They offered temporary life inside a legend, in the presence of a spirit.

My parents had an unhappy marriage. I was a shrimpy little kid. Bright and verbal, but not very happy. It was a rather dark and claustrophobic world, and in many ways the universe of baseball seemed much larger and full of light. It had a heroic dimension that my everyday reality didn't have. It was a magical world, a beautiful and heroic world I could walk into.

If I may, I'd like to close this conversation with a poem of mine. This poem was an attempt to deal with the feelings of a little kid in terms of a baseball game. It's called "The Game," and it has some sort of Tarot card imagery. I was into Tarot cards when I wrote it, about ten years ago.

> Inside my heart the page of pentacles
> unwinds and deals. The stars that thread the ball
> break on the inside corner of the years.
>
> He kicks and fires. I can see his horns.
> The airless Tarot of the stats reveals
> my face must be his own behind the change
> which floats along the sudden wind of time.
>
> I swing and get a piece of it. I run
> through death and shadow hoping for a bad
> hop, a quirk of shortstops in the flow,
> something to eat that's weaker than myself,
> a secret path of lime to lead me back
> to where my boy-size monster in the heart
> roars for October 1st at Ebbets Field
> like falling out and into love again
> and sliding towards the mystery of home.

I've played the game, of course, and I try here to recreate the feeling of batting against the nemesis, the pitcher, who's really the shadow opponent, who's yourself, in a way. In this poem I hit a dribbling ground ball to the shortstop, hoping maybe it won't be cleanly fielded. It's almost the reverse of the childhood fantasy, where I put a drive in the gap every time or hit one off the wall. More realistic. This is real life—hoping for a bad hop, hoping the shortstop won't pick it up cleanly. And then, at the end, there's the sense of the eternal return, the desire to come back home. The object of the game is to go all the way around and come back home, and in the poem I guess I'm going back home to childhood in an attempt to make it better, to come to terms with what I once had to run away from.

When I think of that what I feel is tears. I feel a sense of release that in a younger self I would have unconsciously identified with victory. At this point I don't think it's victory that matters. It's coming back to myself. It's returning to the boy batting against his nemesis, doing whatever he can do, and being satisfied with it. Even if it's just a dribbling grounder.

V. Not Just Fathers and Sons

The idea that baseball is an inheritance, a mythically charged heirloom passed from one generation to the next, principally from father to son, is largely a product of recent literature and film. Donald Hall, in *Fathers Playing Catch with Sons* (1985) and, more recently and far more influentially, the distinctly Hollywood *Field of Dreams*, based on W.P. Kinsella's *Shoeless Joe*, set the terms of what has become a quite lively and widely joined discussion.

The premise of their authors is, in Hall's lyrical, almost rhapsodic prose, that "Baseball is fathers and sons ... the generations, looping backward forever ... the profound archaic song of birth, growth, age, and death." Playing ball, Hall senses, "I walk ... with the ghost of my father." Sons, in other words, inherit their love of baseball from their fathers. Their passion for the game is passed from generation to generation with the toss of a ball in a twilit country yard or city park and thuds firmly into its lifelong place like a fastball in the pocket of that cherished, newly given glove.

In other reminiscences, when they are not bathed in a Hallian glow or floating languidly in liquid dreams, the raft of father-baseball-son is often remembered as a sanctuary, a safe haven in an often otherwise troubled relationship or in generally troubled times. A principal character in the 1991 movie *City Slickers* recalls baseball as the only subject he could discuss with his father at all, a view not far removed from that presented by Abby L. in the section on "Belonging." And Richard Skolnik quotes columnist Lawrence Levy's admission that baseball was "the most dependable, enduring tie between my father and me; it gave us a way to reach each other when all other channels failed, a place for a troubled teenager to meet a strong-willed man."

However varied its nature, the link is often assumed. Attempting to account for the fan's uniquely powerful and intimate relationship with the game, Skolnik lists, among other causes, the likelihood that the fan at one point or another tossed a ball or hit one out to his father, an "act long memorialized as among the most noteworthy and celebrated rituals of father-son relationship (along with attending baseball games together)." But, like all other shapes ascribed to this kaleidoscopic game, all other efforts to account for its special resonance and power, this one fractures under pressure, at least in its universalizing form. Setting out, in *Baseball Fathers, Baseball Sons*, to explore this relationship as it played itself out in the lives of the game's great stars, Dick Wimmer, encumbered perhaps by "the constant link of baseball" that binds him to his own sons, often runs into a wall he does not seem to notice or be troubled by. Asked if baseball brought him closer to his own father, Ted Williams answered blandly, "Not as much as you'd think." Stan Musial's father, a Polish immigrant, knew some baseball, but played none and had little influence on his son's interest or career. Rod Carew recalls encouragement from his mother and an uncle, none at all from his unappreciative father. Ozzie Smith, reared exclusively by his mother, learned nothing of baseball and squeezed no love for it from a father who simply was not there. And so it goes, as many former players denying a substantial connection as affirming it.

Writers, the film and literature more actively and often quite annoyingly on their minds, are often overtly and engagingly contemptuous of the paternal pastoral. Robert Creamer dismisses Donald Hall's description of baseball as a secret rite of passage between fathers and sons as "amiable guff," and Frank DeFord is more graphic and emphatic still. DeFord rejects talk about baseball as a pastoral "about fathers and sons and America and apple pie" as "all that kind of *Field of Dreams* crap" and describes his own commitment in loving but distinctly unfilial terms. Robert Whitney's father found baseball a dreadfully "boring sport," and Jonathan Yardley confesses he was never dandled on the knee of a father who regaled him with stories of boyhood encounters with Honus Wagner. His father, he confesses, was utterly indifferent to sports.*

The truth about baseball as a family legacy lies with all others, broken into fragments and scattered haphazardly across a field too broad to encompass or traverse. All of the above are true, of course. How could it be otherwise? The mistake is not in the affirmation of a father's role in the conveyance of this small but radiant treasure, but in assuming or insisting on it. We go too far not when we notice the father's hand in the iron grip of the game, but when we cannot unclasp them.

If the fans I spoke with are representative, the father, if he is a fan at all, is often the source of the child's first attachment to the game. He ignites the first enthusiasm, determines the choice of his son's or daughter's favorite team or player, and is responsible for that first inspiring visit to a ball park. That beginning, however, is only occasionally prelude to the kind of lasting bond described in the professional literature, still less frequently to the permanent vitalization of a previously moribund connection. A number of the fans I spoke with remembered being taken to their first game by their fathers, some finding it a particularly poignant experience not because it began a lifelong generational bond,

---

All of these testimonies are found in Birth of a Fan, *edited by Ron Fimrite.*

but because their father's cosmic disinterest in the sport magnified the gift. How much he must have loved me to have suffered this for me! For some it permitted, as we've said, occasional entry into the sealed world of an otherwise unapproachable father; for others it provided the only playing field on which the small adoring child might meet the overpowering parent on level ground. What is surprising, perhaps, is that while a fair number of fans cited the parental connection as a decisive source of their impassioned involvement with the game, relatively few placed a parent at the continually beating heart of their experience. More surprising still, two of the small handful who did so were female fans, and for one of these it was the mother who passed the glittering baton and did not let go when the other end was taken.*

In Rebecca A.'s mind, baseball "is almost totally associated with my mother," an at once cerebral and deeply moral person for whom baseball was a mathematics problem, a geographical atlas, and, more than either, a moral proving ground. Baseball, for Rebecca, was principally a learning experience at first, her mother the involved instructor passing on moral lessons the game, more particularly the Brooklyn Dodgers, seemed to embody: that what mattered above all was not winning, but being a good human being, showing tolerance and care, adhering to principle, sticking together as a team, and, recognizing the inevitability of failure, accepting it graciously. What she taught between spoonfuls of geography and math was the "whole ethos of goodness associated with the Dodgers because they were integrated."

For Vivian L., baseball was a father-daughter obsession, moral or moralistic only in the warmth of mutuality, understanding, and closeness they found in their common passion for the game. Here, too, there is learning, but of a very different kind. For Vivian's immigrant father, baseball was critical to his own process of Americanization. And what he passed on to his eagerly attentive daughter was his admiration for the American virtues his double entendred Yankees exhibited and symbolized: youth, strength, agility, and an irrepressible penchant for victory. Himself an encyclopedia of baseball knowledge and statistics, Vivian's father gave her the wedge for her own entrée—not into American life (she was already there), but into the summoning but otherwise resistant world of boys and appealing young men. Mainly, however, baseball was a closed, almost illicitly intimate society, pointedly exclusive of her mother, where Electra and Agamemnon, suited out for a double game, spoke their secret language out of the range of mother's ear.

Tom Z. is a catch-player, a fielding dreamer, his recollections of baseball in the classic mold of fathers playing loving catch with sons. The ball travels, as it should, in both directions, when an adult Tom, returning an unforgotten favor, takes his aging father to the games. Since his father's death, Tom sees his mementos, crowded residents of an entire room in his basement, as reminders of a father

---

For another strong tribute to the father-son bond as crucial to the child's continuing passion for the game, see the opening pages of the conversation with Walter S., pp. 76-77.

he idolized and whom he still associates, intimately and inseparably, with his own throat-catching attachment to the sport. If anything at all separates Tom from the hero of *Field of Dreams*, it is the superior power and credibility of his love for both. Tom's eyes teared up as he spoke of what he'd lost and what, in memory and continuing devotion, he still retained. It was impossible not to be moved by this man, touched so intensely by the past's presence in what he loves.

I'll close this introduction with a brief segment of an interview I conducted with a friend. I will not reproduce Dan I.'s entire interview, but this one reminiscence has a poignancy that demands a place:

> During my father's final illness—he died of stomach cancer at the beginning of July in 1983—I visited him in April for what would prove to be the last time. The doctors said he had anywhere from a year to a year and a half to live. I planned to spend the summer with him in his apartment, where we would watch the Cub games together on television. We watched a couple of games in April when I spent that last week with him, but I remember visiting him in the hospital one afternoon when the Cubs were playing the Phillies at Wrigley and finding the set turned off. My Dad said he didn't feel like watching the game that afternoon, and I should have taken that as a sign. A friend suggested I visit him in June, but I said I had time, planning to spend the summer with him. Four days later he didn't wake up, and by the time I got there he was gone. Pronounced dead that afternoon. I preached the funeral oration and directed the trip to the cemetery—which was located way out west on Addison Avenue, the street that abuts Wrigley Field—and I directed the funeral procession to turn off at Addison and circle the field. I knew he would have wanted to have one last look.
>
> There were many other bonds between me and my father. Baseball wasn't the only one. But in the later years, when I found it a little more difficult to relate to him, it was a principal bond, something we could always go back to. It was a safe place. An absolutely surefire place.

Fathers and sons are not everywhere. But living and dead they still circle the diamond.

Learning What the World Was Supposed to Be Like

Rebecca A. Born 1950. Director of university Women's Studies program. Raised in Brooklyn, New York. Brooklyn Dodgers.

I lived in Brooklyn until I finished college, so most of my childhood memories of baseball were focused on the Brooklyn Dodgers. If you talk to people who come from Brooklyn, you know that if they lived there before 1957 the

Dodgers were central to their growing up. I was 8 years old when the Dodgers left, but those early memories are the most powerful.

The Dodgers were central to my life and to the life of my family. My mother and father were both extremely devoted fans. They weren't kooky people; in fact their lives were very staid and kind of circumspect in almost every other way. But they were pretty avid when it came to the Dodgers. We were what we used to call lower middle class, which I guess is essentially working-class with aspirations to the middle class. Going to games in those days felt very egalitarian. Tickets were cheap, and even people like ourselves without much money could afford really good seats. That was important if you really cared about baseball, and my parents really cared about baseball. So from the time I was 4 years old I went to baseball games. I remember dressing in a Brooklyn Dodgers T-shirt and wearing a Brooklyn Dodgers hat around the house a lot of the time. I have a lot of pictures of me as a kid with this paraphernalia on, this little glove and ball in my hand.

My father was a very quiet man, and the legend in our family was that the heart attack he suffered when I was 6 years old was brought on by the excitement he experienced in the 1956 World Series, which the Dodgers lost. It's probably not true, but that's one of the family legends.

My mother was a more cerebral person and actually taught me more about the game. I had a deep connection with my mother over baseball, and when I was in camp during the summer she would write me every day and send me clippings about what was going on with the Dodgers. It was a summer tradition. Baseball, for me, is almost totally associated with my mother. We talked about it often, and we went to games at Ebbets Field. She was very willing to buy me baseball cards, and another of my mother's family legends was that I learned to read from baseball cards. I certainly knew every player; I had every card; and I remember reading them to her. I remember her asking, years later, what baseball heritage I had passed on to my son. My daughter is not at all interested in baseball, but my son does these kinds of things with me, and I remember doing with him what my mother did with me when I was 4 or 5. I'd hold up a card, name the player on it, tell him the player was born on such and such a date, and ask how old he was. And my son would tell me, just as I'd told her, only a lot more quickly. I associate baseball with learning. That association came from my mother, and I'm passing it on, to a certain extent, to my children. She used it as a learning tool—how to read, how to calculate averages, and geography as well. I also learned geography from baseball. Not as well as one could learn it today, but the geography of the eastern part of the country. When the Dodgers moved west it brought on a flood of anger, but it also led to a geographical awareness of the West Coast. The move became a geographical issue, though of course it was mainly a terrible tragedy and a profound moral issue, a betrayal of everything I thought the Dodgers stood for. It was one of the moral lessons I learned from baseball, and by far the nastiest.

The moral lessons were paramount. Baseball was above all a moral issue—

and a class issue with strong moral overtones. My aunt, my mother's sister, had also moved to Brooklyn, but she was a Yankee fan, even though she lived in Brooklyn. My aunt was much better off than my parents and she was the Yankee fan. That was the message we understood: that the Yankees were the team of the well-to-do, while the Dodgers were the team of the people. I certainly made a very clear connection between my aunt's money and the Yankees and between the Dodgers and a kind of sloppiness. And the main message was: You could be good and play well and be smart, and it didn't matter if you didn't have a lot of money. The Dodgers exemplified that important truth. My mother and her sister used to fight all the time about the Dodgers and the Yankees. My aunt swore that Joe DiMaggio was the greatest player of all time—that was all there was to it—and though there was no comparable Dodger to put up against DiMaggio, my mother loved Gil Hodges. She was one of those people who prayed for him after his heart attack, although she wasn't at all a religious woman. I got the message that this guy was a good human being. He was clean, he never hurt anybody, he did all kinds of good things. My mom died in 1987, and I was really sad she wasn't alive to see Tom Seaver's induction into the Hall of Fame. He said at the ceremony that Gil Hodges had been his role model and his mentor. She'd have loved to hear it. Hodges and Seaver were players who didn't quit and who played the game like gentlemen.

Through the years after 1957 my mother developed a deep affiliation with the Mets, and I guess that says something about my adolescence. When I was 12 I would no longer be rooting for my mother's team. She took the Mets, and though I formed a brief flirtation with the Yankees, I began to drift away from baseball. But that connection, that deep connection between the Dodgers and my mother and me—I'll never forget that.

The great moral allegory of course was Jackie Robinson. It's almost too obvious to state, but for the record, it was a matter of real significance that the Dodgers were the ones who broke the color barrier. Branch Rickey was a great man for doing that, and Jackie Robinson was an extraordinarily courageous man for putting up with all the abuse he had to put up with. My mother always pointed out to us that Elston Howard was the only black man on the New York Yankees, while we had Newcombe, we had Sandy Amoros, we had Jim Gilliam, Joe Black, and you could go on.

There was a whole ethos of goodness associated with the Dodgers because they were integrated. The Yankees may have won more often, but the Dodgers—my mother made sure I understood this—had the higher moral ground. They were better because they had black players on the team and because they tried harder. Winning wasn't really very important. If you were a Dodger fan you couldn't make winning the most important thing. It was more how they played the game and what kind of people these Dodgers were, and the fact that they were a team that stuck together. I bought a book for my son, I guess really for myself, on the relationship between Pee Wee Reese and Jackie Robinson. It's a children's book, and it's pretty typically American in that the white guy has to be the hero. But it focuses on Reese's role in overcoming his own racism and connecting to Robinson as his double-play partner. It made me cry.

Baseball still makes me cry. I'm moved to tears when I read certain things about the game, though I'm not sure I can tell you exactly what. Mainly, I think, it's the theme of reconciliation, which has always been very powerful to me. Perhaps it's connected in my mind with the idea of returning home, going back to the parents we can longer go home to. If a guy gets sold back to his original team or decides he wants to go back, and if there's some kind of emotional response among his old teammates to that desire, I'll feel like crying. The homoeroticism in baseball is astounding. There's a male bonding that doesn't alienate me. I find it very powerful when guys hug each other, after a home run, say. It feels complete, and there's something about it that moves me. Watching the film *A League of Their Own*, I cried and I cried. That was very powerful, especially watching the older women play and seeing their own memories of themselves come back to them. I think the movie underplayed the bond between the women because they were afraid of the lesbianism issue, but the bond was there, it was clearly present. My son wept passionately at that movie. He was really moved by it, and it was deeply thrilling to me that he was able to respond to baseball in a way that wasn't just mathematical or statistical. That's not fair. There are some people for whom the wonder of the math of baseball is totally compelling. That's true to a certain extent of my son, and it's certainly legitimate. But it was good to see him responding so emotionally to the more personal and human side of the game. It set up an ancestry, made the connection to baseball three-generational, with my son returning to the moral and emotional aspect of the game.

I cry at his games. He had a coach whose son played on the team, and their relationship was just god-awful. Never coach your son: that's the first rule. But it ended well. In the last game of the season the son did something that the father approved of, and when he showed that approval demonstratively I started to cry. It was very powerful. It's tied up, I think, to the idea of coming home in baseball. I don't know if that actually works as a metaphor—that in baseball the object is to come back to home—but there's something to it. I associate baseball with the feelings that come with going out on a journey but always knowing that your destination is also where you started from. I feel about baseball the way I feel about that idea.

I don't know if the book about Reese and Robinson affected my son as much as it did me, but there was something special in that story. Reese was a gentleman, a Kentucky gentleman, and that was part of his attraction. Gentlemanliness was a very important value in our home. My father, who was a very quiet man, was a very moral and a very gentle gentleman. He was the model in some ways, and the message of his behavior was clear: you were kind to other people. This affected me in a number of ways. For one, I don't like competition. I find it an abhorrent value. I don't know if that's primarily a woman's orientation—I'm sure that's part of it—but I think some of it goes back to my early relationship with baseball and the Dodgers. It's connected to being a fan of a team that wasn't going to win every year but that would try its best and do well.

Nineteen fifty-five was a whole other kind of experience. They finally won, they finally came out on top after all those years and all that adversity. Through it all, they had done the right thing, and finally good wins out over evil. Even if it's transitory, there is a moment of success. Nineteen fifty-six always comes along and some jerk pitches a perfect game and ruins it. But that's OK, because life is ups and downs. There are moments of great triumph, but there are also defeats, and you have to learn to live with them. The ultimate goal is to live a good life.

In my family, baseball was looked at from the moral perspective. My parents were not religious people, but baseball functioned as a kind of religion for me as a child, a moral scripture. My mother was always pointing out the ball players she thought were the upstanding moral guys. Duke Snider wasn't so terrific, but she loved Hodges and she loved Erskine, who was a major, major hero. Drysdale she could live without because he would bean people, and you know, this wasn't a nice thing to do. Baseball was taught very much in terms of its moral values. It became a substantial part of what I understood the world was supposed to be like.

Not all the lessons were positive. There were also some pretty gruesome object lessons to be found in baseball and among the Dodgers, lessons in how not to behave and what not to do. But these were always seen as aberrations, violations of the basic code. Walter O'Malley ... he was the vicious evil businessman who did not reflect the true values of the Dodgers and their fans. He was going to take them away from their homeland. He was going to send them into exile to that strange place called Los Angeles. The threat that he might take them away was felt as a very deep terror, and it was an enormous loss when it finally happened. It was my very first experience of grieving with my whole family, and to complicate matters my father had grown up in Brooklyn and moved to Los Angeles in the thirties. He was a furrier out there, and he'd married a woman who left him when he went off to the army in World War II. He came back from the war a broken man, so for him Los Angeles wasn't just the place the Dodgers were moving to. It was a place of absolute and total pain and rejection, and to have that earlier loss compounded by this one was simply devastating.

After the Dodgers moved, I switched almost immediately to being a Yankee fan for a while. Bobby Richardson and Gil MacDougald were gentlemen, after all, and so was Elston Howard, who became my favorite black person. My parents just mourned. My father never became a baseball fan again, but after a while my mother switched to the Mets and became the most passionate Mets fan. She was able to transfer her allegiances because to a large extent the Mets took on the Dodger ethos. There was something sloppy, unpredictable, and sentimental about them. They were, if anything, too too human. The gift I gave my mother when she was dying was getting the TV hooked up in her room so that she could watch the Mets games.

We all turned away from the Dodgers in one way or another, because we felt betrayed. My feeling was, if these people were so wonderful they should be there for you. They should show loyalty. Leaving Brooklyn to make more money was clearly a betrayal of that moral trust and responsibility. I don't know anyone in Brooklyn who kept rooting for them or who stayed up late at night listening to the Los Angeles games. My family would have nothing to do with them, and I had absolutely no interest in the Dodgers after that. They betrayed their own values and lost their right to my allegiance.

"An Intimacy Between Me and My Father ... A Secret Society"

Vivian L. Born 1935. Editor. Raised in the Bronx, New York. New York Yankees.

I grew up in the Bronx, on 165th Street between the concourse and Walton Avenue, just a few blocks away from Yankee Stadium. Those days seem rather far away now, but in the 1950s baseball was a very big part of my life. Of course I was a Yankee fan. They were the neighborhood team, and they seemed like a neighborhood sandlot team to me. I prided myself on being one of the few girls who really knew baseball, and I followed the season with a passion. I can't remember the onset of my baseball fever, but I know that all of my high school years it was a very significant part of my life.

My father was a baseball fan, and one of our great pleasures in life was to walk together on Shabbat afternoon—we were quite religious—to the neighborhood right around Yankee Stadium. Near the stadium there were many small lots and fields, Little League and other nonprofessional baseball fields where all sorts of teams played. We would climb onto one of those bleachers to watch the amateur game that was going on, but we would find ourselves a position from which we could see between the grandstands and the bleachers into Yankee Stadium. We could see the scoreboard, so every time a roar went up from the stadium we could tell what had happened. In those days they didn't have transistors, but even if they had, we wouldn't have carried one on Shabbat. But we didn't need one. Since we knew every player's number we knew who was up, and we were able to keep perfect track of the game. That's how we would follow the Saturday afternoon baseball games we'd otherwise have had to miss.

We weren't the only people skirting the rules to feed our baseball passion. There was a phenomenon in the religious community which was quite unbelievable. Very often the World Series would coincide with Yom Kippur. We were in a very religious *shul* [synagogue]. In the Conservative synagogues some people might have gone home, turned on their radios, got the score, and come back and told the others. But in our community you went to a television store. During a break in the service you hung around outside the stores, furtively "happened" to hear the score, and reported it back. As a result, on Yom Kippur everybody in the *shul* always knew what the score was. Somebody would go out, like a dove from Noah's ark, and bring back the information. You could depend on it.

My father was famous for once having snuck into a World Series game by hanging around the gate before the game started, and then waiting for a group of workers, laborers, to be let inside. He pulled up his collar, put his head down, and walked in with these laborers and saw a World Series game. If you understand that this is a religious man who was usually seen in a suit and tie in *shul*, you might get a sense of how much he loved baseball. My father came to America at about the age of 12, and to him learning about baseball was part of his Americanization process, in spades. That was really the crux of it for him as a kid: to learn about baseball in order to have a common language with American kids. It was a really important part of his Americanization process, and he brought this part of America to my grandfather, who never learned English and who sat over his *Talmud* at the dining room table, day in and day out, because he was already retired. My grandfather's children were all out in the world, and they brought the world to him. My father brought baseball to him, to this old *shochet* [ritual slaughterer]—my father was also a *shochet* when he was a younger man—this old, patriarchal grandfather with a long gray beard and twinkling eyes hovering over his *Gemara* and drumming his fingers. That was his contribution, his offering to his father. My father would take a napkin and pencil and draw him a baseball field. Then he would explain the game to him, in Yiddish of course, and my grandfather, who was very intelligent, and playful in his spirit, loved it! He loved hearing about it. Years later I looked back and thought: how quaint, how odd that my father was explaining baseball to this old scholar. But that also gave it value in my eyes. It was an international and a cultural link, and it meant a great deal to me, in part at least because it tied us all together in this way.

The Yankees were as American as you could get, and Mickey Mantle was the Robert Redford of the Yankees. My father would admire these young *schkutsim* [male gentiles]. They represented strength and acceptability. They embodied the values that America loved: they were young, strong, agile, and they were winners. I wasn't an immigrant. I didn't need an entrée into American society. But I must have absorbed this admiration from my father, this sense of the Yankees as magically endowed with the lessons of America. I felt it cast an aura on me to be a Yankee fan. It made me a Yankee, which meant I, too, was young, strong, agile, and a winner, a member of a winning team.

Because of this background, these influences, when I got to the teeny bopper age, the age when most of my friends were collecting autographs of movie stars, I was collecting autographs of ball players, of Yankees to be specific. I used to hang out at the players' entrance after the game, and I would wait to see the idols of my youth go past. I'm not even sure, come to think of it, if I ever got their autographs. I just wanted to see them and sometimes maybe touch them. Tommy Henrich was my first love. I came into baseball in the early '50s, just as Henrich was leaving it. I had pictures of him in my room. Where my friends had movie stars, I had pictures of Tommy Henrich stuck on my wall. When he retired he passed the mantle to Mickey Mantle, and I loyally shifted my allegiance to Mantle. He became the idol of my teenage years.

Now let me quickly jump to the end of my baseball years to give this whole thing a frame, and then I'll go back to details. I'm an editor, after all. I know how these things should be constructed. My baseball fanhood really ended when I met my husband-to-be. He was from the Midwest, from Omaha, and he had no interest in baseball. He thought baseball was ridiculous, and he had no patience for my obsession, or my father's obsession, with it. On these Shabbat walks, when he started coming along with us, he was extremely impatient and edgy and restless. On some of these walks, instead of going to one of the small playing fields, we'd go up to the roofs of nearby buildings and watch games from there. Occasionally my fiancé would come along, though always reluctantly, always grumbling.

I remember one very dramatic World Series game we saw from a rooftop. It must have been against either the Giants or the Dodgers, because it was a subway series. I can't remember which or what the exact circumstances were, but I remember it was a very dramatic game. My father and I were as excited as we could be, and my fiancé, who in those days was a very sober, staid, conservative fellow, was wearing a coat and a hat on this chilly fall day of the World Series season. The wind was strong up there on the roof; his hat blew off, and it went flying down to the street. We had to go down all the stairs because we didn't use the elevator on Shabbat—I think it was six floors—to find his hat. We found it on the street, but he was so disgusted, he was so angry, so derisive—enough adjectives—that he made it quite clear that I'd have to choose between him and New York baseball. And I, being very impressionable and certainly very subject to his dictates at the time, felt that if I had to choose I would take him. From then on, though I still followed baseball in the newspaper, there occurred a very sharp drop in my active participation as a fan. I sort of shifted loyalties, you might say—at first on the surface only, but after a while emotionally as well—from baseball, which I associated with my father, to my fiancé.

The emotional change took a little time, but he sort of mocked my enthusiasm out of me. Look, I was only 17. I got married when I was 18, so when all this took place I was 17. I was already old enough to get over the childish fever, although the most unrestrained baseball fan in my young experience was the mother of a friend of mine. They were Giant fans. The girl was a high school classmate, a Catholic. Her mother was a French Catholic and very straightlaced, except about baseball. About baseball she was like a fish wife! And her sense of values, or her ladder of priorities, was such that she used to write us sick notes for school so we could go to daytime ball games. They were the ones

I phoned on that unforgettable day of Bobby Thomson's home run. I had to phone. They were the Giant fans. It was their *yuntif* [holiday], you know.

That home run was one of the highlights of my life. It was one of the great moments in history, as far as I'm concerned. I'm not kidding. I'm saying this in all seriousness. If I had to list the ten most memorable events of my lifetime that would be one of them. I wasn't a Giants fan, but I hated the Dodgers. I hated them. They're bums, you know. The Dodgers were really dirt in my eyes. No class. But you had to know your enemy, so I learned all about the Dodgers, a lot of it from my father.

In fact I knew a great deal about most of the teams and players and about the game. I was very smart in school. I wouldn't say I was an intellectual, but I did things thoroughly. I think I was the only girl who knew earned run averages, RBIs, statistics like that. When the pitcher came in, I knew everything about him. And I really took to the learning process seriously; baseball was something to know thoroughly. I guess I did it out of a sense of competition, a need to prove myself as good as the boys. I was the one girl they could talk to about things that most of the other girls knew nothing about. Even the girls who rooted for one team or another didn't go into such details. My expertise gave me an entrée into boy culture in those years when the ground rules were quite firm about the plane on which the interaction between boys and girls took place. It gave me a special status. I was always a show off. I was an only child and I was smart, and I was used to being doted on and taken pride in and shown off. So this way of interacting was very usual for me. And when I discovered that this baseball knowledge impressed the boys, I played it all the way. I even studied up just to have something clever to say the next day.

My father was an encyclopedia of baseball. He taught me all these things, so indirectly and through baseball he had a profound effect on my social interactions with my peers and on the early stages of my sexual encounters with boys. He knew all the fine points of the game, all the most arcane rules and strategies, and he'd explain these things to me. I was the only child, and my mother had *nothing* to do with this. My mother was *completely* outside of it, so of course this was an area for my father and I to experience a little Oedipal, or rather Electral, complexity. It was like an intimacy between me and my father which shut my mother out, which was wonderful.

I feel like I'm on the couch now, you know. I don't think I've ever had these thoughts or analyzed these feelings to this extent. I see now, though, that baseball was a kind of closed area of intimacy between me and my father. My father was with me at an Old Timers' game Babe Ruth played in. My father had seen Ruth play as a regular, and as we watched him he would point out Ruth's identifying characteristics: his stance, his walk, the way he ran or held the bat, and I felt I was being introduced to the historic lore of some secret society. That's what we were, a secret and intimate society. On Shabbat afternoons we'd leave my mother washing the dishes and we'd go off to the sandlot field near the stadium. Every Shabbat that there was a home game we would do that. But we were really baseball fans. When the Yankees weren't playing at home, we would go and watch those sandlot games. We just loved the game. We loved to analyze plays and we loved to predict things and we loved to ... we just loved it, for its own sake, for everything baseball so beautifully was. We didn't go to those sandlot games in order to be part of something larger, certainly not to be identified with something glamorous. We loved the game itself, and to this day I think baseball is one of the most, if not *the* most, beautiful sports there is.

Shifting loyalties from baseball to my husband was a metaphor for the shifting of loyalties from my father to my fiancé. My father didn't like my fiancé and didn't want me to marry him. There was a tremendous strain between them always, and my marriage—you've just pulled this out of my unconscious—symbolized my joining the other team, so to speak. So in that way it was very significant. Symbolically, as the Dodgers and Giants would a few years later, I left New York for the West Coast the year I got married. In Los Angeles I went to a Dodger game once—not with my fiancé, God forbid, but with a friend of his who was a baseball fan. It wasn't the same. It wasn't the same at all. First of all because it was the Dodgers, whom I loathed, but mainly because all that youthful glow had been rubbed away—by my husband's contempt for the game, by my having to experience this without my father, and also of course—this is no small matter—because it wasn't Yankee Stadium.

Let me show you a memento. This is the ticket for a ball game I went to this summer, the first time I'd gone to a ball game in 35 years. I went with my daughter who lives in New York. I've lived away from New York for many years, and for one reason or another, although I've visited New York numerous times, I never went back to the stadium. This summer my daughter became interested in baseball and she bought tickets for me, for us. We sat in the boxes, and although the field was full of total strangers I loved every minute of it. We cheered and the Yanks won. They were on a losing streak, but they won that game, and I think I got just as excited as I did when I was a kid. The fires rekindled as if there were embers that had been there all along and just needed a shot of fuel. And the flames exploded—emotionally, the feelings—even though I was with a bunch of strangers, and even though I know that today baseball players are businessmen and Yuppies and so on and so forth. It's not the same crowd that inflamed the fantasies of my childhood, but the field, the green, the fans, the physical surroundings, the uniforms, the whole picture just sparked me off. And I was very happy that my daughter was into it, that she seemed to love it almost as much as I did. We were standing up and cheering every play, and the people behind us were very disgruntled, a couple of Yuppies who thought it was very gauche to stand up and wave your arms and yell. But we paid them no mind. We just let loose. That's how I've always been, a let-looser with no restraints. Funerals and baseball games were the same for me in this way. Both call for no-holds-barred emotion. There's no reason in the world to hold back at either. We just let it out.

The stadium is alive with memories and feelings. When they were starting to take Yankee Stadium apart about fifteen years ago or so, I was visiting my father, who had moved to Brooklyn by then. I had about four days in New York, and when I read in the paper that they were selling seats I said, "I'm going to get one; I'm going to take one back home with me." But I woke up the next morning with a terrible head cold, which was incapacitating, and I was just unable to leave the house. So I didn't get one of those seats, but I really intended to and I wish I had. I would have placed it in my home or on my balcony with great pride and pleasure, and it would have reminded me, every day, of what I felt when I entered the stadium as a child: the excitement, the anticipation, that special feeling of intimacy with my father who shared this great pleasure with me and who had given it to me as a gift.

But you can't go home again, not ever, not really, and maybe the cold I developed came to tell me that. The break with baseball my marriage forced on me would never be fully repaired. I blame my ex-husband, but I was probably outgrowing it around that time, too. At that point in life, if you remain an obsessive baseball fan I think you're clinging to a childish pursuit, although there are plenty of grownups who are steaming baseball fans. To me it represented a sort of break with childhood and a growing up. I suppose if you really pin me down I'd say that as an adult you can be interested in baseball, but not *that* way, not with such an obsessive passion. I don't know why that is, though it does make sense. After all, what is it? Nine big bruisers chasing around after a ball and throwing it around and trying to tag each other. In the end it's just a game, and money aside, you start to wonder about these guys who play it. It makes more sense for them to do it for money than to really care, at that age. They're grownups, too, you know.

I don't know. Perhaps once upon a time it wasn't just another game. Perhaps when I was a child baseball truly was worthy of the love and respect we showed it. When Tommy Henrich retired I reluctantly transferred my loyalties to Mickey Mantle because I had no choice. But I felt I had come in on the tail end of something wonderful, the end of this nostalgic game remembered. I've read a lot of baseball lore, lots of books about baseball, and everything remembered through a hazy screen of nostalgia in the days before my time when the game was simpler and plainer and the players really cared—all that seems to me the essence, the true essence of baseball. I don't know. Maybe this is part of a larger, more inclusive nostalgia for childhood. Nothing is really innocent, nothing could have been as pure and idyllic as the early days of baseball sometimes seem when looked at through this haze. Your brain keeps telling you that, but it's easy to forget. Seeing the movie *The Natural* brought it all back to me, put the game behind that glorifying mist and restored the idyll. The film embodied all these things we're talking about, and in a dramatic way: the passion for baseball, the Americanism of baseball, and the beauty of the game in its earlier days. The sound of the crack of the ball against the bat was like a drug to me. It was something I had been weaned from, but as soon as I heard it it churned me up, even as filtered through the sound system of a movie.

It's like old perfume. It's a sensory experience that triggers a lot of memories and sensations. It's a bit of something so familiar and significant at that early stage of your life. You were part of it and it was part of you. It identified you. It was like your religion, and frankly I gave it a lot more than I gave to my religion. I studied a lot more baseball stats than I studied Torah. I guess you could say I believe in baseball. It was a system of belief that I believed in. Perhaps I'm getting too dramatic, but there was something mythic about the game, and of course the early years of baseball have a special aura about them. What has passed always assumes larger, more mythic proportions.

There's a book called *The True Believer*—I don't remember the author's name—that sets forth some characteristics of the true religious and ideological devotee. It would be interesting to go back to that book to see whether what he says about those believers applies to baseball fans. I think it does. There's a worshipful element in baseball fandom, a form of idolatry. I never collected souvenirs or memorabilia, but if I'd ever caught a baseball at a game, I would be carrying it around with me all the time. It would be a sacred object.

"My Way of Remembering"

Tom Z. Born 1951. Company supervisor. Raised in Philadelphia and Port Richmond, Pennsylvania. Philadelphia Phillies.

My earliest recollections of baseball, maybe to a degree all my recollections of baseball, are connected with my father. He loved baseball and played it when he was a kid. He'd been a water boy for one of the semipro teams down in Port Richmond, and later, when he got into construction, he had a part in the building of the dugouts in Shibe Park. It made me proud to know he'd had a hand in building them. He'd take me out to Shibe Park or to Connie Mack Stadium, and I loved it. Then he'd come home and we'd throw the ball back and forth, and I'd love that, too. Something passed from him to me, this baseball feeling, something you can't describe but you know is there and can't live without.

Living so close to the ball park, going to the games was a central part of our lives. It was something to do all the time. At first I went with my father, then with my friends. We'd go down to the ball park to watch the games and to smell the baseball field. You could smell the popcorn; you could smell the grass; you could almost smell the game. When I'd see Johnny Callison or Richie Allen out there, taking batting practice, I'd beam. When they'd come over to us and shake our hands, I was in awe.

When I think of baseball I think of moments like that and more ordinary moments, too. I remember getting on the 54 bus to the ball park. I remember the little Italian guy who used to sell water ice to us before we'd get on the trolley car to come home. That's what I enjoy thinking about. I collect pictures of Shibe Park to remind me of those things, to take me back to that world, a world that's gone and that will never return. I've collected lots of souvenirs over the years, lots of photographs and paraphernalia, and they mean a lot to me now.

Trying to put it all together, baseball was a kind of fantasy, a world I was proud to be a part of. Proud in part because my dad was part of it. It was his thing, too. I was proud to be a part of it because in a way it seemed too good to be true, and I'm still living it somehow. By having all these little do-dads, I keep my connection with that fantasy, with my childhood when I lived baseball with my father. Maybe it's the kid in me that makes me want to relish those moments. My father passed away nine years ago and I really miss him. He was my idol. He was always there for me. I wish we could sit there again, watching Robin Roberts pitch on opening day.

My love of the game, it starts from there, and it developed as I got older. If I see something that reminds me of those days, that connects me in some way, I just kind of hold on to it: these chairs from Connie Mack Stadium, these photographs, or these beautiful paintings I have here of the ball park. I guess that's what makes the connection: I was here with my dad. I was there; I could name all the players; I could tell you something about all the great games I was at. When I look back at it, I say, "Boy!" It was like *Field of Dreams*. I could really identify with Kevin Costner in that movie. That's the way it was for me, and for a few hours it brought my father back.

Back in 1976, after I graduated from LaSalle University, I went to umpire school. My father used to come out and see every game I umpired. He really got a charge out of that. We started going to the games on a regular basis again, but this time I was taking him. I wanted to repay him for having taken me when I was a kid. Now I bought the season tickets, now I would take him to the game. I had two seats, and he would go with me all the time. It was just he and I going to the games. Come on, Dad, let's go to the ball game. I never took anybody else, because that was my way of continuing the relationship. When he passed away, I just stopped umpiring. It meant a lot to him when he'd have to miss a game I was umpiring. Now he'd have to miss them all. Maybe that's why I stopped.

Baseball for me is all tied up with strong emotion. In September of 1980, my wife and I went to Poland, where she was born. We went there for seven weeks to visit her parents, and you know what happened in 1980. That was the year the Phillies won it all. I didn't find out the Phillies had won until about a week-and-a-half later. I went to the Council in Krakow for a *New York Times*, and when I saw what had happened I had tears in my eyes. I still have the picture. My wife's family couldn't believe I was crying; they couldn't understand it. I was crying for what I had missed. The Phillies had won, and I wasn't there to enjoy it.

I have a shirt that says, "There is no crying in baseball," but there is. There's a lot of crying. It's like there is a heart and a soul in baseball. I don't know how to say it, but there's something about baseball that creates emotions. You sit there and you see the pitcher holding the ball, you feel devotion and loyalty to a certain player, or you anticipate what's about to happen. I don't know how to say it. It's intangible, but there's no mistaking it when it happens. You're suddenly overcome with emotion. Baseball does that to you.

It's just a game; we don't know these guys personally; nothing earth-shattering hangs on whether they win or lose; but none of that matters. We get caught up in it, and the emotions just flow. It's almost too incredible to believe, the feeling that goes through you. It's a part of you, it's ingrained, I just don't know what to say. I sit here looking at some of my pictures. There's Stan Musial, my father's favorite player, there's Robin Roberts and Lenny Dykstra, and Richie Ashburn. Looking at them all I feel young, happy; there's no other word for it.

It perks me up just to talk about baseball. I'm thrilled to talk about baseball. I wish I had my own talk show on radio just so I could talk about it, reminisce with people about what they remember. We'd say, "Do you remember this, or do you remember that?" It would be a great show. Talking about baseball makes me happy. This is a tough world we live in, and we're here only a short time. Only God knows when your time comes. When mine comes I'll be ready to leave, but as long as I live I'm going to enjoy baseball. It's part of my life, my way of remembering and being proud and being happy.

For me it's an honor to be associated with baseball. The game is that great a game, so great that to be at the park is like visiting a marvelous land. When you're talking about baseball, you're in a special little country: the field, the stadium, and the game. It's not one player, it's not the team you're rooting for that matters. It's the game itself that's special. Going to a game is setting sail for a special country, a different world where one feels honored to be. There's something about it that just gets you. It grabs you when you're young, and it doesn't let you go. It's going to be with me all my life, and when they bury me I hope they put a baseball in my coffin.

It's the game that affects me, more than winning or losing, more than the team or any set of players. It's been a part of me for most of my life. I'm 41 years old. I guess if I live to be 82 I'm halfway through. I might not see tomorrow, but for as long as I live, baseball is going to be with me. I love to talk about baseball, love to talk about the game. I love talking to people like you who understand me. Some people say, "This guy is crazy; how can he get so emotional about a game?" But that's the way I am, and I'm never going to change.

This conversation got me thinking about all the hidden, underlying things that give baseball meaning, about what the game means to me and how important it is to me, and why I couldn't live without it. What has baseball given me? What would I have lost if I didn't have it? Maybe I wouldn't be happy. Maybe something else would be controlling me. Maybe I wouldn't be as full of life. Having baseball makes a real difference in me. It was a major part of my relationship with my father, and it's a major part of who I am. I can see myself sitting out there with my dad back in '52, and it fills me with emotion. Everything I know and remember about baseball becomes part of my love for the game and part of me. These artifacts that I have, they take me back to those treasured moments. I sit here and stare at them. I'm getting all emotional now. It's the way I am. I'm passionate about baseball. It's so hard to understand. It's as though baseball is in my soul.

VI. A Sense of Belonging

Aristotle defined man as a "gregarious animal," drawn by his nature to social and interpersonal relations indispensable to his sense of well-being. He also defined the human animal as a featherless biped, but the social definition has shown greater durability. Some 2,400 years later, John Bowlby, the influential developmental psychologist, affirmed what we all now take for granted: that from earliest infancy onward, supportive and satisfying relationships with other human beings is our most fundamental need. "By virtue of his basic human nature," wrote Harold Bernard, man is "incurably social."

The most intense and influential of these relationships are of course the parent-child ties treated in the preceding section. But hardly less powerful and essential are the friendships, peer relationships, and wider connections formed in middle childhood and adolescence. As parental ties loosen during these periods, the need for supportive relationships with peers becomes more urgent. Uncertain of their changing identities and of their place in a nebulously defined and rapidly changing society, most adolescents, as Mussen observed, are plagued by a sense that they "do not belong" and seek within the peer group that elusive and precious sense of welcoming connection.

Although, quite curiously, none of the many studies of childhood and adolescence I have scanned make more than the most glancing reference (if any at all) to the role of shared fandom in the formation, conduct, and solidification of these connections, few living males will slight its importance. Today the field is divided. Shared passion for basketball and football and shared allegiance to an NBA or NFL team is at least as strong a bond and as obsessive a subject as madness about baseball or the Baltimore Orioles. But until fairly recently it was all, or nearly all, baseball. Going to games with friends, listening to them on the radio, watching them together on TV or, perhaps most commonly, recounting highlights of yesterday's game and arguing, fiercely if lovingly, about the relative merits of teams and players, were to early teens what sex and its desirable objects are to older ones. More than school or family, they were *the* topic of conversation, one subject on which virtually everyone you knew held impassioned, informed, and usually unshakable opinions. They were, or often seemed to be, the very stuff of which friendship was made; or, if that is overstated, the glue that, as much as any other, held them together.

Although a number of fans mention this connection and its importance, for most, baseball as a bond among friends is subordinate to other emphases and themes. Abby L. is the only fan I spoke to who views her experience as a young fan principally through this lens. For Abby, baseball was above all else a social activity, something one did or does with other people, particularly with young friends. She speaks of it as a subject that opened to her, at least for pleasing moments, the otherwise closed world of her father and as a way of showing interest in her son's consuming interest. Mainly, however, it was what she did with friends: going to games, trekking with them to a gas station just outside Ebbets Field, where they waited to snare popped fouls that left the stadium, filling scrapbooks devoted to competing stars or collectively writing them starry-eyed and regularly unanswered letters of congratulation or request.

What emerges from these interviews, and what surprises, is how much wider the net of bonding mutuality spreads; also, how much sharper in the fans' memories are these broader, less intimate connections formed around the game than the peer or friendship relations we tend to associate with it. Abby speaks of the Dodgers as a force that united all Brooklyn in its expanded clubhouse and democratically equalized all its residents-fans (the two were synonymous) as it brought them together in a shared preoccupation as certain and reliable as sunrise. And the other fans in this section speak almost exclusively of these more encompassing, typically less intimate, but hardly less vital or satisfying connections.

Pat and Sue J., young adults when baseball first awed them into submission, show us that the game's capacity to provide a wide but still intimate sense of belonging is not exclusively a childhood or adolescent phenomenon. Two wonderfully enmeshed sisters, they speak first of the central role of their shared passion for the Yankees in the cementing of their own enviable bond, but trowel the adhesive in wider and wider circles. Baseball holds virtually the entire extended family together, since "every one of us is a baseball fan." Yankee Stadium is "home," a "home away from home" where they feel a warming sense of belonging. And the fans and workers, whom frequent attendance have made familiar, feel like only slightly more distant relatives. The team too is a family, the wives a part of it, and at the outer reaches, New York City and all America are embraced by a shared devotion for this pastime.

Bennett K., another Yankee fan, though one whose fandom is an object of melancholic nostalgia rather than a source of present pleasure or connection, links the Yankees to an Edenic Bronx, an immigrant neighborhood, and a time that have sadly been extinguished. Tied by resonant association to that lost paradise, baseball is, to Bennett, a romantic idyll, emblematic of an earlier, simpler, and friendlier America. Once played by men who lived and, in the offseason, worked in the community and offering otherwise "odd" immigrants a scorecard passport to Americanization, baseball provided a sense of community and togetherness a harsher America no longer offers or sustains.

For the young Sanford S., an emotional immigrant of sorts troubled by a prevailing sense of otherness and rejection, baseball fandom was a complex fusion of inclusion and exclusion. As a sport he played poorly and as an idealized romantic world beyond his reach, baseball reminded him of his exclusion. Conversely, as a sport anyone, rich or poorer, could tune into and that united an entire city, one whose tragic element and grit brought it down to a reality he could relate to, baseball gave him "a warm and wonderful sense of belonging and acceptance." Sanford's portrait of his neighborhood street, every porch lit up on summer nights by dim lamps and the familiar voice of the Pirates' broadcaster, is evocative and moving. "You could walk from one end of the street to the other and never miss a pitch." And so it was, virtually, throughout all of Pittsburgh, a city given a common and proud identity by its team.

The broadest cast of the net, perhaps, is across the waters of history. One notes traces of this link to the past in Pat and Sue's exalted feeling that on entering Yankee Stadium they participate in a long illustrious history. And it is more strikingly and pervasively present in Bennett's identification of the game with an earlier, simpler, and better America. But the power of baseball to connect us to history, to bind the fan not only to his contemporaries, but to a remote and recent past, is at the heart of Joe N.'s experience and recollection of the game. Witnessing games where records were set or where something remarkable occurred gave Joe a fixed place in flowing time—as though he'd stepped out of his own life into the career of a great ball player and into the glowing history of the game. As with so many others, Joe's perception and appreciation of baseball is another, often the earliest and richest manifestation of a driving preference or value, in this instance his own determination, in his research and in his civic activism, to leave his mark, to be part of history.

What one sees in most of these interviews is the child and adolescent traveling, on the ship of this game, past the peer group through the wider rippling circles of neighborhood, city, nation, and history; past childhood, in other words, into adulthood and participation in the larger society and the greater world. As the British psychiatrist Anthony Storr remarks, "In the course of daily life, we habitually encounter people with whom we are not intimate, but who nevertheless contribute to our sense of self." What they give us is "mutual recognition, acknowledgment of each other's existence, and thus some affirmation ... that each reciprocally contributes something to life's pattern." By contributing so critically to the widening of these connections and giving them an emotional resonance one cannot help but hear in these interviews, baseball enhances this sense of recognition and acknowledgment. It adds richly to our sense of belonging in a world increasingly reluctant to provide such comfort.

This is impressive testimony to the importance of baseball to children and adults. But what is most memorable about these interviews is the beauty and eloquence of their descriptions, the palpable excitement at present relations, the burnished nostalgia for past images and places—all linked intimately to baseball and to the fans' enduring reverence for the game.

"A Social Activity, Something to Do with Other People"

Abby L. Born 1939. Researcher in bio-medicine and women's health care. Raised in Brooklyn, New York; now living in Montreal. Brooklyn Dodgers.

The first thing I can remember about baseball was pitching on the girls' softball team. The girls had to play separately from the boys in the playgrounds in Brooklyn, so we started our own softball team. It was a very informal arrangement, though, and it didn't last very long. So that was part of it. Another part— I'm talking about the late '40s and the '50s—was that my father, who had grown up in the Bronx, was an avid Yankee fan, and baseball was always part of his dinnertime conversation. The third part was Ebbets Field, which at that time, of course, was still there, only a long walk or a bike ride from where we lived. There was a gas station sort of catty-corner to Ebbets Field, and there were always dozens of people in the gas station waiting for foul balls to be popped out of the stadium, hoping to catch them.

For me baseball was never mainly a matter of loyalty to the team. It was a social event: going to the games, sitting in the bleachers, which is where we always sat. I never went to baseball games with my father, and my mother had no interest in baseball. It was always with friends, and for us it was always as exciting to stand outside the stadium waiting for the balls as it was to go inside and watch the game.

There was another component. There were three of us who were very good friends—this was back in junior high school—and each of us adopted a different baseball player as our special possession and followed him through the newspapers and fan magazines. Mine was Mickey Mantle. Jackie's, I believe, was Gil Hodges, and I don't know who Joan's was. But the three of us had scrapbooks dedicated to these players, and I can remember dutifully filling and arranging this scrapbook with every piece of information I could find about Mickey Mantle. I'm not sure why I chose Mickey Mantle, though I remember it was definitely a conscious choice. He was a Yankee and not a Dodger, so that was a pretty radical thing for a Brooklyn girl to do, and I guess it was either because I thought he was good-looking, sexy, or because my father was a Yankee fan and I wanted to make a connection with him through this scrapbook.

Anyway, there was this Mickey Mantle fan magazine, which I'd buy and cut to pieces and paste in the scrapbook with every other picture and story about Mantle I could find. I'd also send him birthday cards and anniversary cards, and I sent him a card congratulating him on the birth of his baby. I never got a response from him. Never. But it didn't discourage me. I kept cutting and pasting and sending cards. We all did this! It lasted maybe a year or two, and then one day—it seemed to happen to all of us pretty nearly at the same time—one day we all just stopped. As mysteriously as we began, we just stopped. I often wonder what ever happened to that stuff I saved, that scrapbook. My mother must have just ditched it. One way or another, though, it disappeared from the face of this earth, and to me it was a reminder that things fall apart and that we're not always aware of what other people cherish. Like my ex-husband's baseball, which his mother gave away without thinking that this was something important and critical in his life.

So that was baseball. It was Ebbets Field and a Mickey Mantle scrapbook ... and those dinnertime conversations. In those I was an observer rather than a participant, because it was really hard-nosed competition about facts and figures and recollections and memories, things I didn't want to have anything to do with. It wasn't important to me to know who had the best ERA or the best batting average that year or who had done what. I stored only enough of that kind of information to allow me to stay at the edges of the conversation. As I do now because I know my son is terribly, terribly interested in baseball.* It was a matter of maintaining connections, being part of the family or the group. I knew just enough to give me another thing to talk about with my father, a subject that was neutral territory and therefore safe. As a way of avoiding charged issues, baseball was an ideal subject. And since it was a consuming passion of his I felt I was showing interest in him by being interested in something he was interested in.

Perhaps it's not too much to say baseball was my way of trying to enter a very closed world I was very anxious to get into. He was not a particularly fatherly father, certainly not a mothering father, and this may have been my way of saying, "Hey, listen to me; I can talk your language." I don't know. I don't think I'm doing the same thing with my son. I guess it is very similar, but with him I'm not trying to earn points. I'm just showing that I respect his interest in this game and that I'd like to share it with him.

What was nice about those scrapbooks was that it was a communal activity, not a competitive one. I shared the experience of being a member of a fan club with two other friends, who were good friends at the time, growing up. I think it was easier that we idolized different players, because that way we weren't competing against each other. We each had our own little territory. We could each do our own thing, and sometimes we would do these things together. Like the cards we sent to Mantle and Hodges, or the letters we sometimes wrote them—we'd write them together. And standing over at that gas station waiting for the balls to come out—that was another communal activity, done with people you knew or got to know.

*Her son is Chris H., whose interview appears on pp. 200–203.

So baseball was basically a social activity, something to do with other people. And for the people living in Brooklyn in those days, the Dodgers were a very, very powerful cultural event, or rather a deep and binding presence. You didn't have to think about them; they were just there. They were a given, part of the landscape. The sun would be there in the morning and so would the Brooklyn Dodgers. You never questioned it. You never doubted it. You never asked about it. And they were *our* Brooklyn, the Brooklyn that mattered most. There was a Brooklyn Botanical Gardens, and there was a Brooklyn Academy of Music and a few other little Brooklyny things. But basically Brooklyn was the Dodgers. The Dodgers were Brooklyn, part and parcel of it, a cultural icon.

The Dodgers kept us together. They were a unifying force, a very democratizing force, because it didn't matter how old you were, how young you were, or what your color was—at least not if you were a fan. The Dodgers were ours, and they made us different from those "other people" in Manhattan and certainly from anybody in Queens. In those days, in the '40s and '50s, the Manhattaners were the sophisticated, rich people. That's how I always thought of Manhattan. You went "into the city" to do the grown-up things. You got dressed, you went to the theater, you went out for dinner. The upwardly mobile activities were associated with Manhattan, and we rarely went there. All these people I've been talking about—we hung out in Brooklyn; we were very definitely Brooklyn hangers-outerers. Queens was sort of the suburbs, the sticks. Staten Island didn't exist, practically, for anybody. And the Bronx was the poor man's equivalent to Brooklyn. We had everybody typecast. As a kid, I don't think I ever went into the Bronx, not once.

Mainly I stayed in Brooklyn, which means the Dodgers were all around me all the time. They were one of several Brooklyn institutions, basically, but they were the one that tied you to other Brooklynites. "Oh, you're a Brooklyn Dodger fan," someone would say, and you'd pick it up from there. It wasn't the same at a concert at the Brooklyn Academy of Music. You know: "Hey, you're a Brooklyn Academy of Music fan." It doesn't have the same ring to it, and of course it was a much narrower community. Everybody was a Dodger fan. There wasn't anything special about being a fan. You'd have been puzzled by somebody who said, "No, I am not a Brooklyn Dodger fan," and I don't remember anybody ever saying that. It was just assumed. The Dodgers are there, the Dodgers are in Brooklyn, and you lived in Brooklyn: Therefore, we're all Dodger fans. It was a closed circle, a perfect syllogism.

So on every level, from friends and family to the entire borough, baseball was a shared activity, a relationship thing. There's probably a woman's issue hidden in here. For me, baseball was a person thing, my way of making contact with other people who were important to me: my father and my son and my friends. It was a matter of relationships rather than competition, though I wouldn't be surprised to learn that in many ways men are doing the same thing, even if they're not always aware of it. Particularly with baseball, which is a team sport rather than an individual sport. Baseball enforces certain relationships between people in a whole variety of ways. My ex-husband wouldn't miss his pickup baseball games in the park, every weekend. They were critical to him, and he made a lot of acquaintances, if not quite friends, among the people he played with. They were probably also into one-upsmanship—who could hit harder and run faster—but at the same time they were establishing certain networks among themselves, though it may not have been as obvious or important to them as it is to girls or women who are doing the same thing. As fans, men seem to be much more statistically oriented. They want to know everything they can find in that book by Bill James, or whatever his name is. And for my ex-husband the conversations about baseball that he would have at the table were a kind of one-upsmanship contest with my son, a game of who knows more? who remembers more? I would absent myself from that little encounter. I have no memory for these things. I didn't know who had more RBI's than who, and if I did get involved, it was only as a way of saying, "Hey, pay attention to me. I know this stuff; I'm here."

Competition on the ball field may also create bonds between people. But I don't think bonds were being created when people talked statistics. It was very divisive and not the least bit integrating. It was a bond only in the superficial sense that it got two people talking to each other. Basically it was a competition rather than a relationship or a dialogue: Who's gonna win? Who's gonna remember the most? To me, that's not what baseball was all about, and it's not what life is all about. To me, what mattered—and what still matters—is your relationships with other people. Being together. Baseball did that for me. It brought me closer to people I wanted to be close to.

At Home in Yankee Stadium

Pat J. Born 1952. Project leader for computer programming department. Raised in Long Island, New York. New York Yankees. Sue J. Born 1958. Medical office manager. Raised in Long Island, New York. New York Yankees.

Sue: My first memories of baseball are from playing it in elementary school. I was a jock and all my friends were jocks. I vividly remember collecting baseball cards. My best friend and I had these big stacks of cards, but eventually he won all of them from me. It didn't do him much good, though, because his mother threw them all out when he was in college. Too bad. I think he had a Mickey Mantle rookie card.

When we were kids, our father always watched the Dodgers on television. He also watched the Yankee games, but only to root for whoever was playing against them. Maybe that's why we became Yankee fans. Since our father was so against them, maybe we felt they needed someone to root for them. I have a brother who is much older than I, and though he would come home infrequently, he would occasionally take us to baseball games. Even though it was the Mets games he took us to, it was still exciting for us. Anything he wanted to do I wanted to do. I just wanted to be with him, and if he said a baseball game, then a baseball game became very exciting. Years later we decided to have a surprise birthday party for my stepfather, and we took him to Yankee Stadium. I'd say it was around 1980—September, 1980—and it was the first time any of us had ever been there. The feeling I had the first time I saw the grass is a feeling I could never describe. All of a sudden I realized I was in the house that Ruth built, and it was overwhelming, it was incredible. I get that feeling to a lesser degree the first time I go every season and see the greenness of the grass. It's just wonderful, so beautiful, and something that just doesn't come across when you're watching a game on television.

Pat: Yankee Stadium is the most beautifully kept park in major league baseball. You feel the history around you when you walk in there. You walk through that tunnel, and suddenly the entire stadium opens up in front of you. It takes your breath away. I love taking people there for the first time and watching their faces when they see it. When the stadium opens up to them in that way, it just fills your heart. It's wonderful.

Sue: We went to the World Series there. There's nothing like going to the World Series. You know the entire world is watching and that you're part of history. I suppose it's the same if you go to the Super Bowl, but this was the Yankees, and that they were in the Series was just the coolest thing in the world. They were playing the Dodgers, who we hate, and Reggie Jackson was there. I'm a big fan of Reggie's. I don't know why. Yes I do. It's the excitement of knowing that every time he steps up to the plate the ball can go anywhere. He could just as easily strike out, and if it was an inside pitch he could do a real dive as though he was gonna get hit. But you always knew there was the chance of that home run. Anybody that can get up three times in a row in the World Series and hit home runs is incredible, and that's what the Yankees are. The Yankees are different from any other team. The Dodgers could have kept that special quality, that distinctness, if they hadn't left New York. Now only the Yankees have it.

Pat: The Yankees are the definition of what it means to be in the major leagues. When anybody talks about getting into the majors they talk about playing in Yankee Stadium. Whenever new players sign up with the Yankees they say that since they were a kid they always dreamed of wearing the pinstripes. I guess I kind of do, too. By going to so many games—we've been going for thirteen years now, on a very regular basis—we kind of feel we've earned our own pinstripes. We feel like we're part of the team.

People at the stadium make you feel that way, too. You probably get that with other teams as well, but getting it with the Yankees—that's what makes you a real fan. You feel you're part of their life at the stadium and part of that long illustrious history. It's funny because even though the stadium has been rebuilt it still echoes with that history. We went to see a Billy Joel concert there a while back, and he felt it, too. He spoke about how amazing it was to sing in Yankee Stadium, and you know, we all feel the same way about just being there. We had tickets on the field, right on the field. And we walk out on that field and the grass is right under our feet and we're going "Wow, this is where Willie [Randolph] stood all those years," and "Hey, Don [Mattingly] was right over here the other night." It was amazing.

In seventeen days, pitchers and catchers will report for spring training. It's like our lives begin again in two weeks because baseball is coming back. It's like Susan Sarandon said in *Bull Durham*: "The cathedral of baseball." And because we go so often it feels like home. We're so familiar with it we can find our seats in any part of the stadium. We always help people find their seats; we could charge for it. We're almost on a first name basis with the ticket-takers in the garage. When we see them it's "Hi, how are you doing?" The atmosphere is wonderful. Once, after a fire in my home, I was forced to move, and I lived in three different places in four months. When I walked into the stadium for the first game of the season it felt great, it felt comfortable. I felt like I was home. I'm somewhere I belong again.

It's so exciting when Mel Hall hits those home runs in the bottom of the ninth to win a game. There's nothing better. It just fills you up; it sends a charge through your system. And since we know the chants so well, we always know what to sing when certain music is played. We know and everybody knows, and we're all shouting together. When you go like we do, on the plans, you know the people that sit around you. You meet these people you'd never meet under any other circumstances, and you look forward to seeing them again.

Sue: I feel safe in Yankee Stadium. A lot of people ask me, how can you go to the Bronx? I would go there by myself before I'd go to Shea any day. I would go myself, no doubt about it, because I know those people; they're somehow like a family and I feel safe there. The stadium is home to me, and it has a kind of sacred quality, like a church or synagogue. I feel that way in synagogue. I'm Jewish because I converted, and I do feel at home when I'm in synagogue, just as I feel there's something kind of sacred about Yankee Stadium, though of course it's a different kind of sacredness.

Pat: This is our home away from home. We go to about thirty games a year, and we love it. We look forward to it, we plan our year around it. If we want to go somewhere else, we have to check: "Oh, do we have a game?" Because if we do we can't go anywhere else. It's a priority in our lives ever since we became fans and began going to the games. From the minute we walked into the stadium in 1980 we were hooked, and it's for life. We know it's for life, because every year it's as strong if not stronger than the season before. It's almost a need to go to a game. We *have* to go to the stadium. We need baseball. We jokingly call it a kind of fix, and it is. It's an addiction. It satisfies something deep in our souls and I see it in a lot of other people, too, so I know we're not unique in that respect.

Sue: Our love for the Yankees and the stadium is beyond explanation. It's an intangible thing. Feelings are hard to explain sometimes. I think that one of the reasons I feel so strongly about going there is that it's something I have with my sister; the time is spent together. My husband hates baseball. He won't even let me watch it on TV, so if I'm not at a Yankee game I don't even know what's going on. Sometimes I get to the stadium after I haven't been there for a while, and if there's a new player on the team I don't even know who he is. So for me going to the game is the only contact I can have with baseball, and it's also part of this bond I have with my sister.

Pat: Many people don't have any kind of a bond with a sibling, but ours is strong, and I just love it. When we were young the 6-year age difference was hard to overcome. But as adults we found we had a lot in common, and that was very important to my whole family. We're all very close, and we work hard at maintaining the relationship. I think it's kind of like that with baseball. You have to make an effort. You have to get up and go to the stadium if you want to maintain the relationship. When you enjoy it and it gives you this satisfaction, it's not a hardship. Sometimes it's completely spontaneous. We just hop into the car an hour before game time, hoping we can get tickets. If we get them, great. If not, oh well. But we have to try because we feel the need to be outdoors, eating hot dogs, listening to the crack of the bat.

Sue: Family is very important to us. We make sure to stay in touch. I talk to my sister three or four times a week. Both my brothers have moved south. One is in Atlanta and one is in Austin, Texas, but we make sure to see them at least once a year. We talk on a regular basis and keep up with their lives, our nephews' lives, because we want to be a part of them. We don't want to see a distance grow between us that we can never close again. We have too many friends whose families have no relationship with each other except a blood connection. You wouldn't know they were related; they don't even like each other. We adore each other, and it's wonderful. We enjoy spending time together, and it makes for a happy life. As it happens, every one of us is a baseball fan. Maybe not to the extent that we are, but it's part of the bond.

Sports and making connections go together for me. I can remember being in sixth grade and reading baseball biographies so that I could get the attention of a boy I liked, and I remember also sitting down and learning the rules of football just so that I'd have something to talk to my father about. Baseball gives people at least one thing they can talk about, and then from there find out they have other things in common. That's why baseball is great. You can talk to anybody about baseball, anybody. Even if they say they don't really follow it, they know the names, they know something about it. Also, almost everybody can talk at least a little about baseball because almost everybody can find a way to relate to it. You can enjoy baseball on a lot of different levels. You can enjoy just watching them play and appreciating the skill and the abilities of the players.

Or you can get into it and say, "Okay now, I bet he's gonna put a hit and run on here" or "watch the second baseman, watch his moves here." So there are different plateaux to the game, and you can enjoy it on any level. You don't have to be an expert to enjoy the game. You can appreciate it without understanding the intricacies of it. That helps to bring fans into it; you learn it as you go along, and the more games you watch the more you learn. A lot of it you absorb without realizing it. All of a sudden you're talking about these different plays and you go "Wow, how did I learn that?" It's just from the exposure.

Pat: Some people are bored by baseball. Sometimes nothing happens for twenty minutes, and you can knit a sweater during a game. But when you're there everything is happening. You're seeing what's happening on the field: the players moving in or to one side when a new batter comes up. The outfielders come in, they move out, the infielders shift. You're seeing all of that happening while you're there, and you feel like you're a part of it. When you're at the game you have more information about what's happening on the field than you get from a camera that shows the batter standing there waiting for the pitcher to come to the mound. Suppose the manager goes out to argue with the umpire. On TV they'll cut to a commercial, but at the stadium we're watching, stomping up and down, kicking and spitting bullets at this umpire. We're going crazy, while at home the announcers just come back and say, "Oh they had an argument, but it's over." You get a lot more out of it when you're there and can see all these things happening.

Sue: Baseball is a game to be a part of. Something that distinguishes baseball from other sports is that it's a sport you can look at and say, "Well, I can do that." Not at that major league level, of course, but it's a game almost anybody can play with at least some competence. Not everybody can play basketball. Not everybody can play football; somebody our size can't go tackle a Lawrence Taylor. But in baseball there's an element of "Yeah, I could do that." I could get up there and I could swing the bat and throw the ball, and I can have fun with it. Knowing that builds an appreciation in the people who do it.

Pat: Every way I look at it baseball is about being a part of something and being together. The game really fosters that feeling. I love watching little ones at the stadium. Their eyes light up when a ball comes within five sections of them. One kid that sits behind us on Sundays comes with his family very early. They watch batting practice, and every week he gets another autograph. I just hope he doesn't become jaded and nonchalant about it, and I hope he never loses that little sparkle he's got. "Wow, I've got Jessie's autograph!" We yell out to the players as they're coming out between innings. One time we were sitting in the front row, about section 23, and Jessie Barfield walked by. About five of us yelled out, "We love you, Jessie," and he turned around and smiled at us. And when he went back at the end of that inning he walked right past us and waved again.

So you actually have an interaction with the players. The fact that the stands are so close to the field makes you feel like you're really right there. With football it seems like you're much farther away.

To me it's all one big family. I got to meet Katie Connor last year, Mark Connor's wife,* and I listened to a couple of the wives talking about the food drives and all the fund-raising they do. During an interview last year, Jessie's wife said, "Well, when I played in Toronto...." I don't know who the announcer was, but he did a double-take. "When *you* played?" he asks. And she says, "Oh well, Jessie was playing, but I was there too." So you see, they feel like they're actually on the team, in the pin-stripes too, and that conributes to that same family feeling. It's obvious the wives get along with one another and spend time together. And when a new wife comes to town it seems they try to help her learn the ropes of this stadium and this town.

I'm sure it's like that on all the teams, and it's wonderful. But there is something special about the Yankees. They have a magic, just because they're the Yankees. The history behind them is awesome; it's never gonna be matched. You go through that monument park and wow, these guys were really something. I wish I could have seen Mickey play. I love old timer's day. I love seeing these guys come out in those old uniforms. I think it's a family thing among the players and between the players. But the fan is in danger because of the money involved. It has become too much of a money-making thing. I can't blame them for asking for four million dollars. If the owners are making money and these guys are putting people in the stands, they deserve to make the money. Whatever somebody is willing to pay, that's what you're worth. But these salaries separate them from the fans. When somebody goes into a slump now, the fans are likely to yell out, "Hey, we're paying you four million dollars a year, you better hit that ball, that was a ten thousand dollar strike out." I don't think it will ever split the fans from the players completely, but it's a growing schism, and sometimes I feel it myself. What's more, those large salaries drive the ticket prices up. It's like forty-five dollars to go to a Knicks game, and I'm afraid the Yankees are going to have to raise the prices beyond what a family can afford to spend on a Sunday at the park. That would be a tragedy. Right now it's thirty bucks, and that's an awful lot of money. For a family of four it's a hundred and twenty bucks.

Sue: Part of this family feeling is identification with the city, with New York. We trashed the Mets a lot, but when it comes to the Mets and other teams you have to stand by New York. I have strong feelings about New York. I don't ever want to live anywhere else. I have friends and family who have moved to lots of places, and that's fine for them. But I really love New York. I think it's the center of the universe. It has everything. We live in the suburbs, but we're close enough so that we can come in here any time we want and take advantage of all it has to offer. I think people who live in other areas, where they don't have the availability of the shows and the art, they're really missing something.

*Mark Connor was a Yankee pitching coach and bullpen coach in the late '80s and early '90s.

I feel a sadness for them. Face it, we're spoiled. We have two baseball teams, we have football teams, we have hockey, we've got basketball, we have it all.

Pat: Let's put it this way: The Yankees are the center of baseball, Yankee Stadium is the center of New York, and New York is the center of the universe, Absolutely. Yankee Stadium is the epicenter of civilization, and yet when you go there you're right at home. It's the center of the universe, but it's also comfortable. When you go often enough and you know your way around, it *is* home. You know how to get to your seats as easily as you know how to get to your sofa. It just kind of wraps itself around you like a security blanket.

Sue: There's also something very American about baseball. Nobody plays it the way America does. It's called America's pastime, but I'm not so sure of that. Americans go to car races as much or more as to baseball games. But baseball has been around for so long. The long, long history of the game gives it a special place in the life of the country. Baseball has probably touched every American's life in one way or another, and as we said before, there are so many different levels to it that everybody can relate to it in some way. It's interesting to watch a parent teach a child the game. "This is why he's gonna sacrifice," or "this is why he's gonna hit away." But you don't have to know that to be able to watch the game and enjoy it. It's part of what keeps America together.

Pat: When Nolan Ryan won his 300th game, we were at the stadium and we were watching the out-of-town scoreboard to see how he was doing. He's still in, it's the eighth inning, and you find yourself rooting for him. Since you know thousands of other fans are doing the same thing at ball parks all over the country, you feel a connection to all of them.

Sue: Or let's suppose you've got bases loaded with Reggie Jackson coming up. The excitement level that comes when the bases are loaded and somebody who has the potential to hit a grand slam comes to bat—oh boy, you can feel it. It's like everybody's sticking his finger in one huge socket. Really. Everybody's thinking, "Oh my god, we're gonna see a grand slam!" And then there's an enormous letdown when he strikes out, and you hear this deflated nooooooo, like air coming out of a giant balloon. Everybody there feels the same way.

Pat: Somebody once asked me if I could imagine life without baseball. The answer is no. Plain and simple, no. I would have to find baseball somehow. Even if it was just playing tapes of games or whatever I could get my hands on. I can't imagine life without baseball. If it disappeared I'd look hard for something to take its place, but I don't know if I'd ever find it. It would leave a terrible void in my life. If we lost baseball or if we never ever had it, we'd have to look for something else, something to connect us and to connect other people. But I don't think anything would do it in the same way. It's a wonderful game.

VI. A Sense of Belonging

"The Tie That Binds"

Sanford S. Born 1946. Museum curator. Raised in Pittsburgh, Pennsylvania. Pittsburgh Pirates.

My first recollection of baseball goes back so far that I can't really pinpoint it. I can remember from a very young age, maybe around 5 or even earlier, having a baseball uniform, a baseball, and a toy baseball mitt. The first important memory goes back to when I was about 6 years old. At the time, I was still playing with all the girls on the street. Where I grew up there were only girls my age to play with, but I always looked up to my big brother, who was five years older, dying to be taken wherever he was going and to play baseball with him and his friends. One day, when I was 6 years old, my brother came home talking excitedly about some other kid my age who was a terrific baseball player. That was an emotional blow to me. I wanted to be out there playing baseball with my brother, so the thought that there was another 6-year-old who could play baseball and who was worthy of a privilege I was unworthy of was hard to accept. It was perhaps the first clue that there were things I was going to be permanently excluded from in life. I was the youngest person in my family, and I was never interested in being a kid. I wanted to be grown up and to do grown-up things. My brother always seemed to be doing these great things, and I could never come along with him. He didn't want his 5- or 6-year old brother tagging along. So I felt like an outsider. I felt excluded from all the really worthwhile and exciting things he and other older people were doing. I had this feeling that people—at least the people who mattered—didn't want to include me, and that turned out to be a psychological issue I'd have to deal with all my life. I'm still struggling with it today.

I'm very sensitive about this. If something is going on among people who are close to me and I'm not invited, I feel pretty bad. Sometimes I need to be more than just invited. I need to be convinced I'm really wanted. I'm too quick to take offense, too ready to conclude that people don't want me, that they're trying to exclude me. So baseball first became important to me as the earliest hard proof of that exclusion, my first memory of that special sensitivity.

For the rest of my childhood, though, it was mainly a source of inclusion, a way of belonging. I can remember listening to the Pirates games on the radio and wanting to be involved in baseball. I guess being involved in baseball was like being O.K. In Pittsburgh everybody was a baseball fan, so my first contact with Major League Baseball was trying to understand it in order to be part of that experience. As a family we went to a lot of games. My uncles owned workingmen's clothing stores. They drove Cadillacs and dressed in fancy clothes, and the business had box seats in Forbes Field, behind third base. I felt very good there. I have very fond memories of Forbes Field. These were our seats, and I guess in some ways I felt possessive of them. We knew the ushers, we knew the people in the seats around us, and I felt at home. That section of Forbes Field was a part of home. It belonged to our family. In general, as I said, I always felt like an outsider, but when I went to those games I felt more like an insider. I felt more grown up going to baseball games, which of course is how I always wanted to feel.

I can remember one summer—I don't know how old I was, somewhere, I suppose, around the age of 7 or 8—a lot of people teaching me, explaining baseball to me. Learning about baseball was an important part of growing up, of becoming the adult or older child I was so desperate to be. It's not an initiation, exactly; it's part of life. Understanding baseball was like being toilet trained or like learning how to read. It wasn't to be initiated into anything. It was just one of the things you learned and were expected to learn. It was one of the things you did in your struggle for maturity and acceptance, one of the skills you had to have if you were to live in that society. You could not function in the society I grew up in without knowing baseball. It was a form of literacy, so if you didn't understand baseball you were illiterate.

Baseball was the national pastime, and it was certainly the Pittsburgh pastime, the one pastime everybody could participate in. On my street on summer nights you'd go out on your porch and you'd hear the game coming from everywhere. Everybody was sitting on their porch listening to the Pirates game, and it felt good to be a part of that. In my generation everybody felt very close to the Pirates. The team members were like parts of your family. Robert O. Clemente was a part of our family. I remember the day Clemente died. It was on New Years Day, though I can't remember what year it was [1973]. I hadn't heard it on the news when I came home. I walked into my parents' bedroom and saw my mother, sitting on the bed, crying. And it didn't seem strange. It didn't seem excessive.

My parents now live in Florida, and while I was down there visiting them for the holiday, we went to see this new Robert De Niro movie, *A Bronx Story*. One segment takes place in 1960, and at one point this little kid, a great Yankee and Mickey Mantle fan, is telling this Mafia guy how much he hates Bill Mazeroski. My mother, who had just had a stroke and who was watching the movie from her wheel chair, was profoundly moved. She's lost a lot of her faculties—there are many things she can no longer do—but Bill Mazeroski still touched her heart! Everybody remembers Bill Mazeroski hitting that home run to win the 1960 Series, so when this kid mentions Mazeroski's name, my mother lights up. She's just glowing with pride and pleasure, remembering his great moment as though he were one of her children.

These people were like members of the family, and I think some baseball players seemed even closer than that. You listened to these people. You followed them. You rooted for them one summer after another, and you became very attached to them. For much of my childhood my grandmother, who had moved to Florida, would come and stay with us every summer. She was an avid baseball fan and a very nervous woman. Every night she would listen to the games on the radio, or watch them if they were on television. My family had these box seat tickets, but she would never go to a baseball game. Why? Because she was so nervous! She would get so excited over the Pirates that she was afraid it would be just too much for her. She was afraid she'd have a heart attack or a stroke or something.

I can remember plenty of summer nights, sitting on the porch with my grandmother. Sometimes my parents were there, sometimes my brother. But often it was just my grandmother and me. In those days everybody had awnings on their porches. But on nights like these we'd pull them up, and you could see your neighbors on their porches listening to baseball. We'd have fruit out. We'd be eating fruit and drinking cold drinks. We had porch furniture, tan porch furniture with cushions on them, decorated with big palms and things like that. And we had these tan lamps with yellow lights. Everybody had them. Up and down the street, on every porch, those small lamps with yellow lights, and the voice of Bob Prince echoing everywhere. You could walk from one end of the street to the other and never miss a pitch. In some ways those memories of listening to baseball on the radio are much more powerful than the memories of watching the games on television. There was this atmosphere, this mysterious aura, sitting there in the dark, the whole street listening together, the yellow lights. And I remember one summer night, sitting there and listening when the lights went out in Forbes Field. We're sitting there listening to Bob Prince describe the scene, telling how the players went out on the unlit field and played what he called gaslight ball, a make-believe game without a ball in the dark of Forbes Field. We wouldn't think of turning off the radio. The lights had gone off in Forbes Field, but we're still sitting there listening, taking in this description of a make-believe game and loving every minute of it.

They were ours, you know; they were our Pirates, as our cousins were our cousins and our uncles were our uncles, though it's not the same since they tore down Forbes Field. When they started making these super stadiums the game really changed. It lost a lot of its personality. It became impersonal, too impersonal. Back then, though, they were family, but at the same time I'm not sure I thought of them as mere people. It was hard for me to think of them as people. They were like gods. Wearing a baseball uniform made them superhuman to me. Superman wore his uniform, and Mazeroski and Clemente wore theirs, and there wasn't all that much difference. I would watch them closely. I'd watch their every move, and I would mimic everything they did, every little gesture. I saw them as the equivalent of Greek gods. Yet at the same time they were like members of the family, and somehow, though it doesn't seem to, that makes sense. People have an intimate association with their gods, you know, and to turn it around, some members of your family may seem like gods. I certainly looked up to my brother when I was a child. I don't know if I'd put him in the same category as Robert O. Clemente, but he didn't seem like an ordinary mortal, either.

The players were examples for us, models of behavior for us to imitate. They were clean-cut Americans. There was never any kind of a scandal around them. Back in those days baseball represented everything clean and good in America. And since they were athletes we thought they were especially clean. We thought they went to bed early, didn't drink and didn't fool around. They were clean livers, clean and pure as America itself.

My love of baseball is tied into my love for Broadway musicals, like *Singin' in the Rain*. I thought that was what life was supposed to be. I thought it was supposed to be like one of those musicals with Gene Kelly and Donald O'Connor and Debbie Reynolds. But it wasn't turning out like that. I kept waiting for life to turn into a musical, a kind of *Oklahoma!* where everybody dresses well and knows how to tap dance, where the men know how to sing a love song to the women, and where there's always a happy ending and everybody falls in love. I thought this was what life was supposed to be, and I ended up becoming an incurable romantic. I have a very romantic view of life, and when I was young baseball was a part of it, another romantic world I wanted to belong to. One of the things I was struggling with at the time was my own physicality, being such a poor athlete. I wasn't an athlete. That kid my brother praised as a great ball player when I was 6 years old, his name was Ricky Sloan, and once, when I was pitching to him, he hit a line drive right back at me, right into my face. I don't think I ever admitted this to anyone, but ever since then I was really afraid of a baseball. I would go out every year for Little League because I thought it was cool to walk around with the uniform, but I knew I'd never make it past the first cut because I was afraid of the ball and wouldn't go after it, couldn't charge it or anything like that. It's funny; I was playing baseball and I was going to the games, but I was never really athletic, and you know, it's difficult for a kid not to be a good athlete. I wasn't turning into Gene Kelly or Roberto Clemente, and I had a hard time dealing with that. It was only when I got older and started looking more deeply into my life and looking back that I realized where I got my idea of what life was supposed to be like—from Broadway musicals, from Rodgers and Hart. And my problem was that I wasn't walking down the street, in the rain, singing. If anything went wrong, if people didn't like me, if I was rejected, or if I wasn't an athlete and couldn't make the team, I felt something had gone wrong and I thought I was not O.K.

So baseball was part of the beautiful romantic world I was excluded from, but only as a player. As a fan, as I said, it gave me a warm and wonderful sense of belonging and acceptance. And being a fan also taught me things that helped me deal with my own limitations and rejections. There's a darker side to baseball, a kind of rough, gritty, tragic side that's very different from its image as the clean and wholesome American pastime. There's tragedy in baseball. There are those days when you get rained out, and there are long stretches when you lose again and again and again. I used to like that poem, "Casey at the Bat," where the hero lets down his teammates and breaks the hearts of his fans. We all saw the movie about Lou Gehrig. We know about players being sent down to the minors, others coming up and not making it, career-ending injuries, and terrible strikeouts at crucial moments. No, baseball definitely has a sad human aspect worlds away from Hollywood and Broadway. I saw that movie, *Field of Dreams*. It was too romantic, and though it appealed to the romantic side of me, it wasn't convincing. Baseball was more complex than that, and one of the things it did for me was temper my idealism. Baseball gave me an opportunity to understand what life was really like. I saw the tragedy in baseball, and I knew it wasn't perfect. Yet it was something you loved, something everybody loved and that deserved to be loved. Maybe the same could be said for me.

Where I grew up in Pittsburgh, clothes were very important. How you dressed was very important. Today it's called "preppy," but we called it Ivy League then, and if you were in the mainstream you dressed Ivy League, you belonged to a country club and you rode around in a convertible. It seemed like everyone I knew had more money than we did, and I grew up wishing for more. So lots of things seemed out of reach. But not baseball. Baseball was within reach, and it was part of a world I wanted to belong to. Back in those days it didn't take any money to be a baseball fan. Anybody could tune in, and when you did you joined all the others who were tuning in, all those neighbors sitting on their porches, lit up by those yellow lights and serenaded by the voice of Bob Prince. That was a world I could be a part of.

If you ask what baseball meant to me as a child, what comes to mind is that it was the tie that binds. It was part of the fiber of life. It was summertime—baseball is inseparable from summertime—and it bound all of us together. My family, everybody on the street, our neighborhood, the entire city—we were all bound together by baseball.

Pittsburghers are very proud. They have very strong feelings about being Pittsburghers and about everything connected with Pittsburgh—like certain celebrities who come from Pittsburgh, like Rolling Rock Beer, Duquesne Beer, and of course the Pirates. The Pirates played a big role in bringing Pittsburghers together and giving them pride in their city. Pittsburghers have a common identity through shared memories, and the Pirates are among the richest, the deepest and the most emotional of those memories. That was baseball in Pittsburgh back in those days: it was something everybody shared. It was a grown-up world—not perfect, but still pretty beautiful, where I felt at home.

Paradise, the Bronx

Bennett K. Born 1950. University instructor in English Literature. Raised in the Bronx, New York. New York Yankees.

I first remember baseball as a good way to stay up at night, under the covers. Baseball itself wasn't the most important thing; rather it was a way not to go to sleep and not have anyone know what I was doing. I was 9 or 10 years old, and I loved listening to baseball under the covers. It was great; it was security, a security blanket, and it included a magic world created by people like Mel Allen and Red Barber who really didn't need a game at all. I remember seeing a television program about Red Barber where, in his earliest days, he would do the game off a ticker tape and make the sound of the crack of the bat by clicking his tongue against his teeth. He was so good at it you never knew he wasn't describing a game he saw in front of him.

He and Mel Allen created a very magic, special world. Their job was to make you feel as if you were there, and they did it perfectly. It's dark in your room; you're young; you're about to fall asleep; and in that twilight state between sleep and waking you get there. You get to that world. It was as if you could see it. They weren't like the announcers are today, killing you with endless statistics; you know: How many times does a guy get a hit after he ties his shoelaces with his left hand? They were much more interested in the drama, especially the eternal conflict between the batter and the pitcher, and they made that drama come alive. That was wonderful, and then, when the ball was hit you had the noise of the crowd. You had their excitement. Why would anyone be disappointed about not seeing a home run if Mel Allen is announcing it? "That ball is going! It's going! It is *gone!*" Kids in the street would do that. You'd hear it all over the place, and you could see the ball in your imagination, sailing over the fence.

Listening to those games I was transported to another world, another life, you might say, where things were not symmetrical but where they were perfect all the same. Baseball is not a symmetrical game, but it's a perfect game. You understand exactly what has to be done in order for justice to triumph and the Yankees to win. There's no ambiguity or uncertainty. The asymmetry in baseball doesn't disturb that. The ball fields are different—different shapes and sizes, different distances you need to hit the ball to hit a home run, and different substances and textures: hard field, soft field, high grass, low grass, when there was grass. That's O.K. That's part of it. What matters is, the game ends after nine innings or after eight-and-a-half if the home team wins, and the path to victory is clear. All you need is one more run than the other team has. There's nowhere to hide, no room for excuses. The ball is right in front of you, coming at you. If you didn't hit it there's nothing you can say. You can't say you were fouled.

I liked this clarity, this lack of ambiguity. I liked knowing exactly what has to be done for justice to triumph, and I knew that this was one place where it did triumph. As soon as they brought my sister home it was clear there was no justice in the world. I would squeeze her head and say, "Ooo! it's just like an orange!" but they attacked me. They said I couldn't do that, so there was no justice in my house, absolutely none. And baseball was a way of setting things straight. It was the world where there were no sisters to deal with. My grandmother also lived with us. There was no chance that Mel Allen or Red Barber would ask me if I wanted a sandwich while I was eating. And if they had been around I'm sure they would have let me boil water by myself. Not at that age, maybe, but at 17 or 18 they'd have let me. The world was too much for me, and baseball was the great escape. It was the place to go.

I guess I was living a late twentieth-century version of the Romantic attitude towards nature. I didn't think about all these things as a kid. I'm just speaking instinctively, probably influenced by some Romantic poetry I've been teaching. For the Romantics, nature was the great solace and retreat from a world they found intolerable, and baseball is a wonderful mid-twentieth-century substitute for nature. Since the Romantic period we haven't been able to see nature as some sort of salvation. You might go on vacation; you might go to the mountains or walk through a forest for a while; but it won't save you. But I think going to a ball game or watching it or listening to it on the radio can give you that feeling of a vacation in nature. And since it's an experience you can have day after day for seven months out of every year, it *can* save you. Two years ago I went to a game at Fenway Park in Boston, and because it still has grass and the old wooden walls and seems to be sagging a little, to this New Yorker it felt like nature. I don't know. Maybe there's something Jeffersonian about it, a return to an agrarian ideal where everyone has a chance to achieve the American Dream, where everyone gets a piece of land. At a ball game we all get to share this piece of land for two-and-a-half, three hours.

And we're united. We're sharing a common experience. People who support the same team usually sit together at the ball park. There may be one or two idiots who don't understand who they're supposed to root for, but basically we're in agreement, we share all this together, and before long you start talking to people. Probably no one talks to anyone else in Yankee Stadium these days. They might be afraid to. You never know when you might be talking to the Son of Sam. But in Fenway they still talk to one another; complete strangers talk to each other about the old days of Williams and Vern Stephens, about Carl Yastrzemski, about what's gone wrong with Clemens. I loved that kind of buzzy friendliness. It's a return to community, to small town agrarian life where everybody knew everybody or felt friendly even towards people they didn't know.

Of course it only lasts for the duration of the game, but that's O.K. It's a really good feeling while it lasts, and it's a welcome refuge from big city life. I've got a cousin, a former police detective, who won't go to Yankee Stadium without a gun. He bribes the parking attendant so he can park in the lot closest to the stadium, even if it's full, because he knows it's dangerous if you have a long walk back to your car after a night game. The stadium itself is still beautiful, but it's hard to forget everything around it. And then there's Steinbrenner, who doesn't do much for the agrarian spirit. So in New York baseball is no longer an escape from the urban plague. Coming to the stadium you realize you're in Bosnia; you're in a war zone with burned down buildings. But it wasn't always that way. For me, baseball and the Yankees the way they used to be is the way the Bronx used to be. It's the very appealing world described in Doctorow's *World's Fair*.

I lived a few blocks away from Yankee Stadium. When there was no game I would go up to the 161st Street train station and peek in. I don't want to tell you where I was standing, but there was a way to lean in and actually see a little bit of the stadium from there, and it was great to be able to do that. When I think of those days I think of the Grand Concourse, which was truly grand.

I just lost my last Bronx relatives—cousins and aunts. They're no longer alive, so I no longer know anyone in the Bronx, and my entire neighborhood is gone. It's almost as though the Bronx is just as lost as the Yankees are.* We left the Bronx when I was about 12, so remaining a Yankee fan after that was a way to keep that neighborhood, that closeness, those great old feelings alive.

In that little world in the Bronx everybody knew everybody else. Even if people weren't your relatives they were your relatives. Everyone was another cousin, another uncle, another aunt. It was a big family with a wonderful community spirit. On holidays there might be 50 people gathered at my grandmother's house, and the Yankees were part of it; they were right there in the community. My father remembers that in the offseason he would buy his clothes from Tony Lazzeri, who was working in a clothing shop nearby because he didn't make enough money as a ball player to support his family. Even in my day a lot of the players were still living and working in the Bronx, and the team was the team of the Bronx. It was the real thing. I don't think you could call the Yankees a team of the Bronx today. They don't even want to be in the Bronx.

Perhaps it's just nostalgic foolishness, but it seemed that they cared about the community, too. Today the question is, "Where can I make more money?" "Where will you build me a nicer stadium?" No one thinks seriously about cleaning up the immediate area around the stadium. It's ugly. It's ugly. I love to go to Yankee games when I go back to New York, but it's certainly not the same feeling. It could never compete with that old feeling, not because of the quality of the players, but because that ideal is gone, that sense of community and togetherness are gone. My father is a very nostalgic person. To him nothing in the present can match the glory of yesteryear. There's no music after Benny Goodman. There's no baseball player after Joe DiMaggio, except maybe, maybe Mickey Mantle. Everything stopped then. I don't know about Goodman and DiMaggio; that's probably overstated. But that sense of the Bronx as a community everyone cared about, with the Yankees at the heart of it—that certainly stopped then, and I'd love to have it back.

To me baseball was an ideal world connected to an ideal or perhaps idealized community. Baseball was orderly and perfect; you knew the rules; you knew what it took to win; and it was a place where justice got done. And it was all set, like a perfectly cut diamond in a ring of community, friendship, and family. To me, it's a throwback to an earlier, simpler, more natural way of life.

I've got to make a distinction. I spoke earlier of baseball as a refuge from a difficult world, a place to escape from if you were looking for order and perfect justice. But that refuge was from my internal world and the chaos of my life at home, though the proportions weren't right. There was too much family and too little baseball. I'd have preferred it the other way around, where you lived in the ball park and could turn your family on on the radio, and then shut it off. My sense of the outside world at that time, of the Bronx and the larger

---

This conversation was held in 1994, before the Yankee resurgence.

family and community, was much more idyllic. So baseball played two roles. It was an escape from what I felt were the craziness and injustices of my life at home, and it was a representation of the purity of the life I saw around me, or thought I saw. I knew my home was flawed. I didn't understand that other people might be having the same problems.

At times, baseball could even bring the harmony of the outside world into my family and change it, at least briefly. It could be not just an escape, but a cure, even if it was only occasional and temporary. I remember going to a World Series game with my father, in 1964, against the Cardinals. I don't remember which game it was, but it was a game [four] the Yankees lost at the stadium, 4–3 on a Ken Boyer grand slam. It was horrible that they lost, but I wasn't overwhelmed by the loss because I was too overwhelmed by being there. If I think about it, the only thing I ever did with my father that you could call a bonding activity would be the five or six times we went to the stadium together. World Series, Yankees, Bronx, and my father—all of this together. It was paradise. It was great being there with my father. This was the one place where we had nothing to argue about. We're here united; we're here for a win; we're on the same side. For once in our lives we have the same goals, the same values. We wanted exactly the same thing to happen, and he showed me the mysteries of keeping score. I would never go to a game without keeping score. I don't understand now why I did that. It's kind of distracting, but it was an obsession. You have to keep score so that you can take the game home with you. You invite Red Barber back to the house, and you replay the entire game. Here's what every batter did and how they ran the bases. You have that record, that permanent record and all those strange signs. And in a way you've brought this sanctuary, that feeling of togetherness, into your home and preserved it a little longer. It was a wonderful feeling and a wonderful way to bond. Even if you have a great father-son relationship, baseball is still something special between you. I love going with my son, and it's important to both of us. First of all, I want him to like baseball. I'm still enough of a sucker for the game to want him to like baseball, however tainted it may have become. Also, because I have such emotional memories of bonding with my father through baseball, I wanted to do it with my son. And it's nice; it works.

So baseball for me was that kind of perfection, that kind of purity, and the player who most represented that ideal, unfortunately, was Mickey Mantle. He was my hero. He was perfect, though of course we know he wasn't. Far from it. Once, when I was 12 or 13 years old, I got my father to take me early to a game, about three or four hours early, so that aside from seeing batting practice I would be able to meet Mickey Mantle arriving at the ballpark and get his autograph. I think he came at around 10:30 or 11:00, probably after a long night of carousing, though at the time I knew nothing about that and would have refused to believe it. I still remember the cardigan sweater he was wearing. I started to run towards him, excited as I've ever been. But he waved his hand at me in a way that said, "Not now, kid, don't bother me," and I froze in my tracks. It was terrible. At first I was mad at myself, thinking maybe if I'd kept going, if I'd persisted, maybe he would have given me the autograph, because there was nobody else around, nobody, just me and Mickey Mantle. But I couldn't go all the way. I couldn't ignore the dismissal of my god, who just wasn't interested, and that was the beginning of the end. It was part of a rite of passage, a major disillusionment that seemed to mark a turning point in my life.

I couldn't look at baseball in the same way anymore. It had lost some of its purity, and it took with it part of the purity I had previously seen elsewhere. I began to understand that mythic heroes were also flawed people, and it's not good for a kid to know that. It may be educational but it's no fun You don't want your mythic heroes to be flawed. Superheroes are supposed to be perfect, and Mantle wasn't perfect anymore. Baseball wasn't perfect, and it was easy enough, as I looked past it, to understand that America wasn't perfect either—a revelation we'd all be forced to deal with not long after that.

Baseball, I think, represents a way for people to maintain a sense of the country's purity. If the game is pure, and if the people who play it are pure, then the country is pure. But of course no one feels that way anymore. Fans aren't dumb. They've seen all the damage caused by strikes; they've seen the greed; and they've learned to despise both sides equally. They're not interested in deciding who's the bigger pig. They understand that it's a double-edged sword, with a pig on each side, and because of the obscene amounts of money involved, sports simply can't play the purifying role we'd like it to play. Nobody pays Superman a salary, right? But what if he began to demand one. Imagine his contract. "I'd like 17 billion dollars for patrolling the world, and some tax shelters." It's not what you want to hear your superhero saying.

I loved the Yankees for all the reasons I've mentioned, but also for the same reason that everyone who wasn't a Yankee fan hated them: because they had this endless, endless tradition of perfection. The Yankees were something reliable, something you could depend on. Their winning year after year was a kind of reassurance. It was part of that perfect world I imagined all around me and longed for at home. It was a rational part of reality, something you could be fairly sure of. They would win, they would do well, and they would drive the people who hated them crazy, which was fine with me. Even after I lost my innocence to the wave of Mantle's hand the Yankees could still be trusted. They could be counted on to win; at least that. And then even that stopped, for a long, long time, and when that happened the last leg was taken out from under me. The stadium is not the stadium. The neighborhood is not the neighborhood, and the team is not the team. They're not winning. They spend a lot of money, but they don't win. And they have an owner who's—well, what could I say that hasn't been said?

But even if the Yankees would start winning again it wouldn't be enough. The Yankees were about more than winning. They were once about community, they once had a superhero, a mythological hero, and they created, for me, a magic place, a magic feeling, and a magic room. As time goes by I think more and more about the Bronx. I don't know why I'm so sentimental, but there was something very beautiful about it. It was a world of strange Americans. My parents were born in America, and it was only a few years ago that I realized that even though they were born in America they were immigrants in a way, because they came from a different world and spoke English a little differently than other Americans. They had different inflections, different syntax. Perhaps I wanted to overlook the fact that they were different. I wanted to believe that if we're all in the same place, we're all Americans, even though they read foreign newspapers, speak another language sometimes, make funny movements and signs with their hands, and yell a lot. It was only much later that I realized they were strange people, outsiders.

I wanted them to be insiders, part of the local scene, and what helped me develop and hang onto that belief was the fact that they were all Yankee fans. Even my grandmother, who was fanatically religious and who prayed every day, was a Yankee fan. And not just in a passive or casual way; she knew about baseball! I had difficulty coming from such odd people and living with them. But the Yankees helped. If my uncle is sitting there reading this funny newspaper in a foreign language but can also talk about the Yankees, then it's O.K.; he does belong, he's an American. My grandmother and my uncle lived together, as bizarre as that might sound. And they also lived right next to Yankee Stadium. You could walk to the stadium from their apartment, and in fact you would walk to the stadium from where I grew up, in the projects. In a way that was a metaphoric walk. It was just a few short blocks from being odd to Yankee Stadium.

Well, this conversation transported me back, far back to the time before they eliminated the 461-foot center field wall in Yankee Stadium. I was back there with the monuments, the shrines to Ruth, Gehrig, and Huggins, which they've hidden behind a 410-foot wall. They can hide them, but they can't erase the memory of Mantle hitting the ball behind the monuments for an inside-the-park home run. I still remember that. I'm still a sucker for those memories and for everything connected with those years in the Bronx. I'd be perfectly happy to go back in time and make everything come out right: to get the autograph from Mickey Mantle, to keep the Bronx alive, not to have Vietnam, not to have Kennedy assassinated, to make everything perfect again. The Yankees would be winning again, and I'd be in Paradise.

A Part of History

Joe N. Born 1964. Does documentation for research and development company. Raised in Lakeside, near San Diego, California. San Diego Padres.

I've been an avid baseball fan since I was 8 years old, but I saw my first game when I was 6. I know it was the Pirates and the Padres because I still have the scorecard, but otherwise I don't remember anything about the game.

I wasn't much interested at the time. The next year, though, when I was in first grade, some of my friends were collecting and trading baseball cards, and somehow that drew me in. I didn't know what any of the stats on the back of the cards meant. I'd only watched a few games on television. But then in 1972 I started listening to the Padres games on the radio, and I couldn't get enough. I must have listened to everyone. I had a portable radio that I carried everywhere.

I liked the Padres because they were the home team. Simple as that. It certainly wasn't because they were a successful team. When I was growing up the Padres never finished out of last place. I enjoyed it when they won, but that was rare, and after a while I got used to their losing and didn't mind it much. If they finished above .500 it was a miracle season, and they didn't win a league championship till I was in college. I loved them simply because they were the home team, the only team I knew. They were the ones on the radio.

Nate Colbert and Enzo Hernandez were probably my favorite players. Colbert was the Padres' top slugger the year I became a fan. That was the year he hit five home runs in a doubleheader. I remember taking the radio everywhere I went that day. I couldn't put it down, couldn't leave it behind. But I missed the grand slam he hit that night because the batteries went dead. It was ironic. I listened to almost every game the Padres played that year; they hit three grand slams and I missed them all. Colbert's because the batteries went dead, Cito Gaston's because it was a day game in Wrigley Field and I was in school, and another by Colbert, I think, because for some reason I just didn't have access to a radio.

I was playing Little League ball myself soon after that, and by that time, by about 1972 or '73, I was in love with baseball. I think what I loved was the fact that it's more than just a physical sport. Even though the home runs require power, first you've got to make contact with the ball and you've got to execute the plays. It's a lot less physical than football, say, or wrestling, and someone like myself, who doesn't have great size or much natural talent can compensate with effort and knowledge. You've heard the term a finesse pitcher, for example, as opposed to a power pitcher, or a contact hitter as opposed to a power hitter. Power and strength are important, but you can compensate with shrewdness and acquired skills for a shortage of natural ability. Since I'm not a particularly big man with tremendous natural ability I appreciate a sport that makes room for people like me.

When I watch a game I focus on defense, on good plays in the field and on the fielder's hustle. Even if it's not enough to get the runner out, I appreciate hustle, the fielder diving for the ball, picking it up and throwing it, all almost in one motion. The other thing that attracts me is the historical aspect of the game. There's something special—I can't explain it, but I feel it—when you're at a game where a historical even takes place, where baseball history is made.

For example, I was in the stands when Mike Schmidt set the record for the most career home runs by a third baseman. I felt like I was a part of Mike Schmidt's career, just being there. I felt as though I'd stepped out of my own life and into his. I'll tell you another story. I was at the Hall of Fame on the 25th of June, 1989, in the National Baseball Library that has a working teletype display. While I was in the next room, watching a video about the Pirates, somebody came in from the teletype room and announced that the judge had granted an injunction to Pete Rose, preventing baseball from taking action against him. It may sound strange, but since I was right there when the information came through I felt I was part of the event, part of that piece of baseball history. Because I was there I remember the event much more vividly than I remember historical events I had no part in.

One of my proudest moments was when I learned two papers I'd written on baseball had been accepted by the SABR Research Exchange. What that meant was that they'd go into the archives of the National Baseball Library in Cooperstown. I got the postcard from SABR's executive director, and it was a real thrill for me. Finding out I was in Cooperstown was one of the proudest moments of my life. From that moment on I became a part of baseball history.

That's important to me, being part of history. Mainly in baseball, I guess, but not only. I've also been a part of civic history in my area. The county tried to put a rehabilitation house with twenty-one families into our neighborhood, which has only one-family homes. Our neighborhood organized and opposed it. We went down to the county seat and fought it, and we won. We got them out, and I played a part in that. I felt I'd played an active part in the preservation of the neighborhood, which is a long-term thing. Also, when I was on the community planning board, the city's planning commission wanted to eliminate a small connector road near San Diego State University. I got involved in the fight to keep the road, and we won that, too. The road is still there, and when I drive past it I feel a certain pride that I helped to keep it there. When things like that happen I feel I've become part of something larger than myself.

But this is a feeling I connect particularly with baseball. Just going to a ball game makes me feel I'm part of history in a way. Every game is recorded. It has a permanent place in the history of the season and the history of the game. But the special events are the most exciting. I've seen a number of players get awards. I've seen records set and nearly set, and I've seen batting championships won and lost. I was at the game when Benito Santiago got a hit in his thirtieth consecutive game. It was an infield hit down the third-base line. It gave me a special feeling to know I was there when Santiago's streak reached 30 games.

I collected baseball cards when I was a kid, partly at least for the same reason. They're a part of history, the history of the game. Every set of cards represents a year in that history, and each card is a kind of memento. Looking at old cards is like looking back into the past, into the history of a player, his team, or the game itself. Back when I started collecting baseball cards in 1971 you could buy a package of 54 cards for 39 cents, a package of 30 for a quarter. Most of the cards I have are from 1971 because they were so cheap. Some would have bubble gum in them, others just the card pack. I'd sort them out by positions, alphabetize them by players, and trade my duplicates.

I don't collect them like I used to because it's no longer fun. It's become an investment rather than a hobby. Still, I'm glad I have these cards because I like the idea of preserving something from the past. I like being part of history, and I like preserving it. That's one of the main pleasures of belonging to the Society for American Baseball Research. As a member I can compile information about some aspect of the history of baseball and put it into more convenient form, more concise and better organized than it was before. When I do a research project like that, combining separate sources into a single document, I make it that much easier for later researchers who will use the information I've collected. Instead of having to go to all the multiple sources I've used, they can just use my compilation. That's my little contribution to future historians of baseball, my small place in the history of the game.

VII. Identification

In my day we crouched like Stan Musial, our bodies coiled, the bat rotating vertically above us like a radar antenna scanning for Messerschmidts. Alternatively, in emphatic imitation of DiMaggio's spread-eagle stance we did near splits at the plate; or, pressing knee to chin and kicking skyward like Warren Spahn, we hoped for the best as we unraveled and, our vision blocked by our own leg, let go. Today's young fans, no doubt, are working their own studious variations on Hedeo Nomo, grabbing a loose piece of sky and, twisting, threatening to toss it into center field before uncoiling toward the plate; or on Jay Buhner, flush to the pitcher posing casually for a full-front portrait, assuming his stance scarcely before the ball is in the air. We had gloves made sacred by the burnt-in signatures of Eddie Mathews, Richie Ashburn, and Preacher Roe. They have theirs, inscribed with the equally magical names of Cal Ripken, Jr., Tony Gwynn, and Roger Clemens. Unfortunately, since modern baseball gloves come with preformed pockets, today's fans are deprived of the secret pleasures of replicating what we believed was the nightly ritual of the stars: With care and devotion we rubbed Vaseline into our mitts, planted a ball where we hoped a pocket might miraculously form, and, tying it with string or scrunching it into the corner of the room where floorboards met, waited for the magic transformation that never took place.

All thoroughly delightful and quite harmless stuff, but to the child and adolescent a very significant ritual and one that extends, as the following conversations indicate, far beyond these narrow physical borders. These acts of repetition and possession and others recounted in the interviews are acts not of simple imitation but of identification. In imitation the child merely takes on the actions of others, most obviously one's parents. In identification—induced and intensified by repeated acts of imitation—the child at least temporarily loses his identity in that of his object or model. He is not merely like Willie Mays or Greg Maddux, he *is* that ball player: "And now, ladies and gentlemen, playing right field, wearing number nine and hitting a very respectable .301, Hank 'The Rugged Ex-Marine' Bau—er!" Yeaaaaaaaaaaa!

Stepping up to the plate to the inevitable cheers and whistles is but the simplest expression of this very important exercise. As we'll see in the following interviews and have already seen in others, fans identify with far more than athletic eccentricities and prowess. They experience, vicariously but with remarkable intensity, triumph and loss, reconciliation and acceptance, dominance and imperfection. Through players and teams they identify with aging, death, and the irretrievability of the past, with sacrifice and suffering, with guardianship of the helpless and care for the weak, with moral principle and courage, and, at the outer reaches, with entire cities, social types and classes, and religious faiths and factions.

Clearly, important work is being done here, for identification is a basic process of socialization and one that lies behind a good deal of what other fans emphasize. It is often identification that makes baseball an effective training ground for morals, an impetus in the quest for excellence, a source of empowerment or the sense of belonging, and so on.

Identification is performed, as Freud remarked, under the impetus of extremely powerful forces, two of which are particularly relevant to the young fan: the adaptation to socially assigned sex roles, typically male in this instance; and the development of conscience. What the child acquires in the act of identifying—whether with parents, social role models, or idolized heroes—is the capacity for empathy, sympathy and understanding that comes with assuming, even for fleeting moments, the identity of another group or individual; the skills, competence, mastery and power that define and elevate the athlete; and the real or assumed moral standards, behaviors, and prohibitions of the model. He also learns, as identification slides toward discovery, many of the joyous and painful lessons of this life.

For identification to occur, the child must want to possess at least some of the model's attributes, and he must perceive at least some similarity between himself and the individual or group whose characteristics and values he absorbs. Both requirements are met with simultaneous ease and intensity in the child's identification with the athlete. That the star athlete possesses the physical competence and mastery the child seeks and that he bathes in a generously lavished admiration and affection the child dreams of is past question. He also exhibits, and to a degree not found in other potential role models, a quite remarkable proximity to the child.

Unlike rock stars, film and media idols, and political heroes, the athlete is playing a child's "game," one the worshipful child himself probably plays, similarly attired and using similar equipment. Wearing a uniform that belongs more to the child's world than the adult's, he is transformed at once into a comic-book hero or superman, while at the same time remaining a kind of enlarged child dressed in an emblemized costume that marks his membership in a totemized adolescent tribe of Tigers, Indians, or Giants. The uniform thus at once exalts and lowers the player, lifts him above—he is an Atlanta Brave after all—as it ties him to both childhood and earth. That the player is number 3 or number 6 identifies him as a particular member of this otherwise leveled organization, highlights his individuality within the blending group in a way the child appreciates. And at the same time it transforms his identity into something symbolic, universal, and transportable. The child who wears that number or summons it for imaginary use assumes that identity. Like the virtues of a cannibalized enemy, the player's nature and skill are appropriated with the wearing of his tribal dress or, since he is often an animal, his "skin."

The athlete, moreover, has all the skills, movements, and energies of the child. He runs, hits with a stick, chases or throws or catches a ball, "plays" on a field, shouts encouragement to his friends and sordid epithets to his adversaries, curses or denounces authority (the umpire), and is engaged, like every schoolboy, in a perpetual competition centered on agility, intelligence, and power. Even more than other athletes, the baseball player, like the child, is bound by rules and restrictions, compelled to wait his turn, and asked to prove himself both as the cooperative, at times sacrificial, member of a group and as an individual singled out for scrutiny. And finally, like the graded schoolchild accustomed to marks and constant assessment, the baseball player—again more lavishly than other athletes—is lathered with statistics, numerical evaluations of his performance and worth. The ball player is, in short, a child-man play-working for men-children or for children waiting to be men and dreaming that the transition may not cost them the pleasures and freedoms of childhood. He is, in this sense, a transitional figure poised between childhood and adulthood, the playing field a transitional and mythical space, a natural or (today) naturalized landscape of passage where the ritualized transition from childhood to adulthood, replete with tribal sacrifice and suffering, is played out. Here one may pass into manhood, even into heroism, yet remain a child.

Thus far the baseball player is almost inseparable from other athletes, perhaps even at a certain disadvantage. Other than the blend of individuality and cooperation and the greater versatility only the cognoscenti are likely to appreciate, his physical gifts may have less dramatic appeal than those of the zigzagging or ram-like running back or the slam-dunking center or power forward. It is in the arena of shared or shareable characteristics that the baseball player reaches out to us, appears to the acquisitive young fan a singularly accessible as well as attractive vessel to inhabit. Unlike his counterparts on the football field or basketball court, the baseball player is rarely a physical phenomenon or merely enviable anomaly. Unlike the football player, he need not be a 220-pound power mower or a 300-pound house of immovable flesh. Unlike the basketball star he need not loom among the branches or know the secret of how to sail above them. A baseball player, as fans frequently note to their satisfaction, looks rather like our fathers, our older brothers, or our probable selves. He may be 5'9" or 10" tall, he may weigh no more than 170 or 180 pounds, he may have a bit of a paunch, even a "healthy" one, and he may run, if he has compensatory virtues, like a pellet-laden frog. The baseball player, then, is a uniquely accessible object of identification. Like the tragic hero, as Aristotle defined him, he is better than ourselves, yet identifiably like us: mortally flawed, imperfect, and therefore a man for whom we can feel pity and fear and through whom we may experience an exalting catharsis.

It is for all these reasons, I believe, that baseball fans identify so deeply, so complexly, and often so agonizingly with the players and the teams they love. The problem, given the game as it has developed over the past three decades or so, is the desirability of such identification, principally in the realm of morals.

It is here that identification offers the youngster his most important acquisition and his most substantial if most difficult rewards. And it is here that the baseball player had, or at least seemed to have, the most to teach us. A good deal of it comes with the territory. Barring evidence to the contrary, those we admire for one set of strengths or virtues, particularly virtues we crave for ourselves, are assumed to have others; the child takes for granted that those who are good in one sense are good in others. In the past, we had little evidence to the contrary and at least some to confirm our wishes and assumptions. Now of course we know too much and have too little to confute it. Branch Rickey and Jackie Robinson are gone. Marge Schott and Albert Belle are with us. We sympathize and identify, alas, with Andrew Zimbalist's son, when he tells his stunned father that he does not wish to play Little League ball this year "because I don't have any role models anymore." His is a lament that threads with a staining color the conversations I had with fans, the youngest speaking for themselves, others for their children or grandchildren. As imitation generates and enhances identification, identification flows toward the development of the child's ego ideal, his internalized model of himself as he wishes to be. Individual players may have little to offer in this arena. But it is a mistake to imagine the benefits of identification confined to hero worship and role modeling. As several of the following interviews (and a number of others reproduced in other sections) indicate, there is a great deal in this still amazing game beyond the individual player-as-imitated-idol the young fan may identify with, much of it of considerable moral and developmental value.

The range of identifications fans experience is remarkable, the intensity inspiring, occasionally comic, at times almost worrisome. For Elliott S. ball players were athletic role models only, extensions, as he puts it, "of our heroic selves, identified with because they were playing the game we played" and playing it so much better. As Elliott understood and experienced his youthful fandom, it was inseparable from the fact that he, too, played the game. You knew how you played it, knew how it felt and how difficult it was to do well, and you identified, admiringly and wishfully, with those who did it so magnificently. A fan, therefore, is player-as-witness, a vicarious participant agonized by his team's habitual defeats—he was and remains a Cub fan—and exalted by their occasional victories because the players are surrogates for the athletically accomplished self.

John D. also identifies principally with the physical agility and power of the players he reveres, but his identifications are at once more active and complete. If Elliott was a watching player, John was a playing or simulating watcher. Not content to participate vicariously, to feel in his relatively stationary body the movements of the players on the field, John enacts and reenacts what he sees and remembers, often in the slow-motion choreography of the replay. At the ball park he winds up with the pitcher in the aisles and responds to the pitch with a batless swing, thereby, he assumes, having at least some small effect on the outcome. At home he does the same, charging through his happily diamond-shaped apartment from room-base to room-base in the adopted bodies of Greg Luzinski, Mike Schmidt, and Pete Rose. Imitative play turns, however, as it often does, to near deadly seriousness when, on Mike Schmidt's retirement, John's identification shifts from the feel of youthful power to the recognition of inevitable aging, decline and the impossibility of return. As John learns, one who loses himself in another's triumphant beginning risks engulfment in the pathos of his ending.

In an interview almost alarming for the scope and totality of its identifications, Erik K., 22 at the time of the interview, speaks of a current habit of identity transference that projects his mind and body onto every figure on the field and in the stands. Principally he is a coach, studying the opposition and the games, running imaginary videotapes through his mind so that he might be more helpful to his Yankees. He does this not for the accolades, but for the altruistic purpose of aiding his then faltering team, and if they are defeated he feels he has let them down. "I'm the coach, I'm in the dugout," telling his pitchers how to pitch, sitting on their shoulders during the ball games and whispering wise counsel in their ears. When one of his players hits a home run, he is there to congratulate him, to pat him on his bottom as he passes third base or crosses the plate. But he is also the hero rounding the bases and receiving these rewards, and he is the fans in the stands on their feet and howling. Small wonder, when the Yankees lose, "I take it personally."

Tim C.'s identification is, like Elliott's, narrowly focused, but it is almost entirely moral rather than athletic.* In an unusual and moving interview, Tim speaks of his identification with the catcher, a hero wrapped in protective armor essential to the performance of his assigned task: that of protecting the umpire, the indispensable god or chess-king of the game. During the course of the interview, Tim realizes that his affinity for catchers and their chivalric assignment is a reflection of his lifelong identification with the helpless or disabled, whose cause became his mission. He recognizes only now that championing the cause of a terminally ill brother or others weak or disabled, "I was being the catcher who protects the umpire from harm." For Tim, as for so many others, what matters to him on the diamond is what concerns him elsewhere. Baseball is less the mirror of life it is often said to be than a mirror of the forming or established self.

Appropriate to his career choice as social worker and psychotherapist, Charles S.'s identifications were richly and distinctly psychological. What he identifies with is neither the physical strength or energies of the players nor the moral symbolism of their tasks. He was identified, rather, with the Baltimore Orioles' cultivation of talent out of their own local material, their reconstruction

---

*In fact Tim's interview might as easily have been included in the section on the expression and development of morality. Fans don't always oblige the writer's or editor's fondness for sharply defined boundaries, though that, as I've argued, is but further testimony to the breadth and variety of their experience of the game.

from within; for that is "something I believe in, something I can relate to personally. I believe in self-reliance." The same connection between his own ideal self-image and what he related to most profoundly as a fan accounted for his powerful identification with victory when the Orioles began to win, and for his difficulty accepting imperfection and poor play. And both are rooted in his driving desire for total dominance. "I think there's a craving for perfection behind all this," he observed. "I'm that way myself." So enmeshed was Charles with his Orioles that when they lost, particularly because of the faulty play of a single player, he did not feel sad for the "goat." Rather, he says, using a revealing present tense, "I get depressed for me. It's like I was out there and I lost the game."

Herb P.'s identifications were distinctly social, economic, and religious rather than athletic or moral, group oriented rather than individual. There's a wry Yiddish humor in Herb's reminisces, but he's clearly serious about what he speaks of so smilingly. "How you felt about baseball, which team you lived and died with," he reports, "had more to do with these matters of group identity and identification than with the pure love of baseball." His "you," of course is a thinly disguised "I," his lack of hesitancy in employing it a mark of how readily we assume the universality of our personal preferences and perceptions. For Herb, an old Brooklyn Dodger fan now past 70, love for "his" Dodgers and hatred of "their" Yankees was a relatively simple matter. Low down, grubby, vernacular, and loud, the Dodgers were the proletarians and the Jews. Rich, prissily meticulous, and restrained, the Yankees were the aristocracy and the "goyim." And who you/I rooted for was clear. Given this public group identity and identification, there is more than metaphoric truth to Herb's insistence that he wanted them to win "because they're mine, because they belong to me. In fact they are me. If they win I win."*

Identification differs from the other categories in that it names a process rather than a benefit or effect. As such, it is the source of a number of the acquisitions and benefits we've already described, and it would have been possible to classify these interviews according to the rewards and purposes identification serves. For John D., identification is, partly at least, with agility and power, while for Charles S. it is a source of empowerment related to the drive toward excellence, even perfection. Elliott S. also feels his physical skills by identifying with more advanced versions of them and adds a sense of belonging also important to Herb, although Herb's identification intensifies a membership he already owns and is certain of rather than extending his circle. For Tim C. and Erik K. the process is an expression, mainly, of the moral self, the desire to help.

A separate category is justified, as I've said, because in most instances—Tim and Herb are possible exceptions—the process seems to edge the purposes off stage. Almost all fans report some degree of identification with players and teams. These differ in the breadth, intensity, and persistence of that identification. The 'what' seems—it certainly seemed when they were younger—more potent than the 'why.'

VII. Identification

A Member of the Team
The Warming Brotherhood of Baseball

Elliott S. Born 1943. University lecturer in English literature. Born and raised in Chicago, Illinois. Chicago Cubs.

Growing up in Chicago I was a devoted fan of the Chicago Cubs. That's the team I enjoyed watching play and followed as a kid in the Chicago area. My first awareness of the Cubs probably came just about the time I started playing baseball myself as a kid—in first and second grade. I started a little early, perhaps, as one of a group of kids I grew up with on the North Side. We were the North Side team, and we were all Chicago Cubs fans. I had very little affinity for the White Sox. For me, Chicago was the Cubs.

Back then—this is about 1949–50—the Cubs were a .500 team, but it was very exciting to go to the games, primarily because it's exciting to go anywhere when you're that young. As I got older I got more and more enthusiastic because I knew what to expect. I knew the stadium; I knew the hot dogs; I knew the goodies I'd be eating; and I knew the game I'd be watching. Wrigley Field is a lovely park, and the beauty of the place impressed me. But the most exciting thing for me was to be part of a large crowd doing the same thing: watching professional players playing well. It was an adjunct to my own playing.

That's what made me a fan, I think: They were playing the game I played, and they were playing it professionally, the way it should be played. It made me feel good to think that in some way I was like them. We all bought gloves with the names of our favorite players on them. The players were extensions of our heroic selves, so to speak. They were people we identified with because they were playing the game we played. This kind of thing affects a kid. Here you were, among your heroes, thinking one day you might be someone else's hero. We all wanted to be sluggers. We bought Louisville Slugger bats, and if we didn't have an autographed mitt, we'd autograph it ourselves, with the name of our favorite player, as a mark of identification. That was the idea: to be like him. I'm not sure it was a personal thing, focused on a single ballplayer above all others. I used to like Hank Sauer. I liked Sauer because, like me, he was an outfielder. My neighbor was the first baseman, so he was Phil Cavaretta. Since neither of us played shortstop we couldn't be Ernie Banks, much as we might have liked to. But for all that hero selection it was basically a generalized experience. It wasn't so much a particular player you wanted to be like; you wanted to be like "them." My neighbor was Phil Cavaretta; I was Hank Sauer; and this other guy was Ernie Banks. But it was the association with the team in general, the Cubs as a unit, that counted more than anything else.

Because you were so completely identified with them, you felt good when they were winning, and I remember how depressed I was when they lost, especially when I'd made the effort to go to the game. Usually you'd have a parent with you, so it was an outing, a big event that aroused big expectations. But then they'd lose, to the Phillies or the Dodgers, or whoever, and you'd come out feeling terrible. If you were out there with them when they lost, you had witnessed their defeat and been a part of it. It was painful, more painful than reading about it in the newspaper. You had seen how it happened, and you'd lived through it with them. When that happened, you didn't walk out of the stadium happy and say, "Hey, buy me another Coke," or something. You were in no mood for that. You had suffered a blow.

You're a booster, you're a fan, and when you're a fan what your team does is important to you. One, because you're doing the same thing in your sandlot or school yard. And two, because you love the sport and the guys who play it. You are their fans and you want them to win. You want them to succeed because you're identified with the team, with the city, and with your better self as an athlete.

We play baseball for fun and excitement and competition; they play it as professionals. They play it very well, and you don't play it all that well, so they are examples for you, role models, though not in terms of personality development. They're athletic role models, showing us how we are supposed to act, behave, and perform on the field.

There were very few baseball players that I remember—Willie Mays, for example, certainly Ernie Banks of the Cubs, and Stan Musial of St. Louis—who seemed transathletic. That is to say these were men who excelled in the sport and who, because of their exposure and their own generosity, wanted to reach out to the community and convey messages about good sportsmanship, good conduct, and good citizenship. But I don't remember other baseball players doing that sort of thing, so I was used to seeing them in an athletic situation only.

The athletic self includes the physical self. As a kid, when you're growing up and trying to be athletic, when you evolve from being a Cub Scout to a Boy Scout or from being a very young 9- or 10-year old to a 13- or 14-year old, you get a sense of your body, your physical appearance, strength, and agility, and you're embarrassed when you're clumsy or inept. You strike out or you run too slowly, and you feel weak. You're conscious of your own body, of what it can do and can't do, and you appreciate the excellence of the good athlete.

Mainly, though, it was a team thing. When they lose you feel sad for them. You feel team sorrow. I identified myself with the Cubs as a team, and I knew when they lost it was a team loss. It wasn't the pitcher who won or lost the game; it was the team. Some fans pay attention to statistics: how many games a pitcher has won or lost, a hitter's average or RBIs. But I never saw it that way; for me it was a team game. The team lost, and they aren't going to the playoffs or to the World Series. I felt sorry for them collectively, as a team.

Perhaps this meant more to me than to others because I was always on losing teams. It wasn't because we didn't try, didn't make the effort, but most of the teams I played on—the school team, the club team—they were all losers. I think my Cub Scout team was the only winning team I ever played on. So I could identify with the Cubs when they lost, and perhaps at a very precocious age I could understand what losing meant and the significance of it. If you were a Cubs fan it was a joke. You were always at the bottom or pretty near it. This was the early '50s, the age of the Brooklyn Dodgers, the Phillies, and the Giants. And we were always middling.

It was all right, though. As a fan, you were part of a group taking part in the game, and you felt good about it. Being a fan meant participating in the game. It was a passive participation, but you were still participating. A fan is one who is a total participant in the sport, one way or another. He shouts, he screams, he yells, because he is participating, and the sport allows him to do that. And he's participating as a fan who also participates as a player. A fan is usually someone who has played the game. I don't know many people who are fans of sports they never played themselves. Being a fan enables you to continue to play the game vicariously through the players on the team. When I was a kid I enjoyed watching the game largely because I also played it. As an older man I enjoy it without feeling that I have to play. There are older guys who need to pretend they're still 18, to prove they can still shag flies and dash down the base paths. I don't need to feel that way. My fandom as an adult no longer requires active involvement as a player, but when I watch or go to a game I still participate in the group and team experience with the same intensity I had when I was a kid. In some measure you're always a kid at a baseball park. There's the team and there's you. The team is out on the field and you're up there in the stands, and there's a relationship between you, a kind of connection, a kind of bond that goes very deep and that's always there. It first formed when you were a kid, and it continues for as long as you love the game.

Catcher in the Rye

Tim C. Born 1956. Employment consultant. Raised in Lincoln Park, Michigan. Detroit Tigers

My first memory as a fan is connected with an older brother who was very sick and who spent a lot of his time in a children's hospital in Detroit. One day—this was in the mid '60s—the whole Tiger team went to the hospital and signed baseballs for the kids there. My brother came home with this autographed baseball, and I thought it was the neatest thing in the world that all these great ball players had gone to visit him at the hospital and signed the ball for him. They'd given him a prized possession and an unforgettable experience. I thought it was great of them to take the time to do that.

Before that I never thought people of that stature would take the trouble to do a thing like that, and I reacted very emotionally. To me—I was about 7 or 8 at the time—these were superior beings from another world who had surprisingly descended to earth. They weren't really touchable, you know; they weren't normal people who did what you and I do. It was as though they lived different lives, separate from our own. I never really thought they had any life other than baseball. I thought that was what they did and all they did: they played baseball, they lived at the ball park, and when the game was over they'd just disappear into the dugout until it was time to come out again for the next game.

Since I lived so close to Detroit I'd have been a Tiger fan in any case, but from that day on, the Tigers were special to me because they had gone to see my brother. They had given him some light in his life and some hope, a bright spot in all that sickness and suffering. My brother had what was called discaratosis congenita, with pansid apnea. It was a bone marrow and blood disease, related to leukemia, though not the same. He didn't survive. He died two or three years after that at the age of 17, but getting that ball made a tremendous difference to him. It put a ray of light into his life. We knew how important it was to him because he talked about it all the time and he displayed the ball proudly to everyone who came into the house. The team meant a lot to him then, and it meant a lot to me that they would come and do that for him. I understood his situation very well. I knew how sick he was, and for a while there the Tigers seemed like saviors.

A few years after that they went into the World Series and won it, and happiness seemed to run in the streets. I remember parties in the streets and confetti and people blowing their car horns for days because the Tigers had won the Series. The victory brought everybody together. It gave everyone the same focus at the same time. They were ours, a precious possession we all shared.

My special favorite on the team was Norm Cash. I liked catchers. I don't know why, but I think it was the equipment: the facemask, the chest protector, the shinguards, and the big glove. They got to wear more than anybody else, and the more equipment you're wearing the more important you are. The logic is, you have to be protected because you're important. It was as though the catcher was the umpire's guardian; his job was to protect the umpire from the ball. The umpire was the most exalted figure on the field, a kind of god who ruled over the game. He made the decisions about what was good and what was bad, what was fair and what was not. Everybody yelled at him when they disagreed, and he could throw you out of the game if he felt like it or stop the game or do pretty much whatever he liked. He had the power, and the catcher was next in the hierarchy, just below the umpire, sent out there as a protector because he was unusually brave.

I never thought about being a catcher myself. I didn't like catching when I played baseball, because most pitchers throw very hard and it would sting quite a lot. But to me that only made the catcher seem more heroic because he could do this; he was able to catch those balls and not show the pain. Or maybe it didn't cause him pain. Maybe he knew a way to catch that ball without experiencing the pain that I felt. Either way, he was special, and he wasn't only protecting the umpire. He was protecting home plate and keeping the runs from coming in. He was the guardian of home plate and a very pivotal person in the game. I never thought of it before, but it occurs to me now that I was identifying with something out there, identifying with the catcher's role as I understood it.

I'm quite a staunch advocate of the rights of the handicapped, and not just because of Lila.* It started with my brother who was always sick and always in a cast. He had some experiences that he shouldn't have had, most of them the result of other people's stupidity or insensitivity. People would talk to him or about him in very thoughtless and sometimes downright cruel ways. I couldn't stand it, and young as I was, I spoke out, I defended him. My brother had his leg in a cast up to the hip and he walked with crutches. Once, after he got off the school bus, instead of going the long way on a sidewalk to the front door of the school, he cut across the grass, and the bus driver yelled at him, "Stay off the grass!" in this very harsh and nasty manner. He had no consideration for what my brother was going through. I remember my brother telling my mother what had happened when he came home from school that day, and my mother reacted the same way I did. We were outraged. How could someone do that? Is he blind? Can't he see this person needs to take the short cut, that he's not doing it because he's lazy?!

Later on, I had friends in high school who had disabilities and I would help them and speak up for them when they were wronged. And then I met Lila. She was perfectly well when we met, and I never expected this to happen to her. But you know, when it did happen it didn't change the way I saw her or the way I felt about her, not at all. I was able to look past the wheelchair and see Lila. I was always able to identify with people with disabilities. I guess living with my brother and knowing how he felt and what he needed, certain things that others didn't need, made me especially sensitive. I could feel their needs as though they were my own, maybe even stronger, and I felt compelled to speak out for them and protect them. I couldn't let it pass. When I developed friendships in school with kids that had disabilities and saw the way other people treated them, I knew in my heart it wasn't right and I would speak out. I would tell people they shouldn't think or speak that way, that they should put themselves in that person's place and try to imagine what it's like.

So I became their guardian in a way, and it wasn't always easy. Other kids would get on you for it. I did feel the pressure of it sometimes, but it didn't stop me. I had a friend all through grade school and high school who had cerebral palsy. Some of the other kids would make fun of him, and when I'd stand up for him, they'd mock me for being Tom Moody's friend, as though that was something to be ashamed of. But I was proud to be his friend, and I was willing to take whatever flack came with it. It didn't hurt, really, or if it did I wouldn't let them know it. As I say this, I realize there's a connection here. In a way I was

---

Tim's wife Lila, in a wheelchair, whose interview appears on pp. 227–231.

being the catcher who protects the umpire from harm, the one who protects home plate and who catches the fastball and doesn't feel the pain or doesn't let it show. This is a pretty stark and surprising realization. I'd never thought of this before.

At home, I have fifty-some autographed baseballs on the shelves near my desk, and when I take a break from work I look at the baseballs and reminisce. I also have baseball pictures and baseball cards. I've kept them all, and I find being surrounded by them very relaxing. They bring back that warm and friendly feeling, that relaxed easy feeling I had when I watched or listened to a game. I never considered myself a very staunch baseball fan before this, but it does seem to have a been a very meaningful part of my life. I love all those cards, those pictures, and those autographed baseballs, but the one I prize most is the ball my brother had. It's there on the top of the stack. That ball means a lot to me because it's a part of him. I don't have my brother anymore. He's gone, and that's what I have left of him. It brings us together. We never were together very much when he was alive. I was the little brother, the pest, the bother, and his room was off-limits. I'd look longingly into his room from the hallway, but every now and then I'd be allowed to come all the way inside, to see and feel his things ... his acceptance. There were those rare moments when he was accepting of me and treated me like I was a person and not the pesty little brother. And when I look at his baseball now, I feel that connection again. His prized possession is now mine. It's a part of him I'll always have.

Even Mr. Replay Can't Go Home Again

John D. Born 1971. Law student. Raised in Cherry Hill, New Jersey. Philadelphia Phillies.

I can't recall exactly when baseball begins for me. It was probably at around the age of 5 or 6, but it seems unconnected to a particular age, as though it was simply there. My family—my sister, my parents, and I—would go to Phillies games every Sunday afternoon, and it's as if, in some timeless way, I just knew everything about every player on the Phillies: their names, their numbers, their statistics, everything, as though I was almost born with that information. I'm not entirely sure what first attracted me to the game, but it had something to do with a game my father made up and played as a child, a game called dice baseball. He was an only child, and when he was a boy he'd play entire seasons of dice baseball and keep records of every game and how each team in this imaginary league made out, year after year. He showed me how to play the game, and I would play it with him.

VII. Identification

At about the same time we were going to the Phillies games. My sister had her Greg Luzinski shirt, the number 19 jersey, and I had my Mike Schmidt shirt, with number 20 on it. We had seats right along the aisle, and I can remember standing in the aisle and acting out what was going on in the game, the whole way through. I'd wind up with the pitcher, swing with the batter, field the ball, run the bases, everything. I'm sure it bothered the people around me to no end, but I can't remember anyone ever complaining, though that may be because I was too deep in my own world to notice. I was particularly fascinated by the home run, the fact that someone had hit the ball this amazing distance and the sight of it going over the fence. I would reenact the scene as though I was part of a slow motion replay. After I'd throw the pitch and swing, if it was a home run I'd replay it in slow motion. I'd hit the ball and then, after watching it rise, I'd move my legs and body in slow motion, as if I was circling the bases. This caused problems when I played Little League ball, because my coaches would always complain that after I hit the ball I would run as if I was moving in slow motion. It was as though I believed the players really ran like that. The television images had become reality for me, the replays more real than the actual events.

My idol was Mike Schmidt. He seemed infallible. I thought he could do anything. I remember thinking he could hit a home run every time up if he wanted to, and I was disappointed whenever he didn't, which of course was about eleven out of twelve times. It was as though it was all under his control, a matter of will, and I felt something similar in my own relation to what was happening on the field. I had the impression I could control what was going to happen in a reverse Murphy's Law kind of way. So if I said to my dad, "This guy's probably gonna strike out," he'd hit a home run. And if I said, "I hope he hits a home run," he'd strike out. I believed in some mysterious way I was affecting the game. I could will things into being, and I think I felt that way when I'd act out the game up there in the aisle. I was somehow making it happen, determining the pitch with my windup and arm movement and affecting the outcome with my swing.

For me, baseball was a superior world, these were the best people, and they could do incredible things out there on the field. When I acted out their movements I was inhabiting their bodies in a way. I was absorbing their talent. I'd imitate players in an incredibly exact way, to the point where, if the pitcher was in trouble I'd pretend I was in the bullpen warming up. I was the whole team, everybody. I can remember watching the '77 World Series on TV, the opening ceremony where they call out the names of the starting players on the loudspeaker one by one. The players trot out of the dugout, tip their caps, and take their places along the baselines, and I'd be standing in my living room acting out the whole thing. They'd say, "Mickey Rivers, leading off, playing center field for the Yankees," and I'd act as if I was jogging out of the dugout, tipping my cap, and taking my place. And then I'd do it all over again for Bucky Dent and for every other player on both teams. I'm about 6 years old, my dad's sitting there watching the game, and I'm running across the room and tipping my cap to the crowd. It was strange stuff. When I'd do a dice baseball World Series I would start off with those introductions, and then I'd act out every important play of the game. It wasn't enough to throw the dice. I'd have to run out every hit.

Our house is built like a sort of diamond, with a square of rooms starting with the hall. The kitchen is attached to the dining room, which is attached to the living room, and the living room comes into the hall again. So it was a sort of diamond. I would stand at one of the corners, hit the ball and run into the next room, which was first base. I would be dodging people, usually my mother as I'd come through the kitchen, and an extra-base hit was dangerous because I'd come around first without being able to tell what was around the corner.

It was great being all the players and running out all the base hits, but later I'd pay a price for all this imitation and identification. My dad's favorite player on the Phillies, Jim Kaat, was getting to be an old man. He'd seen better days and was going to retire, and to me that seemed like the end of the world, a kind of death. He'll retire and then he'll be gone; he won't come back anymore—that's how I saw it. I remember being very moved by that and needing reassurance, so I asked my dad if Mike Schmidt was also going to retire. I needed to know that Schmidt wasn't also about to die, that he'd be carrying on. I got the reassurance I was looking for—Schmidt was only about 27 or 28 at the time—but it didn't last. When Schmidt did retire—I was in the last year of high school—it took me by surprise, and it came as quite a blow. It made me realize how much older I had gotten. It felt like my childhood was gone.

I remember the press conference, and though I have it on videotape I haven't watched it since. It was just too painful. When Schmidt says, "I came from Ohio, a kid of 18, with two bad knees and a dream to play baseball, and I thank God that dream came true," his voice cracks on "dream came true" and he starts bawling. I had to leave the room at that point. It was terrible somehow, and I was crying with him. I was about 18 myself, and I understood that even if my own dreams were to come true, they too would come to an end, as Schmidt's had. That summer they held a tribute for Schmidt at the Vet, and that too was painful. They showed the endless highlights of his career, mainly his most dramatic home runs. I had always loved to watch those clips, but now that Schmidt was retiring, now that it was all in the past, there was something terribly sad and final about it, and I couldn't watch.

Schmidt retired in the spring of my senior year in high school, when I was headed for college and pretty anxious about the transition. I was only going twenty minutes away, to Philadelphia, but I had a sense that I was losing something I could never come back to. When you leave home, even though you know you can come back every summer, whenever you want to, really, home isn't home anymore. It isn't where you live or quite where you belong. When you go back home you expect things to be the same; you want them to be the same as when you left them, but they aren't. The things you want to come back to, you can't, and Schmidt's retirement was symbolic of all that. It was the loss of childhood and living at home. Like Schmidt, I had to go off. That part of my life was coming to an end. Running out the hits is one thing; running out the string is something else altogether, but I guess you can't have one without the other.

"I Talk to the Players, I Talk to the Television"
A Kind of Obsession

Eric K. Born 1970. University student at time of interview. Born and raised in Staten Island, NY. New York Yankees.

I think the first thing I remember clearly about baseball is watching a game at my grandmother's house in Queens. It was 1978, and the Yankees and Boston were playing a playoff game. The Yankees were losing, 3–1, or something like that. I watched until about the seventh or eighth inning, and then I went outside for a little while, just to walk around. I didn't care too much about the outcome because I was just 8 years old, and I wasn't a fan yet. But then I saw it— the big home run. Chambliss crushed it, and I went crazy, and my parents went crazy with me. That was the beginning.

Everybody in my family is a Yankee fan: my father, my mother, and my two brothers. But I'm the biggest. I'm the biggest. I'm devoted to the Yankees. I picture myself as the coach of the team. I put myself in the dugout. I look at the location of every pitch. I look at the way a play is executed and I keep my eye on every pitch. I'm in the dugout and I'm counting pitches. I guess it could almost be called an obsession. I feel like if I watch these pitches carefully and keep tabs on what's being thrown I can help the team, the way a coach would. I try to do that. I try it every game. I talk to the players. I talk to the television. I tell them what I think should happen in a certain situation. I try to call pitches. I'll call a curveball instead of a fastball, or I'll call for a changeup. I try to teach the players, and I try to teach them to play smart. For example, this past Tuesday, when the Yankees had their opening day, I was talking to Scott Sanderson and telling him that he should pitch smart. I know in the past he's had excellent luck against Boston because he's pitched smart, and I told him that if he pitched smart again he'd have a great chance of winning. He shouldn't try challenging a guy like Jack Clark with a fastball, because it's gonna be in the bleachers. He should make smart pitches. If there are runners on first and third and no one out, he should go for the out even if it means giving up a run. It's O.K. if he allows a run instead of throwing a stupid pitch and giving up a double. I didn't get a lot of sleep on Tuesday because of the game. I felt I had a lot of work to do.

When I talk to a player, to Sanderson, for example, I know he can't hear what I'm saying. It's just that if I appeared on his right shoulder he would have a better idea of how to throw his pitch or of what pitch to throw in a certain situation. I know that pitchers and batters are gonna make mistakes, and that's O.K. because they're human. But I think to win a game it takes a lot of smarts, and that's the message I want to get across. Play it smart. Don't overpower them. Use your brains.

If the Yankees lose I take it personally. Especially after a tough loss, I, as coach, will go back to certain plays of the game. It's like I'm watching a videotape of the game, like all the coaches do. And I look back and try to analyze what actually happened to make us lose. I think about everything that went wrong and I get depressed by it, because certain things just shouldn't happen. For example, a sacrifice bunt that isn't executed well, or an error in the field. I know these things happen, but if they start happening every game or every other game, then I feel, as coach, that changes have to be made. We'll have to have extra practices or something along those lines.

I know I'm not really in the dugout; I know I'm not at the game; and I know what I say doesn't have any effect on the players. But if I could have any dream of mine come true, I'd like to be part of the Yankees. I couldn't be a player, but I'd like to be able to help the team the way I do at home. I'd like to be able to talk to them personally and tell them how I think. I'd like to be a coach. It's a dream and I'm sure it's impossible. But I've thought about it a lot, and it would be incredible to me if I was in the dugout and I could talk to the players and tell them the things I feel. I'm sure looking at it on television and looking at it from the dugout are two different things. And maybe I don't know as much as I think. But on the other hand I watch every game on television live, and if I'm not home I try to tape the game and then watch it later. Occasionally I'll watch it and tape it and watch it again. I'll watch the game twice. I want to see what I can learn so that I can coach them better next time.

Each game teaches me something different about the Yankees, and I try to learn about the other teams as well, how to play against them. I know, for example, if they're playing against Toronto in the Sky Dome, it's gonna be hard to beat them. So if the Yankees have an off day before the series I'll talk to them, and I'll tell them I feel that taking two out of three games this series will be fine. But I don't think they should approach the series trying to take two. I think they should always try to take every game, and if they're down five or six to one in a certain game I don't think the game is out of reach. I've seen them come back; the Yankees have a powerful offensive team.

Another thing is, I take the weather of a game into account. I feel like if it's a hot day in New York or if it's in California and the Yankees are playing the Angels I can feel the heat of the stadium, and I know how it affects the game. If they're playing in cold weather in Detroit or some place like that, I take that into consideration, and it helps me to teach the players because it becomes a factor in the game. I take the wind into account when I'm telling a pitcher how to pitch to a certain batter. I picture myself at each game, though I have a lot more trouble doing it if I hear the game on the radio, where I don't have the visual aid I have on TV.

I'm not doing this for the credit. I don't want the players to look at me and say, "Hey, you were right, that was great advice!" I look at myself as an aid to the team, and in the long run I just want them to win. I picture myself at each game, helping the Yankees win, and I feel really good about that because I am part of it. I'm not concerned about the credit for me, because I would feel it inside myself. I'd feel good about myself if they won. I'd feel good about the team, and I'd feel better about myself. Maybe this is why I get so depressed if they start losing. I feel I've let them down. That's really how I feel in my heart, and when I'm away from New York and miss a bunch of games it hurts me that I wasn't there to help. I'll be away for the early part of this season, and I'm just hoping it's not too late when I get home in June. If they're playing .500 ball and they're still in the race, I'll be there for the home stretch in August and September, and I can be a factor in their playing.

My parents are amazed at how closely I keep an eye on each game, and they think I'm a little wacko. But it's important to me. It's become a part of my life in the last couple of years to help the Yankees win again. I'd take some credit for it, I guess, but I have to face reality. I know I'm not there and that the only people they really listen to are Frank Howard and the pitching coach and the manager. It doesn't bother me; I still have that dream: I'll be there, it'll be the top of the ninth inning with the Yankees one run ahead in a crucial game. I'll dictate a sequence of pitches to be thrown, the pitcher will follow my instructions, and the Yankees will win. I just have that dream.

Occasionally after a tough loss I go out in my car alone and I put on some quiet music and have some time to myself. It's like I'm the manager or the coach of the team, and it's depressing sometimes. Especially if they lose because they didn't play smart, didn't listen. I say one thing, and a player does something else. He just doesn't listen. If I was coach, an actual coach of the team and the player didn't listen, there would be a problem. I'm not perfect either, you know; I can make mistakes. But I do everything I can to get things right. I try to picture every possibility and plan for it, I picture a home run for the other team, or I picture a diving catch in the outfield that cuts off our rally. I picture everything. I have to be ready. I have to be ready. It's interesting, because this is the first time I've ever talked about my feelings about baseball. I'm learning a lot about myself like this. And the dream I was talking about before, about actually being there, is becoming a lot more important to me now.

I didn't attend any games this year, and that may seem surprising, because I live only an hour away from the stadium and I have a car and people to go with. I could ride out there, but I prefer looking at the fans on television. I like to see people cheering and standing up and giving standing ovations and curtain calls. That gives me a special feeling and a lot of energy. I imagine I'm a fan at the game as well as a coach in the dugout. Often I stand up at the start of the game when they sing the national anthem. I stand up. I get very into it. I'm not talking about being at the stadium where everybody stands. I do this at home, in my own living room. About five feet from the television I stand up for the national anthem.

I also give curtain calls at home. You know, if a pitcher has a good seven innings and then is taken out in the eighth, and the fans give him a nice ovation while he's walking to the dugout, I stand up, I clap, and I say, "Thumbs up." And I pat him on the butt because it makes me feel good. I like to make a guy who deserves it happy. I want him to feel loved. He can feel love, you know, and I'm gonna be very pleased for helping him feel it. But it's double pleasure for me, because I'm also being cheered and patted on the butt and seeing that thumbs up sign aimed at me. If the game ends on a home run, I picture myself rounding the bases. I hear the crowd cheering me, and I see the whole team coming up out of the dugout and gathering around me, congratulating me.

So if I think about it, I guess I'm not only the coach. I'm also the players. They're all me. I put myself in everybody else's shoes, and I try to perform perfectly and learn from my mistakes. I try to play smart. I feel what the players feel. I feel the pressure of a tense moment in the game. Then at the same time I'm coaching myself, figuring out what to tell myself to help us win. If we do I'll be cheering because I'm also those guys in the stands. I'm right there, even during the national anthem. I'm there, and I'm the first one to cheer and the first one to boo the opposition. As a fan I'm pretty loud. I clap and cheer and scream, but also, in between pitches, I talk to the players in my head. Yeah, I'm everyone. I'm the whole show. That's interesting to me now. I'm a fanatic.

Dominance from Within
Charles S. Born 1945. Psychiatric social worker. Raised in Baltimore, Maryland. Baltimore Orioles.

I became a fan when I was about 10 or 11 years old. I must have been interested in baseball by that time because my mother bought me a book called *Baseball Hall of Famers*, or something like that. Each chapter was on somebody famous, like Babe Ruth, Lou Gehrig, Tris Speaker, or Ty Cobb, and I remember poring over this stuff. It was fantastic. What I loved about it was that each one had something special about him. Babe Ruth hit home runs. Ty Cobb was a ferocious base stealer, and so on. That's the way the book portrayed it. Each one had something unique that he was famous for. They certainly had much better statistics and more going for them than the Orioles had back then. I liked that, too.

I'm not sure what first got me interested in baseball because neither of my parents had any interest whatsoever in any sport. My father was a doctor. His special loves were classical music and literature. That's what he would spend his leisure time on, but I do have a few baseball memories with him. I remember that he took me and my brother to a number of baseball games. Since baseball meant nothing at all to him he must have understood that it was somehow important for children, something we ought to learn about and be exposed to. Once I remember the weather was overcast. They were forecasting thunderstorms, but he drove my brother and me half an hour down to Memorial Stadium for an Oriole game. I can't remember who they played, but I could somehow tell this was very special because here was my father, who cared nothing about baseball himself, taking me to a game in bad weather. I remember another incident of a similar kind. It was 1960, I think, and the Orioles had a string of very young, very talented pitchers who were called the "Kiddie Corps." One of them was Wally Bunker, a rookie pitcher who was on his way to a nineteen and five record. I'll never forget: half way through the season, all of a sudden at the breakfast table my father looks up from the paper and asks me: "Who's this guy Wally Bunker?" I remember being shocked by the question because I thought: "Oh my God, even my father is paying attention to this. It must really be important!"

Living in Baltimore there wasn't much question about which team I'd root for. The Orioles were a fairly new franchise at the time, and there was a lot of excitement about them. They had been the St. Louis Browns before, and they came to Baltimore as the Orioles in 1954. There was a lot of excitement. It was kind of like when the Mets got started in New York. The Mets were a sort of rag tag bunch of guys who made a lot of mistakes and compiled an incredible losing record. That's how the Orioles were, probably for about the first eight or nine years of their history.

My fate was hooked up to this crew of perennial losers. Willie Miranda was their shortstop, and he usually hit about .150 or .175.* He was the best fielding shortstop around, but this guy could not hit, and when Willie Miranda got a hit it was an occasion. He would hit these little loop singles that just barely got out of the infield, but it was a hit, and it was an exciting moment for Orioles fans. Gus Triandos was their catcher. In his best year he hit about twenty home runs,** and he was considered the team's power hitter. I mean these guys really had nothing going for them, nothing at all. They were overachievers when they won. That's how bad it was.

In the 1960s when the Orioles finally began to win, I felt tremendous pride in the franchise because it was clear their improvement was homegrown. All the rookie pitchers in the Kiddie Corps were homegrown. They came out of the Orioles' farm system, so there was pride, hometown pride, in their achievement. The Orioles were beginning to produce a more powerful team of their

---

*In fact, Miranda's lifetime batting average was .221, but he did hit .199 in 1957 and .159 in 1959.
**Triandos hit 30 in 1958 and 25 in 1959. Charles is doing here what fans often do; tailoring the suit of stastistics and details to fit the general body of a general impression.

own making. In the '70s Steinbrenner would buy some pennants for the Yankees, but we had done it on our own, out of our own farm system. Back in their losing days, before they began cultivating new pitchers, they were known for rehabilitating pitchers. Paul Richards, who was their manager, would get these guys with sore arms, bad backs, things like that, guys who were sort of over the hill, and he would rehabilitate them and make them into winners. I always felt proud about that, too. We were doing it ourselves. We were cultivating talent out of our own raw material, and we were bringing old remnants back to life. When they started to win there was tremendous excitement and a lot of pride around the fact that this was a young team that was coached and developed within Baltimore. Nobody came from outside. Except for Frank Robinson, who they got in a trade from the Cincinnati Reds, all the material, all the manpower, was homegrown. There was a lot of Baltimore city pride. This is our team, you know. We've developed it on our own, and we've done it here.

The Yankees had a tremendous amount of talent to trade away, so they could get whatever they needed whenever they needed it. We made our own team. Brooks Robinson, Boog Powell, Ron Hansen, and then Davey Johnson—these guys all came up through the farm system. Milt Pappas, Jack Fisher, Steve Barber—these pitchers, they were also all homegrown products, and they were the core of a winning team. That became a source of great local pride because it showed we didn't have to go out and buy talent. We produced our own. And the Orioles became known for having one of the strongest farm systems in the majors and for developing their own talent. Frank Cashen was the guy. He was a Baltimore man out of the Baltimore system, and he built the team. Later on he did the same thing with the Mets, but he did it first in Baltimore, and we became the model for other franchises to copy. This is how you do it. You build an extremely solid farm system and you grow your own products. I get somewhat disgusted with the current approach to major league success, which is to buy talent. You don't grow it, you buy it. I was raised on this other model, and I guess it spoke to me because it's something I believe in, something I can relate to personally. I believe in self-reliance, independence, being able to take care of your own needs. I believe in hard work and succeeding through your own efforts. That's stuff I admire, and it represents a kind of ideal image of myself. These are strengths I'd love to possess. I don't always find them in myself. In fact often I don't, but these are certainly characteristics I admire, and in those days they were embodied in the Orioles and the way they'd built their team.

The sports teams, the Orioles and the Colts, gave me a sense of pride about Baltimore which otherwise I didn't have. Because of them I was willing to say, "I'm from Baltimore." Since I live in New Jersey now, people assume I must be a fan of one of the New York teams, but I still take pride in saying, "I'm a Baltimore fan. I grew up there. This is my team." Association with a winning team, particularly with one that had made it on its own that way, gave me civic pride and personal pride. Somehow it seemed to raise my own sense of self-worth, and it seemed to do the same for the city of Baltimore.

We accepted them as losers and may even have found a little charm in their bungling, but the glory, the sense of pride and power, comes with being associated with a winner. They were our heroes and we were identified with them. If they're good, so am I. If they're improving, so am I. That's how we felt: like we were all growing together and growing better together. I'm not sure I could have remained a fan if they'd kept losing and losing. There has to be some glory, some hope that things are going to get better. You're always looking for things to get better. There has to be that fantasy, that belief.

But there's a funny process at work here. Once the Orioles began to win, once they became identified in my mind as winners, their losses became very hard to take. When they'd lose I'd get depressed, sometimes deeply depressed. If the team is good you feel that on any given day it should win. You have the potential so you should win. Every time. It's hard to accept that you're less than perfect, and I guess I'm talking as much for myself here as for the Orioles. It's hard to accept that even the best players go into slumps, have off days and play poorly. I think there's a craving for perfection behind all this. You feel that once you're good you should be at your best at all times; you should always win.

I'm that way myself. When I make a mistake I always feel that I should have known better or should have been able to prevent it in some way. There's a kind of perfectionism here that's driving me. It's hard to accept off days, imperfections. One of the hardest things about being a baseball fan for somebody like me is the knowledge that even a good hitter is going to get a hit less than once in three times at bat. It's hard to accept that he's not batting 1.000. Once a team becomes a winner and you've seen how good they can be, it's hard to accept when they let down, when they don't win or play perfectly all the time. I feel particularly strongly about this as a fan because it's how I feel about myself. I'm intolerant of my own defeats, my own falling short.

When a player or the team does badly, I don't get depressed for them. I don't feel sad thinking about how bad they must be feeling. I get depressed for me. It's like I was out there and I lost the game. I threw the pitch that the guy hit for the game-winning home run. It's that sort of thing, a very, very close identification with every player, with the whole team. So they can raise my pride as an individual and as a Baltimorian when they win. But they can also demoralize me as a person and as a Baltimorian when they lose or play badly.

Sports have a particular potency, a particular hold on me in this respect. There are lots of pretty terrible things that go on in the world that won't depress me, that I won't take as personally as I take what goes on on the playing field. If the Orioles lose it will take me a while to come around. It's too depressing. I can't face it. When I see these long articles in the paper rehashing the game, if they've lost I'll just skim the article quickly. I really don't want to read it because I have to relive the whole experience if I do. I'd rather read about the strategies they're developing for the next game. As I think about it it's the loss of hope that seems crucial here. Hope is a very important issue here. I think hope or the fantasy of hope has a great deal to do with how we relate to sports.

Following a team we're always hoping for that moment of glory. When it does come, the moment of glory is short-lived, and even at its peak you begin to wonder: "Can we do it again next year?" Victory is only sweet for a very short time, so there's always the need to maintain or recultivate that fantasy of hope, the hope that things will get better or at least not get worse.

What you really hope for is dominance. You want to be victorious and dominant. That's the important thing. Your pitcher pitches a three-hitter; he's absolutely dominant, and you can feel that power, that command of the opposition. Or you look at your defense, and you see that no matter what they hit, your defense is making these fantastic plays that shatter every threat. It's that sense of dominance that you hope for and appreciate. Maybe this is unique to me or to certain kinds of fans. Perhaps not everyone is so concerned that their team dominate to this extent. Even in their best years the Orioles weren't really a dominant or overwhelming team. They were the kind of team that would win 3–2 or 4–3, close, low-scoring games, usually won with good pitching and tight defense. They'd win like that, but you always hoped for dominance. What you wanted in your heart was a team that would win six to nothing, ten to nothing. You wanted a team that would always shut the opposition out, shut them down or maybe allow them one run.

The object, as I see it, is to dominate, to be in complete command. That's something I can identify with. I'd want to be that way. You don't just want to win, you want to control the game and be dominant. You want to know what's gonna happen, be on top of it. You want to be like Vince Lombardi who, they say, wouldn't just bend the other team's defense, he would break it. It's not enough to be victorious. This is heavy duty. A lot of aggression plays out in these fantasies. I guess I'm playing out aggressive fantasies of my own, probably because I don't see myself as a dominant person in my everyday life.

I'd like to be dominant in terms of professional success and recognition. I'd like to be very much admired, highly thought of, at the top of the field. And I want to do it entirely on my own, through my own hard work and effort. You want to dominate and you want to do it by making the best of what you've got. If you can't quite do it yourself it's nice if your team can be that way. What a wonderful outlet it is to experience that dominance with your team. I hadn't thought of this before, but this is how I feel. My favorite player on the Orioles at that time was Brooks Robinson, and he was dominant at third base. He was considered, and most people still consider him, the best fielding third baseman in the history of baseball. He was tremendous. You couldn't get anything by him at third base. He would dive for these balls hit down the third base line and make these incredible plays time after time. He was amazing. He was really dominant at third base, and he was my hero.

This takes me back to where I started, doesn't it? To that book about the Hall of Famers, each of whom was unique in some way. Each one was dominant in at least one aspect of the game. That's what I loved about them. They were extraordinary in one area. They did something magnificently well.

VII. Identification

Yankee Goyim, Dodger Jews
"You Need to Know Who You Belong With"

Herb P. Born 1925. Born and raised in Brooklyn, New York. Professor of English literature. Brooklyn Dodgers.

I was born in Brooklyn and brought up in Brooklyn—in Brownsville, no less—a hotbed of Dodger fandom, although there were always one or two kids who rooted for other teams. My best friend was a St. Louis Cardinal fan. He fancied himself an infielder, a shortstop, and he admired Leo Durocher and Pepper Martin, so he was a Cardinal fan, the only one we knew. The rest of us were Dodger fans. It was hard even to imagine being anything else. If you lived in Brooklyn you were just a Dodger fan.

There was something called the Knothole Gang back then, and through this organization we could get into ball games relatively inexpensively. You'd buy this one ticket that allowed you to get into a certain number of specified games. So we'd go to those, but it wasn't enough for us. Especially in the summer, when we were free and footloose, we'd sneak into the subway and then sneak into the ball park. We had various ways of getting in, though it was much easier at Ebbets Field than at Yankee Stadium, where they had that unscalable concrete front. Eventually, though, we figured out a way to get into Yankee Stadium as well, though it's appropriate that there was something forbidding about the stadium, something that kept us out. We'd wait for a group of kids to come from a local Catholic school, accompanied by their nuns. They were all going in to see the game, and we'd get on the line and walk in with these kids.

So we'd go to some Yankee games, but only to root against them. I was an anti-Yankee. They were just too glittery, too successful. They always looked so clean in those pinstripe uniforms. And they always struck me as being of a higher class. When they got some real ugly customer, like Moose Skowron or Charlie Keller, I couldn't figure it out. They weren't really Yankees, not true Yankees. A true Yankee was Tommy Henrich, one of those clean-cut, beautiful types who never made any mistakes and who spoke well—although frankly I didn't know how well or how poorly they spoke. I'm sure some of them were illiterate, but I assumed they spoke well because they simply looked like the kinds of people who did.

They were handsome in their uniforms, whereas the guys that we identified with were always dirty. Being brought up in the kind of environment we were brought up in, anyone who appeared all togged out, with a tie and suit, was unusual. We came from a working-class neighborhood where people went to work in work clothes. My father wore a suit to his job, but most of the others wore work clothes and work caps. So anyone who was elegantly dressed seemed somehow alien. They were the gentiles, the *goyim*.

There was a sense, a smell, a feel about the *goyische* neighborhoods that made them different. The house fronts were different. Going there I wasn't exactly fearful, but I had a sense of apprehension, like someone who had strayed into foreign or enemy territory. My grandmother and grandfather lived in that kind of a neighborhood because he was a builder. But they were the only Jews on the block, on the entire *goyische* block. And they lived next to Italians, whom they called the *luchshi*, the spaghettis. The parents were the spaghettis, and the little Italian kids were the farfuls, the *farfuleh*. These Italians were very nice people, and later on they looked after my grandfather and grandmother and took good care of them. They had adjoining stoops, so when we'd visit, we'd always see them there, sitting on their porch, and we'd say hello to Salvatore and to Carmine or whoever. I liked them very much, but I knew they were *goyim*. I knew they were different, though theirs was a different kind of difference. It was the homegrown Catholics and the WASPy Protestants that were the real *goyim*, the real "others," and the Yankees were all WASPy *goyim*, although they had their share of Italians. In my day they had Crosetti and Lazzeri and DiMaggio. But DiMaggio was never an Italian. No, DiMaggio was just this great American folk hero, not a real Italian, whereas the Italians who played on the Dodgers—Carl Furillo, Dolf Camilli, and Cookie Lavagetto—they looked Italian.

The Yankees were upper-class Gentiles, so even their Italians didn't look Italian. I'm kind of playing with the idea of the Jew and the non-Jew here, trying to find out how I felt about them. I knew the Gentiles were different. They carried themselves differently. I was a young second-generation Jewish boy, looking out of his Jewish neighborhood and not admiring everything he found there. I felt different, other, and I knew I didn't want to feel that way. When I was a kid I spoke differently. I didn't speak the way the other kids in my neighborhood spoke because I didn't want to be like them.

The Yankees could have been my ticket into the mainstream, of course, but that would have been a sort of desertion. I still identified with my people and felt more comfortable with them. How you felt about baseball, which team you lived and died with, had more to do with these matters of group identity and identification than with the pure love of baseball. You didn't become a fan because you loved baseball. There are very few people who love baseball, and most of them are full of shit. These guys, like Giamatti. I don't know where the hell they get that stuff. It's so completely aestheticized, all that crap about hearing the sound of the outfield grass. I mean what bullshit that is! Roger Angell is an earthier sort of guy, but he can also become a little overwrought, talking about the beauty of baseball, its endlessness as compared to games that have time limits. Nonsense! You didn't go to games because of the theoretical endlessness of the games or even to see good baseball. You watched a game to see your team win. And being a fan was more a class thing, more a matter of class identification than an athletic involvement. You didn't like a team because they played a better brand of baseball. You liked them because they somehow represented your city or your borough or your social group, your class. And then you wanted them to win. And just like Croats and Serbs and Slovenes, you don't hate others for good reasons. There's no such thing. You hate them because you hate them. Or if there is a reason—if you can call it a reason—you hate them because they're different, they're alien.

The Yankees were always alien in their clean white suits. They could never make a mistake. They never did anything wrong, whereas the Dodgers were always the Bums. I was a Dodger fan before the Boys of Summer, before the '50s. Back then they were hapless, helpless, hopeless things. They were the Bums, and this guy Mullen, the sports cartoonist for the *World Telegram*, captured it perfectly with his cartoon of the Dodger Bum with his hobo hat and his squashed cigar butt.

The Yankees of course were another story. They were at the other end of the social ladder. They were clean and dapper and they couldn't lose. It was frustrating and exasperating. How much can you put up with? When you finally did get a leg up on them you'd make some error and bang, there it went. Mickey Owen's passed ball in the '41 World Series: I can't tell you what this did to us. We cursed; we yelled; we deplored; we wept; we pulled our hair. It was worse than '51 when we lost to the Giants on Bobby Thomson's home run.

I was a grown man in '51, but I kicked the TV set. I wasn't out there appreciating the infinitude or the fine aesthetic points of the game. I wanted my team to win. I'm a grown man. I'm a graduate student at Brown University, and I'm watching this damn ball game and I'm cursing and pulling my hair. Why? Because I was a fan, a Dodger fan. As a fan I'm not interested in good baseball. I'm interested in winning. I want my country to win. I want Jews to be successful. I want my team to win. Now why that should be, I don't know. You need something to identify with. When other identifications are relaxed or loose or go by the boards, you need to know who you belong with. And in a so-called classless society, where there's no real aristocracy, maybe baseball fandom, sports fandom in general, is a way of identifying. And maybe the need is greatest in a secularized society, because there's something religious about fandom. It fulfills a religious need secular people can't meet in other ways.

You watch and you watch and you hope and you hope, and you do stupid things, superstitious things. You change your position, you smoke or you stop smoking when a certain player comes to bat. If you smoke they're gonna lose. If you lean forward and watch him look down for the sign maybe he'll get a hit. You're performing a ritual, and you believe in magic. You're summoning the gods! It's ridiculous. It's ludicrous, and it doesn't come from an appreciation of the finer points of the game. All I know is, I want them to win because they're mine, because they belong to me. In fact they are me. If they win I win. But at the same time, if you always win, like the Yankees, something's missing. Fandom deepens in defeat. It thrives up to a point at least on disappointment and frustration. That's what's wrong with being a Yankee fan. When we were kids we wondered, "How can you be a Yankee fan?" It didn't involve any heartache, any pain. You didn't suffer. They won all the time, so what's the big deal about being a Yankee fan? Anybody could be a Yankee fan. To be a real fan you had to be a fan of a team that had ups and down, and the Yankees never did. They were golden. Golden.

Being Dodger fans, on the other hand, we're proving our mettle. We're showing them we hang on to losers. We're faithful, and we have heart. And at the same time we're admitting, in our identification with this team, that we're fallible. The Yankees were too good. They were perfect. They weren't really human; they were demi-gods or something. I never appreciated that kind of thing. The Henrichs, the Gerry Colemans, the Gene Woodlings, and the Bobby Browns—all these *goyim*. So clean cut. Stroking that ball.

The only *goyische* smoothie we had was Pee Wee Reese. Pee Wee was the Little Colonel. He was not a ruffian. He was the one classy guy among all those ruffians. He wasn't quite a Yankee, but he was clean-cut, nice, a country boy. A *goy*, but an acceptable one. And we enjoyed that. He was a *goy* that we could love. You couldn't love just any *goy*, but you could love Pee Wee. He was lovable because he was a Dodger. He was our *goy*. He played for us.

So in a way baseball is a game of aristocrats and ruffians, and we identified with the Dodgers because they were the ruffians. They were low down, they were the vernacular. They spoke out, and they yelled. They were vulgar. I can't ever remember a Yankee protesting. I can't recall Joe McCarthy ever coming out of the dugout protesting a close call. Joe McCarthy was like the Chairman of the Board. He was always neatly dressed. In the hottest weather he'd come out with this cool blue Yankee jacket on. And then very quietly, deliberately, he'd point something out, and the umpire would say, "Uh huh," and McCarthy would turn his back and walk calmly back to the dugout. He never yelled, whereas in Brooklyn everybody always yelled. In the house you yelled. On the street you yelled. In the subway you yelled. You know, you talked loud. Loud! It often embarrassed me, especially if I were out of Brownsville, on the subway or somewhere, and there was a loud Jewish interchange with some Yiddishisms to give us away. I was very embarrassed at the time, though today I doubt I would be. I have more *chutzpah*.

The Dodgers were a major part of that loudness. They were more like us, more *hamish*. You didn't have to be afraid to scream at Ebbets Field. You were in good company, which is to say you were in bad company. In Ebbets Field you could say whatever you liked, you could do whatever you liked, and you could yell. Yankee Stadium? You could hear a pin drop. Clean, clean. No fuss. They didn't know what to make of Babe Ruth. He was always a little foreign to them. He was a real vulgarian. I mean, he'd show his ass in public; he'd belch and fart. And he always got away with it because he was Babe Ruth. But the other Yankees didn't appreciate that coarser side of him. Fact is, he belonged on the Dodgers. Babe Ruth was really one of us.

VIII. Formation of Identity and Character

In a sense almost every section of this history is this section. Virtually everything we have heard from fans to this point testifies to the importance of their early love for baseball in the formation of their preferences and values, even their personalities and identities as they crystallized with time. Some speak of their early acquisition of moral standards from the game or those who play it, or of the hardening or deepening of values already acquired or formatively taking hold. Others describe their attachment to winning teams, splendid performers, or those who strive and persevere as the foundation of their own developing commitment to excellence and their belief in the value of its pursuit. Those whose conversations appear in the "Empowerment" and "Parent-Child" sections speak openly of baseball as a crucial, at times almost exclusive source of status, power, access, and acceptance. And those for whom baseball fandom was principally an act of (at times consuming) identification record a litany of lessons learned, values absorbed, and skills imaginatively inherited.

Most of the fans whose testimony we have heard this far, however, focus on a single contribution or acquisition. What they remember, principally, is how baseball influenced them morally, how it affected their desire to achieve or their sense of achievement, or how it enhanced their sense of belonging, their status, or self-image. Among fans whose relationship to the sport was principally a matter of identification, the emphasis is more on the process than its result. Although consequences and benefits may be inferred from their intense absorption into various teams, players, and distinctive features of the game, the fan's mind, even in remembering, is typically on the act of identification rather than on how it altered them, on what marks it left permanently behind.*

What distinguishes the fans represented in this cluster of interviews is in some instances the greater variety and importance of lessons learned, in all of them the awareness of deep and enduring impact. They believe that more than simply adding to a store of attributes or values, their experience as young fans,

---

Tim C. is an exception to this, his attention divided between the act of identification and its moral implications and results.

living and dying with their teams, day after day, season after season, in important ways defined their identity and character. As Joe C., whose full interview does not appear here, forcefully expressed it, "Without baseball, I'd probably be a totally different person ... Being a Yankee fan as a child had a lot to do with how my personality developed. It's a basic part of who I am."

Much has been said—in the introduction to this study among a hundred other places—about baseball as a mirror of American culture or a metaphor for life itself. Thomas Boswell, in *Why Time Begins on Opening Day,* identifies baseball as one of our broadest sources of metaphor and describes it as "a heightened and focused form of our common experience." What my conversations with fans suggest, however, is that baseball is more than a mere reflection of who, as a nation or as individuals, we are. It is a formative, channeling, and altering cause as well. Michael Schwartz is correct to call the game "a creation and creator of personal and social behavior and cultural traditions," but one may go farther. For what these fans discover as they speak or long ago realized and wish us to understand is that beyond even the creation of behavior, their devotion to the game in substantial ways defined who they were as children or adolescents and determined who and what they would become. It is difficult to imagine a stronger claim or surer demonstration that this is a game played and watched for pleasure, yes, but also for the highest stakes. "Baseball," George P. reminds himself, "was a lot of fun—we should never forget that, it was fun—but it also seemed important." If his own and other recollections are to be credited, it clearly was.

The range of responses is, as always, colorful and varied. For Chris H. baseball was, in large measure, a way of establishing his identity through otherness and difference. If his father was a Dodger fan, Chris would ally himself with another team. If the Yankees, for all their stumbling, still had the great tradition and the allegiance of most New York fans, Chris would attach himself to the Mets. And when, at age 12, he moved with his family from Manhattan to Montreal, he held onto and actively flaunted his passion for baseball to maintain and accentuate his Americanism, to define his difference from those around him. It was through baseball that he first discovered and then developed his defining inclination to go the other way. And it was also baseball that, in the continuity and similarity of his experiences of the game at different stages of his life, reminded Chris "that in important ways I'm always the same person."

George P. learned a number of important and self-defining lessons from this sport. Principally it provided harsh evidence for what his Catholicism was teaching him: that even for the habitually triumphant Yankees "the world was a tough place, fraught with danger and failure," and that it was best approached with a Hemingwayish stoicism he found in the silent, teeth-gritting persistence of Allie Reynolds, Mickey Mantle, and Hank Bauer. But for George, as for Chris, baseball was also there to inform and remind him who he was. Pressed into service in his early teens as the lonely proof of his shaky masculinity, it became, in a Princeton environment too exclusively and snobbishly devoted to "higher" things, a determinant and reminder of his grittier self. As baseball established Chris as a Met fan among Yankees and an American among Canadians, George's insistent attachment to the game "was a way of preserving my Bronx identity in this new and threatening environment." Baseball, he still believes, "is the commoner in us all ... It keeps us grounded."

Fred C., a city planner who seems to have planned his personality and career almost as deliberately, learned from baseball "what kind of person I wanted to be and how I might become that person." Unlike George, who seems to have fallen on the sword of stoicism—fortunately on its handle—Fred pored over the text of baseball in search of its messages. Part of being a fan, he remembers and believes, is pondering what the game can teach us and how we might be improved by its instruction. The lessons were varied, basic, and critical: the importance of patience and strategic thinking, among others; but perhaps most valuably the chastened understanding that victory and success, always elusive, are less important than the pleasures of pursuit and of "the game."

It is this last discovery that defines Carl T.'s relationship with the old narrow-miss Dodgers and his lasting gratitude to the joyously tragic crew he took them to be. What Carl loved about his Dodgers was their flawed humanity, their un–Yankeelike unpredictability and lack of control. A computer scientist bored with programming and gripped by serendipity, Carl discovered this passionate inclination first in Ebbets Field and has not relinquished it. From the Dodgers, who seemed somehow to love what they were doing, perhaps precisely because they did it so quirkily and imperfectly, Carl learned to take his pleasures as they came and not preoccupy himself with ends. Since, unlike Fred, Carl recoils from analysis as pleasure's foe, he discovered intuitively the secret of the Dodgers and of life itself. In their devotion to pleasure rather than victory, Carl felt he was "watching life the way it should be lived." In that sense, he concludes, speaking for all the other fans in this section, perhaps in this book, "baseball gave me a direction. It helped me understand what life was about."

Identity Through Difference and Continuity

Chris H. Born 1963. Record distributor. Raised in Manhattan and Montreal, Quebec. New York Mets and Montreal Expos

I lucked into becoming a hard-core baseball and Mets fan the year the Mets won the World Series, in 1969, the Miracle Year. Everything was wonderful. I remember putting together a scrapbook day by day, following the standings and the doings of my favorite players from Cleon Jones to Bud Harrelson. My father was a very big Brooklyn Dodgers fan, and it was the traditional father-son thing. We'd compare Pee Wee Reese versus Bud Harrelson and Duke Snider versus Tommy Agee, and though I did feel a certain sense of having the torch passed down, the Mets were my team. Maybe it was my way of establishing a degree of independence, my own identity. Mainly, though, coming from a stereotypical red-lib household with strong left-wing leanings, it was natural to root for the underdog, and the Mets were always the underdogs, even though they were a more successful team than the Yankees at that time. The Yankees were still the great New York team. They had the tradition, the history, and most of the fans. But that would only have driven me harder into the arms of the Mets. As I'd do later in all sorts of things other than baseball, I said to myself: "If that's the dominant way, then I'll go this way." I don't know if a 6-year-old can make a political choice, but that's what it looks like. Here too, in a way, I was establishing my identity through separation and difference. I am who you aren't.

I'm still doing that, perhaps more insistently than ever. We moved to Montreal in 1974, when I was 12, and I'm a more avid baseball fan now than I was as a kid, largely, I think, because it's different, because baseball is an American sport that defines me in terms of what makes me different. I think it's because we're American up here that I've chosen to use my love of baseball as a defining characteristic. I play up the Americanisms and identify myself as an American, as opposed to a hockey-mad Canadian or a Quebecois or a Montrealer. Baseball is the American sport, and it helps me hold onto my American identity; it keeps me from blending in, from disappearing into the environment. Again it's a political decision, but this time a more conscious one than the one I made when I chose to be a Mets fan at the age of 6.

Being an Anglophone in this town is difficult. At various times over the many years we've been here I've felt oppressed, put down. If you're not American, you're lumped in with the Anglophones; you're a member of a not very well-liked minority. Being American, I'm a foreigner, which gives me a more privileged status than the one I'd have as a Canadian Anglophone. If I try to speak French as an American, there's a lot more tolerance for my mistakes than I'd get as a local Anglophone, and if I identify myself as an American, I fit much better into the community than I would as just another English Canadian. And baseball—I'm very much aware of this—is a part of that American identity. On my FAXes, instead of "Sincerely" or "Thank you," I sign off with "Go Expos," and I start counting the days to spring training from January. I find it helps, because throughout my life I've had a need—not so much politically, but psychologically—to have an identity and to stand out. As an American in Quebec, I don't have all that many people to compete with. There's no real stereotypical American up here. Each one of us is as different from the next as anybody else is, and we're not stereotyped. I'm allowed to be who I am, to define myself as an individual, distinct from others.

One of my fondest memories of baseball as a small child is following the game day by day in my scrapbook. I didn't realize until about fifteen years later that when you're young time goes very slowly, and afterwards it seems to whip by. I was going day by day, assembling my scrapbook, and each day was a major chunk of my life. You could talk about it in terms of percentages. Now, each day is a much smaller percentage of my life than it was 15 or 20 years ago, so baseball, which occupied a great deal of my time when each chunk of time represented a much larger percentage of my life, seemed to move very slowly. It seemed almost stationary, as though time was standing in place.

Basically, baseball was for me what they call it: a pastime. It was a pleasurable way to spend time with friends, be it playing a game, which we did every Saturday, or following the season. But as I say, it passed time slowly—pleasurably, yet slowly. Time doesn't necessarily go quickly when you're enjoying yourself. When you're young, pleasure and the slow passage of time are compatible. I'm 29 now, and I'm older than most of the players. When I first realized that, it came as quite a shock. It marked a kind of turning point in my life. When you realize all of a sudden that you're older than the people you're following passionately and that you identified with as a child, you cross a threshold.

It was crossing that threshold that made me realize that I was growing up, getting older and older, faster and faster. There's a world of difference between how time passes now and how it moved when I was young. When I was 6 and keeping the scrapbook, the days used to take forever, and suddenly, boom: I'm 29. Next thing I know I'll turn around and I'll be 35. But baseball helps me put that fact in the background, keep it a dry fact rather than a sign of real change. It helps me slow time down or freeze it, at least for the duration of a game. When I listen to a game on the radio or read about it in the newspaper, age doesn't matter. For the reading skills required I could be 12, I could be 18, I could be 40. When I'm 40 I'll know more about baseball than I do now, and I know more now than I knew when I was younger. But when you're listening to it, concentrating on it, seeing it, age doesn't make a difference.

I could be totally wrong about this, because I'm trying to put titles and meanings on things that I haven't really thought about and it's a shot in the dark, but I would say that when we're worried about getting older and not appreciating things very much, we remember that it's much more fun being young; also, that in as many ways as I can, I attempt to stay as young as possible. Baseball is a way of doing that. It's associated with youth and, if not with agelessness, then with timelessness, a repetition of unchanged and unchanging selves. In the park it doesn't matter if I'm a 4-year-old, a 24-year-old, or a 64-year-old. I feel at the same level. I don't care if the ball player is the same age as me or if I'm older; it doesn't make a difference. The feelings I'm having are the same feelings I had last year and the same feelings I'll have five years from now. If I forget about baseball for five years because the Expos move out of town, I'll get my act together and move out with them; I'll follow them to Buffalo or to Phoenix, and nothing much will change. Overall, there's no difference in my feelings, my sense of being now as compared to what it was then or to what I hypothesize it will be in the future. Sure, as I was growing up I got bigger and bigger, but I was still the same person. I moved from apartment to apartment, but I still have the same things, and it's still my apartment when I'm there. That's probably one of the nicest things about baseball and why it's so significant to me: It's always there, basically unchanged and calling up basically the same feelings in me, year after year. It's like a foundation you can build on. It stays the same, brings out the same feelings, and it serves as a proof that in important ways I'm always the same person.

I may be going out on a limb again, shooting in the dark, but I think I see a connection here. Baseball seems deeply connected to identity. On the one hand I've often used baseball to establish my identity in terms of my difference from others—Yankee fans in New York, hockey fans and Canadian Anglophones in Montreal. On the other it's a way of holding on to my identity through time. It's a string of similar feelings that ties me together as a person and keeps me young. I want to be different from other people, but I also like knowing that basically I don't change. Baseball helps me do both.

"You Sit Down and Think About What Its Lessons Are"
Becoming a Better Person

Fred C. Born 1944. City planner and member of City Council. Raised in Baltimore, Maryland, now living in Berkeley, California. Baltimore Orioles.

My earliest memory of baseball is of going to minor league Orioles games with my father and listening to them on the radio with my brother, usually under the covers late at night when we weren't supposed to be listening. Lights had to be out at 10:00 P.M., but when there were extra-inning games we'd go on listening, feeling closer to one another because we shared this secret. We were tremendously excited when Baltimore got a major league team, and I immediately became an impassioned follower of ball players on their last legs, Vern Stephens in particular on third base. He was supposed to be a home run hitter. In fact he had a grand total of eight home runs that year, but it was enough to lead the team, which tells you that this was not exactly a great ball club. I think they lost a hundred games that first year and almost as many the next.

They did, however, have some young stars that I identified with, particularly a fastball pitcher named Bob Turley. Following that first season, though, the Orioles made this huge trade with the Yankees—it involved about eighteen players or so—and they traded away both Bob Turley and Bill Hunter, my other favorite player. I was probably around 10 or 11 when that happened, and I remember crying for the first time in many years. I was crying at the discovery that a hero of mine could suddenly pick up and leave or be sent away without anyone asking me. In the end the trade worked out reasonably well for the Orioles, but I couldn't know that at the time, and my first reaction was purely emotional—this sense of desertion and helplessness. What I couldn't get out of my mind was the question, "How could they do this without asking me?" It was probably the earliest lesson I learned from baseball, and painful as it was, it was a lesson worth remembering. They can and they will.

I was active in student government at school, and one of the reasons I ran for office was that I knew if they trusted you enough you could take a day off and go to a ball game in the afternoon; they'd think you were at some other school attending a meeting. What helped me get elected, I think, was that I had organized Oriole Days at the ball park through my church group and at school. One of the days I organized probably made me a shoo-in because I happened to bring the whole group to what turned out to be Hoyt Wilhelm's no-hitter, which Gus Triandos won with a home run, I think, in the eighth inning. The success of that outing was probably the beginning of my career as a politician. I felt so good about having given fifty kids the experience of a lifetime that I figured this was the way to go.

Civic-mindedness has always been important to me, and as I think about it I realize that the players I liked best seemed to be decent, civic-minded men. I don't know if I thought of it at the time, but two of my favorite players were Stan Musial and Brooks Robinson, and aside from the fact that they were both first-rate ball players, they also projected a certain image. They were gracious to the public. They were modest, self-denying ball players who never tooted their own horn; they were good family men; and they were strongly involved in serving the community. These were traits my parents were deeply committed to, and everything I knew from both my religious training and my upbringing in general taught me that Stan Musial was the kind of player I should identify with and try to imitate, rather than, say, Ted Williams.

So baseball was tied up early with who I was and who I wanted to be. Going back in time a little, I remember a game when the older veteran Orioles were playing their minor league club from York, Pennsylvania. York had this young kid who was only 17 at the time, a kid named Brooks Robinson. He got three hits against the parent club, and he became my hero instantly, though he was still in the minors. Since I was about 13 myself, the fact that Brooks was a young kid moving up gave me something to identify with. I was a young boy reaching toward adulthood, and Brooks and these other young kids were examples of young people making it in an adult world. They were proving themselves, which is what I was always trying to do. People would often accuse me of trying to be 25 when I was 15, and in fact I constantly lied about my age in order to do a whole range of things I otherwise wouldn't have been allowed to do. So the Orioles had a lot to do with the formation of my identity as a young kid on the make, forcing his way in, elbowing his way into the limelight and succeeding.

The Kiddie Corps was doing that, and so were the Orioles, a new team in the league, so it was easy for me to identify with them. As I recall, the Orioles didn't finally win their first pennant until 1966, which was well after I was out of high school, so I never did get that full sense of identification with success. Rather, it was a matter of seeing young kids make the regular roster and being individually successful. So I learned you could make it on your own, perform well and have respect for your own performance, even if it didn't get you the big prize.

Being a baseball fan was a very formative experience for me. It taught me a lot. It taught me that important as your own performance was, the main thing was the success of the team. It was always clear to me that the guy who ran up good stats but ignored what happened to the team was not the real hero. Musial and Brooks Robinson were because they were outstanding individual ballplayers who still put the team first.

Baseball also taught me patience. You can't learn to like baseball without having patience, without being able to wait for the right moment and to appreciate the waiting as part of the drama of those moments. It's also much better than other sports for teaching analytic thinking and the importance of strategy. Baseball helped me develop a very strong sense of strategy and an ability to think carefully about what I was doing. You never win a game by swinging the bat blindly. Early on you learn to direct where you're hitting the ball. You change your stance, you think strategically, and while I'm sure other sports also involve thinking and strategy, I don't think they emphasize them as much as baseball does, and that was important to me. It was probably more important to me as a player than as a fan, but they reinforced each other in ways that are hard to separate.

Baseball also taught me that you can have fun without being a major winner. If you can learn to live with a team that loses as much as the early Orioles did, you've learned a lot about perseverance. One of the things I learned as a fan is that you have to lose a lot of the time and that the wins surrounded by many losses mean a great deal. So I didn't have the sense that I had to win constantly. You could take losses, it was okay, and you could play well even when your team was losing. Even when things weren't going well around you, you could perform well. I saw a lot of role models out there, guys who played in spite of pain and who never gave up.

You learned that there are different skills by which people can get ahead, that you don't have to be good at every aspect of the game, which is to say you don't have to be good at everything, whatever it is you do. You can be a great fielder like Bill Hunter and be a lousy hitter and still be a major contributor. Early on I had tremendous respect for defense as well as offense, but I also recognized that offense is generally what wins games. I suspect there is some larger truth that was learned there, but it's learned together with a respect for how defense can keep you in a game.

I'm sure there's a lot to be learned from every sport. But for me, part of being a baseball fan was sitting down and thinking about what its lessons were, about what there was to be learned from the game that might make me a better person with a clearer sense of what works and what doesn't, what matters a lot and what matters less. It helped teach me what kind of person I wanted to be and how I might become that person. Also—and this may be the most important thing—it taught me how to accept and adjust to the fact that what I wanted might always be a little beyond my reach.

"Yeah, but It Was Not a Piece of Cake"
A School for Stoics

George P. Born 1938. Professor of classics. Raised in the Bronx, New York, currently living in St. Louis, Missouri. New York Yankees.

My first recollection of baseball is a night game I went to with my father, my brother, and a younger man my father worked with. My father was an immigrant from Italy. He came here in 1920 or '21, a carpenter, and not much of a baseball fan when I was a child, though he later became one. The first game was around 1948–49, when I was 9 or 10, and what stands out is the crowds, being out at night, especially coming out of Yankee Stadium—I guess it was on the north side at 161st Street—and seeing a huge row of buses with people lining up to board them. There was something exciting about that. The other thing that stands out is that the younger man who went with us was with his fiancée. He spent most of the game necking with her, and I think that was the first time I had seen anybody kiss.

My next vivid memory of baseball is of going to a game in the early '50s with a couple of friends. I remember walking into the stadium, coming in from behind home plate so that we could actually see the enormous swell of it and the three decks. It was big and it rose up, and I had a feeling this was someplace special; there was definitely something special about it. It was also special because Allie Reynolds was pitching, and he was somebody I could identify with. I tried to model myself on Allie Reynolds. When we played stick ball I tried to pitch the way he did, which was sort of straight up, big chest. He was the Super Chief and he was doing these almost super-human things. I was not as successful as he was, of course, but he seemed like someone I could emulate. There was something about him, a strength and solidity—nothing passive— and he never betrayed emotion. I prized that. I don't know if I prized that from the beginning or whether I got used to it and sought it out because that's the way the Yankees were. Actually, that's also the way baseball was to a certain extent in the '50s, or at least the way it seemed. People didn't cavort. When they hit home runs they didn't shake their fists or make wild gestures. They just ran around the bases. They didn't have to put on a show. They already had so much respect from fans—particularly because there were so few players at the time—they didn't need to. They seemed above it all.

I knew everybody hated the Yankees, or at least that they were unpopular, mainly because they always won. This was the '50s, when the Yankees seemed to win all the time. But I had a funny feeling as a Yankee fan. All the time they were winning, deep down I always had the feeling that they were going to lose. I think some of that has to do with personality, or a combination of personality and history. I was born at the tail end of the Depression. My parents, especially my father, never really got over the Depression. There was always a fear that it would happen again, and I think I brought that fear to baseball. We lived in an apartment building in the Bronx. My brother and I slept in the living room, on a Castro Convertible like everybody else, and my parents slept in the bedroom. My parents often talked about moving to a bigger apartment, but in the end they never did. They refused to move. It wasn't because we were poor—my father was making very decent money—but there was always a fear of poverty and failure, and I inherited that. I was always very successful at school, but I suffered from a fear it would all fall apart one day and I would fail.

While the Yankees were doing all this winning, what stands out vividly in my own life is that when I was about 12 or 13 I had to go to a doctor to get my stomach looked at because I was nervous and I was biting my nails. I was doing very well in a Catholic grammar school, but while I was doing well in school I would always get anxious before tests, and when I watched baseball games I had the same fears. Despite my fears the Yankees generally came through, except in 1955. I raced home from high school the day of the last game of that Series, just in time to see Amoros make the catch, wheel and get the double play at first base. I saw the third out and started to cry. I don't know why, exactly, but this was the first World Series I had seen the Yankees lose, and there were some other things going on in my life. I guess it was all too much for me. I broke down and cried.

I was 16, I was doing very well in school, but I was socially almost a retard, and I was living in a double world. Here I was, in this tiny neighborhood in the Bronx, where the guys I knew would call me "The Brain." But baseball was also important to me, and sports in general, in maintaining my identity as who I was. When I came home from school I'd go out and play ball, talk baseball, and sound, I guess, pretty much like a jock, like one of the guys. But at school I was taking Latin and Greek, and my friends couldn't quite understand what I was doing. I guess I needed the Yankees and their omnipotence to keep up the masculine end of my identity, to reassure me I wasn't just the Brain who'd never gotten laid and who doubted he ever would.

Also, this defeat in the World Series was clearly a loss. I don't know exactly what it represented, what other losses it called up in my mind, but the message was that nothing lasts, nothing is permanent, and that stayed with me. It joined me to my parents' fear that everything can be lost, that even if you come out of the Depression you can always fall back into it.

I certainly had a reputation at that time and maybe later in college as a kind of negativist, a person who sees the dark side of things. Some of that was sort of trendy. It was the beat thing, part of the revolt of the '50s, not to be an organization man or one of those other-directed types with big grins on their faces. Baseball's the right place for someone with my outlook because you know even the good ones fail seven out of ten times. That wasn't true of the Yankees in the '50s. I grew up watching this team that did win almost all the time. People kept reminding me of that, but I want to tell them, yeah, but it was not a piece of cake. I didn't think of them as invincible. Who did the Yankees have that stood out? Hank Bauer stands out. He was a big, tough guy, strong, but very vulnerable to right-handed pitching. They also had Gene Woodling, but he was a real snot, a little bit on the peachy side, a sweet left-handed hitter who made things look so easy, while I was thinking it isn't easy, it's really very hard.

Then there were the two years when Mantle finally put it all together, in '56 and '57. Everyone idolized Mantle because of all that power, that speed, the switch hitting. But I followed him in part because his career up until then was to me a lot more failure than success. When I think of Mantle what stands out is watching him bat left-handed, facing Early Wynn, who pitched for the Cleveland Indians. Wynn could throw hard and didn't give an inch, and when he faced Mantle you knew exactly what he was going to do: he'd throw inside fastballs and nail him; he'd strike him out.

Mantle was another of those stoics. He had those terrible knees that caused him great pain throughout his career, but he never complained. I saw, in the way these people handled their problems, a kind of pattern I found it useful to follow. It was a big influence on me. I was exposed to Catholic theology at a Jesuit school in the '40s and '50s, and while it wasn't fundamentalist Protestantism, Catholicism also had this idea of original sin and the inevitability of failure without divine intervention. Baseball gave me something in that regard, and I was lucky to have it. A sport where even the best teams lose very often, where almost everybody's out seven or more times out of ten, and where these big tough guys like Mantle and Bauer seemed so vulnerable but never let up— there was something about this that mirrored my own life, and it kept me going. Baseball was telling me what Catholicism was telling me and what I was gradually figuring out for myself. The world is a tough place, full of danger and failure, and the way to handle it is with a kind of stoic toughness.

I read these books and articles claiming that baseball is pastoral, an escape from the real world, but where were these people growing up? They were growing up in western Massachusetts in an academic climate, and I'm growing up in the Bronx. Going down to Yankee Stadium was my first experience of this other side; this was urban life. There were thousands of people from the city flocking to the stadium, and you know, I don't think they felt they were in some kind of green field in the countryside where everything was pure and perfect.

Certainly you were aware in New York that there was plenty of money involved in baseball. People were betting, they were playing for money. The players may not have been making as much as they are now, but what about the World Series? How much money did they get for winning the World Series? A pittance by today's standards, maybe, but big money back then. I didn't think of this as a Homeric contest of warriors playing for honor, what the Greeks called arete. That was made quite clear to me where I grew up. There was a certain amount of romance in it, but not the kind of stuff I read in Giamatti and George Will, growing up there in Champagne-Nirvana with his father the professor and making the Cubs into some metaphysical lesson. Maybe I was getting some metaphysics from the Yankees and from New York baseball, but it was very different, a very different kind of lesson. The virtues I saw, at least in the people I really admired, weren't pastoral virtues. Sometimes it was this stoicism. Sometimes it was plain hard work, with no glamour attached to it. I liked Gil MacDougald. He had a funny batting stance, but he came through; he was a reliable ball player. He went from second to third, and I think I liked that about him. He made a hard adjustment without complaining.

It was a tough world, like the one I lived in, and you had to make your adjustments. But through it all, especially in '57, Mantle was my anchor. That year I went to work in a summer camp run by a cousin of mine in western Massachusetts. I peeled potatoes. At the same time I was attending a special class in my high school, in Greek, and my assignment was to read one book of the *Iliad* in the original Greek. So I spent the summer reading that book of the *Iliad*, peeling about a hundred pounds of potatoes every day, and following Mickey Mantle in his Triple Crown year.

The camp was coed, the waiters and all the campers were Jewish, and the rest of the staff was Italian. I'd been in coed schools until eight grade, but high school was just with guys, and this camp overwhelmed me. I mean the sexuality of the place drove me bananas. The exotic nature of it was that these were Jewish girls, which meant they were different from the Italian girls or Catholic girls I knew. It meant they were better built. I was just so frustrated, but that's not the point. I've spent enough money over the years trying to figure that out, but right now I'm trying to figure out why that summer was so crucial for me. I think I know what it was. I was threatened by something alien out there. I was lost in a strange and different world. There were a couple of girls who were interested in me, and I was terrified, because what do I do? Maybe I won't be able to say no, and then what? Do I give up my religion?

It was so threatening, so threatening, and yet fortunately, at the same time, there was Mantle, sweeping through. He was fighting vulnerability and pain and doing everything right. It was a wonderful example and a wonderful distraction from what was plaguing me. I was reading the *Iliad*, the twenty-second book, where Hector gets killed. Achilles is coming up against him, and Hector bolts. At first he doesn't stand to fight, but then he realizes there's no point in running; everybody dies eventually, so he turns and engages. You know, I was into 17-year-old existentialism, and though my mother never said it directly—she only asked why I didn't become a doctor or a lawyer—what she really wanted to say was, "Why did they put these fuckin' crazy ideas in your head, this idea that there is something sad about everything?" Well, that was the lesson of the Greeks and the lesson of baseball. Something sad, and yet with a stoic way of coming to terms with it and an occasional heroic triumph. Here was Mantle in the summer when he could do no wrong. He was doing some remarkable things. He hit two home runs in Detroit, one right-handed, one left-handed, and they both went out of the ball park. He was hitting incredible home runs, and he could run like a jaguar. He must have been about 27 years old, and he was at his peak. The achievement was extraordinary, and it saved me.

Baseball was a lot of fun—we should never forget that, it was fun—but it also seemed important. Adults took it seriously, so it must be serious, and it dominated radio and television, so who could say it didn't matter. When somebody would say to me, "Come on, it's only a game," I'd say, "Compared to what?" It may only be a game, but if it is, it's a very important one. It was clearly a very influential part of my growing up.

I realize now that I used baseball more than once to protect myself in threatening situations. I did that at camp that summer, warding off those Jewish girls with Mickey Mantle, but I also did it when I was quite a bit older. After I finished college I did graduate work at Princeton, and baseball certainly helped me there, too. It helped to define me in this alien environment, this higher realm of academia where, unlike the Bronx, everybody either knew Greek or did particle physics or something like that. In that world there were very few of us who read sports pages and could own up to it, and I think one reason I held tightly to baseball is that it was a way of preserving my Bronx identity in this new and threatening environment. There was enough defiance in me to think, "I'm not going to sell out, this is who I am and I'm going to hold onto this." So I would go to Yankee Stadium and sit in the right field bleachers with, quote, "real people," guys skipping construction work. Obviously there was a certain amount of snobbism on my part, but I liked the attachment to baseball, and in a way I needed it. It carved out a little place for me where I didn't have to compete with all those other superstars and where I could feel my roots.

There's a lot here that's just me, maybe, but I'm a first generation Italian, and in a way this is also a typical American story. This is like the American dream. I've realized a lot of my father's dreams. Here I am a college professor, and I do all these things that he can't do, that he wasn't allowed to do, and I feel bad. I feel bad that the sum of his life is a feeling that my life is purchased at the price of his life. I was never really able to come to terms with that. The world I came out of, that world of New York in the '50s, not only is it gone socially, it was always going to be gone for me. I was never going to be able to go back there. I took one step out once I started in this direction, learning Latin and Greek, and now I have kids who have no feet in New York at all.

Donald Hall writes about baseball as a way for some fathers and sons to come together, but what he doesn't go into is what baseball meant to those of us who were becoming unfathered. We were entering a world closed to our fathers, and not just closed because of barriers, but because our fathers—I'm speaking personally now—because my father felt he could never get into it and that all he had done with his life was less because of that. The older I become the more I'm bothered by that. I know I'm not talking about baseball now, but I can see how it fits in, how it does help construct a bridge between those fathers and the sons who are leaving them behind. There's a certain kind of continuity in baseball, a kind of glue. It's the commoner in us all. It's what keeps us rooted in the grass, in the dirt, where our fathers messed up their hands, no matter how airy and detached the rest of our lives become. My father's message was always, "You are not to be like me, you are not to speak Italian, you are not to be a carpenter. You are to go out and do something different, something with your mind, something better. This is what the United States is about." But baseball is also what this country's about, and it holds us down. It keeps us grounded. It brings us back to the bleachers.

Quirkiness in Action
Playing Life the Way It Should Be Played

Carl T. Born 1944. Computer scientist. Raised in Queens, New York, now living in Montreal. Brooklyn Dodgers.

I was a fan of the Brooklyn Dodgers. I don't remember exactly how I became a Dodger fan. We lived in Queens, so it wasn't like living in Brooklyn where everyone was a Dodger fan. I think it was just that my father was a Dodger fan and I picked it up from him. It wasn't long till I became almost obsessed by the Dodgers, and it seems that for years and years and years all I did was follow them. I knew everything about them. I'd turn on the radio for the first game of spring training. I really did that. Occasionally I'd get the games from as far south as Florida, and it was great listening to the games, because it meant that even if this was February, the middle of winter, in a sense the season had begun.

At that age, beginning at around 10 or 11, I just lived and breathed baseball. It's all I thought about as a kid. I used to play it in all its different forms—stickball, punchball, softball, handball—and occasionally I would go to see the Dodgers play. I didn't see too many games in person. It was a long trip to Brooklyn, and I guess there were other reasons as well, but for one reason or another I didn't get to see very many games. Mainly, I listened to them on the radio when they played away and watched them on television whenever I could. I remember Vince Scully, a great broadcaster. I'd watch every game it was possible for me to watch, and I'd listen to every game it was possible for me to listen to. All the time. All the time.

I lived and breathed baseball, whether the Dodgers succeeded or not, but I got very, very depressed with them because I sort of knew that they would come close but not quite win it all. They had great athletes, great, great ball players, but for some reason they could never, never, never beat the Yankees when it counted—until of course the magic year, 1955. Until then I always felt they were great, but that there was something missing. It was like a great tragedy. Something would go wrong someplace, and they would always lose the World Series. It was a tragedy, as though they were meant to lose. You knew they were gonna lose; it was only a question of how it would happen. The games would be close, everything would be close, but something would go wrong someplace, and the Yankees would capitalize like a machine and they would win.

I think this sense of tragic doom increased my love for the Dodgers, because it seemed to me that a bunch of human beings was losing to this corporate machine that always won. I could never get intrigued by the Yankees. I knew they were a good team, even a great team, but somehow the players weren't human, whereas I always felt the Dodgers were real human beings, and I loved them for that. Campanella seemed like a really happy player. Before he had his big accident, he seemed like a really happy guy who was born to do what he was doing. And then there was Duke Snider, who was really good and really graceful. He wasn't in a class with Mays or Mantle. He wasn't perfect. He was a human being, not a god, but I liked him better for that. I could relate to him.

I saw all the Dodgers that way. They weren't gods. They made mistakes. I remember Don Newcombe, a very talented fastball pitcher who was often wild. Some days he had it, some days he didn't, and you never quite knew which it would be. That seemed very human to me. He didn't somehow cleverly figure out a way to beat the other guys, calculating their weaknesses and exploiting them. He just tried to overpower the opposition, and some days he could, some days he couldn't. It seemed like life to me, like it was. Like the rest of us the Dodgers had their flaws and their strengths, and they went out there, day after day, and risked themselves. They put their virtues and weaknesses on the line and hoped for the best, while the Yankees didn't take those risks. They always found a way to win.

These were real players, real people, who had flaws and strengths. They had a lot of color in them also, whereas the Yankees seemed pale. To me, to have color is to be human. It's to be not quite completely stable and predictable. That was the Dodgers. They were the guys who were gonna do sort of off-the-wall things. Their games were very unpredictable. You never knew what would happen. They won in weird ways, often with power, rarely with intelligence. They seemed to be all over the place, and they depended on drama and surprise to take them through. A lot of that changed when they got Koufax. I remember him impressing me as a thinker, a guy who planned things carefully and deliberately and who worked things out. He was really organized, a kind of misplaced Yankee: very organized, very efficient, and very much in charge. The other guys weren't thinkers, and they didn't seem to be in charge. They threw their virtues and deficiencies in the air and hoped they landed right. I liked that.

I admired the guys who always won, but they weren't my kind of people. I liked the unpredictable, the quirky, the human, and the Dodgers had more than their share of all three. I've always liked these qualities. I guess I was first attracted to them in baseball, in the old Dodgers, but the appeal has stayed with me. I'm attracted to quirky people and behavior, to the lack of complete efficiency and control. Take mountain climbing or skiing, or any of the other things I like to do. The general view is that people who do these things are very controlled and efficient, but they're actually extremely quirky people. They have to be, because there's no real gain in doing any of these things. They do them simply for the sake of doing them. I studied mathematics, and I guess that was a domain of fairly quirky individuals. But I never quite liked them because I thought a lot of that quirkiness was genuine craziness, nuttiness, the activity of people who couldn't relate to anything or to anyone. That was very hard to take and not very endearing.

I don't know why I like this other, Dodger kind of quirkiness, and I'm not sure I want to know. It might take the fun away. If you think too much about things, sometimes the fun goes; it disappears when you get self-conscious about it. I guess what I'm saying is that I don't want to think too much about why I like people who don't think too much. I don't want to get too self-conscious about why I don't like self-consciousness. The Dodgers had fun and they were great fun to watch because they didn't think too much about what they were doing. What I learned from watching the Dodgers was that you have to just live. You have to feel things and do them and not analyze. When you start thinking about things too much, your tendency is to do things very rationally, in a very controlled way, and that's just not fun and it's just not life. With the Dodgers it all seemed natural, and it seemed like fun. Win or lose, there was something going on out there because they were just playing life. They were playing the game of life the way it should be played, without thinking too much or making too much of an obsession about winning. They let go and didn't think too much. They just played.

Life is this unpredictable thing, this roller coaster you have to ride and enjoy, without thinking too much about what keeps you up there. Don't overanalyze it, because it will take the fun out of it. That's what the Dodgers did, they played. They were playing life, living it the way I like to live and watch it lived. They were a bunch of characters, and they were responding naturally.

Of course I wasn't aware of feeling this way when I was a kid. I never thought about it. It would be completely out of character for me to analyze my reasons and probe my feelings, so I never did. Not till just now. You just made me aware of it for the first time. That was the fun of baseball. It was a very natural thing, and you learned by watching it that winning wasn't mainly what it was about. As far as I'm concerned, Vince Lombardi was dead wrong. To me, not only isn't winning the only thing, it isn't even the main thing.

I guess it seems peculiar that a guy like me, working in computers, would be so attracted to quirkiness and unpredictability rather than to strategy and calculation. But a lot of what interests me about computers is not what most people think of when they think about them: the very strict and logical following of rules. When you're writing a program you have to follow rules and act logically to make the bits work together. But when you're doing research what you're trying to do is to see if ideas work out; and the way these ideas play out, whether something works or doesn't work, is extremely quirky. You never know what will happen, really, and I think at that level it's fun. There's a lot more nonsense going on in computer research than people realize. Once you start thinking conceptually you begin to lose your ability to program. Your taste shifts with your ability, and you're drawn to the freedom that goes with this stumbling, unpredictable kind of thinking.

I loved baseball as a kid for much the same reason. Baseball gave me the Dodgers, and it gave me the chance to watch this sort of quirkiness in action. It was a theater of different personalities where I could watch these players perform. I could see what they did and how they lived and how they played together, and in an intuitive sort of way I understood that what they did was who they were. I think I knew I was watching something real, and it got me very, very involved, even obsessed. I'd just watch or listen to their adventures nonstop, and I felt I was watching life the way it should be lived and might be lived. In that sense baseball gave me a direction. It helped me understand what life is about. It definitely helped me more than school. School was some place I was supposed to go to and get good grades in, but it wasn't life and it didn't excite me. Baseball was a lot more real to me and a much more important source of instruction. It taught me how life was gonna be lived: that there would be a struggle, that sometimes you'd win and sometimes you'd lose, but that somehow it didn't really matter. Often you would lose and you would have to understand that. Almost nobody can win all the time, unless you're the Yankees, but I wasn't the Yankees and I knew that. Neither are most of us, so you had to learn to adapt to life, to take your pleasures as they came along, to enjoy things as they happened and not worry so much about the outcome.

To me, baseball is really a nineteenth-century game. It's something that people go to, that everybody goes to. It's Sunday afternoon in a small town. You take your picnic lunch, you go to the baseball game, and you find your seats. The men who are playing come over to the stands between innings, sit down with their families, and enjoy a picnic lunch with them before going back to play. They can do that because the game is slow enough to allow it, and I think it was meant to be that way.

That simpler time is long past, but the game retains some of that simplicity and reflects something basic, something elemental in our lives. That's one of the beautiful things about baseball. It's an elemental struggle filled with vagaries, with accident, luck, and uncertainty—like our lives. The gods can screw you up, no question about it. Maybe the mound was a little low or bumpy that day, you stepped in the wrong place, and the curveball didn't come out right. But that's life. It's quirky, very quirky. Sometimes you step in the wrong place. Sometimes your curveball doesn't break the way you intended. You have to learn to accept that. More important, you have to be like the Dodgers. You have to enjoy the game.

IX. Rescue, Fun, and All the Rest: A Concluding Miscellany

We will conclude with three uncategorized but climactic interviews: one that makes what are perhaps the most extraordinary and far-reaching claims for baseball's influence on his youth; another that, after all this seriousness, reminds us that baseball is also "sheer absolute fun" and a third that, like a summary or symphonic recapitulation, manages to touch almost all the bases on this crowded infield.

Carl P. claims no less for baseball, more particularly for his beloved Dodgers, than that they "maintained my mental health, those Dodgers, for ten years." Given the family, social, and other stresses of his childhood, he believes, without the sanctuary the Dodgers' reliable presence and relative success opened to him, he "might have slipped below the surface, become totally depressed for long periods and then dysfunctional." That was indeed, as Carl quietly puts it, "no small thing."*

For Kathy, Cindy, and Valerie, two sisters and a friend, baseball is also a refuge, though of a far more communal and exuberant kind. Theirs might easily have been included among the conversations centering on belonging, since for them the great pleasure of baseball is being at the park with one another and with the "friends" they see everywhere around them. At Yankee Stadium "everybody is a fan, everybody is a friend." But the cause is finally less important than the effect, and what all three insist on and sing in chorus at the end

---

Although the Dodgers' general success was an important part of this saving role, the principal factor was their (and baseball's) constancy. The same players, like the game itself, were there for him, day after day, season after season. They created a mythical world he could escape to and one that provided continuity, certainty, and structure. Saying this, Carl places himself with several other fans in a category of fans space prevents me from giving full voice to, but who are represented, in abbreviated form, in the Epilogue. I was very reluctant to exclude or curtail these interviews, but so much has already been written about baseball's order, structure, historical continuity and seasonal omnipresence that this category, more than the others, could withstand abbreviated treatment.

of the interview is that baseball is, above all, pure fun, pure happiness, sheer pleasure. "There's got to be something in this life that's just for fun," effuses Cindy for them all. "And baseball's it."

Lila C.'s interview provides an elegant—though of course temporary—conclusion to this history, touching as it does on six of the eight perspectives defined in the other interviews. For Lila, as a child and teenager, baseball was a boy's language whose mastery offered her access to their company. It was also a game she played as well or better than they did, winning their grudging respect. The sandlot where they played, and which she remembers with a dreamily nostalgic affection, was their home; it was where they went, where they lived, almost, and where they longed to go back to. One of six girls in a family with no boys, Lila was the only ball player. She remembers with fondness and gratitude the games she attended with her father, the special place her skill won her in his favor, and the pride with which he'd tell his brothers what a terrific ball player she was. She was indeed a terrific ball player, but it did not come to her as a gift. Eager to excel, she worked hard at the game, played it well, and learned an early and crucial lesson: that if you want to do something and spend time working at it, you can do it well. Teaching that lesson, which she would apply to other, later, and presumably more important pursuits, baseball was formative; "it set a pattern for the way I would conduct my life." And there was, as she remembers, also a social dimension to her experience. What struck her, in the midst of the 1968 Detroit riots, was the stark contrast between the interracial harmony of the players on the field and the racial mayhem beyond the stadium's walls. What she saw on the diamond were black and white men working together, teaching her, by their cooperation, "about black-white relations in America and how this problem should be dealt with." For Lila, baseball became a model for how America might be made to work, if only the lessons of the playing field could be learned in the street. Finally, in a quite beautiful coda to her reminiscences, Lila "waxes philosophical," as she puts it, but lyrically philosophical, about her sense of destiny, of life as a pattern of woven threads, and of the ties that bind one phase or aspect of our lives to others to form that pattern. Baseball, she believes, "has been one of the threads that holds my life together, that ties one stage to another and gives it direction."

Although almost all the interviews I conducted touch on more than one theme, most have their emphases. As in a sonata movement or in the narrative of our lives when viewed from a distance, minor themes spin from a center or circle it. Lila, who speaks of her life as a weave of knotted threads, moves accordingly. She glides seamlessly from one theme to the next, giving each almost equal importance and attention, in effect collecting and summing them up. Speaking of another set of tales, those Chaucer ascribed to his Canterbury pilgrims, an admiring reader remarked: "Here is God's plenty." More modestly, surely, but something of that, she seems to say. Something of that.

They Kept Me from Going Under

Carl P. Born 1935. Professor of history. Raised in Newark, New Jersey. Brooklyn Dodgers

We lived in Newark, New Jersey, later in West Orange, but my father's entire family, a very large family, came from Brooklyn. He was the youngest of nine children and I have some twenty-odd first cousins, most of them older than I am, seven or eight of them not more than half a year to four years older, and many of them from Brooklyn. When I was a boy we spent a lot of time with these cousins and their families, much of it in Brooklyn, and pretty often we would go to Dodger games in Ebbets Field.

I didn't make friends easily, and the Dodgers filled a major void in my life. When I was 12 or 13 or 14—this is 1947, '48, and '49—before I began to develop social skills, the Dodgers filled a time void for me, a time void and an interest void. They took the place of friends I didn't have, hobbies I never developed. But they did more than that. Living in a rather dysfunctional family—not really dysfunctional, perhaps, though the marriage was dysfunctional—it was very tense in the house, and the Dodgers were an outlet for me, an escape. My father became a Dodger fan, and to my astonishment, with the arrival of Jackie Robinson my mother became an even bigger fan, so there was something we as a family could do together, and there wasn't much else. By '48 or '49 we had our first television set, and when the Dodgers began to televise their games, we used to watch the Dodgers on television. Together.

The arrival of Jackie Robinson and the fact that the Dodgers had undertaken this moral mission meant a lot to me. It seemed to me a kind of crusade, and since I identified strongly with my father's experiences with the CIO as a labor organizer and later a labor leader, crusades appealed to me. There was a nobility that we all attached to the Dodgers in their support for Robinson. It seemed monolithic and simple: Robinson against the world, with the bad guys on the opposing teams and the good guys on the Dodgers. There were no reports on radio or TV of the internal animosities on the team itself and almost nothing of players' private lives or peccadilloes. None of them made a great deal of money in those days, so they were genuine folk heroes, and they had no feet of clay. Rarely would someone be exposed as less than we'd thought him. When Hugh Casey committed suicide a couple of years after leaving the Dodgers or being released by them, it came as a great shock to me. He was 38 years old. I remember very vividly having gone back during the past nine months—I'm working on a book of my own about the Dodgers—pursuing that suicide and the cause of it. It struck me as something very out of the ordinary, to have an idol fall like that. It almost never happened.

It was a very rosy world, this world of major league baseball, this world of the Brooklyn Dodgers, and I needed that rosiness. It was a very ordered world in which, unlike myself, the Dodgers won far more often than they lost. They gave you enough highs by winning pennants in '47 and '49 before the heartbreaking years of '50 and '51. In those years the Dodgers became a winning team, and that was important to me. I identified very strongly with their success. I was a failure academically as well as socially. I was a lousy student, at the bottom of my high school class. What I now know to be marginal dyslexia had something to do with it, though I didn't know that at the time. My academic skills were down there in the cellar vying for last place with my social skills, and identifying with the Dodgers when they were winning was a considerable lift. I don't know to what extent that affiliation was significant in the formation of my view of the world around me, improving my self-image and my sense of the world's basic decency and fairness, but I suspect it had something to do with it. The Dodgers were winners, and I was identified with them. Simple, to the point, and very useful.

What mattered most, though, was the continuity and stability they provided. The Dodgers provided a continuity that nothing else I can think of did. They were an anchor. From '46 and '47 on, especially from '47 on, it was the same team, right through 1956 when I started graduate school. I had done poorly in grade school and the early years of high school, and my father had been taking a belt to me. My immediate world—family, school, friends—was an unsure and unwelcoming place. I needed help working my way through it and around it, and it was the team that took me through that entire ten-year period, from age 11 through age 21. Through this entire rite of passage the Dodgers were a continuum I could count on. They played day after day, they were at or near the top year after year, and season after season they fielded basically the same team. Whatever else was going on, much of it not at all to my liking, I was able to escape into the ball club during the season. Frequently. Regularly. The offseason was emptier for their absence, and I spent much of it reviewing the previous season and waiting for April. The playing season, which included the summer, was a time when you were less engaged in other things, when your time was less structured than it was during the offseason. And during those seasons I had that continuity and structure. The days formed around a game, the weeks around a winning or a losing streak, the Dodgers closing in or falling back, and the months around the entire race for the pennant. Out there, in the mythical world of baseball, was something I loved and could rely on.

So it was more than just a matter of being a fan, rooting for a team you liked and hoped would win. The Dodgers were a kind of crutch I relied on for a great deal of emotional sustenance—if it's possible to say that about being a fan of a ball club. Knowing they were there, basically unchanged, waiting to draw me into that world and give me pleasure, gave me a sense of anticipation, when there weren't many things that could do that. Being a fan gave me a fix on a schedule. When I was in college and I was either driving a truck or working in a shoe store in Newark, I was crafty about arranging my schedule so that

I would be able to watch or listen to a ball game. I was dating then, and I would work my social life around the games I wanted to watch or listen to. If I had to drive to Tom's River to make a delivery, I would do it at a time that would put me on the road during a ball game. To me that was nirvana; that was heaven, or as near as I would get to it. You know, 17 or 18 years old, driving down the highway in my pickup truck, listening to a Dodger game, and making four or five dollars an hour. It couldn't get a lot better than that.

Out there on the road it was just me and the Dodgers. For some kids it was us and the Dodgers or the Yankees or whatever, but for me fandom was never part of a friendship. I never had friends who sat around and listened to the games together. Sometimes, if I were home during the day, my mother and I would watch or listen to ball games together. I remember my mother when Thomson hit his home run in '51. She just collapsed in a heap, sobbing inconsolably for an hour-and-a-half until my father came home. And then she wouldn't cook dinner. She just went to bed and curled up and cried herself to sleep. Incredible!

I wasn't personally involved with the players as people. I didn't have enough information about them, and frankly, I don't think I'd have wanted it. We'd get only nuggets of information. It was announced some time in 1952, in early July, that Carl Furillo had left the team for a few days to return to Pennsylvania to get married, and I was thinking to myself: "Why is he doing this in the middle of a season? Couldn't he wait till the end of the season to get married?" It never occurred to me that he had to get married because his bride was pregnant. It never crossed my mind. I couldn't imagine a ball player screwing. I knew they did that. I mean Eddie Waitkus was shot by some ticked-off girlfriend—the "silver bullet" and all that stuff—but the notion that there was a real world out there that Furillo was a part of and that he had to take a couple of days off to go home and get married—that was beyond me. It never occurred to me that he had a life outside of baseball, and that was how it was in general. You had no sense of these people as people. You were never allowed that kind of insight, so they were never more than one-dimensional. Stars going into Smithers' Clinic for drug problems or for alcohol abuse, suspensions for failing drug tests, blatant wife swapping, people returning to college during the offseason—all that sort of thing was a blank page to us.

Their role, as I think of it, was to live in a mythic world and to help me get from one place to another in the real world. And I was smart enough to know I wasn't the only person they were helping to get around the board. There were millions of us caught up in this addiction to baseball. And if nothing else went right you knew that at 7:30 you could turn on the TV and watch the Dodgers—or whoever it was you got your fix from—play in black and white for two or three hours. Or you could spend a day at Ebbets Field or at Ruppert Stadium, which I did even more often, watching and rooting for the Newark Bears.

It was reliable, something you could count on when all else failed. It provided structure, quality structure, since the Dodgers were a quality team. I suspect

Yankee fans understood that in spades, winning five straight Series, three of them against the Dodgers, between '49 and '53. We were what you'd call lower middle class. We didn't live in homes, we lived in flats and didn't have our own bedrooms. We knew we weren't rich, but we never thought of ourselves as being poor. And though we never wanted for much, materially, we lived narrowly constrained lives. The very notion of going to summer camp, for example, was beyond comprehension. In such a world the Dodgers were a very satisfying thing. They maintained my mental health, those Dodgers, for ten years. No small thing.

It was important, for this purpose, that they be good. Had they been weak or mediocre, it would have been too painful and too closely parallel to what was happening to me personally. I didn't need to have my own sense of failure reinforced by a team's failure. That I could live without. Reading through old material for this book I'm doing, I often wondered about Chicago Cubs fans or Pittsburgh Pirates fans. What did people like me in Pittsburgh and Chicago do? How did they handle it? As children and teenagers our identification, our sense of who we were and what we were worth, was determined in no small measure by the quality and consistency of the team you rooted for. The Dodgers were always at or near the top, and yet at the last moment they habitually got knocked off. They were good, but they were flawed; in the clutch they choked, or were accused of choking. But hell, so did I, so our similarities and entanglements went deep. The Dodgers were my model of constancy and success, but they were also a reminder of human defect and mortality and a legitimation of my own.

The Dodgers provided the constancy, the constancy. None of those people were traded, none of them retired or left the ball club. Joe Black might fail, Branca might fail, but they'd fail over a three- or four-year period before they'd be let go. Mixis and Hermanski would go. Bruce Edwards would go and Campanella would come along. But the only one who cracked that infield was Junior Gilliam in '53. No one else. Nobody replaced Hodges, nobody replaced Robinson, Reese, or Cox. The got to play out their entire careers with the Dodgers. They could grow old and die, in effect, with the team. When Robinson was traded to the Giants he retired.

So the Dodgers provided something reliable, something structured, something out there you could count on. Sometimes I try to imagine my childhood without the Dodgers, but I can't, I just can't. Maybe I'm wrong, but I have a sense that the Dodgers kept me on as even a keel as I was able to maintain and that without them I might have slipped below the surface; become totally depressed for long periods and then dysfunctional. If I say this to people now they won't believe me. I'm a fancy college professor with all this smokescreen around me, so it doesn't seem possible. But I was a bad student in a not comfortable environment at home, with money problems constantly plaguing the family. I was rarely able to sustain friendships until I was somewhat older, till I got to junior high school, and that was pretty late in the game. There wasn't a lot that was going right, and the Dodgers filled a void. They cushioned me somehow.

"Something in This Life That's Just for Fun"

Kathy D. Born 1953. Insurance agent. Raised in Lavalette, New Jersey. New York Yankees. **Cindy D.** Born 1960. Chef. Raised in Lavalette, New Jersey. New York Yankees. **Valerie A.** Born 1960. Bookkeeper. Raised in Flushing, Queens, New York. New York Yankees.

Cindy: I didn't become a fan until I was in college. I don't remember liking or being involved with baseball before that. But when I went to my first Yankee game, that's all it took. One game and I was hooked. The excitement of it, the nostalgia of it. I've taken many people to the games and usually I take them to Monument Park at Yankee Stadium to see those monuments, to begin the experience with the past. The feeling you get at Yankee Stadium is so relaxing and so peaceful and so exciting, all at the same time. You get your adrenaline pumping and you get completely involved with it. You get to know the players and you start to cheer for them. If they're down you want them to do well, and if they're up you want them to keep doing well. You've seen the negative things they do to the players in the newspapers and sometimes in the stands, and you don't like it because you're involved with them.

We really feel we know these guys. You can tell a lot about what they're like after watching them for a while. We've seen them with their families because we've gone down to spring training. We're that kind of a fan. You see them with their families and you see how they are with their kids, and you get a sense of what they're like.

Kathy: I became interested in baseball earlier. When I was in grammar school Mickey Mantle was the king of baseball. I can remember sneaking a transistor radio into grammar school to listen to the World Series. That was the one time the teachers didn't mind because they were interested in the score themselves. I grew up idolizing Mickey Mantle and Roger Maris. For ten years I listened to the games on the radio and watched them on TV, and finally—I don't know what took me so long—finally I went to a game. Once I did I couldn't understand why I hadn't come to the ball park before because it brought the whole thing to life, made it all that much more special. Being at the park is being in the middle of that history, that tradition, and the Yankees pride themselves on tradition. It's gotten a little tarnished over the past couple of years, but it's still there. The fans know it's still there, and I think the real players know it's still there.

Valerie: My parents were Mets fans, so I was exposed to baseball when I was very young. When Kathy spoke about bringing the transistor to school it reminded me of coming home from school and finding my mother glued to the television, yelling and screaming, "You idiot!" or "Get it, get it!" But these were the Mets, and later on Cindy and Kathy converted me into a Yankee fan. I never went to games when I was younger. None of my family did, and I guess that's why I didn't go. I was 12 or 13 when I went to my first Mets game, and I went to a couple of them. But that was about it until I got older and went with Cindy and Kathy. Since then I'm hooked. I know New York; I know what people do in New York; and I know how they are. It's a rough, cold, nasty, ugly place. But in Yankee Stadium—or maybe in any stadium, I don't know—everybody is a fan, everybody is a friend. It doesn't matter who you are or what you do. We go there, we see people in suits, we see people in high heels, we see people in cutoffs, we see people drinking beer, people who don't drink—every kind, color, size and shape—and they're all there for the same reason. They're all cheering, and they're all friendly. There are no hassles about anything, and the feeling is that we're all here for a good time, and that's what we all have. It's great!

Cindy: The feeling she's talking about—it starts from the minute they play "The Star Spangled Banner." I'm notorious for standing up and singing and making everybody around me sing. I haven't been to any other stadium, except for Veterans Stadium in Philadelphia and Shea Stadium, so I can't say whether it exists everywhere. But at Yankee Stadium there's that feeling, the camaraderie. You're there to cheer your team on, and it's your team ... *my* team. I cheer for *my* team, and I cheer for *my* players. I know these players and I want them to do well. I'm one of those people that listens to the game in the car, or if I'm at the beach I have my Walkman on, and I'm listening to the game at the beach. If there's a game on, I have to hear it.

Kathy: We listen to the games all the time. We watch as many games on TV as we can, and my sister and I have this habit during the course of the summer, especially towards the end of the season, of taping games. That way, during those cold January days when we haven't had baseball for a while, we play our games even though we know the outcome. We don't care, and it doesn't have to be a special game. We just sit down and have a hot dog and watch it. Two weeks ago we did that with one of last season's games. We watched it and it was great. It pumps you up again, gets you ready, gets you going.

Valerie: We love going down to spring training. You see them in a different light down there. They're more relaxed. You're more relaxed. They're not working ... well, they're working but they're not working. The barrier is gone. It's almost like it's time to play, to have a good time. And you really feel that because they all become a part of you. You follow these people for so many months, and when it's over it hurts. You become very upset.

Kathy: You get very personal, very involved. They're part of your life, and people on the outside look at you differently. You're a Yankee fan, so you have an identity right then and there. People look at you and say, "Oh, she's a Yankee fan." What does that mean? Well, it means somebody who is very strong, aggressive, tough; somebody who will stand up to anybody. Oh yeah, oh it does, it does.

Cindy: Talking about being tough, I once threatened an entire section when they were booing one of the Yankee players who happened to be one of my favorites. They were booing him because he was having a very bad game, and I stood up and started screaming at these people. This was when George Steinbrenner was at his worst, and I said: "George Steinbrenner uses negative reinforcement. Is that who you want to be like?" And I went on and on, and by the end of the game I had the whole section cheering for the player they'd been getting down on.

Valerie: We talk about these guys as though they're our friends, but it's not quite that way. It's not a close relationship because they are sports people, after all, and there is that barrier. I know they're not my family; I understand the difference. But they play a game that I love and love to watch, and that makes us close. There's a difference between family and sports. Individually, they have their own life, their own family. I have my own life and my own family. But the Yankees as a team, they're my team, and they'll always be my team no matter how bad they play.

If anybody tries to put down the Yankees they shouldn't do it around me because they'll be in for a fight. It'll be a verbal fight. Like I'll say, "Why do you say that? Why are they bad? You tell me why, and I'll tell you why I think they're good or what they have going for them. Or I'll even tell you why they're bad. I'll be the first one to tell you why they're bad, but that doesn't change the strong feeling of identity I have with the team and its history." Being a fan has saved me a tremendous amount in psychiatrist bills. You can go to a game and scream and yell, and you feel great after. You can get all your frustrations out at the game, screaming and yelling to cheer them on, and you don't have to pay a psychiatrist. It's good therapy.

Cindy: I don't know if it's a therapeutic thing for me. I'm not an overly excitable jump-around nut person, but it does something for me, I can say that. I never left a game feeling bad, I can tell you that much. Never. Even if the Yankees get beaten badly; even if we sit in the rain for five innings and they cancel it ... and we've had that happen to us. Once I drove through three hours of traffic on opening day with a stick shift so my leg was asleep, and we got there in the seventh inning. But I was still happy when I left. I only saw two innings of baseball, but I was satisfied. I'm always satisfied at a game, no matter what.

What makes me feel so good at a game? Well, you go with friends, usually, and that's always good, the social aspect of it. Then, too, you're a part of something that's so big, and yet in some way you still feel significant. Why you feel significant is hard to say, but you do. You get recognition in one way or another—from the fan you don't know three seats down when you go: "Yeah, go Bernie Williams!" and he says, "Hey, yeah, Bernie Williams, go!" Somebody else is there saying the same thing you are. It's like a small town, a little community. You're in Section E, Box 7; you're seat number 23; there's number 25, there's number 22. We're all here. Great!

Valerie: You definitely get attached to certain people for certain reasons. To the players as well as to the fans. With some it's for their amazing playing ability. With others it's for their buns. You know, whatever turns you on: if you're a face person, a leg person—there are some good legs out there—a lot of different reasons. You see somebody on a commercial, a guy who's behind a catcher's mask every time you've seen him in a game, and you say, "My God, the man has a face, and it's gorgeous!" You never knew that before, but there it is. There's a physical attraction out there, no denying it. Just as there is for men when they watch female entertainers. I assume that plays a very big part in their enjoyment, and when women watch ball players, well, they are entertainers after all. They're out there with the public, and there's definitely a physical attraction. It's a physical game.

But it's more than just physical. The player has a personality. You know where he's from, you know what he does, and you know what he is. That makes it different. A stranger walking down the street may be a very pretty face, but a man in a uniform with a nice butt—and that's Matt Nokes—hey, that's somebody! You know who he is.

Cindy: In our case especially it's not just the physical bit. We like the players themselves, and we don't just like the cute ones. We're not groupies. There's another side to this woman thing. Growing up in the early '60s, bringing the transistors to school—99 percent of the time it was the boys who brought the transistors. Most of the girls didn't know who Mickey Mantle was or care to know. I have two sisters. We never went to a ball game. My dad never thought to take his daughters. If he had a son I bet they would have gone.

Valerie: One thing that annoys me is that if I'm talking with some guy about baseball he tends not to believe what I tell him, simply because I'm a woman. While I'm sitting there he'll go through ten other guys in the bar to check out what I said, and then he'll come back and say, "Well, you were right." He's surprised. Men tend to look at me the way a female might look at the cute guys on the team. I do that, but like I said, I also know the stats. I know what they're hitting; I know what they can do; and it's a little annoying that men won't take me at my word for something I know. It gets to the point where I'm beginning to understand that's how males are programmed: not to believe a female might know something like that. So you just sit there and tell them what you think, and you smile and watch them walk around the bar and wait for them to come back and admit you were right. Then you say, "You're an idiot. Listen to me next time, I know what I'm saying. I know what I'm talking about." And finally, after a while, certain people will come to me and ask me a question because they know I'll know the answer. It just takes time for men to recognize that and to accept it.

So there are some annoying things, but they're small things, and after a while, as I say, even they give you satisfaction. If I had to sum it all up, I'd say that more than anything else baseball gives you happy times. That's for sure—some great memories, some fun times. It's a good excuse for a bunch of people to get together. There's nothing finer, after a hot summer day, than to go out to the stadium and sit in the cool breeze and watch. Just sit back, put your feet up, have a dog, and watch the game. I think that's one of the nicest ways you can possibly spend your time. It's sheer absolute pleasure.

Kathy: It's a great escape from all the hassles of the day. You can put them in the back of your mind and not worry about them. What you worry about is whether he's going to steal that base or make that hit, and then there's always the possibility, the thrill that you might catch a foul ball. We also tend to stay after the games to get autographs from the guys. That's how we get to know a little more about them. We see who comes and signs, who snubs the fans, who doesn't, and that changes my opinion of a player even more than his face.

Cindy: I don't know if I want anything to be profound about baseball or what it does for me. I want it to be an escape. I want to go to the ball park, and I want to see the players, and as Kathy said, I want to see the players afterwards to see how they treat the fans and to go to spring training to see how they are with their families. I like that. I like to see that, to see what kinds of cars they drive, things like that. I don't want anything to be profound about it. I want it to be pleasure, and that's what baseball has given me. It's given me some incredible wonderful times, some great times with friends, meeting new people at the stadium. You go to the stadium, and if you're sitting in the same section time after time you get to know some of the people sitting in that section. You have a bond with those people, and with the people who work at the stadium. I've gotten to know a lot of the people who work in the different clubs because we've dropped in so often. It's fun to go back and see them and say, "Okay, how are you doing? You got a new restaurant. That's great, that's fabulous. Good luck with it." And you get to know those people, and it's fun. There's got to be something in this life that's just for fun. And baseball's it.

Valerie: It's pure good fun, and there's got to be a place for that. That's what Yankee Stadium is for me. It's a place where I go to have fun. I was thinking about what Kathy said. It's the escape. That's it for me because I actually do escape. I come from New Jersey to go to the games at Yankee Stadium. I don't know if that's escaping over the George Washington Bridge, but it's an escape. It's where you leave, in a way, who you are. I'm the bookkeeper at Advanced Electric, and all of a sudden I'm not. I'm this person in a baseball hat driving across the George Washington Bridge. You're escaping the day, the troubles, anything that's on your mind. You can't sit there and mull over the day's events when you're watching a baseball game. It takes you out. It takes you somewhere else. Even if you've had a very hard day, it's easy, very easy, to forget. We've all had a lousy morning this morning, all three of us did. I had to work, she had to work, and look at us, we're happy! We said, "Hey, we're going to the [Yankee Fan] Festival, and we're gonna have a good time." There wasn't even any question about whether we were going to have a good time. We just knew it.

One of Fate's Threads
Lila C. Born 1958. Executive searcher (head hunter). Raised in Kalamazoo, Michigan. Detroit Tigers.

My earliest recollection of baseball is of taking a little transistor radio into my room to listen to Ernie Harwell call Tiger games at night, and hiding us both under the covers so I wouldn't get caught. My main concern was to learn the game. I played baseball with a lot of boys, and I wanted to be able to speak their language, so this was a kind of learning time for me, each game a new lesson. I wanted to be one of the guys, and this was the way to do it. I was learning to speak their language.

I loved playing the game, and I played it very well. Every day, my main concern after school was to get dinner over with, do my chores, and get my homework done, so I could get out to the little sandlot around the corner. It seemed big at the time, but I've since seen it, and it's very small. Still, it was a special place for me. When I think back on that time it all seems kind of dreamy. It's strange. In a way that sandlot was our home when we were kids. It was where we went, where we lived, almost, and where we longed to go back to. Most of the kids who played were boys, of course, but I could play as well as, or better than, most of them. I have vivid memories of many of the boys with their tongues sticking out at me, angry at having been beaten out by a girl, being picked for a team after I was. I got a kick out of that, not in a malicious way, but because I earned that selection. I wasn't picked first or second because of my baby blue eyes. I could hit the ball and I could play the game, and I liked that feeling of competence, of doing something well.

It was more than that, though. There were other things I could do well, but they didn't have that same emotional significance for me. I was the oldest of six daughters. My father had always wanted a son, and he and my mother were always certain the next one would be a boy. But it never was. My youngest sister is 12 years younger than the next youngest. My parents had her because my mother was certain, just certain, she would be a boy. She wasn't, of course; there were no boys, but my father was determined that this wouldn't deprive him of the kind of parent-child friendship he was so eager to have. I would watch baseball and football games with him, and he would take me to work with him sometimes. He was a carpenter, and he'd let me lay the boards on the saw horses and measure them, things like that. I just loved it. He never treated us as girls or boys; we were just who we were. He was a really great, great father. Sometimes, when we'd have relatives over and my father would be sitting around with my uncles I'd hear him say something like, "Oh yeah, she's a terrific baseball player," and I'd feel good all over. I really liked that; I really liked pleasing him, and my skill as a baseball player gave him special pleasure.

I loved the fact that I was the only one of the six of us who played baseball. I liked to be distinguished, period. Not in an arrogant way; I didn't lord it over my sisters. I just liked to excel at whatever I did, and I found that when I focused my energy on something it usually turned out really well. So I worked at baseball and played it well, and since they didn't play it at all, it added to the prestige I already had as the oldest sister.

I've never thought of this before, but now that it comes up, I guess I was aware of being special and enjoyed that feeling and its privileges. I was special being the oldest, and I was special being the only one who played baseball. And among the boys I was pretty special, too, because I was as good or better than they were. I knew if I invested enough energy and focused on something I could do it really well. And if I couldn't do it well at first I was always willing to go the extra mile, and that's been true of me all my life. I believed that if I made up my mind to do something and wanted it badly enough, eventually I'd be good at it. I got some of that from my mother. I haven't talked about her much, but she has one of the most positive attitudes of anyone I know. She instilled that self-belief in me, in all of us, and I feel very fortunate to have gotten it from her.

It's deeply entrenched in me, something I don't even have to think about, but it shows up in my attitude toward work. I'm a workaholic. When I say I'll go the extra mile I mean I'll do whatever it takes to get something done the way I want it done. And I think baseball was one of the earliest expressions of that, the earliest I can recall. It was a kind of foundation for how I'd later relate to school, to work, to just about everything I did. Baseball was where I first learned that if you want to do something and spend time working at it, you can get somewhere.

I said before that I get kind of dreamy when I look back on those times and think about playing ball on the sandlot, and I do. Those were probably among the very best times of my life, going down to this little tiny sandlot where we played. I *could not wait* to get there every night, could not wait to get there. If I had been a boy, I would probably have thought about a career in the Major Leagues, but I had no such ambitions. For me it was almost a surreal time. It was a really comfortable time at a really comfortable place, and I just loved it. It was a comfortable time in my life, generally, and my home was also a warm and welcoming place to be, but the sandlot was set apart; there was nothing to compare to it.

I can't really explain why because I don't know why, but going there was going to a place where I belonged. It was just a feeling I had. When I was there, whether the boys razzed me or not, I belonged there. I could do this well and their razzing didn't bother me one little bit, because when I got a key hit or hit a home run across the street they'd pull their tongues back into their mouths and cheer for me. I was just one of the guys, and I felt, "This is my place; I belong here." It's not that I didn't belong anywhere else and that this was a place I escaped to. There was no somewhere else because I was there all the time. Where else was there? I was there all the time, every moment I could be there, playing ball. We even played in the rain. I can't emphasize too strongly how impatient I was to get out of the house and get down to the sandlot. I would have spent every hour of every day down there if I didn't have other obligations. Everything else was there just to be done and gotten out of the way so I could go play ball.

Being a Tiger fan kind of rounded things out, because I belonged there, too—under the covers with my transistor and Ernie Harwell's voice. I loved the Tigers. I thought they were outstanding, and at the time they were. I became rabid about the game on the cusp of the 1968 World Series, which was an emotionally charged time where I came from. In school, even the classes were set aside for the Series, and TVs were on in the lunchroom so we could watch. My feeling was, "Boy, this must be very important. They didn't let us out of class and turn the sets on for the Kennedy assassination, so this must be something really special!"

On top of that I had the Tiger owner, John Fetzer, right there in my hometown. He owned the team, my team, and I figured if somebody can come out of Kalamazoo and buy a Major League Baseball team, anything's possible. He was a poor boy who worked himself up from nowhere, and he was proof of what I'd learned down at the sandlot: that if you want something bad enough and put your mind to it, you can have it, you can do it.

But there was another dimension to all this as well, a social dimension. Nineteen sixty-eight was also the year of the riots in Detroit. They were in the news, of course, but I wouldn't have been nearly as aware of what was happening socially in the country or even right there in Detroit if not for my love of the Tigers. I was only ten years old at the time, and ten isn't an age when most kids are very involved in that kind of thing. But I knew what was going on, and it really meant something to me because of the team's involvement. When I saw Willie Horton going out into the neighborhoods and trying to calm things down in Detroit, which was literally burning, I thought he was doing an incredible thing. And when I saw these black men and white men taking the field together and making a dream, a fantastic dream, come true by working together, exactly the antithesis of what was happening outside of the ball park, I felt even more strongly about these men. I felt they were good human beings, and I believed they were showing us the way.

So at ten years old I developed a social conscience that I don't think I would have had if it weren't for the Tigers. It was through them that I learned, in a way I could feel deeply, about black-white relations in America and how this problem should be dealt with. Look how successful they'd been because they knew how to conduct themselves. These people, blacks and whites, were going out and playing together and working together and urging each other on and making something happen. And ultimately something really big did happen for them. They won the World Series, which they couldn't have done if what was happening outside on the streets of Detroit had been happening inside Tiger Stadium. The contrast was striking. On the streets and in the news you were seeing black and white people killing each other, beating each other, burning each other's homes and businesses down. And then you moved inside, to Tiger Stadium, and you saw a joyous reunion of people, black and white and Hispanic, working together for a common goal. Had they been behaving the way those other people were, they'd have gotten nowhere, so this was a clear demonstration to me of how life is supposed to work. Baseball was a clear, clear demonstration and a model. Its message was, if we could learn how to bring that kind of interracial teamwork outside the ball park, we could build a truly great nation.

Willie Horton was a crucial figure in this drama. During the riots there were pictures of him, in the newspapers and on TV, standing in front of a burning building with people milling around him on the streets with rocks and sticks. In the midst of all that chaos Willie was pleading with what he referred to as "his people." "We can't be doing this to one another," he was saying. "This has got to stop." I was full of admiration. That was a really dangerous thing for him to do, but he cared enough to take the risk. He cared about his own people and he cared about America, and seeing him out there had a powerful effect on me. These guys were role models to me then, in a way that I'm not certain they are for children anymore, though I hope I'm wrong.

One more thing comes to mind. I truly believe that all things work together for the greater good. I think we live lives made up of threads, each one attached to the next and that to the next and so on. As we move from place to place and thread to thread, there are ties that bind and sometimes things that sever, but it's the ties that bind that form the patterns of our lives. And what I've found in my life is that from the little 10-year-old girl playing baseball to what I'm doing today there's a very clear path I could never have predicted. It's almost as if the playing was preparation for doing what I do now.* When I first started

*When interviewed, Lila was coordinator of special events for the Detroit Tigers organization.

this job and received calls from people like Willie Horton, it blew me away. I mean, my God! Willie Horton! It was incredible, absolutely incredible! But over the past few years I've talked to baseball players all over the country: Brooks Robinson, Al Kaline, all kinds of ball players, including the best of them, and now I see them for the people they are. They're just people. Wonderful people, for the most part, but no longer superhuman to me, just people like myself, who have their very good points and their flaws, just like I do. I've come a long way: from distant admiration to intimate friendship, from a fantasy of near perfection to a reality I cherish just as much. And since this is the last year I'll be doing this work with the Tigers, I'm feeling a little melancholy. I'm moving on, closing this chapter of my life, and I don't know what my relation to baseball will be after this weekend. One thing seems clear, though: Baseball has been one of the threads that holds my life together, that ties one stage to another and gives it direction. It's different things to me at different times, and it seems to provide what I need at each stage, as though it looks into me and understands.

Yes, I believe in a kind of destiny, that things are somehow meant to be. I feel that way about everything that happens in my life. I believe we meet the people that we meet for reasons, and in retrospect, if not at the time, I can usually see what those reasons were. I often find myself on paths that were entirely unpredictable. I could never have predicted that I would be doing this work. It came about as a direct result of a catastrophic illness that left me unable to walk. I was led to the Tiger organization by connections I made while I was director of public relations and a fundraising person for the Center for Independent Living, an organization based in Berkeley, California, that serves the disabled. Fundraising for the center I met a football coach who preached chapel for the Tigers and who told me that if I ever wanted to do something with the Tiger organization, a fundraising benefit or whatever, I should let him know. Well, I had this idea for a benefit game between Tiger old timers and a minor league club and called him about it. "You're in luck," he said. "Ernie Harwell's giving a talk at Albion College on Sunday. Why don't you come on over? I'll introduce you to him and we'll start there." When I met Ernie—I don't have to tell you what a thrill that was—I asked if he'd do the play-by-play for this game. He agreed, I knew I had a game, and that's how it all got started. The guy whose voice I tucked under the covers with me at night when I was 10 years old, the man who first introduced me to baseball and the Tigers, would be doing a play-by-play especially for me 25 years later, and before long I'd be working for the Tigers myself. Mr. John Fetzer, on the way up.

Sometimes I wax kind of philosophical about things, but yes, I do believe in a kind of destiny. I truly believe, in my life anyway, that I meet the people I meet for a reason and that there is a greater plan than I know of, prepared and set in motion by some greater power. In my life, baseball has been no small part of that plan, and I'm brimming with gratitude for everything it has given me.

Epilogue

Narrative, Drama, and Beyond

As these conversations testify, the aesthetic view of baseball typically includes analogies with specific literary (and occasionally other) forms. John D. compares it to an heroic legend or epic poem, Andy C. to an heroic or archetypal drama, Sanford F., variously, to a coherent and completed play, story, or ballet. At least four other fans I spoke with perceived baseball in these analogous terms, at times centrally, and while constraints of space prevent my reproducing their interviews in full, their descriptions of the game are at once too creative, too wise, and too representative to eliminate altogether. I will therefore deviate, in this one instance, from the pervasive format of this history to present a few summarizing excerpts from these conversations. We will lose much of the texture, drama and narrative flow of their own reflections, but should be able to measure, with greater clarity perhaps, the distinctive angle of their response.

That baseball is dramatic, akin to drama, even melodramatic, has been noted by more than one professional observer. Richard Skolnik praises baseball as the sport which, more than any other, "has learned to manipulate and elevate its dramatic potential." It has, he claims, an "incomparable knack for ... creating dramatic situations, slowly milking them in ways almost shameless and then discharging most suddenly all the accumulated tensions until it's time for the process to repeat itself." Thomas Boswell, responding in *Why Time Begins on Opening Day* to the same unembarrassed excess, argues that the real thing leaves baseball fiction panting on the basepaths. "Actual pennant races," he points out, "are more melodramatic, improbable and all-purpose purple than fiction dares to be. Every first-class pennant race puts the excesses of pulp fiction to shame." For Dennis Porter, to whom baseball is a family or folk drama akin to the fairy tale, baseball is much closer to drama than to narrative art. And while most would perhaps agree with him, the testimony of fans indicates what it always does: that baseball is closer to one thing than another principally because that is where the pointer stands. Baseball is a poem, a painting, theater, and ballet. Self-contained and reflective, it is also a short story or a collection of tales; it is an epic, a comic, heroic, or tragic drama and a melodrama;

and, as we shall see, it may also be a novel or a fairy tale steeped in reality, a construct so real that lesser arts only aspire to its condition.

For Maureen B., baseball was an unending Arabian nightful of stories and a special, quite indispensable language composed chiefly of these sentences or tales. "To me," she remarks, "that's what baseball is about: the great stories that surround it and that pass, like folk tales, from one fan to another or from one to whoever's willing to listen. Everyone has his favorites. There are so many you feel flooded with them." And there is no adequate substitute for them; so basic are they, their absence is all but unimaginable.

> I grew up reading baseball. I grew up hearing it. There was always a game on. The radio was always going, and we loved it. So to me it's like another language I learned as a child. It's very comfortable and familiar to me. So how much would I miss baseball if it were suddenly taken away from me? As much as I'd miss my language. If I had to give up speaking my language, if suddenly I couldn't speak English anymore and had to speak only another tongue, how much would I miss English? That's probably how much I would miss baseball. It's a language to me. And it's a fabulous storehouse of stories. It's like all your family stories. Every family's got these great stories about itself. What if you could never tell those stories again? What if nobody ever wanted to hear those stories again? Maybe that's what losing baseball would be like."

For Hank G., a 65-year-old Tiger fan, baseball is not a collection of related and eminently relatable tales, but, in the shape each game assumes, quite explicitly and formally like a novel. The analogy is apparently something Hank has thought about previously, because it flows into the conversation neatly shaped. "I approach baseball like a novel," he announces.

> The beginning of the game is like the opening of the novel where you meet the characters and the plot begins to move and you begin to understand. In the middle innings things slow down; there are lulls, a little boredom. But that's part of the novel, part of the charm of a good novel. I remember reading Dostoyevsky. There were certain times when I got a little bit bored. But as I went on and on it got more interesting, and you can look at baseball that way. When people say they're bored by baseball I tell them, "Well, approach it the way you approach a novel, because that's what it is. The plot is unfolding in front of you." And when you get to the climax, to the end of the ball game where you're hanging on every pitch, well, there's nothing greater. Basically I get the same feeling from a ball game that I get from a good novel—the feeling of complete and absolute enjoyment. Going to a game is like turning the pages in a book. It's got a beginning, a middle and an end, and it rounds itself off. It comes to a resolution where somebody wins and somebody loses. To me, it's absolutely perfect."

If Hank G. reads baseball like a novel, to Barbara S., a 44-year-old St. Louis Cardinals fan, each game is essentially a two-tiered drama: one level visible to all who care enough to seek it out, the other a running undertext available only to the experienced fan, the literate theatergoer or critic. "Drama," she tells us, "is what I've always looked for in a baseball game and what I responded to most. There's a lot of drama in a game, and only people who don't like baseball don't see the drama. The drama is watching a story unfold and seeing something built. Whether a pitcher is approaching a strikeout record or trying to work his way out of a tight situation, or whether your team will put the tying run in scoring position—that's the drama of the game, and people who can't see or can't appreciate that drama say, 'Ah, baseball's boring. There's no action.'"

That is the surface drama any lover of the game can hook into.

> Part of the drama is kind of hidden under the surface. It's something you feel but can't put your finger on. It's a kind of underground drama the real fan feels below the surface. When I watch a game I pick up little signals and signs here and there and piece them together. I'm tuned into the underground drama, the one growing under the surface and waiting to happen. I'm not necessarily conscious of the process. I'm not making an effort to study the game in this way. I'm just caught up in that hidden drama, anticipating what's going to happen or what I think or hope will happen next. My mind is processing the signs in an unconscious way, the way you do when you're watching a play or a movie or reading a story. After a certain length of time, using your background and your experience, you can anticipate that this team will pull it out in the late innings or that this team is going to get blown to smithereens in this game. It's a drama, and even if your team is out of the running in the pennant race or in a particular game there is still a story going on. Every game is a kind of story, a kind of drama. I can't explain it. I'm probably just rambling instead of making sense, but that's how I feel it. Even an inning can be a story. Take Hrabosky. He could make a single inning into a whole story. I remember one time he walked the bases loaded with nobody out and then struck out the side. Talk about going nuts! The fans went crazy! The game didn't matter. The Cardinals weren't going anywhere. But he did this against the Reds when they were world champions! So that was a great dramatic story right there.

Barry C. sees a similar play differently. For him, too, baseball was a drama, high drama, but it was more powerful and more significant than drama because it was also real. Like John S., in other words, Barry focuses on both the aesthetic shape or quality of the sport and on its capacity, like great art, to simultaneously distill and reflect reality. His Dodgers were in New York State, but not in Albany. Situated in that middle space, "they were close enough to be accessible, yet far enough away to be really different. They were the dream of all I wanted in life, but they were close enough not to be fairy tales. They were real dreams. They were a fairy tale that was also a part of this world, and I think that's what I liked about it: that it wasn't so otherworldly that it got too mystical for me. Baseball was where you lived and what possessed you. It was the realest thing in your own daily life."

Like great art, however, "Baseball was [also] the essence of life," and here Barry works a wonderfully inventive inversion of the old cliché that sees art/baseball as an imitation of life. Listening to him speak, one hears the interchangeability of the two terms, the two distilling mirrors. "A lot of life," he argues, "was like an imitation of baseball rather than vice versa. I always wondered: why does this game control so much of my life and affect me so powerfully? The central concept of life, the notion of rules, the notion of human valor, a certain code of ethics that sometimes exists, that I thought existed, the mixture of joy and sadness—all this is found in baseball and seems to find its purest, least adulterated form there. Everything we're doing—growing up, going to grammar school and high school, our life with families—in some ways it's all a faint imitation of the real thing, baseball, rather than vice versa. Baseball is the essence, it's the core. It reflects all the major values and feelings that life offers, and it does it neatly, concisely, on a diamond in two or three hours, or in a boxscore. It isn't clouded over by all the other messy stuff that confuses life and hides its essence."

At the end of his impressive riff, Barry brings the implicit analogy to the surface, restricts art to its dramatic expression, and gives baseball the nod in a not very tight ball game.

> I'm trying to sum up what baseball meant to me, what it represented. And I think I saw it, and still see it, as this artificial playing ground of life, except I don't think it's artificial. I really do believe it's the real life which everything else would like to imitate. Baseball isn't a play or drama as some people claim. It's more real than drama. It's the real thing; it's what drama aspires to be. Drama, I guess, would like to be the real thing, but the best it can do is write it like a play or put it on stage. This is the real thing. Baseball isn't high drama; drama is high baseball. Or rather it would like to be high baseball; it doesn't quite make it. Baseball is the essence, the purified essence of real life, something art and dream can only aspire to, can only try to imitate. The religious experience, the struggle of the will to overcome weakness and limitation and become better—that was the Dodgers, and that's real life at its purest, its most essential. That's what drama can only hope to capture, though of course to do it, it has to overcome its own limitations, its own artificiality. It isn't baseball, you know. It isn't real.

Continuity and Order: A Final Inning

The continuity and orderliness of baseball have escaped almost no one's notice. Whether or not, as Donald Hall believes, the game joins "the long generations of all the fathers and all the sons," baseball is continuous, as he observes, "like nothing else among American things, an endless game of repeated summers." Different commentators point to different facets of this stately prism. Some call attention to the theoretical interminability of a single game, the atemporal structure that stretches the game toward eternity; some, like Roger Angell, to the statistics and box scores that permit, like the score of a quartet or symphony, precise reconstruction of the game. Others emphasize the long season and the insistent, daily reoccurrence of its games. Baseball, as Tom Boswell remarks, "is always there when we want it."* "Once in season," Richard Skolnik observes, it "is always with us, day after day, week in and week out,

---

*Thomas Boswell, *Why Time Begins on Opening Day*, p. 298.

month after month ... You're in it for the long haul.... Much like a job, you're obliged to stick with it." And almost all who give even the most casual thought to its history take note of the prominence, proliferation, and, despite recent changes, the stubborn persistence of its rules. The game, Bart Giamatti remarks, was basically shaped by the Knickerbocker Baseball club of New York in 1846, its essential rules for place and play established "with almost no exceptions of consequence, by 1895."*

There have of course been changes, almost all in the past three decades, almost all to the shuddering chagrin of purists and traditionalists. The designated hitter does not take the field, and the end of the reserve clause and the institution of free agency have seen to it that increasing numbers of players take different fields in different uniforms with increasing regularity, abandoning their cities, clubs, and fans for wherever the artificial turf is greener. Teams move with augmenting frequency from one city to another, new teams, even new leagues or sub-leagues are added, playoffs grow and multiply, interleague play awaits us, new stadiums are domed, shutting out the sky, and new fields "blossom" with ersatz grass that denies the game's primeval attachment to the natural.

All the same, one might say, while none of the fans I spoke to celebrated these alterations and many regretted them, none felt they had touched the game at its firm ancestral heart. The seats have been repainted, even torn from their hinges and moved to other sections or discarded, but the stadium remains intact. All perceive it as they remember it: as a game of fixed measurements and rules, one that bears on its countenance enough of its great grandfather's lineaments to reassure us that the family has survived, that something in this protean world persists.

For as long as he remembers, Enrico B., a 64-year-old Cincinnati Reds enthusiast, was taken with the continuity of the players' association with his team. At about the age of 8 or 9, he recalls, he and his brother "got hold of some baseball cards and books about baseball and learned the history of each player. And when we looked at these histories we realized that most of the players had been with Cincinnati for some time. Ernie Lombardi, Bucky Walters, Paul Derringer, and Johnny Vander Meer—they'd all been with the team for a number of years, and I liked that idea. It told me things were stable; they don't change every year. At first I thought maybe every year the teams change players, but then I realized that playing baseball was the player's career. It was his job, and like any good player he'd stay at his workplace. I liked that. It made me comfortable. I felt I could count on them."

Continuity in baseball was a matter not only of player association but of the daily reappearance of the games, an availability and regularity that allowed for the formation of a kind of friendship with these players he gradually learned he could rely on always to be there. "There were afternoon games every day,

---

*A. Bartlett Giamatti, "Baseball and the American Character," in The Baseball Chronicles, pp. 355, 360.

and every day I listened, and each day they'd talk about the previous day. They'd say, well, this is the second game of the series, and the Reds won the first. Or this is the third of a three-game series; they split the first two, so this is the rubber game. And gradually, gradually it became familiar. Like a new kid in the neighborhood, this guy's from a completely different background, and at first he's a stranger. But after a couple of months you become best friends. That's how I felt about the game, and about the players."

As is almost always the case with a fan's attraction to the game, it is an expression of his personality, connectable to other preferences, attitudes, and desires, more comprehensively to a weltanschauung. "Every day," he remembers, "it was the same players—in the same order. They didn't change the lineups then as much as they do now. Same lineups day after day. Same players year after year—no free agency then. And the same teams, too. They didn't move. When Brooklyn moved to Los Angeles and the Giants to San Francisco, that brought a certain discontinuity to the game. I guess you have to live with the times, and I guess a certain amount of change is necessary, but I think in a lot of areas it has gone too far. Seeing things cut off that way, whatever it is, undermines your sense of security. And when you're a kid, especially when you're a kid, you need that security."

Enrico found that security in baseball, and while it was once a reflection of the stable world he lived in, it is now, regrettably, an aberration, a tiny but lifesaving raft in a sea of change. It is no surprise that Enrico likes "the fact that baseball has changed so little over the years" and that his reflections on the game lead him to more generalized reflections on the state of modernity and toward self-recognition and understanding.

"The rules have changed less than in any other sport," he is pleased to say,

> so it makes sense to look at records in 1915 and compare them to today. The comparisons are meaningful. You can say, "Hey, this hitter is better than that one." I like that. I like the continuity. Continuity is very important, you know. It creates a sense of closeness, neighborly closeness. People don't know anybody nowadays. They don't even know their next door neighbors. When I was a kid, when somebody would leave our neighborhood, my mother would write to that person for *ten years!* They'd correspond back and forth, though they might never see each other again. If a person moves out now, you never hear from him again, and you probably won't mind because you probably didn't know him very well in the first place. I don't like that. I accept it, but I don't like it. Everything changes so quickly now. In the old days, a popular song would be on top of the charts for six or seven months. Now three months and it's gone. Or one month and it's gone. It's just ... it's almost like a throwaway society. I've been in the same job for thirty-four years now. That gives me something, a feeling of security, familiarity, a sense of continuity. I need continuity. Give me baseball, give me the Cincinnati Reds who've been in one place for more than a hundred years. That's what I love about this game. It's one of the few almost unchanging things you can find.
>
> People complain about the slow pace of a baseball game, but I like that pace. Everybody wants fast fast fast fast fast, which is part, I think, of the

lack of continuity. A person who likes a fast life generally doesn't like too much continuity because he wants things constantly changing. When my son sits in front of the TV he'll change stations fifteen times an hour. How can you learn anything that way? Constantly on the move. I guess maybe it's because I'm old, but I don't like things moving and changing so fast. I don't like the fast pace. I think it's good to sit down and smell the roses. Isn't that the expression they use? If you just walk by, you'll never smell the roses.

Tom F., a 32-year-old fan of no particular team, but a lover and admirer of the game, likewise appreciates the basic ongoing sameness of the game. "I like the game just the way it is," he tells us. "Although I tolerate certain changes in the game, like the designated hitter, I'm very much a traditionalist. I don't want more teams in the playoffs, for example. I like knowing when the season starts and when it ends, and I want the year-long play to be decisive." But Tom, a section manager for a computer company, is more taken with the spatial than the temporal orderliness and regularity of the game. What he appreciates is not so much the persistence of a sameness over long periods of time, but the analyzable structure of a given season, the relationship of component parts to the totality.

> I've always looked at baseball as a 162- or, earlier, a 154-game season, where every game is a piece of the puzzle that has to be seen as an important part of a larger whole. When the whole thing is over you put it all together. You analyze it and see what you've got. I guess I take what you might call a scientific approach. I look at the season with a number of questions in mind: Was it a hitter's year? Was it a neutral year? Was it more of a pitcher's year? What kind of pennant races did we have? What was the distribution of the teams? Were there tight pennant races? If it was a hitter's year, why did it work out that way? Was the weather unseasonably warm? Did they narrow the strike zone?

As with many fans, there is a notable connection between Tom's profession and his interest in baseball and between both and the personality that helps determine and define them.

> The past two years I've written some software to help me study these questions. I'm very much interested in the statistical aspect of baseball, like Bill James or Pete Palmer, and I've written some computer programs that I feed all the raw data into. I like pouring through the numbers when they come out and trying to form some conclusions on the basis of the data, though of course you've always got some opinions beforehand. I've always taken the studious analytic approach to baseball. Even when I was young I'd look at the season after it was all over and dissect it analytically. I'd think about what happened and what it meant, what conclusions I could come to about certain players, certain teams, or about what kind of season it had been. I like doing this sort of analysis. It gives me a sense of pattern and order that I like. I live a pretty structured life. The people I work with might not always believe that, but I have to know where things are, and I try to get into a routine. I try not to be too obsessive about it—that can be detrimental—but order and routine are very important aspects of my life, and baseball is a very important

expression of that orderliness and regularity. I'm especially impressed by players who seem to be in control of their game. Players who lack control annoy me. There aren't many in baseball. The game doesn't lend itself to that kind of impulsiveness or disorder, and that's probably one reason I love it as much as I do.

The control Tom mentions in these last remarks is at the center of "Kit" C.'s appreciation of the game. "What baseball always satisfied for me," this fan reflects, "is the need and the desire for control. Pitching in particular, but baseball in general, appealed to me for that reason. Baseball is a game of rules, and these rules give a sense of control to the game; they keep it under control."

And for Kit, as for others, baseball is connected in odd but revealing ways with formative personal experiences and the character they help construct. "I've never thought of it this way before," he realizes, "but baseball could be counted on to control the bullies—like the girl in my neighborhood who bullied all the smaller kids on my block when I was 5 and 6. It could control the kids whose desire to win transcended the rules. The fact that there are so many rules and that baseball is so carefully defined keeps people in line. And it also provides a structure. To me, the joy of the game, of almost anything, comes from its structure. I've learned as an adult that the more structured you are the more freedom you have. If you don't have the freedom, you're at sea. Things are just out of sync. Baseball has that structure and that freedom. It holds aggression in check, and it provides the structure and harmony that tell you what's permitted and what's forbidden. It gives you clarity, order, a kind of peace."

Representative in these ways as well, Kit's reflections about baseball lead him to musings, often metaphoric and imaginative, about his personal psychology, the nature of his childhood, and his attitudes toward what was and is happening around him.

> Baseball always seemed to me a basically gentlemanly sport, a sport of rules and order and controlled behavior, and I appreciated that. It suited well with the passive and more sensitive aspects of my personality. I realized the dangers inherent in the game, like the possibility of being hit by a hard inside pitch. But basically it was like a romance. Oh, the orderly romance of baseball. I loved the rules. I understood them as a child and I enjoyed playing under their governance. For me, baseball was a romance, an important part of the larger romance of my childhood. It was one of the things that made my childhood very happy, and my childhood, except for my fear of the girl next door, was very happy. People admired me because I did well, and the assumption was, if you played by the rules, if you studied hard and did your homework and were reasonably bright, then the rest would follow. And it did. I won the admiration of my fellow students and my teachers, too.
>
> When the sixties came, I was mystified by the radicalism and the bizarre behavior. Students for a Democratic Society? What the heck are they up to? And what about these Black Panthers and the Student Non-Violent Coordinating Committee? What the heck is this Stokely Carmichael doing? I was astonished by all this rebelliousness, this rude and violent resistance. I knew nothing of dissent, of protest, and I was especially taken aback by the unsa-

vory nature of this protest. These guys weren't saying "no" in a very orderly, gentlemanly fashion. There was something very unruly about them and what they represented. The fabric of America seemed to be disintegrating before my eyes. This wasn't American life the way I'd known it, and I didn't feel comfortable with this new disorder.

As for Carl P. and Enrico, baseball—controlled, rule-governed, and reliable—was the deep-sunk fencepost one grabs onto in the hurricane lashing within and without.

> The '67 season was played against this backdrop, and for me, "Gentleman Jim" Lonborg and the Red Sox restored order. There was comfort to be had in Boston's winning and in Lonborg's doing so well. This was wonderful. It allowed me to put this other stuff out of my mind. It was as though the peaceable kingdom had been restored. Through baseball the peaceable kingdom had returned. Yeah, that's it exactly. It's no wonder I always wanted to be a ball player or a minister. A couple of years ago my parents gave me an old scrapbook of mine they'd been saving. It contains a composition I wrote in fourth grade, where I explain why, when I grow up, I want to be a ball player or a minister. I never became either, of course, but they always seemed to me widely different choices. I guess they weren't; I guess there was a similarity there I'd never noticed.

Bibliography

Books

Angell, Roger, *Five Seasons* (New York: Simon & Schuster, 1977).
_____, *Late Innings* (New York: Simon & Schuster, 1982).
_____, *The Summer Game* (London: Simon & Schuster, 1987).
_____, *Season Ticket* (Boston: Houghton Mifflin, 1988).
Bernard, Harold W., *Adolescent Development* (Scranton, PA: Intext Educational Publishers, 1971).
Blos, Peter, *The Adolescent Passage* (New York: International Universities Press, 1979).
Boswell, Thomas, *How Life Imitates the World Series* (London: Simon & Schuster, 1982).
_____, *Why Time Begins on Opening Day* (New York: Penguin, 1984).
_____, *The Heart of the Order* (New York: Penguin, 1989).
Bouton, Jim, *Ball Four* (New York: The World Publishing Company, 1970).
_____, *I'm Glad You Didn't Take It Personally* (New York: Dell, 1973; first published in 1972).
Bowlby, John, *Attachment and Loss*, Vol. 1: *Attachment* (Harmondsworth, Middlesex: Penguin, 1972; first published 1969).
_____, *Attachment and Loss*, Vol. 2: *Separation, Anxiety and Anger* (London: The Hogarth Press, 1973).
_____, *Attachment and Loss*, Vol. 3: *Loss, Sadness and Depression* (New York: Basic Books, 1980).
Boyle, Robert H., *Sport—Mirror of American Life* (Boston: Little Brown, 1963).
Connor, Anthony J., *Baseball for the Love of It: Hall of Famers Tell It Like It Was* (New York: Macmillan, Inc., 1982).
Damon, William, ed., *Child Development Today and Tomorrow* (San Francisco: Jossey Bass, 1989).
Edge, David, ed., *The Formative Years: How Children Become Members of Their Society* (New York: Schocken, 1970).
Erikson, Erik H., *Childhood and Society* (Harmondsworth, Middlesex: Penguin, 1965; first published 1950).
Evans, Ellis D., ed., *Children: Readings in Behavior and Development* (New York: Holt, Rinehart, and Winston, 1968).
_____, *Adolescents: Readings in Behavior and Development* (Hinsdale, IL: Dryden, 1970).
Feinstein, John, *Play Ball: The Life and Troubled Times of Major League Baseball* (New York: Villard, 1993).
Fimrite, Ron, *Birth of a Fan* (New York: Macmillan, 1993).
Gallen, David, ed., *The Baseball Chronicles* (New York: Carroll & Graf, Inc., 1991).
Gardner, Howard, *Developmental Psychology, An Introduction* (Boston and Toronto: Little, Brown, 1978).

Giamatti, A. Bartlett, *Take Time for Paradise: Americans and Their Games* (New York: Summit, 1989).
Graham, Douglas, *Moral Learning and Development: Theory and Research* (London: B.T. Batsford, 1972).
Guttman, Allen, *From Ritual to Record: The Nature of Modern Sports* (New York: Columbia University Press, 1978).
Hall, Donald, *Fathers Playing Catch with Sons* (San Francisco: North Point, 1985).
Hargreaves, Jennifer, ed., *Sport, Culture and Ideology* (London: Routledge and Kegan Paul, 1982).
Hartup, Willard W. and Zick Rubin, eds., *Relationships and Development* (Hillsdale, NJ: Lawrence Erlbaum, 1986).
Honig, Donald, *Baseball Between the Lines: Baseball in the Forties and Fifties as Told by the Men Who Played It* (Lincoln, NE: University of Nebraska Press, 1976).
_____, *Baseball When the Grass Was Green* (Lincoln, NE: University of Nebraska Press, 1975).
Iser, Wolfgang, *The Fictive and the Imaginary: Charting Literary Anthropology* (Baltimore: Johns Hopkins University Press, 1993).
Kinsella, P. W., *Shoeless Joe* (New York: Ballantine, 1982).
Lewis, Lisa A., ed., *The Adoring Audience: Fan Culture and Popular Media* (London: Routledge, 1992).
Mantle, Mickey, with Herb Gluck, *The Mick* (New York: Doubleday, 1986; first published in 1985).
Mulvoy, Mark, man. ed., *Baseball: Four Decades of Sports Illustrated's Finest Writing on America's Favorite Pastime* (Birmingham, AL: Oxmoor, 1993).
Murdock, Eugene, *Baseball Players and Their Times: Oral Histories of the Game, 1920–1940* (Westport, CT: Meckler, 1991).
_____, *Baseball Between the Wars: Memories of the Game by the Men Who Played It* (Westport, CT: Meckler, 1992).
Mussen, Paul Henry, John Janeway Conger and Jerome Kagan, *Child Development and Personality*, 3d. Ed. (New York: Harper & Row, 1969; first published 1956).
Nixon, Howard L. II, *Sport and the American Dream* (New York: Leisure Press, 1984).
Novak, Michael, *The Joy of Sports* (New York: Basic Books, 1976).
Radway, Janice A., *Reading the Romance: Women, Patriarchy, and Popular Literature* (Chapel Hill, NC: The University of North Carolina Press, 1991; first printed in 1984).
Rosenau, Pauline Marie, *Post-Modernism and the Social Sciences: Insights, Inroads, and Intrusions* (Princeton, NJ: Princeton University Press, 1992).
Schaap, Dick, *Sport* (New York: Arbor, 1975).
Shannon, Mike, *Diamond Classics: Essays on 100 of the Best Baseball Books Ever Published* (Jefferson, NC: McFarland, 1989).
Sheed, Wilfred, *Baseball and Lesser Sports* (New York: HarperCollins, 1991).
_____, *My Life as a Fan* (New York: Simon & Schuster, 1993).
Shieber, Tom, ed. *Baseball Research*, No. 23 (Cleveland: The Society for American Baseball Research, 1994).
Skolnik, Richard, *Baseball and the Pursuit of Innocence: A Fresh Look at the Old Ball Game* (College Station, TX: Texas A&M University Press, 1994).
Smith, Red, *To Absent Friends* (New York: New American Library, 1973).
Spink, G. Taylor, *Judge Landis and Twenty-Five Years of Baseball* (New York: Thomas Y. Crowell, 1947).
Sprott, W.J.H., *Human Groups* (Harmondsworth, Middlesex: Penguin, 1966; first published 1958).
Stone, L. Joseph and Joseph Church, *Childhood & Adolescence: A Psychology of the Growing Person*, 3d. Ed. (New York: Random House, 1973; first published 1957).

Storr, Anthony, *Solitude: A Return to the Self* (New York: Ballantine, 1988).
Voigt, David Quentin, *American Baseball, Vol. III: From Postwar Expansion to the Electronic Age* (University Park, PA: Penn State University Press, 1983).
Wecter, Dixon, *The Hero in America* (Ann Arbor, MI: University of Michigan Press, 1963; first published in 1941).
Weiss, Paul, *Sport: A Philosophic Inquiry* (Carbondale, IL: Southern Illinois University Press, 1969).
Will, George F., *Men at Work: The Craft of Baseball* (New York: Harper Collins, 1990).
Wimmer, Dick, *Baseball Fathers, Baseball Sons* (New York: William Morrow, 1988).
Wolff, Rick, Editorial Director, *The Baseball Encyclopedia: The Complete and Definitive Record of Major League Baseball*, 9th Ed., Revised, Updated, and Expanded, (New York, Toronto, Oxford, et al.: Macmillan Publishing Company, Maxwell Macmillan Canada, and Maxwell Macmillan International, 1993).
Zimbalist, Andrew, *Baseball and Billions: A Probing Look Inside the Big Business of Our National Pastime* (New York: Basic Books, 1992).
Zingg, Paul J., ed., *The Sporting Image: Readings in American Sport History* (Lanham, NY: University Press of America, 1988).

Articles

Altman, Lawrence K., "Mantle's Cancer 'Most Aggressive' His Doctors Had Seen,"*New York Times*, August 14, 1995, p. A1.
Anderson, Dave, "Biggest Loss for Baseball: Do You Care?" *New York Times*, September 15, 1994, p. B11.
Angell, Roger, "Baseball's Horrible Year," *The New Yorker*, October 17, 1994, pp. 65–76.
_____, "Called Strike," *The New Yorker*, May 22, 1995, pp. 46–53.
_____, "Bad Call," *The New Yorker*, August 15, 1994, pp. 2–4.
Associated Press, "Madlock Arrested on Bad-Check Charge," *New York Times*, July 13, 1995, p. B16.
Berkow, Ira, "Dear Mickey: Messages and Prayers for an American Hero," *New York Times*, June 25, 1995, p. S9.
_____, "Play Ball! Hello-o-o-o! Anybody Watching?" *New York Times*, April 23, 1995, Arts and Leisure, p. 31.
Bodley, Hal, "One Year Ago, Baseball Fell Apart at Seams," *USA Today*, August 11, 1995, pp. 1C & 3C.
Bowen, Les, "The Mick," *Philadelphia Daily News*, August 14, 1995, Keepsake Edition, pp. 1–12.
_____, "A Mantle of Majesty and Flaws," *Philadelphia Daily News*, August 14, 1995.
Caraher, Brian G., "The Poetics of Baseball: An American Domestication of the Mathematically Sublime," *American Studies*, 32 (Spring 1991): pp. 85–100.
Chain, Dana, "The Great American Strikeout," *Wall Street Journal*, August 11, 1995, p. 1.
Charnofsky, Harold, "The Major League Professional Baseball Player: Self-Conception Versus the Popular Image," *International Review of Sport Sociology*, 3 (1968): pp. 39–55.
Chass, Murray, "Speed Up. Raise This. Expand That. Whew!" *New York Times*, July 13, 1995, p. B15.
_____, "Reluctant Baseball Owners Approve Pact with Players," *New York Times*, November 27, 1996, p. A1.
Coleman, Lee, "What is American: A Study of Alleged American Traits," *Social Forces*, XIX (1941).
Connelly, Christopher, "At the Top of His Game," *Premiere*, September 1994, pp. 77–83.

Curry, Jack, "A.L. Orders McDowell: Treat Fans to Tickets," *New York Times*, July 21, 1995, p. B9 & B11.
Dawidoff, Nicholas, "What National Pastime?" *New York Times*, August 11, 1994, p. A23.
Elliot, Stuart, "The Yankees Conquered the World, Only to Find That Baseball Doesn't Sell the Way It Used To," *New York Times*, October 29, 1996, p. D9.
Glastris, Paul and Greg Ferguson, "A Sad End to an Amazing Season," *U.S. News & World Report*, August 22, 1994, pp. 24–28.
Grella, George, "Baseball and the American Dream," *Massachusetts Review*, 16 (Summer 1975: pp. 550–67).
Grossberg, Lawrence, "Is There a Fan in the House: The Affective Sensibility of Fandom," in *The Adoring Audience*, Lisa A. Lewis, ed., pp. 50–65.
Guterson, David, "Moneyball!: On the Relentless Promotion of Pro Sports," *Harper's*, September 1994, pp. 37–46.
Harris, Mark, "Introduction" to *The Baseball Chronicles*, ed. David Gillen (1991), pp. xiii–xx.
Hoffer, Richard, "Mickey Mantle: The Legacy of the Last Great Player on the Last Great Team," *Sports Illustrated*, August 21, 1995, pp. 18–30.
Holland, Norman, "Human Identity," *Critical Inquiry*, 4 (1978): pp. 451–69.
———, "Unity Identity Text Self," PMLA, 90 (1975): pp. 813–22.
Jauss, Hans Robert, "The Theory of Reception: A Retrospective of its Unrecognized Prehistory," trans. John Whitlam, in *Literary Theory Today*, Peter Collier and Helga Geyer-Ryan, eds. (Ithaca, NY: Cornell University Press, 1990).
Johnson, Donald R., "The Hero in Sports Literature and Exley's *A Fan's Notes*," *Southern Humanities Review*, 13 (1979): pp. 233–44.
Kennedy, Randy, "In Brooklyn, Sympathy and Dismay," *New York Times*, July 21, 1995, p. B2.
Kleinfeld, N.R., "Parade for the Yankees: The Celebration, A Parade of Pride," *New York Times*, October 30, 1996, p. A1.
Lipsyte, Robert, "In Memoriam," *New York Times*, September 15, 1994, pp. A1 & B14.
———, "The Emasculation of Sports," *New York Times Magazine*, April 2, 1995, pp. 50–56.
Phillips, Cheryl, "Ballpark Figures Slide," *USA Today*, August 11, 1995, p. 3C.
Porter, Dennis, "The Perilous Quest: Baseball as Folk Drama, *Critical Inquiry*, 4 (1977): pp. 143–57.
Roberts, Steven V., with Jim Impoco, and Paul Glastris, "A Bronx Cheer for Baseball," *U.S. News & World Report*, August 22, 1994, pp. 24–28.
Ross, Murray, "Football and Baseball in America," in *Sports and Society: An Anthology*, John T. Talamini and Charles H. Page, eds. (Boston: Little, Brown, 1973): pp. 102–??
Sandomir, Richard, "A Cash Cow Transforms Itself Into a Dead Horse," *New York Times*, September 15, 1994, p. B13.
Saroyan, William, "My Baseball," in *Baseball*, Mark Mulvoy, ed., pp. 284–86.
Schwartz, Michael J., "Causes and Effects of Spectator Sports," *International Review of Sport Sociology*, 8 (1973): pp. 25–45.
Sexton, Joe, "Tax Fraud: Two Baseball Legends Say It's So," *New York Times*, July 21, 1995, pp. A1 & B2.
Smith, Claire, "The Seats Aren't Filled, But They're Not as Empty," *New York Times*, July 2, 1995, p. S5.
———, "Now Baseball Must Seize the Moment and Market Itself," *New York Times*, November 27, 1996, p. B9.
———, "Big Turnout Should Turn the Corner," *New York Times*, October 30, 1996, p. B11.

Starr, Mark, "We Was Robbed!," *Newsweek*, August 22, 1994, pp. 47–52.
Thomas, Robert McG., "Fans' Interest in Baseball Declining, Poll Says," *New York Times*, August 20, 1994, p. Sec. 1, 31.
Ward, Geoffrey C. and Ken Burns, "Game-Time," *U.S. News & World Report*, August 29–September 5, 1994, pp. 61–101.
____, "Baseball the Way It Was," *U.S. News & World Report*, August 29–September 5, 1994, pp. 54–60.
Zingg, Paul J., "Myth and Metaphor: Baseball in the History and Literature of American Sport," in *The Sporting Image*, Paul Zingg, ed.

Index

Aaron, Hank 23, 39, 63, 64, 66, 79
Agee, Tommy 201
Allen, Mel 72, 162–63
Allen, Richie 141
Alou, Felipe 114
Amoros, Sandy 22, 132
Angell, Roger 9, 16, 17, 19, 21, 22, 24, 25, 26, 28, 30, 33, 35, 236
Ashburn, Richie 143, 172
Atlanta Braves 4, 39; mentioned 102–4
Auden, W.H. 18, 110
Averill, Earl 31

Babe Ruth League 124
Baker Bowl 55, 57, 118
Baltimore Colts 191
Baltimore Orioles 1, 5, 30, 145, 176–77; mentioned 189–93, 203–6
Banks, Ernie 178, 179
Barber, Red 162–63, 167
Barber, Steve 191
Barfield, Jessie 155
Barzun, Jacques 14
Bauer, Hank 172, 199, 208
Beatles 98
Belle, Albert 8, 175
Berg, Moe 24
Berra, Lawrence ("Yogi") 9, 22, 45
Bertoia, Reno 34
Biasetti, Hank 46–47
Bird, Larry 113
Bishop, Max 118
Black, Joe 132, 221
Boggs, Wade 8, 78, 116
Boston Braves 105
Boston Red Sox 1, 71, 89, 90, 116, 124, 186, 194, 241; mentioned 76–82, 104–9

Boswell, Thomas 13, 21, 28, 29, 35, 233, 236
Boyer, Ken 166
Branca, Ralph 221
Brett, George 116
Brooklyn Dodgers 1, 16, 34, 73, 74, 89, 129, 138, 139, 146, 152, 177, 179, 180, 199, 200, 216, 235, 236; mentioned 41–46, 52–55, 90–94, 94–99, 111, 122–26, 130–35, 148–51, 194–97, 211–15, 218–22
Brown, Bobby 197
Brown, Jim 19
Browning, Robert 26
Buckner, Bill 78
Buhner, Jay 172
Bunker, Wally 190
Burns, Ken 2, 15, 24, 25
Butler, Brett 28

California Angels 187
Callison, Johnny 141
Camilli, Dolph 52, 54, 55, 195
Campanella, Roy 91, 212, 221
Camus, Albert 42
Carew, Rod 128
Carlton, Steve 60, 61
Carter, Gary 85
Cascorart, Pete 52, 54
Casey, Hugh 218
Cash, Norm 181
Cashen, Frank 191
Cavaretta, Phil 178
Cepeda, Orlando 114
Chamberlain, Wilt 19
Chambliss, Chris 100, 186
Chandler, Happy 28

Chicago Cubs 5, 60, 124, 130, 209, 221; mentioned 178–80
Chicago White Sox 178
Cincinnati Reds 4, 50, 191, 235, 237, 238
Clark, Jack 186
Clark, Will 111, 115, 125
Clemens, Roger 116, 164, 172
Clemente, Roberto 113, 115, 117, 159, 160, 161
Cleveland Indians 31, 76, 208
Cobb, Ty 19, 23, 25, 33, 57, 189
Cochrane, Mickey 118
Colbert, Nate 169
Coleman, Gerry 197
Coleman, Vince 8
Columbia University 37
Connie Mack Stadium 94, 97, 117, 141, 142
Connor, Mark 156
Cooperstown 14, 170
Cousy, Bob 19
Cox, Billy 125, 221
Crosetti, Frank 195
Cuyler, Milt 50

Dean, Jay Hanna ("Dizzy") 29, 30, 32
Dent, Russell Earl ("Bucky") 184
Derringer, Paul 237
Detroit Tigers 21, 33, 56, 68, 234; mentioned 46–51, 180–83, 227–31
Dickie, Bill 73
DiMaggio, Dominic 63
DiMaggio, Joe 8, 19, 28, 33, 41, 42, 56–57, 63, 64, 69, 73, 75, 80, 107, 108, 111, 113, 114, 115, 117, 132, 165, 172
Doerr, Bobby 106, 107
Doubleday, Abner 14
Drysdale, Don 134
Durocher, Leo 33, 54, 194
Dykstra, Lenny 83, 143

Earnshaw, George 56
Ebbets Field 1, 54, 89, 122, 131, 146, 148, 149, 194, 197, 200, 218, 220
Eckersley, Dennis 116
Edwards, Bruce 221
Erskine, Carl 134
Etten, Nick 73

Fenway Park 71, 77, 78, 106, 124, 164

Fetzer, John 229, 231
Fisher, Jack 191
Fitzsimmons, Freddy 54
Forbes Field 158, 160
Ford, Whitey 73
Foxx, Jimmie 57, 76–77
Frost, Robert 9, 15
Furillo, Carl 67, 91, 114, 195, 220

Gant, Ron 104
Gas House Gang 73
Gaston, Cito 169
Gehrig, Lou 33, 42, 57, 76, 100, 161, 168, 189
Giamatti, A. Bartlett 15, 195, 209, 237
Gibson, Kirk 79
Gilliam, James ("Junior") 132, 221
Gooden, Dwight 85
Gordon, Joe 73
Griffey, Ken, Jr. 70, 84
Gross, Jack 55
Grove, Lefty 30, 33, 56–57, 77
Gwynn, Tony 5, 172

Haas, George William ("Mule")
Hall, Mell 153
Hall of Fame 17, 19, 170
Hansen, Ron 191
Harrelson, Derrel ("Bud") 200–1,
Harris, Mark 9
Harwell, Ernie 227, 229, 231
Heath, Jeff 31
Henderson, Rickey 23, 64, 80, 102, 116
Henrich, Tommy 31, 32, 73, 107, 137, 140, 194
Hermanski, Gene 221
Hernandez, Enzo 169
Hernandez, Keith 85, 116
Hershberger, Willard 50
Higbe, Kirby 31, 32
Hodges, Gil 91, 132, 134, 148, 149
Holdsworth, Fred 34
Hoover, Herbert 14
Horton, Willie 230, 231
Howard, Elston 114, 132, 134
Howard, Frank 188
Howe, Steve 8
Hrabosky, Al 235
Huggins, Miller 168
Hunter, Billy 203, 205

International League 75

Jackson, Reggie 152, 157
James, Bill 239
Johnson, Davie 191
Johnson, Ervin ("Magic") 113, 115
Johnson, Walter 19, 23
Jones, Cleon 200
Jordan, Michael 5, 10, 19, 115

Kaat, Jim 185
Kaline, Al 47, 66, 231
Kansas City Royals 4
Keller, Charlie ("King Kong") 73, 107, 194
Keltner, Kenny 33
"Kiddie Corps" 190, 205
Kinder, Ellis 107
Kiner, Ralph 29
Kinsella, W.P. 32, 127
Knickerbocker Baseball Club 237
Knothole Gang 194
Kopf, Larry 30
Koufax, Sandy 28, 117, 212–13
Kruk, John 103

Landis, Kenesaw Mountain 25, 37
Larkin, Gene 103
Larsen, Don 34
Lavagetto, Harry ("Cookie") 195
Lazzeri, Tony 165, 195
Lindell, Johnny 72
Little League 135, 184
Lombardi, Ernie 237
Lombardi, Vince 37, 192, 214
Lonborg, Jim 241
Lopat, Eddie 73
Los Angeles Dodgers 66, 238
Loughran, Tommy 55
Luzinski, Greg 176, 184

Mack, Connie 57, 58, 59
MacDougald, Gil 134, 209
Maddux, Greg 5, 28, 172
Madlock, Bill 8
Mantle, Mickey 3, 4, 5, 6, 45, 66–67, 69, 117, 136, 137, 140, 148, 149, 151, 156, 159, 165, 166–67, 199, 208, 209–10, 212, 222

Marichal, Juan 114
Maris, Roger 46, 222
Martin, Billy 22, 80
Martin, John Leonard ("Pepper") 194
Mathews, Eddie 172
Mattingly, Don 100, 153
Mays, Willie 69, 111, 112, 114, 115, 117, 172, 179, 212
Mazeroski, Bill 159, 160
McCarthy, Joe 73, 197
McCarver, Tim 9
McCovey, Willie 8, 79
McDowell, Jack 8
McGraw, John 30
McGwire, Mark 102, 104
Memorial Stadium 190
Merkle, Fred 30
Milwaukee Braves 63–68
Milwaukee Brewers 4, 103
Minnesota Twins 4, 99, 102, 103
Miranda, Willie 190
Mixis, Eddie 221
Mize, Johnny 74
Montana, Joe 19
Montreal Expos 1; mentioned 200–3
Montreal Royals 90
Monument Park 222
Morgan, Joe 61
Mullen, Pat 48
Musial, Stan 128, 143, 172, 179, 204, 205

New York Giants 41, 42, 56, 75, 100, 101, 108, 137, 138, 139, 180, 196, 221; mentioned 52–55
New York Knickerbockers 156
New York Mets 16, 28, 71, 75, 97, 99, 101, 102, 116, 132, 134, 156, 190, 191, 199, 222; mentioned 82–86, 200–3
New York Yankees 1, 3, 4, 6, 16, 17, 40, 56, 66, 68, 70, 71, 78, 80, 92, 98, 111, 114, 118, 129, 132, 146, 148, 176, 177, 191, 194, 195, 196, 197, 199, 200, 201, 203, 212, 214, 220, 221; mentioned 41–46, 72–76, 99–102, 135–41, 151–57, 162–68, 186–89, 206–11, 222–27
Newark Bears 74, 220
Newcombe, Don 212
Nomo, Hedeo 172

O'Malley, Walter 134
O'Neal, Shaquille 5
Ott, Mel 56
Owen, Mickey 196

Palmer, Pete 239
Pappas, Milt 191
Parnell, Mel 107
Peckinpaugh, Roger 29
Perez, Tony 61
Pesky, Johnny 48, 107
Philadelphia Athletics 41, 47; mentioned 55–59, 117–22
Philadelphia Phillies 1, 39, 40, 55, 58, 97, 102, 118, 179, 180; mentioned 59–63, 141–44, 183–86
Pittsburgh Pirates 4, 59, 147, 168, 221; mentioned 158-62
Polo Grounds 41, 73
Powell, John Wesley ("Boog") 191
Prince, Bob 160, 162

Randolph, Willie 153
Raschi, Vic 73
Reese, Harold ("Pee Wee") 91, 92, 125, 132, 133, 197, 201, 221
Reynolds, Allie 73, 199, 206
Richards, Paul 191
Richardson, Bobby 134
Rickey, Branch 31, 53, 132, 175
Rieser, Pete 54
Ripken, Cal, Jr. 172
Rivers, Mickey 184
Rizzuto, Phil ("Scooter") 41, 42, 73, 107
Roberts, Robin 29, 142, 143
Robinson, Brooks 117, 191, 192, 204, 205, 231
Robinson, Frank 191
Robinson, Jackie 8, 55, 64, 74, 90, 92, 111, 125, 132, 133, 175, 218, 221
Roe, Elwin ("Preacher") 91, 92, 125, 172
Rose, Pete 9, 170, 176
Ruel, Herold ("Muddy") 49–50,
Ruffing, Charles ("Red") 42
Runnels, Pete 51
Ruppert Stadium 220
Russell, Bill 113
Ruth, George Herman ("Babe") 19, 45, 57, 100, 138, 152, 168, 189, 197
Ryan, Nolan 23, 60, 157

St. Louis Browns 190
St. Louis Cardinals 59, 106, 166, 194, 234
San Diego Padres 1; mentioned 168–71
San Francisco Giants 4, 238; mentioned 113–17, 122–26
Sanderson, Scott 186, 187
Saroyan, William 6, 69
Sauer, Hank 178
Schmidt, Mike 27, 60, 61, 169, 176, 184, 185–86
Schott, Marge 175
Scully, Vince 212
Seattle Mariners 124
Seaver, Tom 110, 132
Shea Stadium 223
Sheed, Wilfred 12
Shibe Park 58, 117, 141, 142
Simmons, Al 56, 57, 118
Skowron, Bill ("Moose") 194
Sky Dome 187
Slaughter, Enos ("Country") 73, 106
Smith, Elmer 30
Smith, Ozzie 70, 128
Smith, Walter ("Red") 13, 30
Snider, Edwin ("Duke") 8, 91, 92, 123, 134, 201, 212
Society for Americqan Baseball Research (SABR) 28, 170, 171
Spahn, Warren 63, 172
Speaker, Tris 189
Stanky, Eddie 52, 80
Steinbrenner, George 164, 191, 224
Stengel, Charles Dillon ("Casey") 45, 73
Sternweiss, George "Snuffy" 72
Stephens, Vern 107, 164, 203
Stoneham, Horace 123
Strawberry, Darryl 8, 84, 85

Tartabull, Danny 8
Taylor, Lawrence, 155
Terry, Bill 56
Thomas, Frank 27
Thomson, Bobby 53, 138
Tiger Stadium 230
Toney, Fred 30
Torgeson, Earl 48

Toronto Blue Jays 21
Triandos, Gus 190, 204
Turley, Bob 203
Twain, Mark 15

Unitas, Johnny 19
Vander Meer, Johnny 237
Vaughn, James ("Hippo") 30
Veterans Stadium 60, 95, 102, 104, 223
Vincent, Faye 9

Wagner, Honus 19, 128
Waitkus, Eddie 220
Walker, Dixie 52, 55
Walters, William Henry ("Bucky") 237
Weaver, Earl 123
Whitehill, Earl 56
Wilhelm, Hoyt 204

Will, George 22, 25, 28, 110, 209
Williams, Bernie 225
Williams, Ted 19, 33, 48, 57, 69, 81, 88, 106, 107, 108, 114, 164, 204
Williams, William Carlos 110
Wilson, Mookie 83
Wood, Joe 30
Woodling, Gene 197, 208
Wrigley Field 21, 124, 130, 178
Wynn, Early 208

Yankee Stadium 135, 138, 139, 140, 146, 147, 164, 165, 166, 168, 188, 197, 206, 208, 216; mentioned 151–57, 222–27
Yastrzemski, Carl 81, 164

Zepp, Bill 34